CAMBRIDGE
UNIVERSITY PRESS

CAMBRIDGE
Primary English

Teacher's Resource 6

Sally Burt & Debbie Ridgard

CAMBRIDGE
UNIVERSITY PRESS

Shaftesbury Road, Cambridge CB2 8EA, United Kingdom

One Liberty Plaza, 20th Floor, New York, NY 10006, USA

477 Williamstown Road, Port Melbourne, VIC 3207, Australia

314–321, 3rd Floor, Plot 3, Splendor Forum, Jasola District Centre, New Delhi – 110025, India

103 Penang Road, #05–06/07, Visioncrest Commercial, Singapore 238467

Cambridge University Press is part of the University of Cambridge.

It furthers the University's mission by disseminating knowledge in the pursuit of education, learning and research at the highest international levels of excellence.

www.cambridge.org
Information on this title: www.cambridge.org/9781108771214

© Cambridge University Press & Assessment 2021

First published 2015
Second edition 2021

20 19 18 17 16 15 14 13 12 11 10 9 8 7 6 5 4 3

Printed in Italy by Rotolito S.p.A.

A catalogue record for this publication is available from the British Library

ISBN 978-1-108-77121-4 Paperback with Digital Access

Additional resources for this publication at www.cambridge.org/go

....

....

> Contents

Digital resources

The following items are available on Cambridge GO. For more information on how to access and use your digital resource, please see inside front cover.

Active learning

Assessment for Learning

Developing learner language skills

Differentiation

Improving learning through questioning

Language awareness

Metacognition

Skills for Life

Letter for parents – Introducing the Cambridge Primary and
   Lower Secondary resources

Lesson plan template

Curriculum framework correlation

Scheme of work

Audio files

Diagnostic check and answers

Mid-point test and answers

End-of-year test and answers

Answers to Learner's Book questions

Answers to Workbook questions

Glossary

You can download the following resources for each unit:

Differentiated worksheets and answers

Language worksheets and answers

End-of-unit tests and answers

> Introduction

Welcome to the new edition of our Cambridge Primary English series.

Since its launch, the series has been used by teachers and learners in over 100 countries for teaching the Cambridge Primary English curriculum framework.

This exciting new edition has been designed by talking to Primary English teachers all over the world. We have worked hard to understand your needs and challenges, and then carefully designed and tested the best ways of meeting them.

As a result of this research, we've made some important changes to the series. This Teacher's Resource has been carefully redesigned to make it easier for you to plan and teach the course.

The series now includes digital editions of the Learner's Books and Workbooks. This Teacher's Resource also offers additional materials available to download from Cambridge GO. (For more information on how to access and use your digital resource, please see the inside front cover.)

The series uses the most successful teaching approaches like active learning and metacognition, and this Teacher's Resource gives you full guidance on how to integrate them into your classroom.

Formative assessment opportunities help you to get to know your learners better, with clear learning intentions and success criteria as well as an array of assessment techniques, including advice on self and peer assessment.

Clear, consistent differentiation ensures that all learners are able to progress in the course with tiered activities, differentiated worksheets and advice about supporting learners' different needs.

All our resources include extra language support to enable teaching and learning in English. They help learners build core English skills with vocabulary and grammar support, as well as additional language worksheets.

We hope you enjoy using this course.

Eddie Rippeth

Head of Primary and Lower Secondary Publishing, Cambridge University Press

> About the authors

Sally Burt

I have been involved with education for both children and adults for almost 30 years. I obtained my honours and master's degrees at Magdalen College, Oxford University, and my PGCE at Digby Stuart College, Roehampton, followed by teaching at various inner-city primary schools in London. I was the deputy head at All Saints primary school in London. I moved to South Africa in 1995, where I taught in a junior school for several years. After that, I started my own communications consultancy and since then I have been involved in editing, writing and training across a variety of contexts, including professional communication studies in higher education at the University of Cape Town.

I have worked with Debbie Ridgard for the last 20 years on English textbooks, workbooks, teacher resources, study guides and readers for a range of curricula and publishers, including Oxford University Press SA, Scholastic UK and Cambridge University Press UK. I am also a contributing editor to a professional communications textbook, published by Juta in South Africa.

Debbie Ridgard

I have been involved in education for almost 30 years, since I graduated with a BPrimEd (WITS) in 1992. I spent 17 years teaching Grades 4–7 in a diverse, multi-cultural primary school in South Africa. While teaching I became involved in teacher training and, later, writing educational material. I left full-time teaching in 2010 to focus on writing, but have continued to take on part-time teaching positions at various, diverse primary schools.

I have worked on writing projects with Sally Burt for the last 20 years. Together, we have developed textbooks, workbooks and teacher guides for local and international curricula, as well as literature and spelling guides for various publishers.

> How to use this series

All of the components in the series are designed to work together.

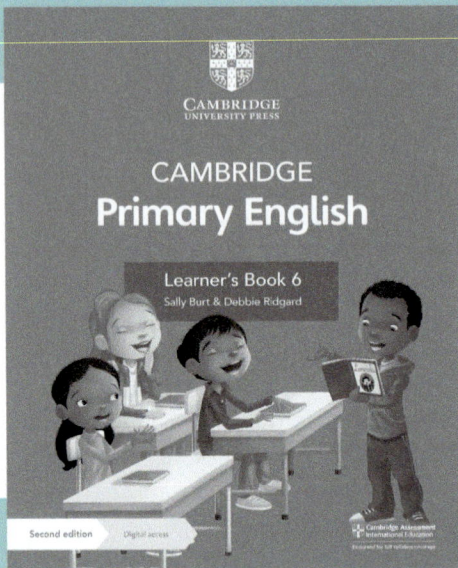

The Learner's Book is designed for learners to use in class with guidance from the teacher. It offers complete coverage of the curriculum framework. A variety of investigations, activities, questions and images motivate learners and help them to develop the necessary skills. Each unit contains opportunities for formative assessment, differentiation and reflection so you can support your learners' needs and help them progress.

A digital version of the Learner's Book is included with the print version and available separately. It includes simple tools for learners to use in class or for self-study.

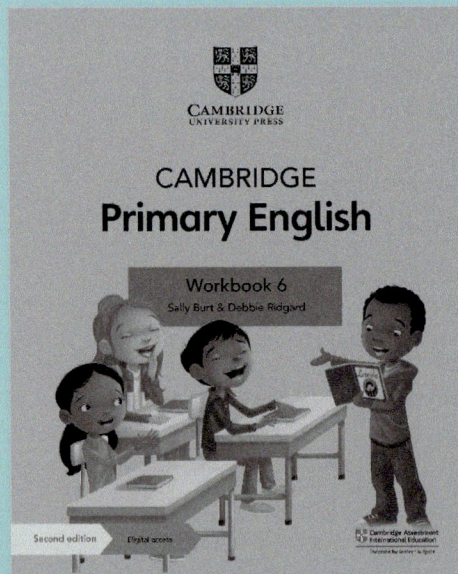

The skills-focused, write-in Workbook provides further practice of all the topics in the Learner's Book and is ideal for use in class or as homework. A three-tier, scaffolded approach to skills development promotes visible progress and enables independent learning, ensuring that every learner is supported. Teachers can assign learners questions from one or more tiers for each exercise, or learners can progress through each of the tiers in the exercise.

A digital version of the Workbook is included with the print version.

The Teacher's Resource is the foundation of this series and you'll find everything you need to deliver the course in here, including suggestions for differentiation, formative assessment and language support, teaching ideas, answers, tests and extra worksheets. Each Teacher's Resource includes:

- A **print book** with detailed teaching notes for each topic
- **Digital Access** with all the material from the book in digital form plus editable planning documents, extra guidance, worksheets and more.

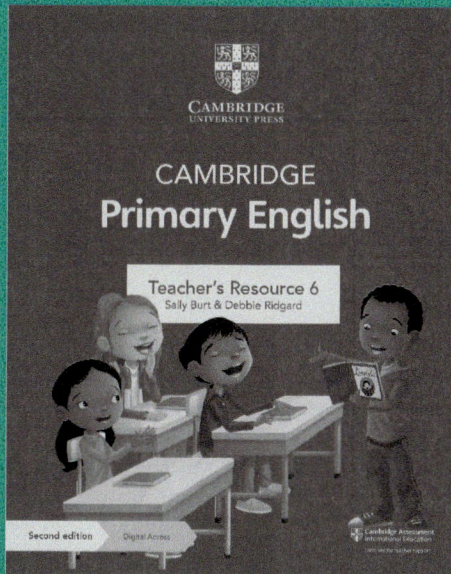

A letter to parents, explaining the course, is available to download from Cambridge GO (as part of this Teacher's Resource).

> How to use this Teacher's Resource

This Teacher's Resource contains both general guidance and teaching notes that help you to deliver the content in our Cambridge Primary English resources. Some of the material is provided as downloadable files, available on **Cambridge GO**. (For more information about how to access and use your digital resource, please see the inside front cover.) See the Contents page for details of all the material available to you, both in this book and through Cambridge GO.

Teaching notes

This book provides **teaching notes** for each unit of the Learner's Book and Workbook. Each set of teaching notes contains the following features to help you deliver the unit.

The **Unit plan** summarises the topics covered in the unit, including the number of learning hours recommended for the topic, an outline of the learning content and the Cambridge resources that can be used to deliver the topic.

Session	Approximate number of learning hours	Outline of learning content	Resources
1.1 What is a prologue?	1	Explore how books start. Read and explore a prologue. Start a learning journal.	Learner's Book Session 1.1 Workbook Session 1.1 ⬇ Worksheet 6.1

The **Background knowledge** feature outlines specific skills, resources, grammar and subject knowledge that you can familiarise yourself with in order to help you teach the unit content effectively.

Learners' prior knowledge can be informally assessed through the **Getting started** feature in the Learner's Book.

BACKGROUND KNOWLEDGE

The early extracts in Unit 1 come from *East*, a book based on an old Norwegian folktale, *East of the Sun, West of the Moon*. The book is historical, being set long ago in a time of wooden sailing ships and travel by horse or foot.

The **Teaching skills focus** feature covers a teaching skill and suggests how to implement it in the unit.

TEACHING SKILLS FOCUS

This unit focuses on many aspects of language awareness, from the nuts and bolts of word class and sentence structure (word order) …

Reflecting the Learner's Book, each unit consists of multiple sections. A section covers a learning topic.

At the start of each section, the **Learning plan** table includes the learning objectives, learning intentions and success criteria that are covered in the section. The learning objectives that are the main focus of the lesson are in bold, followed by those that are partially covered.

It can be helpful to share learning intentions and success criteria with your learners at the start of a lesson so that they can begin to take responsibility for their own learning

LEARNING PLAN

Learning objectives		Learning intentions	Success criteria
Main focus	**Also covered**	• Identify the structure and purpose of a news article.	• Learners can identify a news article structure and purpose.
6Ra. 04, 6Rs.02, 6Rs.03, 6Ri.07	6Rv.04, 6Ri.05, 6Ww.07	• Use reporting jargon.	

There are often **common misconceptions** associated with particular learning topics. These are listed, along with suggestions for identifying evidence of the misconceptions in your class and suggestions for how to overcome them.

Misconception	How to identify	How to overcome
Prologues have to be written from the perspective of a character in the book.	Discuss the prologue to *East* and ask how different it would have been in third-person narrative.	Use learners' responses to stimulate a discussion on the benefits of third- and first-person narrators. Third-person narrative does not allow readers to get inside the head of a character in the same way as first-person.

For each topic, there is a selection of **starter ideas**, **main teaching ideas** and **plenary ideas**. You can pick out individual ideas and mix and match them depending on the needs of your class. The activities include suggestions for how they can be differentiated or used for assessment. **Homework ideas** are also provided.

Starter idea

List words with prefixes (10 minutes)

Resources: Learner's Book, Session 1.2: Getting started; dictionaries online etymological dictionary

Description: In pairs, learners should list words with the given prefixes.

Using the words as context, learners should discuss what the prefixes mean. Point out that using the root word can help decode the prefix when the whole meaning is considered. Learners can check using a dictionary.

Main teaching ideas

1 Looking for clues in the prologue (25 minutes)

Learning intention: To make inferences using evidence from more than one point in the text

Resources: Learner's Book, Session 1.2, Activity 1; *East* prologue (Learner's Book, Session 1.1); Track 02

Description: Before learners start the activity, review what they remember of the prologue and previous discussion from Session 1.1. Encourage

The **Language support** feature highlights specific vocabulary and uses of English throughout the unit that learners might not have encountered before, or may struggle with. It contains suggestions on how to approach these with your class and helpful examples to help them better understand.

LANGUAGE SUPPORT

The vocabulary in this session builds on the previous session which will support some learners. At the end of the session, more work is done on word origins and prefixes.

The **Cross-curricular links** feature provides suggestions for linking to other subject areas.

CROSS-CURRICULAR LINKS

Geography: Gather reference books on Africa, particularly Zimbabwe and Zambia in the area of the Victoria Falls and Bulawayo.

Digital resources to download

This Teacher's Resource includes a range of digital materials that you can download from Cambridge GO. (For more information about how to access and use your digital resource, please see inside front cover.) This icon ⬇ indicates material that is available from Cambridge GO.

Helpful documents for planning include:

- **Letter for parents – Introducing the Cambridge Primary and Lower Secondary resources:** a template letter for parents, introducing the Cambridge Primary English resources.
- **Lesson plan template:** a Word document that you can use for planning your lessons.
- **Curriculum framework correlation:** a table showing how the Cambridge Primary English resources map to the Cambridge Primary English curriculum framework.
- **Scheme of work:** a suggested scheme of work that you can use to plan teaching throughout the year.

Each unit includes:

- **Differentiated worksheets:** these worksheets are provided in variations that cater for different abilities. Worksheets labelled 'A' are intended to support less confident learners, while worksheets labelled 'C' are designed to challenge more confident learners. Answer sheets are provided.
- **Language worksheets:** these worksheets provide language support. Answers sheets are provided.
- **End-of-unit tests:** these provide quick checks of the learner's understanding of the concepts covered in the unit. Answers are provided. Advice on using these tests formatively is given in the Assessment for Learning section of this Teacher's Resource.

Additionally, the Teacher's Resource includes:

- **Diagnostic check and answers:** a test to use at the beginning of the year to discover the level that learners are working at. The results of this test can inform your planning.
- **Mid-point test and answers:** a test to use after learners have studied half the units in the Learner's Book. You can use this test to check whether there are areas that you need to go over again.
- **End-of-year test and answers:** a test to use after learners have studied all units in the Learner's Book. You can use this test to check whether there are areas that you need to go over again, and to help inform your planning for the next year.
- **Answers to Learner's Book activities**
- **Answers to Workbook activities**
- **Glossary**

In addition, you can find more detailed information about teaching approaches.

🎧 **Audio** is available for download from Cambridge GO (as part of this Teacher's Resource and as part of the digital resources for the Learner's Book and Workbook).

Name _____ Date _____

Worksheet 6.5: My writing process

Follow this process to complete any writing activity. Tick ✓ each step as you go.

Stage in process	✓	My notes and comments
Choose a topic		
Identify audience, purpose, language, format		
Brainstorm ideas and interesting vocabulary		
Write a first draft		
Edit using a checklist and a dictionary		

Cambridge Primary Englis...

Name _____ Date _____

Worksheet 6.2: Personal goals

My personal goals	Term 1
My strengths	
My areas for improvement	
My goals for this term	
New words	
My personal goals	Term 2
My strengths	
My areas for improvement	
My goals for this term	
New words	
My personal goals	Term 3
My strengths	
My areas for improvement	
My goals for this term	
New words	

Cambridge Primary English 6 – Burt and Ridgar...

Name _____ Date _____

Worksheet 6.3: Reading strategies

1   Match each reading strategy to its purpose and write it on the line.

Look through a text quickly to get the main idea.

Pay attention to every detail in the text.

Search for specific details to locate information.

predict

read in context

scan

skim

Understand unfamiliar words from how they are used.

...marise

...d closely

Work out what is going to happen.

...e & evaluate

...r knowledge

Weigh up the meaning, purpose and usefulness of the text as a whole.

...ual literacy

Date _____

...sheet 6.4: Features of fiction and ...ction texts

...he features of different text types as you meet them throughout the year.
...ples of these texts types as you come across them:

	Features	Examples
	• Command verbs	
	• Numbered steps in sequence	
	• Clear, plain language	
	• Narrative and/or dialogue	

...dge University Press 2021

Name _____ Date _____

Worksheet 6.1: Learning journal

Trim this page neatly and stick it into the front of your notebook.

Ideas for my learning journal

Possible section	Suggestions for what to include
A reading log	• Title, author, fiction/non-fiction, genre • My response and opinions • Techniques to use again
Model extracts	Extracts (copied or pasted in) I particularly enjoy …
Other examples	Examples of techniques and skills in different contexts and media (fiction, non-fiction, novels, e-books, magazines, comic books, graphic novels, newspapers, brochures, pamphlets, posters, advertisements, online articles, etc.).
My writing experiments	Try new writing techniques and styles, e.g. looking at: character development; narrative voice; tenses; voices and moods; suspense techniques; punctuation and layout experiments, etc.
My word bank	Words that interest me that I want to use again: • from books, a thesaurus, dictionaries or online • with definitions or examples of how the words are used.
Idiomatic phrases and proverbs	Note down idioms and proverbs to help me add 'colour' to my writing. (Remember to write down what they mean!)
Tips for speeches and presentations	A note of: • what other people do well • what works for me • techniques I would like to try.
Spelling	A note of: • useful strategies, rules and letter patterns • words and word families I find useful • word origins.

Cambridge Primary English 6 – Burt and Ridgard © Cambridge University Press 2021

> About the curriculum framework

The information in this section is based on the Cambridge Primary English curriculum framework (0058) from 2020. You should always refer to the appropriate curriculum framework document for the year of your learners' assessment to confirm the details and for more information. Visit www.cambridgeinternational.org/primary to find out more.

The Cambridge Primary English curriculum has been designed to help learners to become confident communicators. They will learn to apply reading, writing, speaking and listening skills in everyday situations, as well as developing a broad vocabulary and an understanding of grammar and language. Through this curriculum, learners will develop evaluation skills, learn to appreciate texts from different cultures and learn to write for different audiences and purposes.

The Cambridge Primary English curriculum framework is split into three strands: reading, writing and speaking and listening. For more information, visit the Cambridge Assessment International Education website.

A curriculum framework correlation document (mapping the Cambridge Primary English resources to the learning objectives) and scheme of work are available to download from Cambridge GO (as part of this Teacher's Resource).

> About the assessment

Information about the assessment of the Cambridge International Primary English curriculum framework is available on the Cambridge Assessment International Education website: **www.cambridgeinternational.org/primary**

> Approaches to learning and teaching

The following are the teaching approaches underpinning our course content and how we understand and define them.

Active learning

Active learning is a teaching approach that places learner learning at its centre. It focuses on how learners learn, not just on what they learn. We, as teachers, need to encourage learners to 'think hard', rather than passively receive information. Active learning encourages learners to take responsibility for their learning and supports them in becoming independent and confident learners in school and beyond.

Assessment for Learning

Assessment for Learning (AfL) is a teaching approach that generates feedback which can be used to improve learners' performance. Learners become more involved in the learning process and, from this, gain confidence in what they are expected to learn and to what standard. We, as teachers, gain insights into a learner's level of understanding of a particular concept or topic, which helps to inform how we support their progression.

Differentiation

Differentiation is usually presented as a teaching approach where teachers think of learners as individuals and learning as a personalised process. Whilst precise definitions can vary, typically the core aim of differentiation is viewed as ensuring that all learners, no matter their ability, interest or context, make progress towards their learning intentions. It is about using different approaches and appreciating the differences in learners to help them make progress. Teachers therefore need to be responsive, and willing and able to adapt their teaching to meet the needs of their learners.

Language awareness

For all learners, regardless of whether they are learning through their first language or an additional language, language is a vehicle for learning. It is through language that learners access the learning intentions of the lesson and communicate their ideas. It is our responsibility, as teachers, to ensure that language doesn't present a barrier to learning.

Metacognition

Metacognition describes the processes involved when learners plan, monitor, evaluate and make changes to their own learning behaviours. These processes help learners to think about their own learning more explicitly and ensure that they are able to meet a learning goal that they have identified themselves or that we, as teachers, have set.

Skills for Life

How do we prepare learners to succeed in a fast-changing world? To collaborate with people from around the globe? To create innovation as technology increasingly takes over routine work? To use advanced thinking skills in the face of more complex challenges? To show resilience in the face of constant change? At Cambridge, we are responding to educators who have asked for a way to understand how all these different approaches to life skills and competencies relate to their teaching. We have grouped these skills into six main Areas of Competency that can be incorporated into teaching, and have examined the different stages of the learning journey and how these competencies vary across each stage.

These six key areas are:

*   Creativity – finding new ways of doing things, and solutions to problems
*   Collaboration – the ability to work well with others
*   Communication – speaking and presenting confidently and participating effectively in meetings
*   Critical thinking – evaluating what is heard or read, and linking ideas constructively
*   Learning to learn – developing the skills to learn more effectively
*   Social responsibilities – contributing to social groups, and being able to talk to and work with people from other cultures.

Cambridge learner and teacher attributes

This course helps develop the following Cambridge learner and teacher attributes.

Cambridge learners	Cambridge teachers
Confident in working with information and ideas – their own and those of others.	**Confident** in teaching their subject and engaging each learner in learning.
Responsible for themselves, responsive to and respectful of others.	**Responsible** for themselves, responsive to and respectful of others.
Reflective as learners, developing their ability to learn.	**Reflective** as learners themselves, developing their practice.
Innovative and equipped for new and future challenges.	**Innovative** and equipped for new and future challenges.
Engaged intellectually and socially, ready to make a difference.	**Engaged** intellectually, professionally and socially, ready to make a difference.

Reproduced from Developing the Cambridge learner attributes *with permission from Cambridge Assessment International Education.*

More information about these approaches to learning and teaching is available to download from Cambridge GO (as part of this Teacher's Resource).

Approaches to learning and teaching English

In this new edition of Cambridge Primary English we offer an integrated approach to language skills (speaking, listening, reading and writing). This means that in each English lesson you can expect a focus on learning objectives from each strand of the curriculum framework. Each Learner's Book contains nine units: two long units and one shorter unit per 10-week term. Each long unit of 12 sessions has been designed to be delivered over four weeks, with three lessons per week, plus a revision session. If your timing is different we hope the materials are flexible enough for you to be able to fit them to your requirements. The shorter units of six sessions are intended to be delivered over two weeks, plus a revision unit. The units per term may be taught in any order with progression being built in per term, rather than unit-by-unit, to add further flexibility for the use of the programme and to allow for more cross-curricular matching.

Listening and speaking are a focus for effective communication, but also underpin reading and writing skills too. We consolidate and develop the sub-strands including: making yourself understood; showing understanding; group work and discussion; performance; and reflection and evaluation. We have included additional listening activities in this edition and there is enhanced support for developing listening and speaking skills in authentic and exciting contexts. Audio tracks actively promote good pronunciation of English and you will find recordings of all the texts from the Learner's Book in this Teacher's Resource.

Across each stage for reading and writing we introduce a wide range of fiction and non-fiction texts including fiction genres, poetry and non-fiction text-types for different purposes. There is a broad selection of authentic texts from around the world, which have been included to promote reading for pleasure as well as an understanding of meaning and the conventions and features of different types of writing.

For reading and writing we orchestrate rich coverage of each sub-strand and are still mindful to integrate listening, speaking, reading and writing skills as follows:

Word structure (phonics and spelling): We assume schools have followed a systematic phonics programme with decodable reading books and that increasingly learners are encouraged to enjoy and explore texts with less restricted word choice. We believe that phonics knowledge is a strong basis for reading and spelling, and that learners need to be both taught and have time to explore spelling patterns, rules and exceptions. By actively focusing the learners' attention on activities and useful rules in the context of the lesson, this course aims to improve the average spelling age in your classroom. Phonic workbooks are provided for Stage 1 and may be of some use for learners who need further or repeated practice in basic phonics at Stage 2.

The downloadable spelling lists in this Teacher's Resource are a supplement to the spelling activities at the back of the Learner's Book. Embedded throughout the notes are **Spelling links**; these are intended to suggest opportunities at which the indicated spelling areas can be looked at in greater detail.

There are three spelling spreads included at the back of each Learner's Book. Each spread contains specific spelling activities to address some of the spelling objectives in a systematic way to ensure complete coverage of all the objectives. They can be used at the teacher's discretion as part of a wider session or as part of a dedicated spelling session. The answers to the spelling activities are included at the end of this Teacher's Resource.

A suggested spelling session format

- **SAY the word and SEE the word.** Introduce words both orally and visually so the children see each word and hear the sound simultaneously to develop auditory perception. Use flash cards, words appearing on a screen or written on the board.

- **PLAY with the word.** They write it in the air or on their desk with a finger, mime it to a partner, write it on a slate or paper and hold it up, do visual memory activities with a partner: look at a word, close eyes and spell it. These activities provide immediate feedback and develop visual memory. Clap the sounds to demonstrate how the word is broken into syllables. Let the children find their own associations to help them remember words e.g. *ear* in h*ear* or *ache* in head*ache*.

- **ANALYSE the word.** Spelling rules can be helpful here to explain how words are built up, why letters move, how sounds change from one word to another and how patterns fit into words.

- **USE the word – make up a sentence.** Activities are provided in the Learner's Book but you can add to these by playing spelling games. Younger children enjoy spelling 'snap' or 'bingo'; older children might enjoy a spelling challenge/ladder or a competition that involves winners.

- **LEARN the word.** They commit the word to memory while writing it out in a wordbook or personal spelling notebook. Tests or assessments need not be repetitive weekly activities but learners do need incentive to internalise the spelling of words and to see they are making progress.

Vocabulary and language: We provide multiple experiences and strategies for securing vocabulary, including saying a word and then writing it, exploring context, grammatical features and a word's relationship to other words (word families, prefixes, suffixes etc.). We also explore texts with learners to reflect on writers' choices of vocabulary and language. In the final sessions of each unit we then innovate on the text vocabulary or language to apply learning and try out new found skills and knowledge.

Practical ideas for the classroom

Words and spellings need to be highlighted and enriched at every opportunity in the classroom.

1 Encourage personal wordbooks or cards: include words covered in spelling sessions and ones they look up in the dictionary. At the back, suggest learners develop a bank of words they would like to use (especially powerful, descriptive or unusual words). Word meanings can also be included. Some children may benefit by using colours or underlining/ highlighting to identify tricky bits or root words.

2 Have a classroom display of aspirational words or themed words around a topic (any learning area).

3 Have plenty of large spelling resources – online and print dictionaries, thesauruses, etc.

4 Set up spelling buddies as a first line of check if a dictionary or thesaurus does not help.

5 Play word games such as word dominoes or phonic pairs on a set of cards as a memory game.

6   Highlight and discuss word origins and have a merit system for anyone with interesting words or word information to share.

7   Display lists of words with similar sounds or letter patterns (either at the start, middle or end) – write the words large in the handwriting taught at the school joined up if appropriate to stimulate visual and kinaesthetic knowledge.

8   Have an interactive word list of interesting words, or words that match a spelling rule or word pattern being focused on. Add to it whenever anyone comes across a relevant word.

9   Consider an alphabet of vowel sounds and consonant sounds as a display or frieze around the walls.

10 If handwriting lessons are timetabled, add word patterns and sounds into those sessions.

11 Research free web resources to create your own crosswords and word searches linked to vocabulary in themes and spelling rules you are working on.

Grammar and punctuation: Whilst being mindful of reading for pleasure and text coherence, we focus on the grammar and punctuation arising from a text so that learners experience new learning in context. We have respected both teacher and learners' capacity for understanding and using correct metalanguage in the classroom and especially in writing activities.

Structure of texts: An exciting range of authentic texts is provided for discussion, performance, reflection and as models for learners' own writing. This is especially true in the final sessions of each unit when learners aim to write within the support of frameworks or scaffolds.

Interpretation of and creation of texts: Whilst the units provide a rich and broad selection of texts, it is also expected that learners are enjoying texts outside of the course, but aligned in some way to the topic or theme. Differentiation within each activity ensures that all learners can explore authentic texts and experiment with creative ideas and writing.

Appreciation and reflection of reading: We support the ethos of reading for pleasure and encourage learners to reflect and evaluate their wider reading from an early age. Links to Cambridge Reading Adventures (CRA) series are provided and offer a perfect bridge for learners between the texts in the Learner's Books, Book Band graded reading books in CRA and the wider world of authentic texts. We adopt 'assessment for learning' strategies to encourage learners to work independently and in pairs or groups to discuss their reading (and wider learning), to share experiences and to respond to others' ideas and experiences.

Presentation and reflection of writing: We encourage learners to adopt a write, reflect/evaluate and improve cycle of working from an early age. We encourage them to present their own work and listen for feedback as well as to talk about their own ideas and others'. Handwriting is an important part of writing and this series encourages best practice in handwriting but does not teach it explicitly. We recommend using the *Cambridge Penpals for Handwriting* series alongside *Cambridge Primary English* for teaching handwriting.

> Setting up for success

Our aim is to support better learning in the classroom with resources that allow for increased learner autonomy while supporting teachers to facilitate learner learning. Through an active learning approach of enquiry-led tasks, open-ended questions and opportunities to externalise thinking in a variety of ways, learners will develop analysis, evaluation and problem-solving skills.

Some ideas to consider to encourage an active learning environment are as follows:

- Set up seating to make group work easy.
- Create classroom routines to help learners to transition between different types of activity efficiently, e.g. move from pair work to listening to the teacher to independent work.
- Source mini-whiteboards, which allow you to get feedback from all learners rapidly.
- Start a portfolio for each learner, keeping key pieces of work to show progress at parent–teacher days.
- Have a display area with learner work and vocab flashcards.

Planning for active learning

We recommend the following approach to planning. A blank Lesson Plan Template is available to download to help with this approach.

1 **Planning learning intentions and success criteria:** these are the most important feature of the lesson. Teachers and learners need to know where they are going in order to plan a route to get there.

2 **Plan language support:** think about strategies to help learners overcome the language demands of the lesson so that language doesn't present a barrier to learning.

3 **Plan starter activities:** include a 'hook' or starter to engage learners using imaginative strategies. This should be an activity where all learners are active from the start of the lesson.

4 **Plan main activities:** during the lesson, try to: give clear instructions, with modelling and written support; coordinate logical and orderly transitions between activities; make sure that learning is active and all learners are engaged ; create opportunities for discussion around key concepts.

5 **Plan assessment for learning and differentiation:** use a wide range of Assessment for Learning techniques and adapt activities to a wide range of abilities. Address misconceptions at appropriate points and give meaningful oral and written feedback which learners can act on.

6 **Plan reflection and plenary:** at the end of each activity and at the end of each lesson, try to: ask learners to reflect on what they have learnt compared to the beginning of the lesson; build on and extend this learning.

7 **Plan homework:** if setting homework, it can be used to consolidate learning from the previous lesson or to prepare for the next lesson.

To help planning using this approach, a blank Lesson plan template is available to download from Cambridge GO (as part of this Teacher's Resource).

For more guidance on setting up for success and planning, please explore the Professional Development pages of our website **www.cambridge.org/education/PD**

> 1 Different voices – different times

Unit plan

Session	Approximate number of learning hours	Outline of learning content	Resources
1.1 What is a prologue?	1	Explore how books start. Read and explore a prologue. Start a learning journal.	Learner's Book Session 1.1 Workbook Session 1.1 ⬐ Worksheet 6.1 ⬐ Worksheet 6.2
1.2 Delve into detail	0.5+	Explore the prologue detail. Explore mood. Work with prefixes and word origins.	Learner's Book Session 1.2 Workbook Session 1.2
1.3 Focus on technique	0.5+	Explore writing techniques. Identify the effect of textual features. Build a picture of a character and setting.	Learner's Book Session 1.3 Workbook Session 1.3
1.4 Write a short prologue	0.5+	Plan a prologue for a reading book. Write, edit and improve a prologue. Share and evaluate each other's prologues.	Learner's Book Session 1.4 Workbook Session 1.4 ⬐ Worksheet 6.9 ⬐ Worksheet 6.11
1.5 White bears	0.5+	Read an extract for detail. Answer questions using evidence from various points in the text. Plan and write a fact file.	Learner's Book Session 1.5 Workbook Session 1.5
1.6 Short and long sentences	0.45	Explore sentence types and sentence length. Investigate the impact of short and long sentences. Extend sentences using phrases.	Learner's Book Session 1.6 Workbook Session 1.6

Session	Approximate number of learning hours	Outline of learning content	Resources
1.7 Review word classes	0.5+	Explore word classes. Identify and use the definite and indefinite articles. Investigate homographs and homophones.	Learner's Book Session 1.7 Workbook Session 1.7
1.8 Review dialogue	1	Read and perform dialogue. Explore direct speech. Explore reported speech.	Learner's Book Session 1.8 Workbook Session 1.8 ⬇ Worksheet 6.3
1.9 Voices	1	Read about events from different perspectives. Explore standard and colloquial English. Infer character from detail.	Learner's Book Session 1.9 Workbook Session 1.9 ⬇ Differentiated worksheets 1A–C
1.10 Finding out more about flashbacks	1	Listen for information. Explore how flashbacks work. Express a personal opinion.	Learner's Book Session 1.10 Workbook Session 1.10 ⬇ Worksheet 6.12
1.11 and 1.12 Create Voice 4 at the museum	1.5	Plan Voice 4 at the museum. Write Voice 4 at the museum. Edit and improve writing.	Learner's Book Session 1.11 and 1.12 Workbook Session 1.11 and 1.12 ⬇ Worksheet 6.6 ⬇ Worksheet 6.13
Cross-unit resources			
Diagnostic check Learner's Book Check your progress Learner's Book Projects Unit 1 Language worksheets End-of-unit 1 test			

BACKGROUND KNOWLEDGE

The early extracts in Unit 1 come from *East*, a book based on an old Norwegian folktale, *East of the Sun, West of the Moon*. The book is historical, being set long ago in a time of wooden sailing ships and travel by horse or foot. The book includes plenty of context about the time in which it was set, including information on hand-made map making, compasses, compass roses indicating the path of the winds – essential for sailing ships – and information about Inuit life and survival in the frozen North.

Edith Pattou, the author, has written a sequel to *East* (called *West*), also steeped in Scandinavian folk tales, which can be recommended to learners.

TEACHING SKILLS FOCUS

Language awareness

Language awareness is a critical aspect of acquiring competence in a language.

This unit focuses on many aspects of language awareness, from the nuts and bolts of word class and sentence structure (word order) to different registers attached to writing and speaking in different contexts. It is critical to be aware of some learners who will need greater support when working with figurative or idiomatic/colloquial language. In many respects, learners find standard English easier than figurative or colloquial English because the rules are clearer and they can learn subject–verb agreement, word classes and standard sentence structure (simple, extended, compound and complex).

Encourage learners to be aware of language as a means of communication – how rich it is and how differently we communicate in different contexts. Put up charts of commonly used figurative expressions and even slang expressions commonly used by the learners in those contexts. Regularly invite learners to re-express things in either more or less formal language so they become increasingly aware of how many different ways we can communicate the same thing.

When learners work at exploring and writing from different perspectives on the same event, focus on how the language used expresses not just content but also personality with meaning beyond the literal. This can be very difficult for some learners but the more familiar they become with different modes of communication, literal and figurative, formal and informal, the easier it will become.

When learners communicate with you as the teacher, encourage a more formal register, correct errors, for example in subject–verb agreement or tense, and give them the chance to rephrase what they intended to say correctly. Keep corrections light-hearted, but encourage learners to be aware of how they communicate in different contexts, which will help them to develop the skills of reading between the lines and inferring meaning that is not explicitly expressed.

1.1 What is a prologue?

LEARNING PLAN

Learning objectives		Learning intentions	Success criteria
Main focus	**Also covered**	• Explore how books start.	• Learners can talk about how books start.
6Rs.01, 6Rs.03, 6Ri.06, 6Ra.02, 6Wc.06, 6Wp.03, 6SLg.03	6Rv.02, 6Rv.03, 6Ri.02, 6Ri.03, 6Ri.08, 6Ri.10, 6Ra.01, 6Ww.03, 6Wv.06, 6Wp.01, 6Wp.02, 6SLm.03	• Read and explore a prologue. • Start a learning journal.	• Learners can read and discuss a prologue. • Learners can start and fill in a learning journal.

LANGUAGE SUPPORT

Using the word *prologue* as a springboard, the session highlights word origins, in this case, ancient Greek. The word is separated into its component parts – a prefix and a root word – to show how the word developed. It is useful to have access to an online etymological dictionary so that whenever words arise, especially those with clear component parts such as prefixes and suffixes, you can demonstrate how the

word originated and developed into the current form. Learners will do further work on word origins, prefixes and suffixes in later sessions and units.

Learners work on a prologue that comes from a book based on a Norwegian folktale. It would be useful to find images of runes to show what they look like. Images of skeins of wool, ships logs and sheaves of music would help learners understand the vocabulary.

Starter idea

How does it begin? (5 minutes)

Resources: Learner's Book, Session 1.1: Getting started; independent readers and other library books

Description: Organise learners into pairs to analyse how their reading books begin. Allow them to look at a range of other library books to explore how they begin as well.

Share how their books begin as a class – encourage learners to read out their book beginnings. Discuss any unusual or interesting beginnings. Point out that a traditional opening such as *Once upon a time* may indicate a particular genre of book, e.g. a folktale, traditional tale or fairy story – or even a story based on one of these genres.

Main teaching ideas

1 Read the opening paragraph (10 minutes)

Learning intention: To read an opening paragraph that is a flashback and express a personal response to the text

Resources: *The Middle of Nowhere* (Learner's Book, Session 1.1, Activity 1); Track 01

Description: The opening paragraph from the novel *The Middle of Nowhere* by Geraldine McCaughrean is extremely figurative right from the opening sentence. The novel is set in the Australian outback during the 1950s and 1960s. Incongruously, a piano is delivered to a remote telegraph station at a very difficult time for the family.

Encourage learners to notice the play on words relating to music (*a sweet note, jangled, unstrung,* etc.) suggesting things could have gone well but turned out badly. The mood is reflective and sad, with the narrator looking back. Although *if* clauses are covered later in the year, this is an opportunity to point out an *if* clause and show how it can be used to suggest how things could have been different – but cannot change now as time has passed.

Encourage discussion on whether the first paragraph is attention-grabbing. Explore how this short flashback to a moment the narrator has pinpointed as the start of events is a technique foreshadowing the type of story it is likely to be – in this case, one where events clearly go wrong.

Play the audio of *The Middle of Nowhere* (Track 01).

> **Differentiation ideas:** Provide additional support to learners to support their understanding of the techniques. Challenge learners to rewrite the short paragraph without using figurative language or imagery. Discuss whether it achieves the same effect.

Answers:
1   a   Figurative language about the sky falling in and images of music related to the piano – *sweet note, jangled, unstrung*, etc.
    b   Sad and reflective – accept any sensible answer.
    c   The narrator is looking back, which is clear from the past tense and use of the *if* clause followed by *as it was*.
    d   Learners' own answers.

2   Read and talk about a prologue (25 minutes)

Learning intentions: To read and respond to a prologue; to explore word origins

Resources: *East* prologue (Learner's Book, Session 1.1, Activity 2); Track 02, online etymological dictionary

Description: Discuss the character's speech bubble about the origin of *prologue*. Look at the ancient Greek script and explain that the ancient Greek alphabet was different from modern Greek, although there are similarities. Compare the Greek script to the runes mentioned in the prologue.

Explain that as well as the word *prologue* coming from ancient Greek, the ancient Greeks developed the concept of a prologue – really for plays, as they did not write novels then. The prologue was often performed by the chorus to foreshadow events, hinting especially at bad things or tragedy to come.

Encourage learners to use the Booktalk feature in the Toolkit at the end of the Learner's Book to discover more about the various elements of books. Explain that while a *prologue* is part of the story, a *preface*, written by the author, is not. A preface explains how a book came to be written and often acknowledges important people in the writing.

A preface is more common in non-fiction, whereas a prologue is strictly a fiction device.

Remind learners when talking in pairs to listen to each other in turn rather than interrupting with what they think or want to say. Explain how they can then build on what each other has said rather than just each having their own ideas.

Many of the fiction units in this stage demonstrate how writers manage the concept of time – going backwards or forwards in time, using flashbacks (mini ones, as in the opening extract in Activity 1 in this session or more major ones involving significant portions of the book, either interspersed with the main story or comprising it). Encourage discussion about time in books. Discuss how story narrative is generally written in the past tense, implying some form of looking back on events that have already occurred in contrast to dialogue, which represents words exactly as they are spoken at the time.

East's prologue has someone looking back to someone else looking back by including a note written by a person at some earlier stage. It is clear from the prologue that the story will focus on the author of the note and her journey rather than on the narrator of the prologue. Discuss with the class how the prologue gives clues about the story. If nothing else, it clarifies that the note writer survives her journey.

Play the audio of the prologue from *East* (Track 02).

> **Differentiation ideas:** Support learners by encouraging small groups to read the prologue together. Encourage more confident readers to look up unfamiliar vocabulary independently.

Answers:
2   a   Before the main story starts.
    b   Learners' own answers but can include giving clues as to the story and foreshadowing.
    c   Learners' own answers.

3   Start a learning journal (10 minutes)

Learning intention: To start a learning journal to record reading, writing techniques, ideas, predictions and useful words

Resources: Learner's Book, Session 1.1, Activity 3; Worksheet 6.1; notebooks

Description: Learners have been encouraged to maintain a record of their reading, but by Stage 6 this should be more of a learning journal, expanded to become a personal record of each learner's development as a reader and a writer. See the

Toolkit at the end of the Learner's Book for more extensive ideas on how learners might use their journals.

Aim to encourage creativity and help learners enjoy reading as writers, noting techniques writers use from sentence structure to imagery and more extensive devices such as prologues and flashbacks. If you are using the worksheets, use Worksheet 6.1 Learning journal at this point.

You may not want to be too prescriptive about how learners use their journals or how they organise them and lay them out and some level of differentiation might be appropriate.

Encourage learners to write more than just a list of titles and a simple comment. Model how they might choose words they particularly like, how to copy an extract with a comment explaining a particular technique or use of language they would like to use in their own writing or how to insert other examples from magazines and books to compare techniques into their journals. They can also draw impressions of characters or add images from magazines to make it more of a multimedia journal.

> **Differentiation ideas:** Vary the level of expectation for class learning journals. Support learners on a one-to-one basis by talking about what they are writing and prompting them as needed. Encourage more confident learners to write independently in their journals without being prompted.

Answers:
3   a–c Learners' own answers.

Plenary idea

Making predictions (5 minutes)

Resources: *East* prologue (Learner's Book Session 1.1); Worksheet 6.2

Description: Hold a plenary on what learners have gathered from the prologue.

Ask: *Who will be the main character? What is the main event in the story? What clues are given?*

Share ideas and end by asking learners to share predictions about what could have started *with a pair of soft boots.*

> **Assessment ideas:** Use learners' responses to assess how well they have understood both the explicit and implicit messages and clues in the prologue.

Use the session, especially if it is the first session of the year, to assess which learners settle well to tasks and which appear to need guidance.

Make informal notes on which learners participate regularly in discussion and ask questions either with a partner or as a class, and which learners need to be encouraged or given more opportunity to express themselves.

Make a note also of learners who struggle to listen to instructions or to partners. You can use Worksheet 6.2 Personal goals to set personal goals with each learner to revisit during and at the end of the year.

CROSS-CURRICULAR LINKS

Geography: Gather books on Norway and other Scandinavian countries and mapmaking.

Art: Gather information on weaving, tapestry and stories 'written in cloth'.

Homework ideas

Learners can complete the Workbook activities for Session 1.1, focusing on word origins and prefixes. Go through the answers in class the following day.

Learners can write about independent readers in their learning journals (Worksheet 6.1), giving a personal response.

Answers for Workbook

1   a 3   b 2   c 3   d 4   e 1
2   Learners' own answers.
3   a antibody   b Antarctic   c antisocial
    d anti-climax   e antibiotic   f antifreeze
    g antithesis   h antiseptic   i antidote
    j anticlockwise
4   Possible answers:
    a   *overcast* – on top of/covering
    b   *infrastructure* – below
    c   *perimeter* – round, about
    d   *postpone* – after in time
    e   *octagon* – eight
    f   *hyperactive* – beyond, more than normal
    g   *prepare* – before in time
    h   *exclude* – out
    i   *submerge* – under
    j   *synchronise* – in union, together

1.2 Delve into detail

LEARNING PLAN

Learning objectives		Learning intentions	Success criteria
Main focus	**Also covered**	• Investigate the prologue detail.	• Learners can identify relevant detail.
6Rv.02, 6Rs.03, 6Ri.01, 6Ri.10, 6Ri.11, 6Ri.14, 6Ww.03, 6Wv.03	6Ri.02, 6Ri.03, 6Ri.06, 6Ra.02, 6Wc.06, 6Wp.01, 6SLm.03	• Explore mood. • Work with prefixes and word origins.	• Learners can talk about mood and how it is created. • Learners can work with prefixes and word origins.

LANGUAGE SUPPORT

The vocabulary in this session builds on the previous session which will support some learners. At the end of the session, more work is done on word origins and prefixes. Encourage learners to notice that familiar school subjects, such as *biology*, might have names with ancient Greek origins. Encourage learners to think of other words with the prefix *bio-*, such as *biosphere, biometric, biodegrade, biopic* and *biography* – a text type covered later in the year (as well as *autobiography*). The prefixes learners explore in the Starter activity mean the following: *sub* – under, *trans* – across, *mono* – single, *micro* – very small, *auto* – self.

Common misconception

Misconception	How to identify	How to overcome
Mood in writing is just about whether it makes you feel happy or sad.	Ask learners what mood they are in now, at home time, when they read a scary story or when they are with their friends.	Use learners' reading books to help establish the many different moods created in the stories, whether adventure, suspense or humour.

Starter idea

List words with prefixes (10 minutes)

Resources: Learner's Book, Session 1.2: Getting started; dictionaries online etymological dictionary

Description: In pairs, learners should list words with the given prefixes.

Using the words as context, learners should discuss what the prefixes mean. Point out that using the root word can help decode the prefix when the whole meaning is considered. Learners can check using a dictionary.

Share answers as a class, using the online etymological dictionary, if time.

Main teaching ideas

1 Looking for clues in the prologue (25 minutes)

Learning intention: To make inferences using evidence from more than one point in the text

Resources: Learner's Book, Session 1.2, Activity 1; *East* prologue (Learner's Book, Session 1.1); Track 02

Description: Before learners start the activity, review what they remember of the prologue and previous discussion from Session 1.1. Encourage learners to work with a partner initially.

Focus on the prologue's role and the clues that answer the questions or foreshadow events to come. Learners should find evidence in the text for their responses, from more than one place; you may wish to produce an example answer in response to part a, showing how to back up your answer using evidence from more than one part of the text.

Encourage learners to notice the prologue's mood. Many prologues are sombre, hinting at difficulties to come. This prologue creates a sense of mystery, suspense and curiosity about things past.

Learners should respond to part e individually in their notebooks. Remind them to use their own words and to give reasons for their view.

> **Differentiation ideas:** Learners can support each other by talking through their answers in small groups before they write in notebooks. Differentiate the activity further by allowing learners to work orally only. Pair more confident learners together and encourage them to write down their answers after talking.

> **Assessment ideas:** If learners write the answers in their notebooks, this activity can be used to assess their comprehension of the prologue content, structure, purpose and position in the story.

Answers:

1 a
   - The author of the note because the note's author was asked to write everything down.
   - A story of a journey is referred to.
   - Papers in different languages; diaries; maps; ships' logs, skeins of wool, small boots made of soft leather; sheaves of music tied with faded ribbon; long, thin pieces of wood with map-like markings on them; dried-up mushrooms; woven belts; even a dress the colour of the moon – all the things in the box.
   - The writer of the note's brother (because Father is also mentioned). Accept sensible suggestions.
   - To set things right.

   b
   - Fiction – it is talking about a story and is not written factually. Also, prologues do not appear in factual books.
   - Fantasy, adventure or any sensible suggestion backed by clues in the text.

   c
   - Learners' own answers – accept sensible choices backed by reasons from the text.

   - The first part of the prologue is more mysterious, full of suspense and evoking curiosity
   - The second part is sadder and more wistful, expressing some level of regret or thoughtfulness looking back.
   - Learners' own answers but could change the mood by changing the verbs, removing the italics in the first part, taking away the hearing voices not being good and adding words like adverbs, e.g. *excitedly*.

   d   Flashback giving readers clues.
   e   Learners' own answers.

2 Decoding ancient Greek words (10 minutes)

Learning intention: To explore word origins and prefixes

Resources: Learner's Book, Session 1.2, Activity 2; online etymological dictionary

Description: Many English words have foreign origins, especially ancient Greek, Latin and French. Discuss familiar words in your region with non-English origins (e.g. *frankfurter, baguette, pasta*) that have been adopted into English. Explain that the ancient Greek civilisation was followed by the Roman civilisation which shared many things and adopted many words from ancient Greece. In addition, Britain was conquered first by the Romans, then by the French, so many foreign words came into the English language.

Discuss how the words *pro* and *logos* come together and have changed over time to become the English word *prologue*. The Toolkit at the end of the Learner's Book has an example of a word from an etymological dictionary definition for *autobiography* which is a conjunction of several words derived from ancient Greek. Use it as another example of parts of a word coming together like a jigsaw puzzle. If you have access, encourage learners to explore word origins using an online etymological dictionary.

Many prefixes have Latin or Greek origins. *Pro* may confuse if learners are more familiar with its meaning *for* from contexts such as the *pros* and *cons* of an argument. Ask if learners are *pro* or *anti* homework as another contrast of prefixes.

Spelling links: Discuss other common prefixes that mean *before* and *after*: pre–, post–, ante–, etc. Build a list of root words and word families on the board or wall display, e.g. *logic, logical, logically*.

Point out the hard *g* sound created at the end of the word *prologue* and ask what makes it a hard *g* sound (the *u* before the *e*) to revise the soft/hard *g* and *c* sounds. There are more activities on prefixes, word origins and root words in the Spelling section in the Toolkit at the back of the Learner's Book.

> **Differentiation ideas:** Support learners by providing a list of words to look up in the dictionary if they do not know what they mean or what they are the 'study of'. Encourage more confident learners to write sentences using the words.

Possible answers:

2   a   *Pro-homework* – Favouring or in support of. *Prominent* – Before in time, place or order (place).
    b   Learners' own answers. Examples: sociology, archaeology, anthropology, astrology, geology, zoology, ideology, theology.

Plenary idea

Apologies (5 minutes)

Description: Write *apology* on the board. Ask learners how *apology* uses the root *logos* and what the prefix *apo*– might mean (away – a speech in one's own defence – taking blame away).

Learners can think individually and then share with a partner before convening ideas as a class. They will not find *apo*– as a prefix in the dictionary – discuss why not.

> **Assessment ideas:** Assess learners' ability to use the meaning of word roots and prefixes with origins in another language to understand the meaning of whole words.

Homework ideas

Learners can complete the Workbook activities for Session 1.2. Go through the answers in class and listen to learners' *phobia* sentences.

Invite learners to find out if anyone at home has a phobia and to share it with the class.

Answers for Workbook

1   a   An irrational or extreme fear of something.
    b   noun   c   *c.*1786   d   Came into English possibly by the French word *phobie*, but originally from the ancient Greek suffix *phobia* from *phobos* meaning fear, panic or terror.
    e   Learners' own answers.

C	L	A	U	S	T	R	O	P	H	O	B	I	A	U
Z	E	K	I	T	G	F	E	G	J	B	V	J	I	X
K	M	R	A	R	D	H	H	R	A	G	S	T	B	C
T	Y	I	B	L	O	J	M	A	X	M	J	H	O	A
M	U	D	U	M	R	H	M	P	O	L	F	Q	H	R
I	B	I	B	L	I	O	R	H	O	B	I	A	P	N
A	B	L	U	T	O	P	H	O	B	I	A	U	O	O
K	K	X	G	O	U	R	Q	R	M	O	F	A	B	P
L	T	D	F	V	D	V	Z	H	O	N	G	S	R	H
O	A	I	B	O	H	P	O	O	Z	R	T	T	E	O
F	R	I	G	O	P	H	O	B	I	A	E	L	Y	B
A	P	I	O	P	H	O	B	I	A	K	H	D	R	I
F	X	W	K	N	J	S	N	A	J	K	W	L	I	A
A	I	B	O	H	P	O	T	C	O	O	U	W	F	S
Q	C	V	S	X	F	Z	E	B	F	U	O	R	L	B

2   *graphophobia* – fear of writing; *verbophobia* – fear of words; *bibliophobia* – fear of books; *apiophobia* – fear of bees; *zoophobia* – fear of animals; *octophobia* – fear of the number 8; *siderophobia* – fear of stars; *claustrophobia* – fear of small or enclosed spaces; *frigophobia* – fear of the cold; *arithmophobia* – fear of numbers; *carnophobia* – fear of meat; *ablutophobia* – fear of washing.

3   a–c   Learners' own answers.
4   a   philosopher; b   philately; c   philanthropists; d   bibliophiles; e   philharmonic.

1.3 Focus on technique

LEARNING PLAN

Learning objectives		Learning intentions	Success criteria
Main focus	**Also covered**	• Explore writing techniques.	• Learners can identify and discuss different writing techniques.
6Rv.04, 6Rg.08, 6Ri.08, 6Ri.09, 6Ri.10, 6Ri.11, 6SLg.02	6Rv.02, 6Rg.01, 6Ri.02, 6Ri.14, 6Ww.03, 6Wv.03, 6Wc.06, 6Wp.01, 6SLs.01	• Identify the effect of textual features. • Build a picture of a character and setting.	• Learners can discuss the effect of textual features. • Learners can build a picture of a character and setting using clues in the text.

LANGUAGE SUPPORT

Once again learners break down a word into its component parts – prefix and root – looking at word origins. They then use this knowledge contextually to suggest whereabouts in a book an *epilogue* would come (at the end). Learners are still building on the vocabulary encountered in Session 1.1.

Starter idea

Where does an epilogue come in a book? (5 minutes)

Resources: Learner's Book, Session 1.3: Getting started

Description: Learners use the etymological dictionary entry to predict where an epilogue might appear in a book and why a writer might use one. It is not dissimilar to a prologue in that it is usually set out of the time of the main story. It frequently features a character looking back on the events of the story and sometimes includes events set in the future to further resolve the story. Invite learners to give ideas for what they might include in an epilogue to their own reading books.

Main teaching ideas

1 Identify writing techniques (25 minutes)

Learning intention: To identify and explore writing techniques and features

Resources: Learner's Book, Session 1.3, Activity 1; *East* prologue (Learner's Book, Session 1.1); Track 02

Description: The prologue from Session 1.1 is in two parts – in the first part, a character looks back to finding a chest of items containing clues that will be important in the main story. It is written in first-person narrative. Discuss with learners its features in addition to first-person pronouns, e.g. show the thoughts of the narrator. In the second part of the prologue, the narrative is taken up by the writer of the note – it is also first-person narrative looking back at earlier events. This part is written in italics to differentiate it from the main prologue. Neither section reveals whether the narrator is male or female. Ask learners to predict this, giving reasons for their ideas.

Read through the Language focus box and discuss the difference between hyphens and dashes. Two of the dashes are used to provide additional information to the sentence (Other sounds came then – whispering ...; *more patience than I've got – or rather, than I used to have*) and one is more of an aside (*Hearing voices – this isn't good*). Discuss how the semicolon (;) is used. The first one in the prologue separates two parts of a sentence, keeping them closely linked rather than making them into two separate sentences. The semicolon is also used like this in the note. The second use of the semicolon is to separate items in a list. Encourage learners to note the use of the colon to introduce the list.

The handwritten note is mainly written in the present tense (and within parts in the past tense). Discuss the effect of this with the learners. It makes the letter more intimate and immediate, as if the writer is talking directly to the reader – perhaps as she writes the letter.

Encourage learners to notice when the writer uses short sentences for effect, e.g. towards the end of the first part of the prologue where the short sentences increase the sense of mystery and suspense. The note writer also uses a combination of short and long sentences, sometimes for emphasis and sometimes to reflect how the writer is almost thinking aloud. Discuss how when we think and talk, it is often not all in long sentences; we often have short truncated thoughts. The combination of different sentence lengths reflects this.

Remind learners that even though they discuss the answers to the questions before writing in their notebooks, they do not have to agree or write exactly the same thing. It is interesting for them to discover that not everyone has the same reaction or response.

> **Differentiation ideas:** Support learners by organising them into pairs to answer the questions.

> **Assessment ideas:** Informally assess learners' knowledge of the different writing techniques to establish planning where further work is required.

Answers:
1 a • Both parts in first-person narrative.
       • It allows the reader to get inside the thoughts of the narrator.
   b Learners' own answers. No clues are given – accept all sensible answers and reasons.
   c • To emphasise and to add drama.
       • To indicate that it is the note and not the same narrator as in the first part of the prologue.
   d To add additional information; an aside – talking to the reader; adding additional information and emphasis; adding additional information; adding additional information and emphasis
   e To create a longer pause than a comma linking two parts of a sentence that are too closely related to be separate sentences – adding additional information; to separate items in a list; to create a longer pause than a comma linking two closely related parts of a sentence – adding additional information.
   f Mainly present tense. It makes it more immediate, drawing the reader into the writer's thoughts as she has them.
   g The short sentences add emphasis – building suspense. In the second part, the short sentences reflect how the writer is thinking – unevenly in short truncated thoughts mixed with more meandering thoughts.

2 Building a picture (15 minutes)

Learning intention: To draw plausible inferences and make predictions

Resources: Learner's Book, Session 1.3, Activity 2; *East* prologue (Learner's Book, Session 1.1); Track 02

Description: To build a picture of the note writer, learners need to initially identify explicitly stated facts the writer includes. Discuss with the class what they have discovered and together make inferences about the character. For example, ask: *Is the writer male or female? Why do you think this?*

Making inferences will help learners work out what they do not know and what they would like to find out. What they do not know can be as interesting as what they do know.

Make sure learners give reasons when predicting who will be the main character – the first narrator or the note writer. The weight of inference would suggest it is the note writer who will tell his/her story of the journey he/she undertook.

While nothing specifically identifies the story as set in the past, nothing mentioned makes it appear that it is set in the present. Furthermore, in the prologue, the initial narrator finds things from the past, possibly a long time past. The note talks about events that have already happened, but these are the recent past for the writer. No modern gadgets or items are mentioned. While it is not impossible that the writer of the story could have woven his/her story into a cloth hanging, it is an activity that is more likely to have happened in the past before machines.

Allow time for pairs to discuss their reasons and then compare them with another pair before sharing ideas as a class.

Whenever learners work together in pairs, groups or even as a class, it is helpful to remind them of their core listening skills – to listen respectfully to each other's ideas and this year especially, to try to build on each other's ideas to develop a discussion rather than each learner just stating their own view. In groups, it is important for learners to encourage each other to take turns and to listen while waiting for their own turn. Listening is often taken for granted but listening is an active skill that requires learners to focus and pay attention and even respond, rather than just being there.

> **Differentiation ideas:** Support learners by helping them to draw up a character mind map for the note writer that they can add to when they read later extracts of the story. Encourage more confident learners to work individually and add more details and illustration.

> **Assessment ideas:** Ask learners to complete their answers in their notebooks and use them to assess how well they are able to make plausible inferences from the text.

Answers:
2   a   Learners' own answers but should include things like the note-writer is good at weaving, went on a journey to set things right, does not consider himself/herself a good storyteller, the writer has a brother (probably) and a father. The note-writer blames himself/herself for the death of someone loved.
    b   Learners' own answers; probably mainly whether the writer is male or female.
    c   Accept sensible, backed-up answers but it is most likely to be the note-writer, although of course it could be split between the narrators.
    d   Accept sensible, backed-up answers, but they should work out that it is more likely to be set in the past because of the things mentioned (and the lack of modern things mentioned).

Plenary idea

What do we know? (5 minutes)

Resources: *East* prologue (Learner's Book, Session 1.1); Track 02

Description: Hold a plenary to summarise what the prologue has suggested the story will be about. Gather information learners have explored in the Getting started and two main activities.

Review what they know about the two narrators in the prologue and what they do not know.

Encourage predictions about the genre of the story being introduced and invite comment on whether learners would like to read more of the story and why.

> **Assessment ideas:** Use learners' responses to informally assess how much they have understood in relation to the content and techniques in the prologue as well as about the prologue's purpose and what this might suggest about the story.

Homework ideas

Learners can complete the Workbook activities for Session 1.3. Go through the answers in class and survey learners to find out how confident they feel using hyphens and dashes correctly.

Learners could research the Bayeux Tapestry as an example of a famous story woven in cloth.

Answers for Workbook

1   a   hyphen   b   hyphen   c   dash
    d   hyphen   e   dash
2   Possible answers – accept sensible variations.
    a   The box was full of interesting things – things I had never seen before.
    b   My school – the one on the corner – is the largest in the area.
    c   Gardening – my favourite hobby – is a relaxing weekend activity.
    d   We managed to build the model aeroplane before everyone else – working together.
    e   I wish my friend – the one from Kuala Lumpur – would tell me some of the folktales from her region.
3   a   climax   b   additional information
    c   aside or comment   d   climax
    e   additional information

1.4 Write a short prologue

LEARNING PLAN

Learning objectives		Learning intentions	Success criteria
Main focus	**Also covered**	• Plan a prologue for a reading book.	• Learners can plan a prologue with various features for their reading book.
6Rv.04, 6Rg.03, 6Wv.04, 6Wg.01, 6Wg.04, 6Wg.08, 6Ws.02, 6Wc.01, 6Wc.04, 6Wp.04, 6Wp.05	6Rg.01, 6Rg.08, 6Rs.01, 6Ww.06, 6Ww.07, 6Wv.02, 6Wv.06, 6Wc.03, 6Wp.01, 6SLp.01	• Write, edit and improve the prologue. • Share and evaluate each other's prologues.	• Learners can write, edit and improve their prologues. • Learners can share, evaluate and discuss each other's prologues.

LANGUAGE SUPPORT

This session focuses on the learners' writing and ability to put into practice what they have learnt about writing techniques and prologues over the past sessions. Remind learners about the requirements of standard English and when to deviate from it for effect.

Common misconception

Misconception	How to identify	How to overcome
Prologues have to be written from the perspective of a character in the book.	Discuss the prologue to *East* and ask how different it would have been in third-person narrative.	Use learners' responses to stimulate a discussion on the benefits of third- and first-person narrators. Third-person narrative does not allow readers to get inside the head of a character in the same way as first-person. However, it can be seemingly omniscient and give clues that characters could not know about what is to come – looking forward as well as looking back.

Starter idea

Flashback or flash forward (5 minutes)

Resources: Learner's Book, Session 1.4: Getting started; independent readers

Description: Ask learners to spend a few minutes refreshing their memories of the characters and plot of their independent readers. If they have only just started one, suggest they use one they have already finished. In pairs, they can then discuss their books and what clues they might like to include in a prologue. They should think about whether their prologue would be a flash forward or a flashback and whether it would be written in first- or third-person narrative.

Main teaching ideas

1 Plan and write a prologue (25 minutes)

Learning intention: To plan and write a prologue to a reading book

Resources: Learner's Book, Session 1.4, Activity 1; Worksheet 6.11; A4 paper

Description: This should be a fun writing activity. Explain that at the end, groups will try to match each prologue to the correct book; learners must not sign their work and must write it out on A4 paper, neatly and legibly. You could ask learners to type their prologues to avoid handwriting clues.

Ask learners to choose either their current book or a favourite book they know well. Encourage them to read the blurb and then jot down questions about their book: *Who is the main character? Where is the book set? What is the main idea in the plot? What issue must be resolved?* Allow learners to discuss their questions and answers with a partner – they may find it easier if their partner asks questions they can answer. Partners can take notes for each other. Make sure they do proper planning.

Once learners are confident about the storyline, they can decide on the type of prologue to write. If it will provide hints and predictions with an omniscient or all-knowing, third-person narrator, suggest clues related to the key issue in the plot: *If only they had known …* If learners plan a flashback, encourage them to discuss what events could have happened before the story that might have led to the events of the story taking place. Be creative with suggestions and do not worry if learners write something similar to the model in the textbook. For more guidance on this, refer to Worksheet 6.11 Write a prologue.

Discuss a suitable structure for the paragraphs – one paragraph to introduce the gist of the story; the second to add more details with a few hints; the last to make predictions with *would, could* and changing from the past to the present or future tense. Encourage a mixture of long and short sentences.

> **Differentiation ideas:** Support learners by providing them with a frame for their paragraphs, after discussing their reading book.

Differentiate the activity further by suggesting one or two writing techniques to be included, e.g. italics or short sentences.

> **Assessment ideas:** Use Worksheet 6.11 Write a prologue to assess what learners have written to see if they have included the writing techniques and proofread carefully.

Answers:
Learners' own answers.

2 Discuss, edit and improve prologues (15 minutes)

Learning intention: To edit and improve prologues based on proofreading and feedback

Resources: Learner's Book, Session 1.4, Activity 2; Worksheets 6.9 and 6.11; A4 paper

Description: Partners swap prologues and read each other's aloud. Encourage them to read through first so they can read aloud fluently and add expression, especially if it has a mood of suspense. Encourage them to ask each other questions about the book. Consider modelling a question-and-answer session with a volunteer.

Once the prologues have been written or typed out, display the class's reading books and prologues for groups to try to match prologues with books. If more than one prologue has been written on the same book, read them out and discuss the different aspects that have been picked up.

> **Differentiation ideas:** Support less confident learners by setting them fewer success criteria in Worksheet 6.9 Writing assessment sheet so that they can focus on one or two aspects of their writing.

> **Assessment ideas:** Use Worksheet 6.9 to assess learners' handwritten or typed prologues. They can be kept for portfolio purposes to assess how well learners have understood prologues, and as an example early in the year of their writing capacity and level of sophistication, as well as whether they can maintain a consistent narrative voice and tense throughout their paragraphs. Example success criteria:

- *I must write a three-paragraph prologue.*

- *I must use a consistent narrative voice (first or third person).*

- *I must include several writing techniques.*

- *I must choose words carefully for effect.*
- *I must use a variety of sentence lengths for effect.*

Answers:
2 a–c Learners' own prologues.

Plenary idea

What about an epilogue? (5 minutes)

Resources: Reading books

Description: Ask learners to think about what might be in an epilogue to their reading book. Ask: *Could a character be looking back some time later at the events of the book with something meaningful to say? Could the epilogue be some later events after the end of the story that shows what happened to the characters?*

After a few minutes, invite volunteers to present ideas for an epilogue. They should show the class their reading book and give a summary of events, before suggesting ideas for the epilogue.

> **Assessment ideas:** Assess learners' ability to handle time through their ideas for the epilogue. Ask: *Are you able to suggest events that occur beyond the end of the plot? Can you place the narrator forward in time looking back to the events of the story with comments and reflections?*

Homework ideas

Learners can complete the Workbook activities for Session 1.4. Go through the answers in class, inviting volunteers to share what they have written.

Learners can ask at home if anyone has read a book with a prologue.

Answers for Workbook

Possible answers

1 **a** present **b** It gives the sense of immediacy, as if the action is happening as the reader reads. **c** It is talking about something in the past. **d** The future tense is used in the last sentence – to foreshadow what is to come.

2 **a** First person **b** Use of the personal pronouns *I* and *we* **c** For emphasis – to make the reader realise there is something special about *the old way* **d** It makes them stand out and it emphasises that *They*, although not named, are somehow real and present. **e** It allows readers to fill in their own ideas about what will happen. **f** Learners' own answers.

3 Learners' own answers but certainly fiction.

4 Learners' own answers.

1.5 White bears

LEARNING PLAN

Learning objectives		Learning intentions	Success criteria
Main focus	**Also covered**	• Read an extract for detail.	• Learners can read an extract for detail.
6Rv.04, 6Ri.01, 6Ri.02, 6Ri.07, 6Ri.11, 6Ri.14, 6Ra.02, 6Ws.04, 6Wc.06, 6Wp.03, 6Wp.04	6Rv.01, 6Rv.02, 6Rv.03, 6Rs.03, 6Ri.03, 6Ri.06, 6Ri.12, 6Ri.16, 6Wv.01, 6Wg.08, 6Wp.02, 6Wp.05, 6SLm.03	• Answer questions using evidence from various points in the text. • Plan and write a fact file.	• Learners can answer questions drawing on evidence from various points in the text. • Learners can plan and write a fact file drawn from the text.

The extract from *East* in this session contains a glossary which includes the word for polar bear in Norwegian. Some of the Norwegian names and what the white bear is called may be challenging for some learners, especially as the names are in some cases figurative.

The extract also contains one or two phrases which may be unfamiliar, e.g. *driving blizzard* or *deep winter months*. Both *driving* and *deep* have a more figurative meaning when combined with *blizzard*

or *winter*. Encourage learners to predict what the phrases mean based on the context.

Otherwise, the extract contains largely factual information about white bears. Discuss with learners whether the inclusion of this factual information still makes this part of a fiction story. Point out that although the extract refers to white bears, learners may be more familiar with calling them polar bears.

Starter idea

Polar bears (5 minutes)

Resources: Learner's Book, Session 1.5: Getting started; reference books about polar bears and their habitat

Description: Ask learners what they know about polar bears, e.g. their colour and where they live. Then give learners a few minutes to discuss with each other anything else that they know about polar bears, e.g. what they eat, how big they are and whether they hibernate.

Share ideas as a class to build up a fact file of prior knowledge about polar bears, allowing learners to browse the reference material.

Main teaching ideas

1 Finding out about white bears (20 minutes)

Learning intention: To scan for detail to answer questions and analyse the extract's features

Resources: *East: Neddy (1)* (Learner's Book, Session 1.5, Activity 1); Track 03

Description: Learners should be able to predict that the extract will be in first-person narrative as each chapter is told from a different character's point of view.

Learners can read the extract in pairs aloud, with one person reading the narrative and the other reading the peddler's words. You could also use audio of the extract (Track 03).

Discuss with learners that the note writer in the prologue said that Neddy was the real storyteller in the family, that both Neddy and 'father' had written down their versions of the story and that the note

writer was also talking about writing down the story. Learners may find it challenging to talk about Neddy's voice in the extract, but he is clearly telling a story of the past. He is not reminiscing or looking back and talking about feelings as the note writer was. If anything, his voice is more similar to the first narrator in the prologue who is also recording events – although more mysterious ones. Neddy is recounting almost factual information that does not seem mysterious or have any particular mood attached to it – it is more serious and matter of fact.

Learners should be able to predict that the note writer is Rose, Neddy's sister.

Bring learners together to go through the questions and remind them of the difference between facts and opinions so that they are able to recognise the extract as factual.

In part c, ask whether the name 'He Who Walks Without a Shadow' is literal or figurative.

> **Differentiation idea:** Support learners by asking them to write answers to the questions in their notebooks before coming together for a class discussion.

Answers:

1 a First person, because it is like a diary or journal with Neddy telling this part of the story. It also uses first-person pronouns.

  b • Accept all sensible answers backed up by reasons for the differences.

     • The note-writer is Rose, Neddy's sister. Accept all sensible explanations, especially that the note-writer mentions *Neddy* and *father* and so it is likely that the character, Rose, will be his sister.

- Accept sensible words for the mood, e.g. thoughtful, matter-of-fact and serious.
- Learners' own answers about their choice of words.
- The extract is factual because it provides objective information.

c
- Neddy wanted to find out about white bears after one had saved his sister Rose. A white bear had saved her from drowning in a frozen pond, although that is not mentioned here.
- Accept sensible answers about the bear's name, e.g. the white bear is white against a backdrop of snow – white on white.
- Learners' own answers on their favourite Saami names.

2 Draw up a mind map (20 minutes)

Learning intention: To write a mind map using information from the extract

Resources: Learner's Book, Session 1.1, Activity 2; *East: Neddy (1)* (Learner's Book, Session 1.5); Track 03

Description: Encourage learners to make notes as they scan the extract to find factual information to include in their mind maps.

Do not be prescriptive about how learners display their work. They may not want to use a mind map. They could also use a table or other way to organise their notes – whatever seems appropriate to them. Encourage use of bullets, headings and colours to make the information stand out. If possible, give them the opportunity to source images of polar bears to include in their notes, either from the internet or from reference books which they could scan or copy.

Encourage learners to compare their work to a partner's, and, if necessary, allow time for them to add any additional information to their own notes. Encourage them to give each other feedback on layout as well as content, making suggestions for improvement.

> **Differentiation ideas:** Support learners by allowing them to work in pairs to draw up the mind map. Limit how much information learners need to

find according to ability, e.g. three or five facts. Encourage more confident learners to present their mind maps or notes using IT. For example, learners could source a short video to include in a PowerPoint presentation.

> **Assessment ideas:** Use this activity to see how well learners are able to change the text from one format into another – from story to fact file. It is a good opportunity to see what textual features learners consider appropriate for a fact file, e.g. a table, picture or bullets.

Answers:
2   a–b   Learners' own fact files.

Plenary idea

How different would it be? (5 minutes)

Resources: *East: Neddy (1)* (Learner's Book, Session 1.5); Track 03

Description: As a class, discuss whether learners enjoy stories written in first-person narrative or whether they prefer third-person narrative.

Invite volunteers to read out sections of the extract, transforming it into third-person narrative. Discuss what changes need to be made and whether the effect is different.

> **Assessment ideas:** Note whether learners can successfully translate first-person narrative into third-person narrative.

> **CROSS-CURRICULAR LINKS**
>
> **Science:** Gather reference books and information on polar bears and their habitat.

Homework ideas

Learners can complete the Workbook activities for Session 1.5. Go through the answers in class, inviting learners to share their sentences from Activity 2.

Learners can do additional research into polar bears and their environments.

Answers for Workbook

1 a **knead**: press and shape the mixture firmly and repeatedly with your hands to make bread; **need**: something you must have or do; **kneed**: hit someone with your knee

   b **vain**: too interested in your own appearance or achievements; **vane**: flat, narrow part of a fan, propeller, etc. that turns because of the pressure of air or liquid against it; **vein**: tube that carries blood to the heart from the other parts of the body.

2 Learners' own answers.

3 a adjective; antonym: heavy; own example.

   b noun; antonym: none; own example.

   c adjective; antonym: burdened, heavy, down, heavy-hearted; own example.

   d adjective; antonym: awkward, clumsy; own example.

   e adjective; antonym: dark, intense; own example.

   f noun; antonym: dark, darkness; example given.

   g noun; antonym: none; own example.

   h verb; antonym: snuff out, put out, smother; own example.

4 Learners' own answers.

1.6 Short and long sentences

LEARNING PLAN

Learning objectives		Learning intentions	Success criteria
Main focus	**Also covered**	• Explore sentence types and sentence length.	• Learners can identify and discuss different sentence types.
6Rg.03, 6Rg.08, 6Wg.08	6Ri.01, 6Ri.03, 6Wg.04, 6SLm.03	• Explore the impact of short and long sentences. • Extend sentences using phrases.	• Learners can talk about the effect of a writer's choice of long or short sentences. • Learners can extend sentences using phrases.

LANGUAGE SUPPORT

While learners should be familiar with what constitutes a sentence, it is useful to consolidate early in the year as a base for building compound and complex sentences later. There are three main sentence types: statements, questions and commands. Exclamations are sometimes considered a sentence type, although they are not strictly sentences as they do not have a subject and finite verb. When learners work through the activities on re-ordering the words to make sense of the sentences, encourage them to search for the verb first and then to identify the subject, before looking at what is left which will be the object or remainder of the sentence.

Learners may need to be reminded that phrases are groups of words that work together and do not contain a verb, which differentiates them from sentences and clauses. Phrases can do the work of various word classes such as adjectives, adverbs and nouns.

Starter idea

A sentence or a phrase? (5 minutes)

Resources: Learner's Book, Session 1.6: Getting started

Description: Give learners time to use their prior knowledge to explain the difference between a phrase and a sentence to each other.

Learners can then give each other examples of sentences that contain one or more phrases. They can also identify whether the phrase is doing the job of an adjective or an adverb.

Invite pairs to share their sentences with the class.

Main teaching ideas

1 Writers use a variety of sentences (20 minutes)

Learning intentions: To revise sentence structure and sentence types; to extend sentences using phrases

Resources: Learner's Book, Session 1.6, Activity 1

Description: Give learners time in groups to build on the Getting started activity and work out what makes a sentence. Then, bring the class together and develop a class definition on the board, clearly identifying the key sentence features and optional features, such as objects or descriptive phrases.

For part a, invite volunteers to list the different sentence types, giving examples of each. Break down each example into component parts: subject, finite verb, object, descriptive phrase etc.

Still in groups, learners reorder the words in part b to make sense of the sentences. Remind them to focus on finding the finite verb first, then the subject and then the remainder of the sentence. Some sentences may take different word orders (e.g. a phrase might go in different positions). In part c, learners make phrases into sentences.

Learners then extend some simple sentences using phrases, adverbial or adjectival, both at the beginning and the end of the core sentences. Remind learners that even when you extend a simple sentence with numerous phrases, it is still a simple sentence if it only has one finite or complete verb.

> **Differentiation ideas:** Support less confident learners by working together in small groups to ensure that they understand what constitutes a sentence and that they are confident at identifying phrases to extend sentences.

> **Assessment ideas:** Assess learners' grasp of sentence features and the difference between a sentence and a phrase.

Answers:

1   a   • Learners' own answers but must include a subject and a finite verb, and make sense on its own.
      • Statements begin with a capital letter and end with a full stop. Questions begin with a capital letter and end with a question mark. Commands begin with a capital letter and end with a full stop or an exclamation mark, often start with a command verb and have an implied subject.
    b   • The bear caught a fish. Statement.
      • Do white bears live in snowy regions? Question.
      • Find out as much as possible about white bears. Command.
      • White bears have a strong sense of smell. Statement.
    c   Learners' own answers but must include a subject and a verb, and make sense.
    d   Learners' own answers.

2 Writers use sentence length for effect (20 minutes)

Learning intention: To explore the effect of short and long sentences

Resources: Learner's Book, Session 1.6, Activity 2; *East: Neddy (1)* (Learner's Book, Session 1.5); Track 03

Description: Learners re-read the extract *Neddy (1)* closely to answer the questions. Encourage discussion around the effect of the short sentences, reminding learners that there may be no 'right' answer and that the writer is deliberately choosing to use a combination of short and long sentences.

In paragraph 2, the list of items introduced by a colon would normally be separated by commas, but each is separated by a full stop. This, however, does not make them sentences as they do not have the features of a sentence – some are just single words. Again, they are a deliberate choice by the writer. In fiction, writers often diverge from the normal rules of writing and standard English to create a particular effect. Encourage learners to suggest reasons why the writer chose full stops to separate the list items.

Explore the reasons behind the writer's use of long and short sentences in the rest of the extract. Then encourage learners to add this writing technique to their learning journals, with examples from the extract to demonstrate its effect. This will remind them to use the technique in their own writing.

> **Differentiation ideas:** Support learners by encouraging small groups to discuss answers rather than write them. Work with less confident readers and writers on their learning journals so they have a useful reference and can copy techniques to support their writing more easily. Encourage more confident learners to work alone, writing the answers in their notebooks before sharing ideas with a partner.

Answers:

2   a   • It has two short sentences and three long
             sentences.
         • Learners' own answers about the effect.
             An example might be to contrast what he
             knows and what others know.
     b   • No, each item is not a sentence because
             they do not contain the features required to
             make a sentence.
         • For a list, you would usually use commas,
             but possibly semicolons.
     c   Examples in Paragraphs 4 and 5 – 4 is the
         better example containing the Saami saying.
     d   Neddy is giving factual explanations using
         sentences that must be modified to link
         ideas and so become longer sentences.
     e   To emphasise the power and strength of the
         bear and how dangerous it is.
     f   Learners' own answers.

Plenary idea

Extend me (5 minutes)

Resources: A simple sentence of your choice, e.g. *The white bear lifted its head*.

Description: Write your chosen simple sentence on the board and invite learners to extend it using phrases.

Ask learners how many phrases they can add to the beginning and end of the sentence, and then identify the role each phrase is playing: adverbial phrase or adjectival phrase – or even noun phrase.

See if you can add a phrase of your own at the end.

> **Assessment ideas:** Use the activity to assess whether learners know the difference between sentences, phrases and clauses.

Assess also learners' understanding and facility with adverbial phrases. You can build on this later when you revise and develop compound and complex sentences with dependent clauses.

Homework ideas

Learners can complete the Workbook activities for Session 1.6, practising short and long sentences and phrases. Go through the answers in class, inviting learners to share their sentences in questions 3–5.

Answers for Workbook

1   a   White bears have an excellent sense of smell.
     b   I interviewed anyone who had ever seen a
         white bear to find out more.
     c   The Saami believe you should know
         everything about the white bear before
         hunting one.
2   **b** and **c**.
3–4   Learners' own answers.
5   Learners' own answers.

1.7 Review word classes

LEARNING PLAN

Learning objectives		Learning intentions	Success criteria
Main focus	**Also covered**	• Explore word classes.	• Learners can identify different word classes and their purposes.
6Rg.05, 6Rg.08, 6Ww.04, 6Wg.08	6Rv.02, 6Rv.03, 6Wv.02, 6SLm.01, 6SLm.03	• Identify and use definite and indefinite articles. • Investigate homographs and homophones.	• Learners can use definite and indefinite articles appropriately. • Learners can differentiate homophones and homographs by using them appropriately in context.

LANGUAGE SUPPORT

This session consolidates learners' prior knowledge of word classes by revising them and their purposes. Traditionally, there are eight parts of speech: *noun, verb, pronoun, adjective, adverb, conjunction, preposition* and *interjection*. Some of these have been extended, such as conjunctions into *connectives* and adverbs to incorporate *adverbials* in general. Learners are often unfamiliar with *interjections (Oh! Wow!)*, traditionally one of the eight parts of speech but often omitted when learning about word classes.

The session extends into *homographs* and how the different meanings for a word may even encompass different word classes. This can be challenging and is different to synonyms which would automatically share the same word class.

The session also provides specific guidance on using the definite and indefinite articles correctly. Some learners find articles difficult, but using articles correctly is critical.

Starter idea

Remember word classes (5 minutes)

Resources: Learner's Book, Session 1.7: Getting started

Description: In pairs, learners try to remember the different word classes. Encourage learners not only to give each other examples of the different word classes, but also to create sentences that use most if not all the different word classes.

Allow time for pairs to compare their lists with partners in case they have omitted any word classes.

Main teaching ideas

1 Identify and understand word classes (20 minutes)

Learning intentions: To explore word classes and their purposes; to use the definite and indefinite article appropriately in context

Resources: Learner's Book, Session 1.7, Activity 1

Description: Words and sentences are the building blocks of good communication. Learners may read and see widespread use of abbreviated communication, especially on ICT platforms. A strong understanding of the word classes/parts of speech and how elements of sentences fit together will help them to build effective sentences and paragraphs whether writing fiction or non-fiction. Grammar can appear dry and pointless if it is not attached to good examples and will not seem meaningful to learners. However, some drill is beneficial, particularly for those who learn best by repeating an activity until they have mastered it.

Encourage discussion about the boxed words: what they do and how they add to a sentence. For example, adjectives qualify a noun: *a flower, a beautiful flower, a budding, blue flower, a fragrant, delicate, exotic flower.* Encourage learners to come up with sentences that use as many of the word classes as possible and display them for everyone to enjoy.

If learners are unsure of a word class, they can use a dictionary to check. If the word belongs to more than one word class, many dictionaries provide a contextual example. If possible, suggest learners try out online dictionaries, e.g. the Cambridge Learner's Dictionary.

Remind learners of the importance of context and that some words may belong to more than one word class – e.g. *in* can be both a preposition (*put it in the box*) and an adverb (*please come in*).

Supplementary teacher information: In some regions, *articles* are part of a class of words known commonly as *determiners*, which includes words like *this, that, those, my, your* and *their* – these determiners are also sometimes known as demonstrative adjectives (*this, that, those*) and possessive adjectives (*my, your, their*).

Spelling link: Point out that the indefinite article is *a* for words beginning with a consonant, but *an* for words beginning with a vowel, and that the pronunciation of *an* elides into the noun.

> **Differentiation ideas:** Support less confident learners by making time to go over the concepts, different word classes and their purposes with learners who are finding them challenging.

Answers:
1 a Learners' own answers.
  b Learners should comment on the difference between any fish or pine needle and a specific fish or pine needle – one that has previously been identified.
  c Learners' own answers.
  d noun, adjective, verb, adverb, preposition.
  e Learners' own answers.

2 Understand homographs and homophones (20 minutes)

Learning intention: To explore homographs, homophones and easily confused words

Resources: Learner's Book, Session 1.7, Activity 2; dictionaries and thesauruses

Description: Homographs can confuse learners if they are not aware of or looking out for them. Discuss the word origin from ancient Greek: *homo* meaning 'same' and *graph* meaning 'something written'.

Homographs are spelt/written the same way and so look the same, although they do not always sound the same, e.g. *record* (n) – *record* (v); whereas homophones (*homo*/same and *phone*/sound) sound the same but are not spelt alike, e.g. *sight/site* and some are easily confused. Writing the homophones in the context of sentences will help entrench the spelling with the meaning.

Some homographs share a word class, e.g. both might be nouns; others are different word classes. The activities cover both. Encourage learners to use a thesaurus and a dictionary.

> **Differentiation ideas:** Support less confident learners by limiting the number of answers required in each question to allow more time to focus on the word classes and meanings.

> **Assessment ideas:** Use Activities 1 and 2 to generally assess learners' understanding of and competence with the different word classes. It is an important foundation for the year's learning.

2 Answers:
  a Possible answers:
     • pupil: a school student; the black centre of the eye.
     • club: an organisation for people who want to take part in a sport or social activity together, or the building they use for this; a long, thin stick used to hit the ball in golf; a heavy stick used as a weapon; a place open late at night where people can dance.
     • ring: a round piece of jewellery to wear on your finger; something that is the shape of a circle; the sound a bell makes.
     • bank: an organisation or place where you can borrow or save money; the land along the side of a river; a large pile of snow, sand or soil.

- bat: a piece of wood used to hit the ball in some sports; a small animal like a mouse with wings that flies at night.

b   Learners' own answers.

c   Possible answers:
- adventurous: adj. synonym possibilities: daring, bold, brave, courageous, audacious.
- disturb: verb. synonym possibilities: interrupt, distract, bother, disrupt, annoy, intrude.
- warily: adv. synonym possibilities: cautiously, suspiciously, carefully, thoughtfully.
- guardian: n. synonym possibilities: carer, protector, caretaker, keeper, guard.

d   Learners' own answers.

Plenary idea

Sentence challenge (5 minutes)

Resources: Small pieces of paper

Description: Give each learner a few pieces of paper and a few minutes to write their name and as many sentences as possible that use all the word classes – or ones that you specify. They should write each sentence on a different piece of paper. Collect the sentences.

Write some of the sentences on the board to share with the class, identifying the different word classes.

> **Assessment ideas:** Use this activity to assess learners' ability to identify and use the different word classes appropriately in context. You can do this orally and by taking in the pieces of paper.

Homework ideas

Learners can complete the Workbook activities for Session 1.7. Go through the answers in class. Encourage learners to use the prepositions in Activity 4 correctly in sentences.

Answers for Workbook

1   a the   b a   c no article   d a   e the

2   b verbs   c pronouns   d prepositions   e nouns   f adjectives   g adverbs   h interjections

3   Learners' own answers.

4   between; in front of; through; across; beside; under; over; below; next to; above; outside; beyond.

1.8 Review dialogue

LEARNING PLAN			
Learning objectives		**Learning intentions**	**Success criteria**
Main focus	**Also covered**	• Read and perform dialogue.	• Learners can read and perform dialogue with appropriate expression.
6Rg.07, 6Ri.10, 6Wv.04, 6Wg.02, 6SLm.04, 6SLp.01, 6SLp.02, 6SLr.01	6Rv.05, 6Rg.01, 6Ri.02, 6Ri.16, 6Ra.01, 6Ra.02, 6Ra.03, 6Wv.02, 6Wv.05, 6Wc.01, 6Wc.03, 6Wp.04, 6SLm.05, 6SLr.02	• Explore direct speech. • Explore reported speech.	• Learners can write and correctly punctuate direct speech. • Learners can change direct speech into reported speech.

LANGUAGE SUPPORT

In this session, learners focus on the dialogue and what it reveals about the characters. The term 'register' is introduced to help learners compare the features of narrative and dialogue – standard English in narrative versus less formal speech patterns in dialogue.

They are also introduced to an ellipsis which appears in Neddy's speech. An ellipsis is a specific punctuation mark that marks where words have been omitted, e.g. when not all a quote is relevant. More frequently in fiction, however, it represents a pause, either in what someone is saying or in the narrative. It can also show a character or narrator trailing off, leaving the reader to fill in the missing thoughts or actions.

Starter idea

How do you punctuate direct speech?

(5 minutes)

Resources: Learner's Book, Session 1.8: Getting started; a selection of reading books containing dialogue

Description: Learners will be familiar with punctuating dialogue from previous stages, but may need to revise the specific grammatical and punctuation rules.

Ask learners to explain the rules as they remember them to each other and allow them to consult their reading books, or a selection that you provide, to help them remember the rules.

Allow learners to compare their rules with another pair and discuss any differences.

Main teaching ideas

1 Read the dialogue aloud (25 minutes)

Learning intention: To explore narrative and dialogue and infer character.

Resources: *East: Neddy (2)* (Learner's Book, Session 1.8, Activity 1); Track 04; Worksheet 6.3

Description: Authors do not usually describe characters in their entirety – they allow readers to infer from the way characters speak and act. Encourage learners to make suggestions about what the characters are like.

Explain that you do not want learners to read out the connecting narrative but rather they must use the connecting narrative as stage directions to help them know how to speak and act – e.g. *She jabbed a finger toward the cloak*. Discuss how to read with expression and to empathise with each character. Encourage learners to recall what they know of Neddy and Rose from previous sessions.

Use the audio of the extract (Track 04).

Ensure learners skim the passage to check they understand context before they focus on their own parts to check understanding of the words and how to pronounce them. For guidance on skimming, refer to Worksheet 6.3 Reading strategies.

Encourage body language and gestures to accompany voice expression. Every good reading is in some ways a role play. Ask one or two pairs to demonstrate their reading. Invite feedback on what was enjoyed and suggestions for improvement.

Ask learners to draw a mind map of their character using the character's words to build a character profile. Share mind maps and discuss ideas about the characters.

Learners should then be able to read the dialogue with even more expression. Swapping characters will give them a different perspective on the same events.

> **Differentiation ideas:** Support less confident learners by limiting how much of the dialogue in the extract pairs need to read so they can focus on interpretation. Provide learners with photocopies of the extract so they can underline and annotate their parts.

Answers:
1   a   Learners' own answers.
    b   They show him trailing off, not wanting to say everything. They show his hesitation and how uncomfortable he is. He would leave pauses where the ellipses are if speaking.
    c   He was beginning to realise what was going on. The phrase is figurative – truth does not glimmer and *dawn on me* links to the sun rising and light bringing understanding – he can **see** what is going on.
    d–f   Learners' own answers.

2 Revise dialogue and punctuation skills (20 minutes)

Learning intention: To explore dialogue and punctuation

Resources: Learner's Book, Session 1.8, Activity 2; *East: Neddy (2)* (Learner's Book, Session 1.8); Track 04

Description: Get learners to discuss the dialogue and develop a memo before having a class discussion to find out how much they remember about punctuating dialogue. Pull the activity together by drawing up a class memo for the wall on punctuating dialogue.

Do the same for reported speech.

Learners can now put into practice what they have revised about punctuating dialogue when they continue the dialogue (and narrative) between Neddy and Rose. Remind learners that the narrative will be in the past tense, but the dialogue may not necessarily be. In addition, learners should use a less formal register for the dialogue than for the narrative – trying to keep in character according to the earlier part of the conversation in the extract.

Remind learners that details make all the difference – they should think about word choice, expressions, colloquialisms – even figurative expressions, sentence structure and so on.

Giving their dialogue to another pair to perform will show learners how well they have given 'stage directions' through the narrative.

> **Differentiation ideas:** Organise pairs of less confident and more confident learners as the activities are a mixture of reading, writing and performing. Challenge learners to write independently.

> **Assessment ideas:** Assess learners' dialogue for content, punctuation and interesting connective narrative. Negotiate relevant success criteria with learners. For example:

- *We are to extend dialogue in the extract involving the same characters.*

- *Each character must speak at least twice.*

- *We must keep the dialogue 'in character' from our prior knowledge of them.*

- *We must punctuate the dialogue according to the rules we developed.*

Answers:

2   **a**   Learners' own answers but should include speech marks around the words actually spoken; dialogue introduced by a comma and the dialogue beginning with a capital letter; a new line for each speaker; a comma inside the speech marks at the end if followed by narrative indicating who is speaking or otherwise, a question mark/exclamation mark inside the speech marks at the end. If the speaker continues after narrative ending with a comma, no capital letter is used.

    b   Rose slowly asked Neddy why he had kept their secret from her. Neddy shook his head and replied that she would not have understood. At least that was what he had thought.

    c   Learners' own answers but should include that the reported speech is often introduced by *that*, and that the rest of the speech goes a tense further into the past, e.g. *have* goes to *had*. Pronouns also often change.

  d–e   Learners' own answers.

Plenary idea

Let's hear it (5 minutes)

Resources: *East: Neddy (2)* (Learner's Book, Session 1.8); Track 04

Description: Invite pairs to read the dialogue between Neddy and Rose to the class, adding the dialogue they wrote themselves.

Encourage other learners to give pairs feedback on what they enjoyed and what they learnt about the characters from the reading. They can also give suggestions for improvement.

> **Assessment ideas:** Assess learners' ability to read aloud confidently and fluently and to convey ideas about characters through speech, gesture and expression. Also make notes on how successfully learners give each other constructive feedback as they will be doing so throughout the year.

Homework ideas

Learners can complete the Workbook activities for Session 1.8 on working with dialogue and word endings. Go through the answers in class the next day. Invite volunteers to read out their dialogue for Activity 2.

Answers for Workbook

1 a 'Don't forget to bring your soccer ball tomorrow,' [own word, e.g. *reminded*] Javier.

  b Ava [own word e.g. *begged*], 'Please may I go to the party? Everyone will be there.'

  c 'What on earth have you got there?' [own word, e.g. *laughed, enquired*] Sebastian.

  d 'Give me that!' [own word, e.g. *demanded*] Nesmah. 'It's mine.' (or *mine*! optional exclamation mark at the end)

2 Learners' own answers.

3 electrician, competition, mansion, invitation, session, musician, technician, discussion, expansion.

4 Learners' own answers.

1.9 Voices

LEARNING PLAN

Learning objectives		Learning intentions	Success criteria
Main focus	**Also covered**	• Read about events from different perspectives.	• Learners can read and appreciate the same events from different points of view.
6Rv.04, 6Rg.03, 6Rg.07, 6Rs.01, 6Rs.03, 6Ri.10, 6Ri.14, 6Ri.16, 6Wg.08, 6SLm.01, 6SLm.04, 6SLp.02, 6SLr.02	6Rv.01, 6Rv.05, 6Ri.02, 6Ri.07, 6Ri.11, 6Ri.17, 6Ra.01, 6Ra.02, 6Wv.02, 6Wv.04, 6SLp.01	• Explore standard and colloquial English. • Infer character from detail.	• Learners can identify and talk about standard and colloquial English. • Learners can infer what characters are like from details in the text.

LANGUAGE SUPPORT

The session focuses on the differences between standard and colloquial English – a difference in register. While the text is written as first-person narrative, the format is of each person 'speaking' and so the register is less formal than might be expected in ordinary narrative accompanying dialogue. Learners are expected to infer characterisation in part through how each character speaks – the register – and in part through the level of standard or colloquial English. In the text for Voice 3, text and word effects are also used as visual clues.

This work on standard English builds on earlier work identifying aspects of standard English such as subject–verb agreement, full sentences and sentence structure, no contractions and correct pronouns.

Common misconception

Misconception	How to identify	How to overcome
People recounting the same events include the same details.	Invite two or three learners to recount an event that they all participated in, e.g. something that happened at assembly or in the classroom. Listen to each account and then invite the rest of the class to identify differences in their accounts.	Help learners to realise that people remembering events differently or different details does not mean they are not telling the truth, although someone could be telling just some of the truth. Use the voices to show learners that when recounting the same events, different characters focus on different aspects – they have different perspectives.

Starter idea

What is standard English? (5 minutes)

Resources: Learner's Book, Session 1.9: Getting started

Description: Allow learners a couple of minutes to recap on what constitutes standard English and to give each other examples.

Come together as a class and discuss the different occasions when standard English is used and when it may not be. Also discuss what is not standard English – e.g. colloquialisms, idiomatic speech, contractions and non-standard sentence structure. Point out that some figurative language may form part of standard English if it is used within standard sentence structure.

Main teaching ideas

05 1 Explore the extract (25 minutes)

Learning intentions: To understand perspective and point of view; to infer a timeline from different narratives of the same event

Resources: *Voices in the Museum* (Learner's Book, Session 1.9, Activity 1); Track 05; recording device to record the readings and role play

Description: *Voices in the Museum* tells the same events from three different points of view. A fourth person is mentioned in the events. Learners piece together Voice 4 by inference during the following sessions.

Use the audio of the text (Track 05).

Learners should work in groups of three, with one person for each voice. Each learner skims their voice to get the general idea, then summarises the key points for the others before they infer an overall timeline drawn from all three voices.

Encourage discussion on the different points of view and what they noticed – what information seems the same and what appears only in one voice. Use this opportunity to differentiate between the writer's voice and the narrator's voice. Discuss how many narrators there are (three) and yet there is one writer. Talk about how each 'voice' narrates a version of events in first person - showing how the writer 'becomes' each voice. Look back and compare this style with the extracts from East which is also written in first person. Now ask learners to look at their independent readers and identify the narrator. Is it a character (first person) or an outside narrator (third person) that is outside the story? Compare the techniques and how the writer's voice as an external narrator can know things a character as the narrator cannot. Find out which technique they prefer to read.

They can also discuss their initial impressions of the characters. If appropriate, pool the class's impressions of the voices before they read aloud. Ensure learners have correctly inferred that Jax (Voice 3) is Voice 2's teenage daughter. They can infer this from the text and then gain a clearer impression of her age from the picture and the text effects in her writing. If possible, let groups record themselves reading aloud so they can listen and discuss how to improve expression and characterisation. Allow them to practise before recording a final version. If no recording device is available, groups can practise in front of each other to get feedback.

To get in character, encourage learners to get into position physically as they read, e.g. sit as if on a bench, constantly looking around for Maximilian. If learners imagine the body language, expressions and gestures, this should come out in the reading when they hear it played back.

The voices describe events that happened in parallel rather than in sequence, so learners need to scan each voice carefully to piece together a sequential timeline of the events. There is some flexibility in how they interpret the sequence, e.g. it is not clear whether the lady arrives before the supervisor, but learners can infer that he sits down after she does, from her reaction.

Learners can draw the timeline, with caption notes above and below. Start with a discussion about what happened first, then allow groups to construct the timeline. Groups can compare timelines for accuracy and discuss differences.

Learners can use a mind map or other organisational tool to build a profile of each voice; the important skill is to find evidence in the text to support their inferences.

A class discussion about their favourite character rounds off the session well. Learners should express their preference giving reasons and evidence; focus on their reasoning so they become confident at justifying an inference.

> **Differentiation ideas:** Encourage the formation of groups that mix less and more confident readers for the reading and character analysis. Allow more confident groups to form if they occur naturally but challenge them to work harder at their reading and character analysis.

Answers:
1 a Learners' own answers.
  b An older lady (Voice 1) is taking her charge, possibly her son or grandson, Maximilian, on an educational outing to the museum. She seems fussy and uptight as she sits on a bench and disapproves of Maximilian going to the kiosk rather than studying the dinosaur. Voice 2 is a supervisor at the museum who is just coming off shift, waiting to meet his (probably) teenage daughter, Jax. Jax (Voice 3), is probably a teenage girl who meets Maximilian in the kiosk queue where he is anxiously looking towards Voice 1 because he knows she will not approve of him going to the kiosk instead of studying the dinosaur.
  c Learners' own answers.
  d Timeline to include at least the following: Voice 1 arrives with Maximilian at the museum and goes to the Dinosaur Hall. Voice 1 sits down on the bench near the Tyrannosaurus Rex, while Maximilian wanders off to look at the exhibits. She notices something odd about the dinosaur. After Voice 1 has sat down, Voice 2 sits down on the other end of the bench, having come off shift at the museum. He either has or has not already met up with his daughter who is queuing at the kiosk to get coffee for him. Meanwhile Maximilian wanders away from the dinosaur and joins the kiosk queue. While trying to hide from Voice 1, he begins to get on the nerves of Voice 3 although she finally asks if he wants a drink, after noticing something slightly strange about the dinosaur. While they are both in the queue talking, Voice 1 notices that Maximilian is no longer looking at the dinosaur and is queuing at the kiosk, so she gets up to make her way over to him.
e–f Learners' own answers.

2 Think about how we express ourselves (20 minutes)

Learning intention: To explore the link between standard and colloquial English styles and characterisation

Resources: Learner's Book, Session 1.9, Activity 2; *Voices in the Museum* (Learner's Book, Session 1.9); Track 05; Differentiated worksheet pack

Description: Supplementary teacher information: Standard English can be a difficult concept for learners, especially as English varies from region to region and in general, standard English has become much less formal than it was 10–20 years ago. However, it is still important for learners to be able to recognise what is generally regarded as standard English with complete sentences, paragraphs, correct grammar and punctuation, subject–verb agreement and no colloquialisms such as contractions, slang or idiomatic expressions. English is an extremely figurative language and so it is not entirely appropriate to say that standard English contains no figurative expressions at all. However, it does not usually contain idiomatic expressions.

This would be a good place to use Differentiated worksheets 1A–C on working with figurative language and idiomatic expressions.

Allow learners to work initially in pairs and then go over part a as a class to ensure everyone is clear before they write the sentences in their notebooks.

Each character recounts the events as if they are speaking, so learners can consider the 'voice' of each character in terms of standard English, slang and colloquialisms. In the case of Voice 3, textual features also indicate how she speaks and something of her character.

Learners should notice that Voice 1 uses the most correct or standard English, which fits with other evidence about her: her formal way of dressing and behaving, and what she thinks Maximilian should be doing. Voices 2 and 3 use the most idiomatic, non-standard English. This could be due to age, regional accents/dialect, an informal context or more relaxed personality type – the grandmother being the most old-fashioned and proper, probably due to her age, emphasised by her more formal dress. Voice 3 reflects the voice and writing style of a teenager in the use of terms like *sooooo*.

There are no right or wrong answers, but learners should draw inferences about characters from how they speak in the text. However, be sensitive about guiding learners to recognise that speech does not necessarily reflect all there is to know about a person, e.g. in relation to speech difficulties, accents or how people choose to express themselves.

Encouraging learners to role play the different characters will help them reflect on the different ways we choose to express ourselves either naturally or by choice.

> **Differentiation ideas:** Support learners by working in a small group with those who find it hard to infer characterisation from the speaking style and to identify non-standard English constructions.

> **Assessment ideas:** Use learners' reading/role plays to assess understanding of characterisation and how we choose to express ourselves. Keep recordings for their portfolios, focusing on how well learners reflect variations in speech and appropriate use of standard English; how well they convey ideas about characters in drama in different roles and scenarios

through speech, gesture and movement; and how well they vary vocabulary, expression and tone of voice.

Negotiate relevant success criteria with learners. For example:

- *We should summarise each character's account of events to find out about them.*

- *We should use body language, gesture, and tone of voice to reflect our characters.*

- *We should include our knowledge of their use of standard English into our characterisation.*

- *We can record ourselves so we can discuss our performance and improve it.*

Answers:

2   a   Possible answers:
- I would have asked [her] if she was alright but I was exhausted.
- I thought I would ignore the lady in the purple coat until Jax came with my coffee.
- Jax knows every bone well, and has done since she was a young child!
- Would you like a cool drink?

     b
- Voice 1 – it fits her proper appearance and how fussy she is.
- Learners' role plays. They should feel that standard English changes Voice 2's character and does not reflect the same person.
- Learners should notice the text effects, e.g. *sooooo tired* [informal spelling for emphasis]; we always do the *dinos* [underlining for emphasis and informal abbreviation]; *She must have been sweltering – didn't she look outside this morning?* [rhetorical question for emphasis]; *ON MY NERVES* [capitalisation for emphasis]; *The Purple Coat* [nickname and italics for mischief and emphasis]; *You up for a cool drink, then?* [casual expression]; *broke the ice* [idiomatic expression]; also the contraction *We'd* and use of an ellipsis at the end to allow the reader to imagine what happened when the Purple Coat arrived. All these points together imply a teenage speaker.

     c
- calm and unworried; do fake crying; very expensive; miss out on something by being too late; have second thoughts

about something; sort yourself out and get organised; be in trouble.

- Voices 2 and 3 use the most idiomatic/colloquial or non-standard English. Accept all sensible suggestions for reasons based on the text.

d Learners' own answers but should justify it either way – Voices 1 and 3 contain both narrative and dialogue but all the narrative sounds like someone speaking – recounting their observations and thoughts.

Plenary idea

Who is Voice 4? (5 minutes)

Resources: *Voices in the Museum* (Learner's Book, Session 1.9); Track 05

Description: Hold a class discussion to discover everything the learners can find out about Voice 4 – the boy, Maximilian, who is mentioned by Voices 1 and 3.

Invite suggestions about what he might have said if he had been recounting the same events and his speaking style.

> **Assessment ideas:** Informally assess how learners are able to infer information and detail about character from various different points in the text. They will need this skill when they actually create Voice 4, so it would be helpful to know who will need extra support.

Homework ideas

Learners can complete the Workbook activities for Session 1.9, working with standard and colloquial English. Go through the answers in class the next day. Learners can mark each other's work.

Learners can do their own research on dinosaurs.

Answers for Workbook

1 a true b true c false d true e false f false g true h false i true j true

2 a second sentence b first sentence c second sentence d second sentence e second sentence f second sentence.

3 a proverb b proverb c idiom d proverb e idiom f proverb g idiom

4 a–c Learners' own answers.

1.10 Finding out about flashbacks

LEARNING PLAN			

Learning objectives		Learning intentions	Success criteria
Main focus	**Also covered**	• Listen for information.	• Learners can listen for detail to answer questions.
6Rs.02, 6Rs.03, 6Ri.07, 6Ri.14, 6Ra.02, 6SLs.01	6Rv.03, 6Rv.05, 6Rv.06, 6Ri.02, 6Ri.09, 6Ri.10, 6Ra.03, 6Ws.01, 6Wp.02, 6SLm.03	• Explore how flashbacks work. • Express a personal opinion.	• Learners can talk about how flashbacks work. • Learners can express personal opinions based on what they have read or listened to.

LANGUAGE SUPPORT

The listening extract does not contain especially challenging language, so no learners should be disadvantaged. The focus of the activities is listening for detail and ordering events chronologically when presented in the extract out of sequence.

Common misconception

Misconception	How to identify	How to overcome
Flashbacks are always a separate chapter.	Use the listening activity to ensure that learners understand that a flashback moves to an earlier part of the story and events that have happened previously. Ask how a reader would know that they had suddenly started reading a flashback.	Use the discussion to help learners see that authors can manage flashbacks in a variety of ways, including separate chapters and differentiated text, e.g. italics. In addition, ask learners how the flashback section of the listening text begins – *The whole episode started three weeks before …* thereby locating the following section earlier in time.

Starter idea

Flashback (5 minutes)

Resources: Learner's Book, Session 1.10: Getting started

Description: Allow learners a few minutes to talk in pairs or small groups about any flashback experiences they may have had. Explain that it can be very brief – when doing something, they might have a sudden, vivid memory of some earlier event or conversation triggered by what they are doing at the time.

Share any experiences of your own before inviting learners to share their experiences.

Main teaching ideas

🎧 06

1 Listen for detail (30 minutes)

Learning intention: To listen for information and detail

Resources: *Oliver Strange and the Journey to the Swamps* (Learner's Book, Session 1.10, Activity 1); Track 06; Worksheet 6.12

Description: Flashbacks may be more familiar to learners from films rather than in novels and the concept can be difficult for younger learners. Flashbacks can be short inserts or even the main story, as is frequently the case in Michael Morpurgo's books.

If you have access to the internet, *The Piano*, a two-minute animation by Aidan Gibbons, set to music by Yann Tiersen, is a fabulous way to introduce flashbacks. An old man is playing the piano and the film traces his life in a sequence of flashbacks. Be aware that the mood of the film is emotional, and it includes wartime scenes; you will need to judge whether the content is appropriate for your class.

The novel is about a boy, Oliver, who travels to Southern Africa from Tooting, an area of London, to search for his professor father who has gone missing while researching an extremely rare but poisonous frog. The book opens while Oliver is already on his way to Africa, so the flashbacks occur regularly throughout the book to explain some of the background and how a young boy happens to be travelling to Africa on his own.

Talk about what learners think a flashback could be and how it would work in a novel before explaining and reading the extract. The extract comes from the end of Chapter 4 and the beginning of Chapter 5 of the novel. Oliver flashes back to how it all began, after everything started to become strange. You can use Worksheet 6.12 Oliver Strange – a timeline of events to support this activity

Make sure learners read the text extract in the Learner's Book first to give context. Play the audio (Track 06) or read the text aloud with learners listening. Although this is designed as a listening activity, you may want to provide a copy of the text to allow less confident learners to follow as you read. Remind learners that listening is an active process that requires them to sit properly to listen, to focus and to interpret what they hear before responding. Listening is a core skill and you can assess the quality of their listening through their ability to respond appropriately – not just listening for explicit meaning but for underlying meaning as well. The more they develop this skill, the more successful they will be in all areas of the curriculum. Add your own questions to the questions in the activity to challenge them further if you feel it is appropriate.

Play or read the extract once, then discuss what learners remember. Now ask them to read the questions before you play or read it again. The questions are largely concrete and require concentrated listening and note-taking of explicit information rather than interpretation. Remind learners that note-taking means writing key words rather than full sentences.

Let learners go over their notes and work out where they need to listen for more information, then play or read the extract once more for them to complete their answer notes. Remember that listening is a skill that learners need to practise, so they do not need to be too concerned about getting everything right. When you go over the answers, build them as a class using contributions from everyone rather than marking the activity as right and wrong individually.

Before learners draw up the timeline, discuss the sequence of events, particularly with groups of less confident learners helping them to see that the end of Chapter 4 is set after the events at the start of Chapter 5 (the flashback). Make sure they do not think they are just focusing on the list of things that have happened to Oliver in the first part of the extract.

> **Differentiation ideas:** Support learners by providing access to the recording as often as they need to, in order to answer questions and draw up the timeline. You can also provide a copy of the text. Encourage more confident learners to write full answers to the questions rather than taking notes only.

> **Assessment ideas:** Assess learners' listening ability, either via the class discussion or by looking at their notebooks or Worksheet 6.12 if you have used it.

Audioscript: *Oliver Strange and the Journey to the Swamps*

He turned away from Zinzi. He wasn't the one who was weird. This was what was weird:

1   His aunt hadn't been in Bulawayo to meet him.
2   He was travelling with a python.
3   A creepy, sinister man was following him.
4   Ilalaland wasn't a place after all.
5   The plans he'd made with Grandma in Tooting had gone upside down.

6   Tooting was far away … a zillion, million miles away. Another life.
7   And worse than everything, he wasn't any closer to finding his father than before. Now his father had truly disappeared.

Chapter 5 Tooting, London – Wanted Alive

The whole episode started three weeks before when he'd stared down at the globe on the kitchen table in Tooting.

"He's gone, Grandma!"

"Who?"

"Dad! He's completely and utterly disappeared."

His grandmother looked up from her sudoku puzzle in *The Times*. "Disappeared? What do you mean, utterly disappeared?"

"He's gone. It happens, Grandma. People disappear."

"Objects disappear, Oliver. *People* don't!"

"Yes, they do!"

"Not people like your father. It would be hard to make him disappear."

Ollie spun the globe. The colours blurred under his hand. The pattern of red dots snaked like an intricate belt around the earth's middle. Each dot was a red sticker that he'd stuck to the globe to mark a place his father had been to.

The stickers encircled the world. There was no beginning and no end to them.

The red snake began in south China. Then it wriggled its way through Vietnam, Cambodia and Thailand, then stretched across to Madagascar, and coiled up through Mozambique, Tanzania and over the Congo, across the ocean through the Amazon to Peru and ended up by catching its own tail as it slithered its way through the islands of the Pacific Ocean.

His father had travelled just about everywhere in the world.

All in the quest for frogs.

Why? Why was he so *obsessed* with frogs?

Dianne Hofmeyr

Answers:

1 a • He is in Zimbabwe, on his way to Victoria Falls.

 • His aunt hadn't been Bulawayo to meet him. He was travelling with a python. A creepy, sinister man was following him. Ilalaland wasn't a place after all. The plans he'd made with grandma in Tooting had gone upside down. Tooting was far away. He wasn't any closer to finding his father than before; his father had disappeared.

 • The flashback is set in Tooting, London – three weeks earlier. Oliver is with his grandmother.

 • His father had visited south China, Vietnam, Cambodia, Thailand, Madagascar, Mozambique, Tanzania, the Congo, (through the Amazon – could include Brazil), Peru and the islands of the Pacific Ocean. He went to research frogs.

 b Basic events to be included: Oliver's father gets interested in frogs; he travels the world to research frogs; he disappears; Oliver tells his grandmother he thinks his father has disappeared; Oliver goes to Africa to find his father.

2 Exploring flashbacks (15 minutes)

Learning intention: To explore how flashbacks work in a story

Resources: Learner's Book, Session 6.10, Activity 2; *Oliver Strange and the Journey to the Swamps* (Learner's Book, Session 6.10); Track 06; Worksheet 6.12

Description: If necessary, play the audio or read the listening text once more before this activity. Ask learners to think about the point of the flashback and what role it plays as they listen.

Ask some general questions about the text's features, such as the style in which it is written, features that they recognise, the simile and figurative language of the red dots becoming like a snake and finally the rhetorical questions at the end.

Explain that the flashback was contained in a chapter on its own and discuss other ways writers could indicate that a piece of the writing is a flashback, such as using italics or introductory phrases as this one does – *The whole episode started three weeks before …*

Encourage learners to think about how stories are normally presented in time sequence. Ask: *How would the book be different if the Chapter 5 flashback had been Chapter 1?* Encourage them to see it as an author choice to withhold information from the reader to make the story more exciting.

Invite learners to predict why Oliver's father is so interested in frogs. Enable learners to infer this aspect of the plot might be resolved in a flashback or in the main story.

Encourage learners to share their opinions and personal responses to stories with flashbacks, whether they enjoy the idea of them and whether they might normally choose to read this book or could be encouraged to read it based on what they have heard. They should add their views to their learning journals.

> **Differentiation ideas:** Encourage the formation of mixed groups of more and less confident learners to discuss the answers to the questions before sharing ideas as a class. Draw reluctant learners out to help them feel more confident about giving their opinion.

Answers:

2 a Chapter 4 is the main story and Chapter 5 is the flashback.

 b For example, the text could be in a different font or in italics.

 c • Readers learn that Oliver normally lives in Tooting (England) with his grandmother and his father disappeared several weeks ago. Oliver's father has travelled all over the world searching for frogs.

 • This information could have been at the beginning of the story –i.e. in time sequence.

 d • Learners' own answers about the obsession with frogs.

 • Learners' own answers about finding out but ask for reasons.

 e Learners' own answers.

Plenary idea

What happens next? (5 minutes)

Description: Talk as a class about how the story might progress in Chapter 6 where the main story resumes. Pick up on some of the questions that arise from the end of Chapter 4, such as why his aunt had not been there to meet him, why he was travelling with a python, a girl called Zinzi and a bushbaby.

Invite suggestions as to what Oliver will do when he reaches Victoria Falls to help find his father and whether learners think Zinzi will help him.

〉 **Assessment ideas:** Use the discussion to informally assess how much detail learners have picked up and their ability to draw inferences from the text and make predictions.

CROSS-CURRICULAR LINKS

Geography: Gather reference books on Africa, particularly Zimbabwe and Zambia in the area of the Victoria Falls and Bulawayo.

Homework ideas

Learners can complete the Workbook activities for Session 1.10 to consolidate their understanding of flashbacks. Invite learners to share their finalised flashbacks the next day in class.

They can discuss films at home and with friends that they think contain flashbacks to share at school.

Answers for Workbook

1–3 Learners' own answers.

1.11 and 1.12 Create Voice 4 at the museum

LEARNING PLAN

Learning objectives		Learning intentions	Success criteria
Main focus	**Also covered**	• Plan Voice 4 at the museum.	• Learners can plan what happened to Voice 4 at the museum.
6Rg.07, 6Rs.03, 6Wv.02, 6Wv.04, 6Wg.04, 6Ws.02, 6Wc.01, 6Wc.04, 6Wp.04, 6Wp.05, 6SLm.01, 6SLp.01, 6SLp.02, 6SLr.01	**6Rv.05, 6Ww.06, 6Ww.07, 6Wv.05, 6Wv.06, 6Wg.08, 6Wp.01, 6SLm.04, 6SLm.05, 6SLp.03**	• Write Voice 4 at the museum. • Edit and improve writing.	• Learners can write to bring Voice 4 to life, sounding authentic. • Learners can edit and improve their work incorporating feedback.

LANGUAGE SUPPORT

Learners again focus on register when writing Voice 4 in the museum. Be clear that although Voice 4 is likely to contain informal or colloquial speech patterns, learners still need to understand the rules that apply to standard English and how they can break some of them effectively in order to create an authentic boy's voice. Encourage the use of figurative language including idiomatic speech, supporting learners who may find this challenging.

Common misconception

Misconception	How to identify	How to overcome
You do not need to consider standard English when writing dialogue.	Encourage learners to re-read Voices 1 to 3 in the text in Session 1.9 and discuss with them which ones use standard English. Learners should note that although Voice 1 uses almost exclusively standard English, and the other voices use colloquialisms, the rules of standard English underlie them all.	Encourage learners to notice examples of standard English such as subject–verb agreement, word order, sentence structure and so on in Voices 2 and 3. Enable them to see how standard English is interspersed with colloquial English and how language rules are broken only with care to create effect.

Starter idea

Non-standard English (5 minutes)

Resources: Learner's Book, Session 1.11 and 1.12: Getting started

Description: Rather than focusing on standard English, allow learners a few minutes to talk about language that would not be considered standard English, e.g. idiomatic speech, some figurative expressions or language, slang, jargon, subject–verb disagreement and general colloquial manner of speaking.

After learners compare their ideas with another pair, share ideas as a class and link what they have said to register. Explain that spoken language or dialogue is usually less formal in register and often less technically correct than narrative and so they are likely to use it in conversation with each other or in families and friendship groups, whereas they would use a more formal register when speaking to a teacher.

Main teaching ideas

1 Build a profile of Voice 4 (35 minutes)

Learning intentions: To role play different characters; to build a profile of Voice 4

Resources: Learner's Book, Session 1.11 and 1.12, Activity 1; *Voices in the Museum* (Learner's Book, Session 1.9); Track 05

Description: Recap events from the *Voices in the Museum* extract and explain that learners will develop Voice 4 – the fourth character – from clues in the story. This is an opportunity to demonstrate how much information can be established or inferred by asking the right questions. Encourage learners to add their own questions to elicit details. For example: *What was odd about the dinosaur? What could Voices 1 and 4 have noticed that was odd about it?* Learners might find the information useful when they begin to plan their flashback later in the session.

The role play will help learners to think about the characters; what Voice 4 might have said about the other characters and what they might have said about him.

Make it clear that although learners can find out some information about Voice 4 from the other voices, they will also have to use their imagination to fill in the unknown parts. Learners may make simple inferences, but challenge them to think of other possibilities. Say for example: *What if the lady is a palaeontologist who thinks the dinosaur may not be what it seems, is trying to prove it and is worried about Maximilian getting mixed up in the business?* Encourage imagination. This session is designed to spread over two lessons so allow plenty of time.

⟩ **Differentiation ideas:** Challenge learners by asking them to role play what the other voices might have said about Voice 4 if they were asked to remember him specifically from the day at the museum.

⟩ **Assessment ideas:** Assess learners' ability to role play and adapt their speaking style to reflect their character.

Answers:

1   a   •   Voice 4 is Maximilian. He is related to the lady in the purple coat, Voice 1. He is not related to Voices 2 and 3 but he meets Jax, Voice 3, at the kiosk and strikes up a conversation.
        •   Voice 1 suggests he was not keen: *Maximilian dragged his heels as he always did on days like these.*
        •   He slipped away from the dinosaur to the kiosk when Voice 1 was not concentrating on him and met Jax in the queue.
        •   Accept any sensible suggestion – he probably kept glancing at her because he knew he was supposed to be looking at the dinosaur and not going to the kiosk and that she would tell him off if she saw him there.
    b–c   Learners' own answers.

2   Plan and write a flashback for Voice 4 to the museum (45 minutes)

Learning intention: To plan, write and edit a flashback

Resources: Learner's Book, Session 11.11 and 11.12, Activity 2; *Voices in the Museum* (Learner's Book, Session 1.9); Track 05; Worksheets 6.6 and 6.13

Description: The writing activity is effectively Maximilian's reflection on the same events at the museum as the other voices. His reflection though is now a flashback in a different story – *The Missing Dinosaur Bone*. If any learners find the flashback hard to think about, get them to plan Voice 4 as if it was just like the others. Once they have planned

what they are going to say, discuss what the mystery of *The Missing Dinosaur Bone* could be about and whether there were any clues in Voices 1, 2 and 3 that something was wrong with the dinosaur. Learners do not have to write the entire story, so they can be as creative as they like with the flashback idea and what Voice 4 might have remembered as he thinks back to those moments in the museum and meeting Jax, who knows everything about the dinosaur.

Remind learners that they are writing in the first person and encourage them to include details and a speaking style that would match a 10–12-year-old boy, including colloquialisms, slang or informal text and punctuation features. You can use Worksheet 6.13 Voice 4 in the museum at this point.

Learners should read their drafts to a partner once or twice to get feedback on the speaking style, whether the content matches the other voices, whether he remembers a 'clue' that could help him in his new adventure. Tell them it is like he is talking to himself – asking himself questions (as Jax did) – even if they end up being rhetorical questions without an answer.

Allow learners time to edit their drafts, maybe incorporating feedback and proofreading for errors using dictionaries or online tools, and they can also refer to Worksheet 6.6 Check, check and check again. Remind them to use their word lists in their Learning journals and remind them to use their own strategies for deciding how to spell words correctly.

⟩ **Differentiation ideas:** Encourage more confident learners to write the entire story of *The Missing Dinosaur Bone*. It can be an ongoing task for extension. They can type it up and illustrate it by hand or use ICT to produce it as a short novel, dividing it into chapters.

⟩ **Assessment ideas:** Assess how well learners maintain a consistent narrative voice in their first-person narrative flashback.

Negotiate appropriate success criteria with the learners. For example:

*   *We should write Voice 4's version of events at the museum.*

*   *We should write in first-person narrative.*

*   *The content should fit in with the other voices' versions of events.*

- *The 'voice' should suit the style and personality of a young boy through the language and style.*
- *It should be a flashback and contain at least one clue that would fit The Missing Dinosaur Bone story.*

Answers:
2   a–d   Learners' own creations of Voice 4.

Plenary idea

The mystery (5 minutes)

Resources: Learners' Voice 4 texts from Activity 2

Description: Looking at their writing of Voice 4, invite learners to make suggestions about the mystery relating to the missing dinosaur bone. *Which bone was missing? How had it ended up under Maximilian's bed? How would he put it back? Would anyone find out?*

Be prepared to add ideas of your own, and together sketch out the basic planning for a story with flashbacks.

Invite learners to write the story as a chapter book, which they can work on in class, whenever there is spare time or for homework.

⟩ **Assessment ideas:** Informally assess learners' grasp of how flashbacks work through the learners' ideas for the story. If any learners write the whole story, invite them to read it out in front of the class and discuss how well the flashbacks work.

Homework ideas

Learners can complete the Workbook activities for Session 1.11 and 1.12 for additional practice at writing about events from different perspectives. Invite learners to read out what they have written in class.

Encourage learners to write the entire story of *The Missing Dinosaur Bone*.

Answers for Workbook

1–3 Learners' own answers.

CHECK YOUR PROGRESS

1   a   An introduction to a book, film or play.

   b   Accept sensible answers along the lines of 'to interest the reader in something to do with the plot, possibly giving clues about the story to come'.

   c   Two of: first or third person; short; related to the story to come; often set in a different time to the main story.

2   a   Learners' own answers but along the lines of 'an autograph is a signature you write yourself – your signature'.

   b   Possible examples: automatic, autobiography, automate, automobile, automotive.

3   Learners' own answers.

4   a   Learners' own answers.

   b   Learners' own answers. **Examples:** *I am going to give you a fine for dropping litter.* noun; *I fine you five cents for talking in class.* verb; *It is a fine day.* adjective; *That will be fine.* adverb.

5   a   Neddy said to Rose that he had learnt all about white bears since she saw one.

   b   Rose replied, "I have seen another white bear in the woods."

PROJECT GUIDANCE

Group project: Learners can research one or two dinosaurs to prepare a presentation for a younger class. One of the primary focuses is the choice of media and how to set out their presentation. Remind learners that they have done many presentations in previous stages and they should draw on prior knowledge of what works well and what doesn't. Be available for advice. Learners should practise to each other before presenting to a younger class – the target audience. They should give each other feedback not just on the clarity and interest of the presentation but also on the content and whether it is clearly laid out and presented. Once learners have had feedback, they can practise their presentation again before finally presenting to younger classes.

Pair project: Learners choose a dinosaur to research and write a fact file on for a younger class. Encourage them to plan what they want to put in a fact file to help them work out what information to look for. Remind them that the fact file is for a younger class so they should think about what younger learners would be interested in knowing and how easy it will be for them to find the information. Remind them of fact file features such as headings, bullets and illustrations or diagrams to help with layout and accessibility.

Solo project: Learners choose any dinosaur to do a presentation on. Reassure them that there is no right or wrong about how to do the presentation. They should draw on their prior knowledge of presenting. Provide suitable reference books or organise visits to the school library, as well as providing access to suitable internet sites for information. The focus is on making notes to use for a presentation. Remind them of different ways of making notes: mind maps, tables, headings and so on. Allow them to present to a small group or to the class. Give learners a time limit if they need one.

>2 People in the news

Unit plan

Session	Approximate number of learning hours	Outline of learning content	Resources
2.1 Making headlines	0.5+	Analyse headlines. Identify language techniques used to make an impact. Make up catchy headlines.	Learner's Book Session 2.1 Workbook Session 2.1 ⬇ Language worksheet 2A ⬇ Language worksheet 2B
2.2 Read all about it	0.5+	Read a news report for information. Identify facts and opinions. Share opinions in a group discussion.	Learner's Book Session 2.2 Workbook Session 2.2 ⬇ Worksheet 6.1
2.3 Layout and purpose	0.5+	Identify a news report structure and purpose. Learn and use reporting jargon. Summarise the main idea.	Learner's Book Session 2.3 Workbook Session 2.3 ⬇ Worksheet 6.1 ⬇ Worksheet 6.7 ⬇ Worksheet 6.14
2.4 Report a story	0.5+	Identify language features of a news article. Write a mini news report. Conduct a news broadcast.	Learner's Book Session 2.4 Workbook Session 2.4 ⬇ Worksheet 6.4 ⬇ Worksheet 6.14 ⬇ Worksheet 6.15
2.5 Explore biographies	0.5+	Explain the prefix bio–. Compare features of a biography and a news report. Identify the viewpoint of the writer.	Learner's Book Session 2.5 Workbook Session 2.5 ⬇ Worksheet 6.1 ⬇ Worksheet 6.4

Session	Approximate number of learning hours	Outline of learning content	Resources
2.6 and 2.7 Make a start	1.5	Identify relative pronouns. Use information to inform writing. Write a mini biography.	Learner's Book Session 2.6 and 2.7 Workbook Session 2.6 and 2.7 ⬇ Worksheet 6.5 ⬇ Worksheet 6.6 ⬇ Worksheet 6.16 ⬇ Worksheet 6.17 ⬇ Language worksheet 2A
2.8 Another life	0.5+	Explain the prefix *auto–*. Compare an autobiography and a biography. Start an autobiography in an interesting way.	Learner's Book Session 2.8 Workbook Session 2.8 ⬇ Worksheet 6.1 ⬇ Worksheet 6.4 ⬇ Worksheet 6.17 ⬇ Language worksheet 2B
2.9 Conduct an interview	0.5+	Read a biography and answer questions. Make up questions for an interview. Role play an interview.	Learner's Book Session 2.9 Workbook Session 2.9 ⬇ Worksheet 6.1 ⬇ Worksheet 6.10
2.10 Practise reporting	0.5+	Change a text from direct to reported speech. Include a quotation using correct punctuation. Make sentences with quotations.	Learner's Book Session 2.10 Workbook Session 2.10 ⬇ Differentiated worksheets 2A–C
2.11 and 2.12 Write a news article	1.5	Use questions to gather information and plan. Organise information into relevant sections. Proofread and present a news article.	Learner's Book Session 2.11 and 2.12 Workbook Session 2.11 and 2.12 ⬇ Worksheet 6.9 ⬇ Worksheet 6.14 ⬇ Worksheet 6.15

Cross-unit resources
Learner's Book Check your progress
Learner's Book Projects
End-of-unit 2 test

BACKGROUND KNOWLEDGE

Recounts are a common form of non-fiction writing useful throughout the curriculum. Your learners will be familiar with recounts that focus on retelling what happened in the first person (if it is a personal recount) or the third person (if the events happened to others). When teaching recounts, it is important to remember that effective recounts rely on the ability of the writer to relate events in interesting ways. Recounts can be combined with other text types, e.g. a news article can include other textual elements like explanations or directions.

This unit explores various recounts including news reports, autobiography and biography. Learners will recall and analyse the style and format of these recounts and understand that writers write from a particular point of view to influence the reader. Learners will express their views about issues raised and compare texts, noting differences in purpose, language, style, audience, format and tone.

As your learners plan an autobiography, write a short biography and present a news report, focus on developing their vocabulary, language and comprehension skills to ensure they become better readers and ultimately better writers.

TEACHING SKILLS FOCUS

Cross-curricular learning

Cross-curricular learning gives learners the opportunity to apply their language skills in other subject areas and make links between topics and experiences. Personal recounts, including news articles, biographies and autobiographies, are the most common form of non-fiction text available to the learners and lend themselves to cross-curricular opportunities. Use this unit to explore other areas of the curriculum in the following ways:

- Display newspaper articles from events in history and link them to recent news articles to show that history is part of our lives.

- Invite learners to find news articles of recent events relating to places covered in Geography and keep track of what happens.

- Use news articles to identify famous characters in other subjects and research them. Learners can role play interviews, read or write biographies or write an autobiography from another person's perspective.

- Display a large map of the world in the classroom and invite learners to find news articles from places around the world. Ask them to mark these places and discuss information they have found out about them.

CONTINUED

- Encourage learners to think about their role in society and what their biography might look like one day. Introduce obituaries – usually written when someone dies. Use examples to discuss features.

- Watch films and documentaries about people in the news (biopics – another form of biography).

- Visit the library to find biographies and autobiographies written for this age group. Many famous people, including authors and music stars, have written autobiographies that learners will enjoy.

2.1 Making headlines

LEARNING PLAN

Learning objectives		Learning intentions	Success criteria
Main focus	**Also covered**	• Analyse headlines.	• Learners can analyse headlines.
6Ra.04, 6Rv.04, 6Wg.04, 6Wv.02, 6SLg.04	6Ri.05, 6Rv.01, 6Rg.03, 6Rg.06, 6Rg.08, 6Wg.05, 6Wc.06, 6Wc.07, 6SLg.03	• Identify language techniques in news articles. • Write headlines that make an impact.	• Learners can identify language techniques used to make an impact. • Learners can make up catchy headlines.

LANGUAGE SUPPORT

Some learners may need to be reminded that headlines aim to make an impact and inform the public with current news. They are usually short – one or two key words, phrases or short statements and explanations; sometimes a question is used. Punctuation enhances the impact and adds meaning. Exclamation marks can be used at the end of commands and statements to show surprise, shock or urgency. Headlines use active or passive voice to create a different effect, e.g. *Child wins award or Mount Everest conquered!* Point out that headlines have a different effect and impact for different readers. Readers might react differently to the same headline depending on their context.

Revise active and passive voice. In the active voice, the subject does the action; in the passive voice, the object becomes the subject and has the action done to it. Some learners may find this challenging and need further support. Write reminders and rules on the board for easy reference.

Some learners may also need a reminder that a compound sentence has two or more clauses of equal importance. A complex sentence has one main clause and one or more subordinate clauses. Compound and complex sentences can also be statements, questions or commands.

Starter idea

Something to talk about (5 minutes)

Resources: Learner's Book, Session 2.1: Getting started; examples of other headlines if possible

Description: Read the headlines in the Learner's Book and include others if you have more available.

Address the questions in the Getting started activity and invite learners' responses. Remind them that the purpose of a headline is to get the reader's attention. Ask: *How do these headlines get your attention?*

Encourage learners to share their ideas and opinions. Point out that headlines can be positive or negative. Invite examples.

Talk about how the newspaper industry has changed over time. Whenever you have a discussion, remind the learners to take turns to speak and listen. Whether in pairs or groups or as a class, the basic rules apply. Discuss and display some of these rules. Ultimately you want to see learners encouraging each other to take turns to express their ideas and accept other opinions. Also encourage active listening where learners listen carefully and interpret explicit and implicit meaning.

Main teaching ideas

1 Discuss and analyse headlines (10 minutes)

Learning intention: To comment on a writer's choice of language, demonstrating awareness of the impact on the reader

Resources: Learner's Book, Session 2.1, Activity 1; Language worksheet 2B

Description: Discuss the purpose and impact of headlines. Ask: *Are they always noticeable? Are they easy to read / difficult to ignore?* Headlines aim to draw readers in and persuade them to read further.

A headline can be biased, neutral, figurative or literal.

Revise punctuation marks. Ask learners to explain the punctuation used in each headline and its effect. While most news reports are in standard English, headlines are often not. They often use everyday language and even word play to get readers' attention.

You could ask learners to write the example headlines as complete sentences by including missing articles, subjects, connectives and

punctuation. Revise sentences using the Language focus box in Activity 2. Discuss why a complete sentence may reduce the impact of a headline.

Discuss the effect a headline has on the reader and how different words have a different impact. Discuss how readers might react differently to the same headline, depending on their context and personal situation or beliefs. Use Language worksheet 2B to revise and build words that make an impact.

Spelling link: A compound word is made up from two or more other words, creating a word with a new meaning. **Examples:** *news + paper = newspaper; head + line = headline; to + day = today.*

Compound adjectives are hyphenated.

Examples: *short-term, blue-eyed, thin-necked*

Ask learners to add compound words to their learning journals.

> **Differentiation ideas:** Support learners through a mixed group activity. Ask the group to make a news headline collage by collecting headlines that show various language and punctuation techniques. Learners then make a poster to fit their notebooks or display on the classroom wall. Challenge learners further by asking them to carry out independent research analysing other headlines about famous events or people.

> **Assessment ideas:** Informally assess the group work and discussion. Check whether learners can express themselves confidently. Check that learners know what a headline is and understand its purpose. Observe how well learners encourage each other to take turns in a discussion – in pairs or groups or as a class.

Answers:

1 Accept reasonable answers based on the text
   a Learners' own answers. Different headlines appeal to different people based on their context – age, interests and life experiences.
   b • Mostly informal, both positive and negative.
      • Usually short with key words, phrases or sentences using punctuation for effect.
      • Headlines use strong words and language to get the reader's attention, draw the reader in and persuade the reader to read further, buy the newspaper or subscribe online. For example, they might use exclamation marks for joy and surprise,

speech marks for emphasis, brackets for additional information or ellipses to create suspense.

c   Readers' own ideas. Headlines have a different impact in different contexts.

d   Learners' own answers, for example: Match rained off! Tuckshop changes menu. Victory at last! Hurricane damage. Concert excitement grows.

2   Review headline techniques and write your own headlines (30 minutes)

Learning intentions: To explore and discuss grammatical features; use words and phrases to convey shades of meaning

Resources: Learner's Book. Session 2.1, Activity 2; Language worksheet 2A; local and international newspapers

Description: Display (appropriate) local and international newspapers and headlines to use in discussion.

Read the Language focus box together. Review the techniques listed and explain further with examples.

Discuss the questions in the Learner's Book and then let the learners write the answers in their notebooks so you can read and assess their ability to write effective headlines that make an impact.

> **Differentiation ideas:** Support learners by practising the active and passive voice using Language worksheet 2A. Challenge learners by asking them to analyse online headlines (using age-appropriate online sites). Learners decide if they are negative or positive.

> **Assessment ideas:** Read and assess learners' written headlines by asking: *Does it make sense? Does it get the reader's attention? Does it use correct and interesting punctuation?*

Answers:

2   a   Accept any correct answers like:
Statement: Teens awarded Nobel Prize
Exclamation: Everest conquered!
Question: Who's next?

b   No. Headlines aim to make an impact using short, simple sentences or phrases.

c   Learners' add their own examples to the following:
Active voice: *Teen awarded Nobel Prize!*
Passive voice: *City struck by tornado.*

Plenary idea

Read all about it (5 minutes)

Resources: Learners' headlines from Activity 2

Description: Learners read out their headlines and reflect on which ones have the most impact and discuss reasons why.

> **Assessment ideas:** Give feedback and offer ways to improve.

Homework ideas

Learners can complete the Workbook activities for Session 2.1.

Ask learners to find further examples of headlines, bring them to school and create a class poster.

They can make up fun headlines to do with daily activities happening around school and home like: *Noodles for supper – again!*

Answers for Workbook

1   Example answers:
   a   A new season – A NEW TEAM!
   b   **PANIC** as lights go out …
   c   100% vote **'YES'**
   d   Rain, rain, go away …
   e   Is there *thyme* to cook?

2   Example answers:
   a   A new team has been selected.
   b   Something went wrong with the power and people were left in the dark.
   c   There was a referendum and everyone agreed on the outcome.
   d   It has been rainy and gloomy for a long time.
   e   Something about using herbs in cooking.

3   Learners' own examples and notes.

2.2 Read all about it

LEARNING PLAN

Learning objectives		Learning intentions	Success criteria
Main focus	**Also covered**	• To read a news article for information.	• Learners can read a news article for information.
6Ri.12, 6Ri.14, 6Ri.17, 6Wv.02, 6Wv.06, 6SLg.04, 6SLm.03	6Rv.03, Ri.04, 6Ri.06, 6Ri.07, 6Ri.08, 6Ri.10, 6Ri.11, 6Ri.13, 6Ra.02, 6SLg.02, 6SLg.03, 6SLp.01	• To distinguish between facts and opinions. • To share opinions in groups.	• Learners can identify facts and opinions. • Learners can share opinions in a group discussion.

LANGUAGE SUPPORT

Being able to distinguish between facts and opinions in modern, digital times can be tricky. It has become an important skill since social media contains a lot of distorted news that is not always correct, true or objective. Some learners may find this more difficult as it demands critical reading skills. Be aware that they may need further support in basic reading comprehension skills in order to distinguish between the two.

'Fake news' is false news – news that is not real or true. With modern technology it is easy to produce fake news. Teach learners to be analytical when they read or hear about events or people. Asking the right questions and doing further research are skills that will help them find out the truth.

Common misconception

Misconception	How to identify	How to overcome
News is always correct and true. Facts are always clear.	Write the following on the board: *Child conquers Everest.* *Child forced to climb Everest.* Discuss the possibility of this being true or false. Ask: *How obvious is fake news?*	Find news that is: • clearly true • clearly false • might be either. Discuss things to look out for and make a poster entitled *How to spot fake news.*

Starter idea

Is it true? (5 minutes)

Resources: Learner's Book, Session 2.2: Getting started; examples of age-appropriate local and international news articles

Description: Display examples of news articles from newspapers and online news. Ask if anyone reads the news and in what form. Find out what types of news the learners enjoy.

Discuss the questions in the Learner's Book in pairs or small groups then have a class report back to share opinions.

Ask: *Do you believe everything you read?* Find out how aware they are of 'fake news'. Discuss ways to ensure you learn the 'real' story, such as checking various sources, using online sites that verify news items and checking the validity of the paper/site or writer.

Suggest some age-appropriate news and magazine websites. Learners review and discuss them.

Main teaching ideas

🎧 **07**

1 Read a news article and answer questions to get the main idea (15 minutes)

Learning intentions: To explore explicit meanings; to locate relevant information from one or more points in a text

Resources: *The Daily News article* (Learner's Book, Session 2.2, Activity 1); Track 07; Worksheet 6.1; dictionaries

Description: Read the headline of the news article. Ask: *What does it tell the reader?* Find out if anyone knows about this event and share personal experiences.

Read the article aloud. Learners can take turns to read each sentence or paragraph.

Use the questions in the Learner's Book to generate a discussion about the article and gather information about what happened. Ask: *What is the main idea? Give some details. Where is Mount Everest? What is special about this mountain and this event?* Remind learners to encourage each other to take turns in the discussion and to listen actively and politely to others.

Point out the different names used in this and other accounts of the story: Poorna Malavath also called Malavath Purna, Malavath Poorna or Purna Malavath. Discuss reasons why a person's name might change in different contexts. Consider cultural or transliteration differences.

Learners use dictionaries or onscreen tools to find definitions for words they do not know.

They choose words from the list of adjectives to describe the style and register or tone of the article. (Ensure learners understand all the words in the list). Ask: *Does every news article sound the same? How do news articles differ in tone and impact on the reader?*

Learners add the news article to their learning journals and look for other news articles of interest. Describe the style and tone of each and their impact on the reader.

> **Differentiation ideas:** Support learners by using the text to practise reading aloud. Challenge more confident learners to practise their reading and comprehension skills using other news articles.

> **Assessment ideas:** Use the text to assess reading aloud and comprehension skills.

Assess written responses to check learners' understanding of the text.

Answers:
1 a It summarises the main idea – a young girl has climbed Mt Everest.
   b A girl of 13, Poorna Malavath. Her parents, her friend Sandhanapalli Anand Kumar, the previous record-setter Jordan Romero, a retired policeman who introduced her to mountaineering.
   c 25 May 2014. Mount Everest.
   d It is very dangerous and difficult and unusual for such a young person to do.
   e Interesting, factual, current, inspiring
   f Learners' own answers.
   g Learners add to their learning journals.

2 Explore facts and opinions (25 minutes)

Learning intentions: To distinguish between a fact and an opinion; to express an opinion and show consideration of another view

Resources: Learner's Book, Session 2.2, Activity 2; *The Daily News article* (Learner's Book, Session 2.2); Track 07

Description: Write the words *fact* and *opinion* on the board. Discuss the meaning with the class. Display a question for learners to think about during the lesson: Ask: *When does an opinion sound like a fact?* (When you use persuasive language like *You will love this place* or *Scientists agree that …*) Ask: *What role does language play in changing the reader's mind?* (Persuasive language techniques, including punctuation, can change the impact and effect on readers.)

The news article is mainly factual, but the writer has an opinion. Ask: *What is the writer's opinion of this event? Is it positive or negative?* Use the questions in the Learner's Book to guide a discussion about the facts and the opinions in the article.

Learners identify the different ways the writer describes Malavath. Consider the shades of meaning in the different words used.
Ask: *Does it matter if the article uses the words 'young girl' or 'person' or 'mountaineer'? What message is the writer aiming at?*

Invite learners to conduct a group discussion giving their opinions on this event. Remind learners to encourage each other to take turns in the discussion.

> **Differentiation ideas:** Support learners by encouraging small groups to use a thesaurus to reference other words for 'person' or 'child' and explore shades of meaning.

Challenge learners by asking them to summarise the news article using key words.

Identify figurative language that could be used to describe this event, or the people involved like: *She is as brave as a lion.*

> **Assessment ideas:** Listen as learners discuss and express their opinions. Ask: *Do they show consideration for other opinions?* Observe how well learners encourage others to take turns in a discussion.

Answers:
2   a   Accept any facts.
    b   13-year-old, daughter, youngest person, teen. Learners' own synonyms. Different

words imply different things and have a different impact on the reader.
    c   The food. Others might experience different challenges.
    d   She felt overcome with awe and beauty and felt grateful and happy to climb the mountain.
    e   •   The journalist wants the reader to have the facts and possibly be impressed.
        •   Readers will react differently depending on their own ideas and beliefs about what is right or wrong.
    f   Group responses.
    g   Group summary and report.

Plenary idea

Facts versus opinions (5 minutes)

Description: Invite groups to report back to the class, expressing their opinions on the news article.

Invite learners to reflect on the questions on the board: *When does an opinion sound like a fact? What role does language play?*

Discuss why it is important to distinguish between facts and opinions. The reader should be aware of the language used by the writer, especially where the writer shifts from narrating events to giving more of a personal opinion or response to events.

> **Assessment ideas:** Learners listen to each other and discuss each other's views and responses.

CROSS-CURRICULAR LINKS

Geography: Explore and research more about Mount Everest and the events mentioned in the news article.

Homework ideas

Learners can complete the Workbook activities for Session 2.2. They could also collect news articles of interest and add them to their learning journals.

Answers for Workbook

1 Facts underlined:

a <u>Punishment is a penalty for wrongdoing</u> and I think it should be used sparingly.

b <u>There are 24 hours in a day</u> but I think some days feel too short.

c I think vegetables are delicious <u>and they contain lots of vitamins.</u>

d I think it is good to get up early when <u>the sun rises in the morning.</u>

e I think kids should do compulsory sports because <u>exercise makes you fit.</u>

2 Learners' own work.

3 **a** sick **b** lie **c** bad **d** crashed **e** ruined **f** naughty **g** disastrously **h** fail

4 Learners' own work.

2.3 Layout and purpose

LEARNING PLAN

Learning objectives		Learning intentions	Success criteria
Main focus	**Also covered**	• Identify the structure and purpose of a news article.	• Learners can identify a news article structure and purpose.
6Rs.02, 6Rs.03, 6Ri.07, 6Wp.02, 6Ww.06, 6SLm.02	6Rv.04, 6Ri.05, 6Ww.07	• Use reporting jargon.	• Learners can learn and use reporting jargon.
		• Summarise the main idea of a news article.	• Learners can summarise the main idea of an article.

LANGUAGE SUPPORT

Learners should be familiar with the structure and features of news articles covered in Stage 5. However, for those needing support, you may need to go over it again.

Journalists use a particular text structure for a particular purpose – to inform the readers of the most important facts of a story, to get their attention and to draw them in to read further. The headline and *lead* (or lede – jargon used by journalists) present the main points. The *lead* is the opening paragraph (or the first sentence or two) of a news article. This is where the main questions are answered about the event – *Who, What, Where, When, Why and How?* These questions are often referred to as the *5W1H* questions.

Lead versus lede: The spelling lede is often used in journalism jargon for the introduction of a news story. It is the first sentence or short portion of an article that gives the main idea of the story and contains the most important points readers need to know.

Common misconception

Misconception	How to identify	How to overcome
A news article must be short.	Ask: *How long must an article be?* Discuss responses.	*Learners read articles of different lengths.*

Starter idea

Ask the right questions (5 minutes)

Resources: Learner's Book, Session 2.3: Getting started; newspaper and/or magazine articles

Description: Write the words *Who? What? When? Where? Why?* and *How?* on the board. Ask if anyone can think of a short way of remembering this set of questions. Discuss ideas before suggesting *5W1H*.

Learners practise making up questions using these question words – about a news event or article.

Write some examples on the board.

Main teaching ideas

1 Analyse the structure of a news article (10 minutes)

Learning intention: To explore and recognise the key features of text structure and organise a text into sections

Resources: Learner's Book, Session 2.3, Activity 1; Worksheets 6.1 and 6.7

Description: Draw an inverted pyramid on the board and ask learners to describe the shape (upside down triangle / inverted pyramid). Leave it on the board for further discussion.

Read the Language focus box together. Explain tricky vocabulary. Then use Worksheet 6.7 Analysing non-fiction texts to reinforce the features of this type of text.

Learners discuss the questions in the Learner's Book with a partner and then report back to check their responses.

Spelling link:

- The *h* in the *wh* consonant blend is silent.

- In the common blend *wr* as in *wrong* and *write*, the *w* is silent.

Learners can add to these lists of *wh* and *wr* words to their learning journals (Worksheet 6.1) as they come across them.

> **Differentiation ideas:** Learners can support each other by working in pairs to make a poster showing and describing the structure of a news article. Encourage more confident learners to find news articles and analyse them according to the inverted pyramid. Use coloured pens to highlight the different sections.

> **Assessment ideas:** Learners can write their own responses to the discussion questions for you to check and assess.

Answers:
1 a Organised into sections, information flows from most important to least important.
   b A journalist finds facts and uses the 5W1H questions to decide which information comes first.
   c The least important information is extra detail about the event including information that is not confirmed or people's opinions.

2 Identify the main ideas and make notes (30 minutes)

Learning intentions: To make notes using the structure provided; to present a summary

Resources: Learner's Book, Session 2.3, Activity 2; *The Daily News article* (Learner's Book, Session 2.2); Track 07; Worksheet 6.14

Description: Ask learners to guide you as you label the inverted pyramid on the board. Learners can use this as a reference.

In pairs, learners re-read the news article from Session 2.2 and match the information to the news article structure.

In notebooks or on whiteboards, learners make notes to summarise the information according to the structure. Use Worksheet 6.14 Inverted pyramid to guide this activity.

Remove the original news article and let learners write a summary in their own words using their notes.

2 PEOPLE IN THE NEWS

> **Differentiation ideas:** Challenge learners to use other news articles to make notes and summarise according to the structure provided.

> **Assessment ideas:** Check and assess learners' note-taking skills and ability to summarise the main ideas.

Answers:
2   a–c   Learners' own answers.

Plenary idea

Sum it up (5 minutes)

Resources: Learners' summaries from Activity 2

Description: Learners share their summaries and compare them. Ask: *Is every summary the same? What changes? What is the same? Are they all reliable? Is a summary a reliable way of recording information?*

Invite learners to reflect on why it is helpful to practise summarising.

> **Assessment ideas:** Learners listen to each summary and suggest ways to improve.

CROSS-CURRICULAR LINKS
Geography, History, Science, PHSE, Current Affairs: Learners practise note-taking and summarising in other learning areas.

Homework ideas

Learners can complete the Workbook activities for Session 2.3.

Answers for Workbook

1–3 Learners' own work.

2.4 Report a story

LEARNING PLAN

Learning objectives		Learning intentions	Success criteria
Main focus	**Also covered**	• Identify the language features of a news article.	• Learners can identify the language features of a news article.
6Wc.06, 6Wg.02, 6SLp.01, 6SLp.03	6Ri.04, 6Wc.07, 6Wp.03, 6SLm.04, 6SLm.05, 6SLr.01, 6SLr.02, SLm.02	• Write a mini news report.	• Learners can write a mini news report.
		• Conduct a news broadcast.	• Learners can conduct a news broadcast.

LANGUAGE SUPPORT

Some learners will need reminding of the link between the purpose, audience, layout and language (and register) of any text. The purpose and audience determine the layout and the type of language used.

Register is the style of language used for a particular purpose. Informal language is used when speaking or writing to someone familiar or when entertaining an audience. Formal language is used when communicating with a stranger or someone with an important position or role.

Remind learners that direct speech is when we use quotation marks to show someone's exact words. Reported speech (or indirect speech) is when we report what someone says. When changing from direct to indirect speech, the meaning stays the same but the structure changes in the following ways:

- The punctuation changes. Direct speech is written using quotation marks; indirect speech does not use them.
- The verbs change from the present tense to the past tense and from the past tense to the past perfect tense.

  Examples: *'It's high!' she said. = She said it was high.*

  'She was excited,' her teacher said. = Her teacher said she had been excited.

- The future forms *will* and *going to* change to *would* or *was going to*.
- Pronouns change. *I* becomes *he* or *she*; *we* becomes *they* and *you* becomes *him, her, us* or *them.*
- Adverbs of time change: *yesterday* becomes the day before; *here* becomes there; *tomorrow* becomes the following day.

Starter idea

Link language (5 minutes)

Resources: Learner's Book, Session 6.4: Getting started

Description: Learners discuss the link between purpose, audience, layout and language. Remind learners to take turns to speak and to listen actively to others.

Have a class report back to share ideas and give examples.

Revise vocabulary. Write the word *register* on the board and explain it using the following questions:

How would you greet a friend? Your teacher? An adult you do not know? The emperor?

Main teaching ideas

1 Identify language features of a news article and write a mini report (30 minutes)

Learning intention: To write for a specified audience, using appropriate content, language and punctuation

Resources: Learner's Book, Session 2.4, Activity 1; *The Daily News article* (Learner's Book, Session 2.2); Track 07; Worksheets 6.4, 6.14 and 6.15

Description: Use Worksheet 6.4 Features of fiction and non-fiction texts to record the news article features and compare them to other texts they come across throughout the year.

Revise formal and informal register. Learners read the article from Session 2.2 again and find examples to share with the class. Write some on the board. Discuss them.

Check that learners remember the rules for punctuating direct speech. Write examples on the board and invite volunteers to demonstrate what to do when indirect speech includes a quotation. Learners practise punctuation by writing the sentences into their notebooks.

Invite learners to think of an event to report on. They should focus on the headline, lead and one more paragraph with some details. This is a mini report, so they do not need to write more. They should simply focus on answering the 5W1H questions and important details. Use Worksheet 6.14 Inverted pyramid and the criteria in Worksheet 6.15 News report assessment sheet to guide this activity.

Afterwards learners check their work for a headline, answers to the 5W1H questions in the lead, language that is formal and in the past tense, and quotations using correct punctuation

> **Differentiation ideas:** Learners work individually or in pairs (to write their report) according to the level of support required.

Answers:
1 a • Third (and first for quotations)
       • Past (and present for quotations)
       • Mainly reported speech. Speech marks show quotations.
       • Mainly formal but the relaxed/local language with quotations is mainly informal.
   b–c   Learners' own written work. Accept one or two paragraphs.

2 Be a reporter (10 minutes)

Learning intention: To show awareness of different audiences by using the appropriate register to deliver a news report

Resources: Learner's Book, Session 2.4, Activity 2

Description: Learners work in small groups to prepare a group broadcast of their news items. Learners take turns to read their news aloud. They should practise presenting it as if for radio or television. Ensure learners understand the variations in communication needed for these different platforms. Discuss the similarities and differences and make notes on the board to remind them. For example presenters on radio do not need eye contact with their audience but do need to read with clarity. TV presenters must keep eye contact with the camera, use appropriate expressions and look and sound formal.

If time permits, each group can present their broadcast to the class or another audience.

> **Differentiation ideas:** Support learners by providing other news articles for them to practise reading aloud in an authentic manner. Pay attention to expression, pace, volume and tone. Differentiate the activity further by creating a checklist of news article features to use to analyse other news articles or broadcasts.

Answers:
2 a–c Learners' own work.

Plenary idea

Listen up (5 minutes)

Resources: Learners' news broadcasts from Activity 2

Description: Learners present their news broadcasts for the class to enjoy and assess.

Invite learners to reflect on which broadcasts worked well and why.

> **Assessment ideas:** Learners listen to each group and assess their overall performance. Also assess individual reports to check learners have included the 5W1H questions. Check that learners have understood the variations in communication when presenting on different platforms.

CROSS-CURRICULAR LINKS

Other subjects: Ask teachers from other subjects to organise a 'news show' in their learning area.

Homework ideas

Learners can complete the Workbook activities for Session 2.4. They could also watch or listen to news shows and check for the features mentioned.

Answers for Workbook

1 Example answer: Both broadcasts and articles report news that is current and interesting to the general public. Both include facts, opinions and quotations of things people have said. Since news is about what has already happened, both use the past tense but sometimes a live broadcast is about something that is taking place at that time so the reporter might use the present tense. In a live broadcast, the reporter may use a more friendly or familiar register than in a written article.

2 Example answer: Speak clearly, look at the audience/camera, give the facts, answer the 5W1H questions.

3 Learners' own work.

2.5 Explore biographies

LEARNING PLAN

Learning objectives		Learning intentions	Success criteria
Main focus	**Also covered**	• Explain the meaning of the prefix *bio–*.	• Learners can explain the prefix *bio–*.
6Ri.05, 6Ri.16, 6Rs.02	6Ri.04, 6Ww.03, 6Wv.02, 6Wv.03, 6Ww.07, 6SLm.03, 6SLp.01, 6SLs.01	• Compare features of a biography and a news report.	• Learners can compare features of a biography and a news report.
		• Identify a writer's viewpoint.	• Learners can identify the viewpoint of the writer.

LANGUAGE SUPPORT

A *biography* is a type of recount. Recounts focus on retelling what happened. They have the same key features as stories. The main difference is that, while stories are fiction, biographies are non-fiction. Explain how and why different viewpoints are expressed in different versions of the same story, such as a news report, a biography and a film.

A *biopic* is a biographical film that retells the story of someone's experience.

The word 'biopic' is a portmanteau word (a word blending the sounds and combining the meanings of two others). It combines the words 'biography' (or 'bioscope' meaning cinema or film) and 'picture'. Start a poster with a list of common portmanteau words.

Common misconception

Misconception	How to identify	How to overcome
A biography is always true.	Write the words *true* and *false* on the board. Make some statements about a TV personality and ask learners to decide if they are true or false. Some things they will not know.	Explain that a biography is written from one person's perspective and that the narrative voice can sometimes be objective and sometimes not, revealing the writer's own voice.

Starter idea

Shades of meaning (5 minutes)

Resources: Learner's Book, Session 2.5: Getting started; dictionaries

Description: Recall the meaning of *bio–* and use dictionaries to find other words with this prefix. Explore the general rules for adding prefixes to root words and discuss spelling strategies.

Write the following on the board: *Malavath is a child. She is a mountaineer.* Invite learners to explain the difference in meaning. Ask: *Are both words* (child *and* mountaineer*) correct?* (yes) *Do both words mean the same thing?* (no) *Do the words have the same impact?* (no). Share other examples.

Explore words that can change the impact of a text.

Main teaching ideas

1 Discuss the opening paragraphs of a biography and compare this to the news article (20 minutes)

Learning intention: To identify, discuss and compare the purposes and features of different non-fiction text types

Resources: *Poorna Malavath* biography (Learner's Book Session 2.5, Activity 1); Track 08; *The Daily News article* (Learner's Book, Session 2.2); Track 07; Worksheet 6.4; biographical materials – books, articles, film poster/reviews

Description: Read the biography of Poorna Malavath together. Identify the facts. Ask: *Are they the same as the news article facts?*

Discuss the similarities and differences between news articles and biographies. Remind learners that both text types are written by someone else. It is someone else's perspective and point of view. Ask: *Does it matter who writes a person's biography? Why?*

Discuss and compare the purpose, audience, layout and language. Learners will notice that the layout is different, but the purpose, audience and language is similar.

Use Worksheet 6.4 Features of fiction and non-fiction texts to record the features of a biography and compare them to features of other texts they come across throughout the year.

Explore the difference between fiction and non-fiction texts and those that can be either. Ask: *Can you tell if a biography is fiction or non-fiction?*

> **Differentiation ideas:** Support learners by allowing them to work in pairs to read the biography aloud and then take turns to tell each other about Malavath and ask questions.

Challenge learners by asking them to read a biography of someone that has inspired them. They could also explore other types of biography, such as obituaries.

> **Assessment ideas:** Assess how well learners compare the texts. Check if they can explain the difference between fiction and non-fiction texts. Use the text to assess learners as they read aloud. Check their pace, volume, expression, tone and fluency.

Answers:

1 a Accept any facts from the text. The biography has more detail about Poorna's character and attitude, and includes more about her background.

b The writer's viewpoint is expressed – it is a personal viewpoint.

c The layout is different, certain details are included or excluded, a report is impersonal but a biography is personal, the style of a biography is more like a story. (Learners give examples.)

d Accept any reasonable answers like positive, informative, personal.

e Accept any reasonable answers that show similarities or differences between the text types. Examples of similarities: Viewpoint: The writer's voice and opinions describe what happens to someone else. Language: Both use mainly the past tense and third-person narrative. Layout: Facts and events are usually in chronological order. Examples of differences: A news article has a headline and gives up-to-date information on daily events while a biography relates events from the past often in sections with headings.

f A biography or newspaper article is usually non-fiction but can be fictional. It depends if the text is based on a real person and events which can be proved.

2 Listen to a film review and discuss the questions (20 minutes)

Learning intention: To listen for detail, identify the point of view and compare books to films

Resources: *Poorna* film review (Learner's Book, Session 2.5, Activity 2); Track 09; *The Daily News article* (Learner's Book, Session 2.2); Track 07; *Poorna Malavath* biography (Learner's Book, Session 2.5); Track 08; Worksheet 6.1

Description: Discuss films versus books. Ask: *Would you rather read a book or see the film? Which is better? What are the pros and cons of each?*

Discuss the meaning of 'biopic'. It is a portmanteau word that combines the words *biography* and *picture*. Use this opportunity to make spelling links with other portmanteau words.

Play the audio of the *Poorna* film review (Track 09). Learners listen for details about when it was released, who produced it, who acted in it, etc. After listening, they should make up questions to ask each other to check their listening skills.

Spelling link: Portmanteau words combine two words to make a new word like lunch and breakfast = brunch. Make a list of commonly used portmanteau words, check the spelling patterns and add them to the learning journal (Worksheet 6.1) – for (tween from teenager and between, email from electronic and mail, internet from international and network.)

> **Differentiation ideas:** Learners can support each other by watching the film (or other biopics suitable for their age and context) together. Challenge more confident learners to write a review of the film.

You could differentiate the activity further by setting them the task of exploring other portmanteau words and adding them to their spelling rules.

> **Assessment ideas:** Use the questions provided to assess their listening skills and comprehension.

Also check the learners can explain how and why different viewpoints are expressed in different versions of the same story.

Audioscript: *Poorna*

A biographical film about Poorna Malavath was released in 2017. This biopic, called *Poorna,* is based on the true story of a 13-year-old girl from a humble village in India who became the youngest girl in history to climb Mount Everest. Her extraordinary story is retold and written by Prashant Pandey and Shreya Dev Verma with stirring music to complement it. The potential of the film was realised by Rahul Bose who agreed to direct and star in it. Aditi Inamdar, who plays Malavath, was chosen from over 100 young girls. The setting of the film is Pakala village in India where the real Malavath grew up. This inspiring Hindi film is proof that a simple story can have a profound impact to challenge and change people's ideas and motivate others to be brave.

Answers:

2 a A biographical film, a film about real, a non-fictional person.

   b It is the true story of Poorna Malavath – the youngest person to climb Mount Everest,

played by Aditi Inamdar – an actor used to represent the real person. The film makers used an actor because they needed someone who looked 13 years old and could act.

   c One is written (biography) and one is a film (biopic).

   d Any reasonable answers.

   e Learners listen, write and discuss the questions.

   f Learners' own responses with reasons.

Plenary idea

Listen and respond (5 minutes)

Description: In groups, learners take turns to ask a question and choose someone to respond.

Invite learners to reflect on the value of reading or watching a story about someone else.

> **Assessment ideas:** Learners take turns to ask and answers questions then give feedback on the quality of each other's listening skills.

CROSS-CURRICULAR LINKS

Science and other subjects: Research biographies and biopics on famous people.

Homework ideas

Learners can complete the Workbook activities for Session 2.5.

Learners choose and read a biography and then write a review to share with the class.

Answers for Workbook

1 Learners' own words and definitions.

2 Poorna Malavath is a brave young girl who believes that with confidence and focus you can achieve anything, no matter who you are. She is a true example because she is the youngest person in the world to summit Mount Everest.

   At the age of 13 when most children are at school, playing games or watching TV, she had her eyes fixed on making a difference in her community and changing the views of society. Her story is an inspiration to anyone from any background, young and old.

   On 10 June 2000, Poorna Malavath was born in a small village in India where her parents worked on a farm. She attended the local school that taught mountain climbing as a subject. This sparked her desire to take up the ultimate challenge – to climb Mount Everest, a mountain on which many lives have been lost.

3   Learners' own summary.

2.6 and 2.7 Make a start

LEARNING PLAN

Learning objectives		Learning intentions	Success criteria
Main focus	**Also covered**	• Identify relative pronouns.	• Learners can identify relative pronouns.
6Rg.04, 6Wg.07, 6Wc.06	6Rg.05, 6Wp.01, 6Wp.02, 6Wp.03, 6Wp.04, 6Wp.05, 6Ws.01, 6Ws.02, 6Ws.04, 6Wg.08, 6Wc.04, 6Wc.07, 6SLp.01	• Use planning and information to inform writing. • Write a mini biography.	• Learners can use information to inform their writing. • Learners can write a mini biography.

LANGUAGE SUPPORT

Some learners may need reminding about the different types of pronouns. The following pronouns are useful when writing a biography (or autobiography).

Personal pronouns refer to people or things: *I, me, we, us, you, he, she, it, they, them.*

Reflexive pronouns reflect back to the noun or the pronoun: *myself, yourself, herself, himself, itself, ourselves, yourselves, themselves.*

Relative pronouns perform the function of a conjunction by connecting one part of a sentence to another. There are six: *who, whom, whose* (referring to people) *that, which, what* (referring to animals and objects).

Possessive pronouns indicate ownership: *mine, yours, his, hers, its, ours, theirs.*

Starter idea

Plot the details (5 minutes)

Resources: Learner's Book, Session 2.6 and 2.7: Getting started; paper or whiteboards

Description: In pairs, learners work together to plot important details about their lives on a mind map.

In groups, learners take turns to tell their group about their partners.

Afterwards, discuss the challenges of telling others about someone and having someone else talk about them.

Main teaching ideas

1   Practise relative pronouns (30 minutes)

Learning intention: To revise pronouns, explore relative pronouns and use relative pronouns to introduce additional detail

Resources: Learner's Book, Session 2.6 and 2.7, Activity 1; *Poorna Malavath* biography (Learner's Book, Session 2.5, Activity 1); Track 08; Language worksheet 2A

Description: Write the word *pronoun* on the board. Invite the learners to give a definition and examples. Use the Language support box (above) to help you recap pronouns and explain their purpose.

Read the Language focus box in the Learner's Book together to introduce relative pronouns. Write them on the board and ask: *Which pronouns refer to people? Which words refer to animals or objects?* Give examples.

Skim the *Poorna Malavath* biography in Session 2.5 and identify the relative pronouns used to replace a noun and used as conjunctions. Use Language worksheet 2A and the activities in the Workbook for further practice if there is time in class.

> **Differentiation ideas:** Support learners by revising all the different types of pronouns. Challenge more confident learners to use another text to find examples of pronouns, particularly relative pronouns.

Differentiate the activity further by asking learners to join their sentences using relative pronouns.

> **Assessment ideas:** Check the learners' understanding and use of pronouns. Use the answers provided to assess their use of relative pronouns.

Answers:

1 a   Examples from the text:
       Poorna Malavath is a brave young girl who believes that with confidence and focus you can achieve anything, no matter who you are.
       She attended the local school that taught mountain climbing as a subject.
       A mountain on which many lives have been lost.

   b   • Malavath is a young girl whose motto is 'You can achieve anything'.
       • Mount Everest was the ultimate challenge that she felt called to attempt.
       • They are proud of their friend who loves to climb mountains.
       • She attended a village school which is where she learnt to climb.
       • There was a team of climbers, of which one was 13 years old.
       • She is a humble person whom not many have heard about.

   c   • Mount Everest was the ultimate challenge. She felt called to do the challenge.

       • They are proud of their friend. Their friend loves to climb mountains.
       • She attended a village school. A village school is where she learnt to climb.
       • There was a team of climbers. Of the team of climbers, one was 13 years old.
       • She is a humble person. She is a person not many have heard about.

2 Use a fact file to write a biography (60 minutes)

Learning intention: To take notes, develop writing and proofread for grammar, spelling and punctuation errors

Resources: *Poorna Malavath* fact file (Learner's Book, Session 2.6 and 2.7, Activity 2); Track 10; Worksheets 6.5, 6.6, 6.16 and 6.17

Description: Learners scan the fact file about Poorna Malavath. Ask questions and invite the learners to find the answers.

Together, practise making up sentences using the key words. Remind learners to keep their writing formal, use correct pronouns and vary the sentence length.

Discuss how to plan their writing. They can make notes on a mind map and then add information from other sources. Invite learners to choose how to make their notes to suit their thinking and planning style.

Learners work individually to write three short paragraphs about Poorna Malavath. Learners use the criteria in Worksheet 6.16 Plan a biography to guide, plan and check their work. Learners can also use Worksheet 6.5 My writing process to guide the planning and editing process.

In pairs, learners check and edit each other's work then do a final self-check using Worksheet 6.6 Check, check and check again.

Learners write their biographies in their notebooks using neat handwriting. Encourage learners to develop a personal style that is legible while reasonably paced.

> **Differentiation ideas:** Support less confident learners by allowing them to write two or three sentences only for each section of the biography, and to develop only one of the three paragraphs.

Challenge more confident learners to do further research and write extra paragraphs about Malavath.

⟩ **Assessment ideas:** Use the criteria in Worksheet 6.17 Biography and autobiography checklist to guide and assess their planning, editing and writing.

Answers:
2   a–e   Learners' own writing.

Plenary idea

Present a biography (5 minutes)

Resources: Learners' biographies from Activity 2

Description: In groups, learners read their biographies aloud.

Write criteria for a biography on the board for learners to check as they listen.

⟩ **Assessment ideas:** Learners listen and offer ways to improve.

Homework ideas

Learners can complete the Workbook activities for Session 2.6 and 2.7.

They can also interview an adult member of the family or a family friend or a teacher and then use the information to write a short biography.

They can make a family tree and find out information about close or distant relatives.

Answers for Workbook

1   a   they – the apples
    b   he – the interviewer, them – the questions
    c   they – the guides, them – the climbers
    d   whose/her – the brave girl
    e   myself – I, we – my team and I
    f   this – the school, she – the young climber

2   Example answers:

Amelia Earhart was born in 1897 on 24 July in a small town in Kansas, US.

In 1932, she became the first woman to fly solo across the Atlantic Ocean.

She was also the first person to cross the Atlantic Ocean twice.

In 1937, on 2 July, she went missing in a plane over the Pacific Ocean.

She was declared dead in 1939, on 5 January.

3   Learners' own work.

2.8 Another life

LEARNING PLAN

Learning objectives		Learning intentions	Success criteria
Main focus	**Also covered**	• Explain the meaning of the prefix *auto–*.	• Learners can explain the prefix *auto–*.
6Ww.06, 6SLs.01	6Ra.03, 6Rg.03, 6Ri.01, 6Wv.03, 6Ww.03, 6Ww.07, 6Wp.02, 6Wc.02, 6Wc.06, 6Wc.07	• Compare the purpose of texts. • Start an autobiography.	• Learners can compare an autobiography and a biography. • Learners can start an autobiography in an interesting way.

LANGUAGE SUPPORT

Check your learners remember what a prefix is. Revise common ones used in this session: *auto–* means 'self' or 'by oneself'; *bio–* means 'life' or 'the study of life'.

Starter idea

Viewpoint matters (5 minutes)

Resources: Learner's Book, Session 2.8: Getting started; dictionaries

Description: Display the words *autobiography* and *biography*. Ask learners to explain the difference.

Learners discuss the meaning of *auto–*. Use dictionaries to find other words with this prefix. Explore the general rules for adding prefixes to root words and discuss spelling strategies.

An autobiography is written from the writer's perspective. The writer and narrator are the same. Sometimes the writer may simply relate events and at other times the writer reflects on events. Discuss what it means to have a personal viewpoint. Talk about the pros and cons of writing an autobiography or having someone else write your biography.

Main teaching ideas

1 **Listen to the start of an autobiography and discuss questions (15 minutes)**

> **Learning intention:** To analyse a personal account and identify language features and viewpoint

> **Resources:** *Another Life* (Learner's Book, Session 2.8, Activity 1); Track 11; Worksheets 6.1, 6.4 and 6.17; online etymological dictionaries

> **Description:** Find out if any learners have read any of Jamila Gavin's books (*The wheel of Surya, The Blood Stone, Blackberry Blue and Other Fairy Tales*). If possible, read some blurbs or reviews.

> Active listening involves good concentration and interpretation. Learners should aim to focus on the speaker and on the explicit and implicit meaning of what is being said. Remind learners that meaning is found in what a speaker says and how it is said.

> Listen to the extract from *Another Life* (Track 11). Explore how the story begins. Ask: *Is this a good place to start? Is it a usual or unusual beginning? Is it an interesting beginning? Are there other ways to begin an autobiography?*

Discuss the register and compare it to the biography of Poorna Malavath in Session 2.5, Activity 1. Ask: *Is the autobiography in the audio chattier and friendlier than the biography extract?* Discuss reasons.

Make notes on the board as you discuss the features of an autobiography: a personal account, first-person narrative, flows from one event to another, factual but conversational. Discuss the similarities and differences to a biography. Ask: *Is one more reliable that the other?* Use Worksheet 6.17 Biography and autobiography checklist to guide the discussion.

Use the questions in the Learner's Book to check learners' comprehension and listening skills. Once you have discussed the questions, the learners can write the answers in their books.

Learners add the autobiography to their learning journals (Worksheet 6.1). List other autobiographies they might enjoy.

Learners can also use Worksheet 6.4 Features of fiction and non-fiction texts to record the features of an autobiography and compare this to other texts they come across throughout the year.

Spelling link: The words *autobiography* and *biography* come from Greek words *autos*, which means 'self', *bios* meaning 'life' and *graphia* meaning 'record' or 'account' (or *graphein* meaning 'to write'). Learners can use online etymological dictionaries to help them find the origins of words and add them to their learning journals.

> **Differentiation ideas:** Support learners by including other questions based on the text: *In this passage, who is speaking to whom?* (Jamila is speaking to her peers on the playground, they ask questions which she answers and she speaks to the reader – to tell the story and say what her peers said and thought.) *What events were in the news when she was growing up?* (Events included the Second World War and the struggle for Indian independence and the death of Mahatma Gandhi.) *List three facts mentioned in the extract that are not based on the author's opinion.* (She came from India, was born in the Himalayas and had

not seen a tiger but followed its footprints along the Brahmaputra River.)

Encourage learners to find out more about Jamila Gavin and the places where she lived. Ask them to find out what she is doing now.

Challenge learners to read some of Jamila Gavin's books or other autobiographies and write a short review. See the Workbook for some ideas.

> **Assessment ideas:** Check that learners understand the meaning of *auto–* and *bio–* and they can explain the difference between an autobiography and a biography.

Use the comprehension questions to assess their comprehension and listening skills.

Audioscript: *Another Life*

Chapter 1: Boasting

I used to boast about many things when I was a child, especially on the occasions that we came over to England from India – three times before I was 11 years old – and each time I had to start making friends all over again in a new school. So when I was asked questions about myself in the different school playgrounds I got to know, it would often go as follows:

Q: "Where do you come from?"

A: "India."

I knew they thought of tigers and elephants and monkeys and fakirs sleeping on beds of nails.

Q: "Where were you born?"

A: "In the Himalayas."

That impressed them. They imagined my mother giving birth to me on the icy slopes of Mount Everest some twenty-nine thousand feet up, when in fact I was born about six thousand feet up in the Community Hospital, Landour, Mussoorie which was in the foothills of the Himalayas.

Q: "Have you ever seen a tiger?"

I may have been a boaster, but I wasn't a liar, and to this day I can't say that I have. But I still managed to make it sound glamorous and dangerous.

A: "Not exactly, but I've seen its footprints in the mud and followed it all along the banks of the Brahmaputra River, and I've seen the long grass

crushed where it has just lain, and I've seen the remains of its dinner still fresh, and known that it was not far away – maybe even watching us."

Answers:

1 a
- The story begins with a conversation in the school playground at a new school.
- Challenges: living in two countries, starting a new school, making new friends, starting conversations with strangers.
- She boasts about being born in India in the Himalayas, following tiger footprints
- A boaster but not a liar.
- She was trying to impress her peers/new friends. She wanted to make friends / sound interesting / make them jealous / fit in.
- 'and' is repeated. The longer sentence gives a sense of gathering enthusiasm.
- Register: relaxed, funny

b Two main features of each: Autobiography: personal recount, factual, first-person narrative. Biography: personal recount, factual, third-person narrative.

c Learners add to their learning journals

---

2 **You are never too young to start an autobiography (25 minutes)**

Learning intention: To plan, make notes and write an interesting beginning

Resources: Learner's Book, Session 2.8, Activity 2; Worksheet 6.17; Language worksheet 2B; learners' timelines from Session 2.6 and 2.7; thesauruses

Description: Remind learners that making notes is helpful when planning a text. Learners can use the timelines they created in Session 2.6 and 2.7 Getting started to share biographies. Ask: *Why is a timeline a good way to make notes for this activity?*

Share ideas for an interesting way to begin their autobiographies. Consider the ideas in the Learner's Book and add others. Write some autobiography starters on the board. Discuss who their audience will be – this is a key factor in planning their writing.

Recall register, also covered in Unit 1. Remind them to think about their language, vocabulary and style of writing. Ask: *Do you want to sound like a young child or an older child? Do you want to sound mischievous, studious, chatty, formal, popular or lonely?* Use thesauruses to explore words and synonyms.

Use Language worksheet 2B to revise and build words that make an impact.

Once they have chosen their style and where to begin, let them write the first paragraph.

Remind learners to improve the flow of their writing by using pronouns to avoid repetition, linking sentences and paragraphs with connectives and ordering events correctly.

> **Differentiation ideas:** Vary the level of expectation for the writing activity: learners can write the introduction only; write one or two paragraphs; or write a whole chapter.

> **Assessment ideas:** Use the comprehension questions to assess their comprehension skills.

Check learners' planning and use Worksheet 6.17 Biography and autobiography checklist to assess their autobiography introduction.

***

Answers:
2   a–e   Learners' own work.

***

Plenary idea

This is me (5 minutes)

Resources: Learners' autobiography starters from Activity 2

Description: Learners sit in groups and share their autobiography starters.

Choose to share some with the class.

> **Assessment ideas:** Learners listen to each other and give constructive feedback, offering ways to improve.

Homework ideas

Learners continue to write their autobiographies.

Learners can complete the Workbook activities for Session 2.8.

Here is a list of autobiographies that the learners might enjoy reading:

- *Under the Royal Palms: a childhood in Cuba* by Alma Flor Ada
- *Mao's Last Dancer* by Li Cunxin (Young Reader edition)
- *My life with the Chimpanzees* by Jane Goodall
- *Chinese Cinderella* by Adeline Yen Mah
- *Boy: Tales of Childhood* by Roald Dahl
- *The Story of My Life* by Helen Keller

Answers for Workbook

1   Learners' own words and definitions.

2   Answers:

1	bio	6	both
2	auto	7	both
3	bio	8	bio
4	auto	9	auto
5	bio	10	auto

3   Learners' own work.

2.9 Conduct an interview

Learning objectives		Learning intentions	Success criteria
Main focus	**Also covered**	• Read a biography for information.	• Learners can read a biography and answer questions.
6Ri.04, 6Ri.11, 6SLm.05	6Rs.03, 6Rv.04, 6Ri.06, 6Ri.07, 6Ri.08, 6Ri.09, 6Ri.10, 6Ri.16, 6Wc.06, 6Wc.07, 6SLg.01, 6SLm.01, 6SLm.04, 6SLp.03, 6SLr.01	• Make up questions. • Conduct an interview.	• Learners can make up questions for an interview. • Learners can role play an interview.

LANGUAGE SUPPORT

The person asking the questions in an interview is the *interviewer*. The *interviewee* is the person being interviewed. For some learners, you may need to revise open and closed questions, which are used in interviews to gather information. A closed question requires a short answer, usually 'yes' or 'no' or one word. An open question requires detail, a description or someone's opinion. An interview can have both types of questions but should have more open questions to give the interviewee a chance to talk about the topic in detail.

Common misconception

Misconception	How to identify	How to overcome
Interviews should be formal.	Ask learners to interview each other and ask: *Is it formal or informal?* Encourage learners to look or listen to a variety of interviews on television or radio – especially on children's programmes.	Encourage learners to describe the difference between the interviews they have seen or heard. Encourage them to talk about the register, the body language and the types of questions asked.

Starter idea

Purpose – audience (5 minutes)

Resources: Learner's Book, Session 2.9: Getting started

Description: Write the following on the board: *Purpose – audience.*

Discuss the questions in the Learner's Book about why people write biographies and the point of view of the writer. Discuss the link between the purpose of a biography and the audience. Ask: *Who is a biography written for? Can biography give a negative viewpoint of someone?*

Talk about famous people in history and identify some who might have a positive or negative biography.

Main teaching ideas

1 Read a biography and discuss the questions (20 minutes)

Learning intentions: To read aloud with accuracy and confidence; to explore explicit meanings in a text

Resources: *Tenzing Norgay biography* (Learner's Book, Session 2.9, Activity 1); Track 12; Worksheets 6.1 and 6.10; dictionaries; pictures of historic events relating to Mount Everest (if possible)

Description: Show a picture of the first team to summit Mount Everest. Check the learners' general knowledge.

Read the biography together. Discuss difficult words. Use the glossary or dictionaries to find their meanings.

Discuss the viewpoint of the writer who gives Tenzing's perspective.

Talk about the formal register used in the text. Ask: *Does the language match the purpose?*

Explore explicit meaning. Identify facts in the text by asking direct questions like *What year did this event occur?* or *How many years ago did this event take place?*

Explore implicit meaning and opinions. Ask: *Why was this such an important event at the time? Why was it more of a challenge then to climb the mountain? Do you think the writer of this biography thinks one climber is more important than the other?*

Discuss the structure and flow of the text. Ask learners to point out how the text is organised and how events are described in order. Each paragraph deals with a different aspect of Tenzin's life.

Read and discuss the questions. Remind learners to take turns and listen carefully to each other. If time permits, learners write the answers in their notebooks.

Learners add to their learning journals with a list of people they would like to research further.

> **Differentiation ideas:** Support learners by discussing the questions informally or get them to write the answers in their notebooks to assess. Practise reading aloud.

Challenge more confident learners by adding other questions to the comprehension activity, and encourage them to research other people of interest by finding and reading other biographies.

> **Assessment ideas:** Use the text to assess reading aloud. Check for pace, fluency, expression and tone or use Worksheet 6.10 Reading, speaking or performing assessment sheet.

For the comprehension, use the answers provided to check their comprehension skills.

Answers:
Accept any reasonable answers supported by the text:
1 a • Tenzing Norgay was Nepalese Indian and Edmund Hillary was from New Zealand.
      • A reconnaissance is a mission (usually by the military) to get information about something.
      • Failure due to any of these: Poor weather conditions, poor equipment, poor planning, illness, food shortages
      • Key to success: Proper planning and favourable weather conditions
      • Details unclear because his parents were uneducated, he was one of 13 children, and did not keep records.
      • Yes, it was harder because their equipment and clothing was not as sophisticated as it is today.
    b Organised with headings and paragraphs, flows in order of events, linked with connectives
    c Learners add to their learning journals.

2 Role play an interview (20 minutes)

Learning intention: To ask questions, take on roles and perform an interview in front of the class

Resources: Learner's Book, Session 2.9, Activity 2

Description: In groups, learners assign roles to play the interviewer and interviewees.

Groups discuss open and closed questions for the interviewer to ask, and possible answers.

Remind learners to use the correct register – discuss what this might be. Consider the context and language of the time.

Learners practise their interviews and then present them.

> **Differentiation ideas:** Support learners by allowing them to work in pairs to interview one of the team.

Challenge learners by asking them to research and interview a different team member like Colonel John Hunt.

> **Assessment ideas:** Listen as learners discuss and express themselves in groups. Assess how well learners conducted themselves as an interviewer or interviewee. Learners use the 'How are we doing' questions to assess each other.

Answers:
2   a–d   Learners' own work.

Plenary idea

Listen and assess (5 minutes)

Description: Discuss important criteria to consider when performing. Write them on the board.

Learners present their interviews to the class.

> **Assessment ideas:** Learners listen to their peers and use the criteria to assess and give feedback. Possible criteria:

Did everyone speak clearly? Did the questions and answers make sense? Was the language appropriate?

Homework ideas

Learners can complete the Workbook activities for Session 2.9.

They can conduct interviews with adults in the family to find out about their greatest challenge.

They can watch interviews on TV, analyse them and write a comment on what they noticed.

Answers for Workbook

1–3 Learners' own work.

2.10 Practise reporting

LEARNING PLAN			
Learning objectives		**Learning intentions**	**Success criteria**
Main focus	**Also covered**	• Change a text from direct to reported speech.	• Learners can change a text from direct to reported speech.
6Wg.02	6Rg.07, 6Rg.08, 6Wg.08, 6Wp.05, 6SLm.03	• Use correct punctuation.	• Learners can include a quotation using correct punctuation.
		• Write sentences with quotations.	• Learners can make sentences with quotations.

LANGUAGE SUPPORT

Direct and indirect speech is handled in Unit 1 with a focus on narrative text. In this unit, learners will apply the rules to indirect speech in a news article. Review the following guidelines.

When you change from direct to indirect speech, the meaning stays the same but the structure changes:

The punctuation: direct speech uses speech marks, indirect speech does not.

- Verbs change from the present to the past tense, and from the past to the past perfect tense.

- The future forms *will* and *going* to change to *would* or *was going to*.

- Pronouns change. *I* becomes *he/she; we* becomes *they, you* becomes *him/her/us/them*.

- Adverbs of time change: *yesterday* becomes the day before; *here* becomes there; *tomorrow* becomes the following day.

- The word *that* often precedes the reported speech.

Starter idea

Report it (5 minutes)

Resources: Learner's Book, Session 2.10: Getting started

Description: Write this sentence on the board: *The teacher said to her class "**You will** go out to play tomorrow."* Invite the learners to change it to reported speech. Share ideas.

Write the answer on the board: *The teacher said to her class __that__ __they would__ go out to play the **following day**.* Invite them to analyse which words change (the words in **bold**), what was added (that) and what was taken away (the punctuation).

Discuss the rules (see the Language support box above). Display the rules on the board.

Main teaching ideas

1 Change a text from direct to reported speech (20 minutes)

Learning intention: To change sentences from direct to reported speech using accurate language and punctuation

Resources: Learner's Book, Session 2.10, Activity 1; Differentiated worksheet pack

Description: Revise the work done in Unit 1 on direct and reported speech. Ask: *Do the rules change for fiction and non-fiction texts? What is different about direct speech in fiction and news reports?*

Read the Language focus box in the Learner's Book together. Use examples to explain the rules, to those needing extra support (see the Language support box above).

Read the sentences together and use the example to explain the activity. If necessary, give learners another example or two to try before they continue on their own.

Learners complete the sentences on their own.

> **Differentiation ideas:** Use Differentiated worksheets 2A–C on reported speech to build and reinforce the language skills covered.

> **Assessment ideas:** Use the answers provided for the activities to assess learners' written work.

Answers:
1 a • She told us __that__ **she would** be there.
   • He said __that__ **he was** happy to be home safely.
   • The team reported __that__ **they were** overjoyed.
   • He explained __that__ **they would** begin **the following day**.
   • They announced __that__ the mission **was** accomplished.
  b Learners' own examples.

2 Include a quotation using correct punctuation (20 minutes)

Learning intention: To use the conventions of standard English appropriately to write sentences in reported and direct speech

Resources: Learner's Book, Session 2.10, Activity 2

Description: Ask: *What is the difference between direct speech and a quotation?* Invite their responses.

A quotation is speech that is repeated by someone other than the original speaker.

Complete an example on the board to demonstrate the activity and remind learners that the punctuation marks and rules for quotation marks are the same as those for direct speech.

In pairs, learners discuss the sentences provided and think of interesting quotes to add.

On their own, learners complete the activity using correct punctuation.

> **Differentiation ideas:** Support less confident learners by encouraging them to scan other news texts for sentences with quotations and copy them into their notebooks using correct punctuation. Challenge more confident learners by inviting them to complete and punctuate their sentences in their notebooks.

> **Assessment ideas:** Listen as the learners explain how to change speech from direct to reported speech (covered in Unit 1). Check their understanding and if they can apply it.

Use the answers provided for the activities to assess their written work.

Answers:

2 a Example answers:
- An eyewitness told reporters, "I couldn't believe my eyes."
- As he said in his own words, "The mission was a success."
- "I was part of a great team," she said of her role in the mission.
- To quote one of the team members, "We are safe and that's all that counts."
- "Keep back please!" they told onlookers.

b Learners' own examples.

Plenary idea

Just checking (5 minutes)

Resources: Learners' answers to Activity 2

Description: Learners share their answers in groups.

> **Assessment ideas:** Learners mark each other's work.

Homework ideas

Learners can complete the Workbook activities for Session 2.10.

Answers for Workbook

1 a "I had an amazing experience," she told the interviewer when she returned.

b A classmate said of her friend, "She is brave and focused and a wonderful friend."

c The children chanted, "She's our hero," as they gathered to greet her.

d Her parents commented, "We are overjoyed and very proud of her."

e The headline "Welcome home!" filled the front page.

2 Example answers.

a Everyone said that they were ready to go.

b She declared that their adventure had begun the day before/already begun.

c The teacher told the children that they must have completed the homework by the following day.

d The mother told her son that he should (have) packed/pack his bags for school.

3 Learners' own sentences.

2.11 and 2.12 Write a news article

LEARNING PLAN

Learning objectives		Learning intentions	Success criteria
Main focus	**Also covered**	• Gather information.	• Learners can use questions to gather information and plan.
6Ws.01, 6Ws.02, 6Ws.04	6Ri.01, 6Ri.07, 6Ri.12, 6Ri.14, 6Wc.02, 6Wc.04, 6Wc.06, 6Wc.07, 6Wg.08, 6Wv.02, 6Wp.01, 6Wp.02, 6Wp.05, 6SLp.01, 6SLg.03	• Organise information into sections. • Proofread and present a news article.	• Learners can organise information into relevant sections. • Learners can proofread and present a news article.

LANGUAGE SUPPORT

One of the key skills to focus on in this activity is organising information into the correct sections of a news article to make the article flow. Use the inverted pyramid (see Session 2.3) to remind learners of the different sections and their purpose. Use the 5W1H questions to help them structure the lead and first paragraphs. Remind learners to organise the information from the most to least important. This may take some practice and some learners may need extra support to identify more and less important information.

Starter idea

Read and recall 5W1H (5 minutes)

Resources: Learner's Book, Session 2.11 and 2.12: Getting started; examples of news articles

Description: In pairs, learners discuss the features of news articles and consider which question words they would use for open and closed questions.

Hand out some news articles for learners to read and recall the structure.

Recall the difference between fiction and non-fiction. Discuss how we can tell if a news article is fiction.

Main teaching ideas

1 Use questions to gather information and make notes (30 minutes)

Learning intention: To ask questions, research and make notes

Resources: Learner's Book, Session 2.11 and 2.12, Activity 1; *Tenzing Norgay biography* (Learner's Book, Session 2.9); Track 12; books/information about the first Everest summit

Description: Write the words *Who, What, When, Where, Why, How* on the board. Brainstorm questions learners might have about the Everest expedition like *What was the weather like? What*

food did they take? What clothes and equipment did they have in those days?

In pairs, learners read the biography on Tenzing Norgay and extract the information about the expedition. If possible, they can research other information to add to this.

> **Differentiation ideas:** Challenge learners by asking them to use onscreen tools to research more information about the historical expedition.

> **Assessment ideas:** Observe as learners discuss. Check they remember the 5W1H questions and inverted pyramid structure.

Monitor their note-taking. Check they include important facts and information.

Answers:
1   Learners' own work.

2   Use the inverted pyramid to organise your information (60 minutes)

Learning intention: To use planning to inform writing, organise information into sections and present work neatly

Resources: Learner's Book, Session 2.11 and 2.12, Activity 2; Worksheets 6.14 and 6.15; dictionaries and thesaurses

Description: Draw the inverted pyramid (see Language focus box in Session 2.3) on the board and invite the learners to help you label each section.

In pairs, learners use their notes to organise their information into the relevant sections.

Brainstorm ideas for a catchy headline. Remind learners to use catchy words and phrases to convey meaning and point of view.

Learners aim to work individually to write their news article using their planning to inform their writing. They can use dictionaries and thesauruses to improve and check vocabulary.

Learners use Worksheet 6.14 Inverted pyramid and Worksheet 6.15 News report assessment sheet to guide their writing and assess it.

> **Differentiation ideas:** Support learners by encouraging them to work individually, in pairs or in groups, according to their pace and ability.

> **Assessment ideas:** Use Worksheet 6.14 Inverted pyramid and Worksheet 6.15 News report assessment sheet to guide and assess their news report. You can also use Worksheet 6.9 Writing assessment sheet to help you assess this activity.

Answers:
2   Learners' own work.

Plenary idea

Read all about it (5 minutes)

Resources: Worksheet 6.15

Description: Discuss criteria for news articles and write a list on the board or use the list in Worksheet 6.15 News report assessment sheet.

Learners display their articles for everyone to read or pass them around and/or the learners can take turns to read their articles to everyone. Invite positive feedback.

> **Assessment ideas:** Learners check and assess each other's work using criteria provided in Worksheet 6.15.

Learners decide which articles worked well and which ones need more attention. Offer ways to improve.

Homework ideas

Learners can complete the Workbook activities for Session 2.11 and 2.12.

They can read more news at home.

Learners watch and view news shows.

They can do research on 'fake news' to understand what it is and how to identify it.

Answers for Workbook

1–3 Learners' own work.

CHECK YOUR PROGRESS

1 a Active voice. **b** Passive voice.

2 a This is the team <u>that</u> is going to climb the mountain.

   b I am the one <u>who</u> is better prepared for the job.

   c She attended the local school, <u>which</u> is where she heard about it.

3 a third person

   b third person

   c first person

4 a self, oneself,

   b life, the study of life

5 **a and b** Onlookers heard them saying, "We can do this together."

The words, "Welcome back!" decorated the school when she returned.

PROJECT GUIDANCE

Group project: Learners create a class newspaper that includes news from the school and the community. Learners can interview each other, others in their class, teachers or peers from other classes. Once they have gathered stories about events in school or at home, they should work together to plan and present an authentic, interesting and relevant newspaper for everyone to enjoy. Invite them to include advertisements, TV or film reviews, sports results, crosswords and competitions.

Pair project: Learners research a famous event (from the past or present) that made the news. Both learners will research and find facts and opinions and different points of view about the event. Remind learners to record their sources of information. Once they have all the information, they will plan and present an objective news article reporting what happened in the third person. To be authentic, learners should pretend they are writing the day after the event. Remind learners to organise the news article according to the features learnt in this unit and include pictures, quotations, a headline and paragraphs.

Solo project: Learners use available books and online resources to research an explorer or adventurer of their choice. Remind them to take notes using key words and mind maps, and then use the information to write a biography. The autobiography should include pictures, be organised into sections with headings and be written in the third person. They can present the information as a large, colourful poster to display in the classroom or as an onscreen slideshow.

>3 Personification and imagery

Unit plan

Session	Approximate number of learning hours	Outline of learning content	Resources
3.1 *The River*	1	Read a poem. Analyse its features. Explore its mood and theme.	Learner's Book Session 3.1 Workbook Session 3.1 ⬇ Worksheet 6.1
3.2 Compare poems	0.5+	Read and explore two river poems. Interpret them imaginatively when reading aloud.	Learner's Book Session 3.2 Workbook Session 3.2 ⬇ Worksheet 6.10
3.3 Look deeper	1	Analyse poems. Compare their features. Give a group presentation.	Learner's Book Session 3.3 Workbook Session 3.3
3.4 *Right Here was the Ocean*	1	Listen to find out about a famous poet. Explore one of her poems. Analyse poetic technique and impact.	Learner's Book Session 3.4 Workbook Session 3.4 ⬇ Worksheet 6.1
3.5 Explore figurative language	1	Read a poem. Explore figurative language. Practise writing figurative language.	Learner's Book Session 3.5 Workbook Session 3.5 ⬇ Worksheet 6.1
3.6 Write your own poem	1	Re-read a favourite poem. Use it as a model for writing a poem. Perform a poem.	Learner's Book Session 3.6 Workbook Session 3.6 ⬇ Worksheet 6.9

Cross-unit resources
Learner's Book Check your progress
Learner's Book Projects
Unit 3 Language worksheets
Unit 3 Differentiated worksheet pack
End-of-unit 3 test

BACKGROUND KNOWLEDGE

Unit 3 focuses on figurative language and poetic technique. Learners have encountered metaphors and similes, alliteration and onomatopoeia in previous stages. In this unit, learners read poems with personification among other features. Personification technically refers to giving human characteristics to things or ideas, although some people extend the concept of personification to giving human characteristics to animals. While it would give learners the idea of how to use the technique, giving animals human characteristics is called 'anthropomorphism' – not a word that learners need to know.

TEACHING SKILLS FOCUS

Metacognition

Metacognition helps learners develop the skills to understand what effective learning looks like for them and how they learn best.

Help learners to think about learning objectives such as 'develop my understanding of personification' rather than just 'find out what personification is'. Ask learners to think about their learning throughout the lesson and follow how their understanding develops.

Encourage them to use prior knowledge in the Getting started activities to get them thinking and talking, for example, about figurative language techniques. They can work in pairs to find out what they already know about a new topic. Use their prior knowledge to plan your next steps.

Try to talk less to give more time for discussion. Ask open questions to get extended responses and monitor these discussions for evidence of learning.

For example, are learners demonstrating critical questioning when drawing inferences from the poems or seeking implicit meaning?

Spend time reflecting on learning that has taken place. Use the reflection opportunities in the Learner's Book to help learners to think about the learning process they used to come to their conclusions. *What did they already know and what did they find challenging?* Talk about how they could use this knowledge to help them in future.

Use learners' learning journals to help them become more independent, reflective learners. As well as noting poems read and their responses, they can create a self-learning or learning process section. Ask them to write about what they have learnt. Ask: *What did you find easy or challenging? What did you do when you were stuck? What helped you learn?*

3.1 *The River*

LEARNING PLAN

Learning objectives		Learning intentions	Success criteria
Main focus	**Also covered**	• Read a poem.	• Learners can read a poem with understanding.
6Rv.03, 6Rv.04, 6Rv.06, 6Rs.02, 6Ri.08, 6Ri.11, 6Ri.15, 6Wv.02	6Ri.06, 6Ri.10, 6Ri.14, 6Ra.02, 6SLm.01, 6SLm.03, 6SLp.01	• Analyse its features. • Explore its mood and theme.	• Learners can talk about its features. • Learners can identify the mood of a poem and how it is achieved.

LANGUAGE SUPPORT

Before starting Unit 3, learners may need to be reminded about the figurative language techniques they learnt about in previous stages: similes, metaphors, alliteration, rhymes and rhythm. In this unit, learners are introduced to **personification**. Help them to break the word down into its component parts, person, person**ify** and personifi**cation**, to help them understand how it is the technique of turning a non-living thing into a person. This is done by attributing human characteristics to the non-living thing. Point out how the *y* changes to an *i* when the suffix *–cation* is added to the verb.

Common misconception

Misconception	How to identify	How to overcome
Poems have the same number of lines in each stanza.	Ask learners what a stanza is in poetry and then ask if stanzas have any innate features such as length or punctuation. Put a selection of multi-stanza poems on the board to illustrate how they differ.	Use the poem *The River* to show that stanzas do not have to match each other in length. Encourage learners to become aware of how poems are structured throughout the unit and discuss possible reasons for choosing different-length stanzas.

Starter idea

Shades of meaning (5–10 minutes)

Resources: Learner's Book, Session 3.1: Getting started; images of different-sized rivers in different stages of flow

Description: Look at the images of rivers to provide context. Allow initial class discussion to draw on prior knowledge to order the words in terms of size. Suggest also interpreting the sound of the words;

e.g. *torrent* has an onomatopoeic feel of a large rushing river. Point out the diminutive suffix, *–let* in *rivulet* and *streamlet*, and think of other examples, such as *booklet* and *tartlet* (noting that not all words ending in *let* are diminutives).

Learners could check words in the dictionary during the discussion. Some words are unusual or regional (*beck*: a small river; *burn*: a small river or stream (of Gaelic origin – Scotland); *runnel*: a small stream; *rill*:

a small stream (and a channel formed by soil erosion). Find out if there are any local words for rivers and streams in your region.

Orally revise alphabetical order by ordering the river words if time.

Main teaching ideas

1 Respond to the poem (25 minutes)

Learning intention: To explore a poem's theme and features

Resources: *The River* (Learner's Book, Session 3.1, Activity 1); Track 13; pictures of the Mississippi River

Description: Sara Teasdale is a classic American poet, who often wrote about what she knew well. She was brought up near the Mississippi, one of the world's largest rivers. Although her poem was written over 100 years ago, the timeless subject helps the poem remain accessible and the sentiments unchanging. Show learners images you have sourced of the Mississippi River to provide context.

Learners read silently in pairs first to get the main idea and then aloud, choosing who does which part or even together. Allow them time to experiment and practise as you walk around listening. Reading aloud will help them get the feel of the poem's voice and theme.

The poem can be read on a number of levels, but keep it simple at first and focus on the first-person narrative bringing the river to life and ascribing it longing and yearning, followed by regret and helplessness in the face of the inevitable. When you bring pairs back to class discussion, talk about the extended metaphor of the river's personification. Personification separates the voice of the poet from the narrator of the poem. The poet's own feelings are expressed through the narrator – the river.

Revise features of poetic form so that learners are comfortable talking about lines, stanzas and rhyme scheme. Point out the convention of starting each line of the poem with a capital letter.

Spelling link: Discuss how some words are spelt differently in different parts of the world. More will be picked up in later units. Ask: *How is* grey *(UK) /* gray *(US) spelt in your region?*

Discuss spelling strategies for difficult words like Mississippi, e.g. spelling the letters out to a particular rhythm (*mi-ssi-ssi-ppi*); speaking a word aloud enunciating unstressed syllables and silent letters (e.g. *Feb-ru-a-ry*) or rhymes: *Mrs M, Mrs I, Mrs Double S I, Mrs Double S I, Mrs Double P I.*

ICT opportunity: Show learners how to set their word processing language before doing a spell check depending on whether you require US or UK spellings. If you have a smart board or projector demonstrate how US spellings show up as errors if the language is set to English UK, for example, but not if it is set to English US. Discuss whether an author's work ought to be adapted for the common spelling in each location.

> **Differentiation ideas:** Vary the level of expectation by allowing some learners to write answers in their notebooks in full, while others write their answers in note form. Provide extra support by talking about the answers with small groups of learners before they write in their books.

Answers:
1 a Learners' own reading.
   b • Three stanzas of four lines each; an end rhyme scheme: ABCB.
      • Learners' own answers but something along the lines of following one's dream which turns out to be not what was hoped for.
      • The source is sunny, windless valleys.
      • The river wanted to reach the sea, because it thought it would bring it peace.
      • It wanted to go back where it came from as it did not like the look of the wild sea or how it affected its freshness.
   c The river
   d Learners' own answers but something like: The river is given thoughts and feelings like a human – yearning to go to the sea as it thought it would bring peace. It is fearful of the sea when it gets there and sad that its freshness has been contaminated by seawater.
   e Learners' own answers.
   f Tasting unpleasantly sharp.

2 Match a proverb (20 minutes)

Learning intention: To understand how a theme is portrayed both explicitly and implicitly

Resources: Learner's Book, Session 3.1, Activity 2; *The River* (Learner's Book, Session 3.1); Track 13; Worksheet 6.1

Description: Proverbs are useful for talking about deeper, implicit meanings because they have a discernible, literal message but can be applied metaphorically in other contexts. Help learners to differentiate between idioms and proverbs.

Discuss really wanting something and finding that it turns out not to be quite what you imagined, such as the crazes learners are prone to. Ask: *Could the river have done anything about its fate?* (Link to the geographical aspect of rivers starting at the source and flowing to the mouth.) Ask: *Could it have changed its course had it known?*

Discuss the literal meaning of the proverbs, how they might have come about and their lessons. The first two imply longing for something, but the second is the more appropriate because the river does not covet what something else has. It wants something that *glittered* in its mind, but that turned out not to be as imagined. It carries the idea of not being able to turn back once set on a course of action; decisions may have irreversible consequences.

Encourage learners to add thoughtful entries to their learning journals (Worksheet 6.1).

Spelling link: Point out how many of the adjectives end in *ful* (with one *l* and not two). Show how many nouns – particularly abstract nouns – can be turned into adjectives by adding *ful*: *joyful, sorrowful, helpful, graceful*, etc. Brainstorm others.

Help identify nouns underlying adjectives in the box (*wistful* derives from the obsolete English word *wist* meaning intent, possibly linked to wish and wishful).

> **Differentiation ideas:** Support less confident learners by talking about the lessons of the proverbs compared with their literal meaning. Ask: *Can you think of analogies/similar situations in a different context in your own lives?*

Challenge more confident learners by discussing layers of meaning in more depth with selected groups. Ask them to think of contexts in their own lives that match the poem's sentiments.

> **Assessment ideas:** Use learners' discussions and work on proverbs to assess ability to read for deeper meaning.

Answers:
2   a   Learners' own answers.
    b   *Grass is greener*: what other people have looks better than what we have. *All that glitters*: things that appear valuable might not have the value we assume. *Pride comes*: if we are too proud and do not see what is really happening around us, we may do or say something we later regret. Learners' own answers on which one suits the poem best.
    c–d   Learners' own answers.

Plenary idea

Share your proverb (5 minutes)

Description: Invite volunteers to explain the proverb they chose in Activity 2b, giving their reasons. Allow learners to ask questions linked to the deeper meaning of the poem.

Do a class survey of who chose which proverb. Share your ideas as well.

> **Assessment ideas:** Assess whether learners are able to link the deeper meaning of a proverb to the poem's theme.

CROSS-CURRICULAR LINKS

Geography: Gather information on different kinds of rivers and discuss their features.

Homework ideas

Learners can complete the Workbook activities for Session 3.1. Share ideas as a class the next day.

Answers for Workbook

1   Personification: The washing machine coughed and spluttered before stopping. The window flung itself open and breathed in the fresh air. The icicle shivered and its teeth chattered. The sun beamed as it tiptoed its way across the sky.

2–3 Learners' own answers.

3.2 Compare poems

LEARNING PLAN

Learning objectives		Learning intentions	Success criteria
Main focus	**Also covered**	• Read and explore two river poems.	• Learners can read and compare poems.
6Rs.02, 6Ri.03, 6Ri.07, 6Ri.15, 6Ra.02, 6SLm.03, 6SLm.04, 6SLs.01, 6SLg.01, 6SLp.02, 6SLp.03, 6SLp.04	6Ri.02, 6Ri.11, 6Ri.13, 6Ri.17, 6Ra.01, 6Ra.03, 6SLm.01, 6SLg.02, 6SLp.01	• Give a personal response to a poem. • Interpret them imaginatively when reading aloud.	• Learners can give a personal response to the poems. • Learners can give an imaginative presentation on one of the poems.

LANGUAGE SUPPORT

The language in the poems is not too challenging but the imagery is created in different ways. Spend time talking with learners where possible, especially learners who may find the imagery more challenging, to help them articulate their understanding and response to the poems. Encourage the use of specific poetic terminology when talking of poetic devices.

Starter idea

Have you seen a river? (5 minutes)

Resources: Learner's Book, Session 3.2: Getting started; pictures of rivers

Description: Encourage learners to describe any rivers they have ever come across to each other. If they cannot think of a river, allow them to browse through images and books with pictures of rivers.

Having described literally what they can remember or see, encourage them to describe the river figuratively using similes, metaphors or personification. They can also choose vivid and descriptive words.

Share ideas and imagery as a class.

Main teaching ideas

🎧 14
🎧 15

1 Read two more river poems (25 minutes)

Learning intention: To explore theme and imagery in poetry

Resources: *Mawu of the Waters* and *A River Poem* (Learner's Book, Session 3.2, Activity 1); Tracks 14 and 15; Worksheet 6.10

Description: The two poems in this activity come from different continents to the American poem in Session 3.1, but they all share the topic of water and rivers.

Each learner reads one of the poems and retells it to a partner, as a narrative. Emphasise that they are to summarise the poem's 'story', say who tells it, how they know who the narrator is and the main things said by the narrator.

In discussing the structure and features, learners should identify poetic devices based on examples rather than guesses. Neither poem has a rhyme scheme or a rhythm. In the second poem, point out how the sentences run on across the lines (enjambment: a technique they will cover in more detail in Unit 9).

Learners need to develop the skill of articulating personal preferences supported by evidence from text. Comparing poems and deciding what they prefer is an ideal opportunity. Remind learners to be respectful of each other's views even if they disagree or have a different view.

Invite volunteers to share their responses. Extend learners' thinking where appropriate (without undermining their initial responses). For example, in *A River Poem*, discuss the theme of water as the source of life and how it is cyclical. The sky, cloud and sun could be reflected in the river, but the cloud is also water in the water cycle. Explore the idea that by drinking the river, one is also drinking the sun, sky and clouds reflected in it.

Take a vote as to which poem is the class favourite.

> **Differentiation ideas:** Pair more confident with less confident learners; ensure the more confident partner reads *A River Poem*, the more challenging of the two. *Mawu of the Waters* includes personification, similes and first-person narrative as with the first two poems, so should be more manageable.

> **Assessment ideas:** Adapt Worksheet 6.10 Reading, speaking or performing assessment sheet, selecting criteria from each of the categories and adding something on additional media. Use it to assess learners' performances. They could also assess each other.

Answers:
1   a–c   Learners' own answers. Example answers:

Mawu of the Waters: Mawu describes how she creates the different forms of water, flinging oceans around her and becoming a waterfall, letting it run through her fingers, cupping it, throwing it and letting it flow through her as a spring or river. It is narrated by Mawu (first person). We know this because of the use of pronoun *I* and what she says. Personification is used throughout, e.g. *I am Mawu of the waters* (i.e. the source of the water); metaphors include *mountains as my footstool*. Similes include *like a shawl*.

A River Poem: The narrator describes what is in the river and that the river can be played with and drunk by the narrator – that they are one, ending with the question – *who is in who?* Learners could be allowed to see the second poem as literal rather than figurative but accept any sensible response.

2   Do a dramatic presentation (20 minutes)

Learning intention: To dramatise the poems using body language, expression and other media

Resources: Learner's Book, Session 3.2, Activity 2; *Mawu of the Waters* and *A River Poem* (Learner's Book, Session 3.2); Tracks 14 and 15; recording devices; music players; props (optional)

Description: Both poems offer opportunities for a dramatic reading and cross-curricular or multimedia work. If possible, play music inspired by water, such as Handel's *Water Music*, or local songs or music linked to water.

Learners do not need to perform in front of an audience unless they want to. You could arrange an assembly performance with some learners joining in with choral reading and others dramatising the words. Allow learners to choose the media for their presentation.

If possible, record their dramatic presentations to allow learners to watch themselves and improve their performances.

> **Differentiation ideas:** Support learners by using recordings to show how they could improve specific aspects of their presentation or drama skills.

Answers:
2   Learners' own answers.

Plenary idea

Share your presentations (5 minutes)

Resources: Recordings of learners' presentations from Activity 2 (if possible)

Description: Invite volunteers to give their dramatic presentations to the class.

Organise the room to create a suitable atmosphere for the presentations.

If possible, also play a recording of their presentation from earlier to allow learners to see if they have improved.

> **Assessment ideas:** Learners can assess whether groups have improved by watching the recordings of their earlier performances.

CROSS-CURRICULAR LINKS

Geography: Source reference material and images of rivers and link them to the water cycle of water going to the sea as well as coming from clouds.

Homework ideas

Learners can do the Workbook activities for Session 3.2. Share answers in class the next day.

Answers for Workbook

1 Possible answers:

optimism	silliness	sadness	peace
elated	crazy	despondent	composed
enthusiastic	daft	gloomy	cool
exultant	foolish	melancholy	passive
happy	hare-brained	mournful	placid
hopeful	light-hearted	regretful	quiet
jubilant	mad	sad	relaxed
positive	ridiculous	solemn	serene
sunny		wistful	tranquil

2 a Possible answers:
   - the end of winter and the coming of spring into summer.
   - It is winter.
   - Learners' own answers for mood.

   b Possible answers: the sounds in the first line of the poem are a little harder and colder.

   c The words gradually soften to represent the coming months and new life associated with the rosebuds.

3 a Learners' own answers.

   b Wild and piled.

   c They are in the middle of the line.

3.3 Look deeper

LEARNING PLAN

Learning objectives		Learning intentions	Success criteria
Main focus	**Also covered**	• Analyse poems.	• Learners can analyse poems for theme, and explicit and implicit meaning.
6Rv.04, 6Rv.06, 6Ri.03, 6Ri.06, 6Ri.08, 6Ri.10, 6Ri.11, 6Ri.15, 6SLs.01, 6SLg.01, 6SLp.03, 6SLp.04, 6SLr.01	6Rs.02, 6Ri.02, 6Ri.14, 6Wg.08, 6Wc.06, 6Wp.02, 6SLm.01, 6SLm.02, 6SLm.03, 6SLm.05	• Compare their features. • Give a group presentation.	• Learners can compare poems' features. • Learners can take part in a group presentation, following criteria.

LANGUAGE SUPPORT

Learners should be familiar with the explicit meaning of the vocabulary used in the two poems in Session 3.2. In this session, they look for implicit meaning and how the theme is portrayed, comparing the two poems. Some learners may need extra support as it is more challenging to read for deeper meaning and to make inferences that rely on implicit meaning.

Starter idea

Give your opinion (5 minutes)

Resources: Learner's Book, Session 3.3: Getting started

Description: Give learners an opportunity to discuss in small groups the river poem they enjoyed the most. They should explain why to each other; remind them to use appropriate technical vocabulary to discuss theme, mood and figurative language.

Survey the class and find out which was the most popular poem, with volunteers giving their reasons.

Main teaching ideas

1 Analyse the poems in more detail (25 minutes)

Learning intention: To compare the features, theme, imagery and mood of two poems

Resources: Learner's Book, Session 3.3, Activity 1; *Mawu of the Waters* and *A River Poem* (Learner's Book, Session 3.2); Tracks 14 and 15

Description: Ask learners to re-read each poem before answering the questions. Encourage them to to visualise the image that the words bring out, e.g. *reap* in the fourth line of *Mawu of the Waters* gives the vision of Mawu reaching down into the water to gather its harvest and in so doing creates lakes of water, which gives an impression of vastness. Point out the exclamation mark in the middle of the fifth line – this is a form of poetic licence as it is not technically grammatically correct.

Mawu of the Waters creates many images relating to a different type of water flow. Invite learners to share what they find appealing.

A River Poem uses less figurative imagery in terms of personification but creates images through vivid description and ideas. Invite learners to share their understanding of the extract. Ask: *Have you ever seen a reflection in water destroyed when, for example, a stone is thrown in or a finger ripples through the calm surface?*

Discuss the old-fashioned contraction *o'er*; the poet uses it to create a different sound effect in place of the two-syllable word *over*, wanting to create a particular rhythm and flow to the lines.

Invite learners to talk about the poem's final question. Ask whether a scientific or a figurative answer is required.

After discussion in pairs, groups or as a class, learners should be ready to write a comparative paragraph. Remind them about useful comparative connectives such as *whereas, on the other hand, in contrast* and *similarly*.

Allow time for learners to swap paragraphs with partners to give each other feedback and see if they agree with each other and to discuss any differences.

> **Differentiation ideas:** Support less confident learners by allowing them to write notes rather than a full paragraph. Learners who would benefit from extra challenge could write the answers to the questions in full in their notebooks.

Answers:
1 a • Possible answer: I put my hands down into the water and, look, as I bring them up, I hold lakes in my cupped hands.
   • 7: lakes, oceans, waterfall, springs, rivers, streams, seas
   • Alliteration of the letter S. It gives the impression of water swirling and swilling about. Onomatopoeia could be considered.
   • Learners' own favourite images.
   b • It means the sky, cloud and the sun are reflected in the river.
   • over: To make it a one-syllable word to create a different sound, flow or rhythm in the line.
   • Learners' own answers to the last line.
   c and d • Learners' own paragraphs and discussion.

2 Give a group presentation (20 minutes)

Learning intention: To give and evaluate a group presentation

Resources: *The River* (Learner's Book, Session 3.1); Track 13; *Mawu of the Waters* and *A River Poem* (Learner's Book, Session 3.2); Tracks 14 and 15

Description: Learners compare the poems read so far. The *Critic's choice* box is a guide and an assessment possibility combined. Explain that the marking scheme is for learners to assess whether they need more help and that it is not a 'right–wrong' assessment. Assess each question as fully answered / partially answered / not answered at all (2, 1 or 0 marks).

Allocate 5–10 minutes for instructions, and just over half the remaining time for preparation of presentations. Each presentation is no more than five minutes. Set a time limit for feedback. Appoint a timekeeper in each group. To achieve 2 marks for each question, the group must both select and perform extracts to illustrate their point. If time, model giving feedback and scoring with a volunteer group.

If possible, record the presentations as a baseline and to allow learners to watch and set themselves goals.

> **Differentiation ideas:** Support less confident learners by using recordings to show how they could improve their presenting skills.

> **Assessment ideas:** Use the learners' *Critic's choice* presentations and assessments to review their presentations comparing the poems for their understanding of theme, poetic form and features.

Answers:
2 a–b   Learners' own answers.

Plenary idea

What's your image? (5 minutes)

Description: Ask learners to imagine that they are a river, stream, lake or sea and to write down a few lines imagining they are that water narrating some story or aspect of itself.

Remind them that using first-person narrative, as if they were the water, is personification. They can describe the human-like actions or feelings.

Invite volunteers to share their lines of imagery.

> **Assessment ideas:** Learners can give feedback on the imagery and say how or why they find it effective and how it could be improved.

> ### CROSS-CURRICULAR LINKS
>
> **Geography:** Gather reference books, images and video clips of rivers, seas, lakes, oceans, streams and waterfalls.

Homework ideas

Learners can complete the Workbook activities for Session 3.3, revising aspects of poetic technique. Share answers as a class, especially the answers in Activity 3.

Answers for Workbook

1 a   DUM de DUM de DUM de DUM (7 syllables) / de DUM de DUM de DUM de (7) / DUM de DUM de DUM de DUM (7) / de DUM de DUM de DUM de (7)

   b   Learners' own answers but should be along the lines of jolly and upbeat.

2 a   End rhymes: Learners could say there is no end rhyme pattern if they have not picked up the half rhymes *after* and *water*. End rhyme pattern is in lines 2 and 4, giving ABCB.

   b   Internal rhymes: Line 1 has *hill* and *Jill*; line 3 has *down* and *crown*.

   c   Half rhymes: *water* and *after* are a half rhyme at the end of lines 2 and 4.

3 a   Onomatopoeia: Using words that include sounds that are similar to the noises the words they refer to.

   Alliteration: Using words, especially in poetry, of the same sound/s, especially consonants, at the beginning of several words that are close together.

   b   **1** uses alliteration, e.g. *cunningly creeping* and *spectral stalker* (but could also be onomatopoeia as *cunningly creeping* and *spectral stalker* are both suggestive of the actions). **2** uses onomatopoeia, e.g. *SHUSHES, hushes, flitter-twitters*. **3** uses alliteration, e.g. *Cook, could, cookies*. There is also a resonance of the same sound with the word *good* – a hard *G* just to match the hard *C*. (It could also be referred to as assonance the same *oo/ou* vowel sound.) **4** uses both alliteration and onomatopoeia, e.g. *cobbles, clattered, clashed* or *horse-hooves* and *clattered, clashed, tapped, tlot tlot* (also a made-up word).

3.4 *Right Here Was the Ocean*

LEARNING PLAN

Learning objectives		Learning intentions	Success criteria
Main focus	**Also covered**	• Listen to find out about a famous poet.	• Learners can listen for information.
6Rv.04, 6Rv.06, 6Ri.03, 6Ri.10, 6Ri.11, 6Ri.15, 6Ra.02, 6Ww.07, 6Wc.06, 6Wp.04, 6Wp.05	6Rv.01, 6Rv.03, 6Rs.02, 6Ri.02, 6Ri.06, 6Ri.07, 6Ri.08, 6Ri.13, 6Ri.14, 6Ra.01, 6Wv.06, 6Wg.08, 6SLm.01, 6SLp.01, 6SLr.01	• Explore one of her poems. • Analyse poetic technique and impact.	• Learners can read aloud and talk about one of the poems. • Learners can analyse poetic technique and its impact.

LANGUAGE SUPPORT

The poem in this session also uses personification but not in first-person narrative this time. Some learners may need support to recognise the technique in action. Go through the vocabulary in the poem to check that learners understand it beyond the words that are glossed in the Learner's Book Session 3.4.

Common misconception

Misconception	How to identify	How to overcome
Listening for information is difficult.	Ask learners whether it is easier to listen for information or to listen for imagery, as when listening to a poem. Find out what makes listening for information challenging, e.g. the speed of the audio or too much detail.	Use the listening activity to show that listening for information is easier if they follow simple steps. First, learners must read the questions and visualise the sort of answer they are looking for, for example, an age or a reason. Second, they must listen carefully and jot down notes if they are not to hear the audio a second time. Third, they must try to answer the questions with the information they can remember or their notes and identify any missing information to listen out for if the audio is played a second time.

Starter idea

🎧 Hear about Zehra Nigah (10 minutes)

Resources: *Zehra Nigah* (Learner's Book, Session 3.4: Getting started); Track 16

Description: Tell learners that you are going to play an audio giving biographical information about a poet from Pakistan. Explain that you will play the audio twice.

Ask learners to read the questions they will have to answer. This will help them know what type of information to listen out for. Four of the five questions require listening for explicit information; the final question requires some interpretation. They can either note the information in their heads or jot down notes. The disadvantage of the latter approach is that while writing, they may miss some other information.

After learners have read the questions, play the audio for the first time, and allow learners a few minutes to review their notes or their memories and assess whether they still need to find out any information. After a few minutes, play the audio once more.

Decide whether to discuss the answers in class or whether to ask learners to write the answers in their notebooks for a more formal assessment.

Audioscript: *Zehra Nigah*

Speaker 1: Zehra Nigah was born in Hyderabad, India in 1937. When she was ten years old, she and her family moved to Pakistan after the 1947 partition of India. Today she lives in Karachi, Pakistan. Zehra believes she was lucky to have a family that were so interested in creative arts. Her father, a civil servant, enjoyed poetry, her mother music and her maternal grandfather the classical poets. When she was as young as four, her grandfather encouraged Zehra, her sister and two brothers to learn great works of poetry by heart – sometimes bribing them with a reward of 5 rupees. He was strict and wanted them to learn not just the lines but the correct pronunciation and style of reciting the poetry. By the time she was 14, Zehra had learnt the works of most of the great poets by heart.

Speaker 2: Zehra began writing poetry as young as eight or nine years old. She was unusual because there were few female poets at the time in Pakistan as it was considered to be something men did but not women. She often performed her work in *mushairas* or poetry recitals both in Pakistan and India. These performances developed her confidence in herself because people wanted to hear her read her poetry. When asked about being a female poet, Zehra said, 'Nature does not discriminate between a male and a female when it awards competence and abilities – only society does.'

Answers:
1 Ten years old
2 Because of the 1947 Partition of India
3 He encouraged her to learn great poetry by heart.
4 Mushairas
5 She said 'Nature does not discriminate between a male and a female when it awards competence and abilities – only society does.' Accept all answers giving the same idea.

Main teaching ideas

1 Read the poem aloud in pairs (15 minutes) 🎧

Learning intention: To read the poem aloud fluently, with confidence and expression

Resources: *Right Here Was the Ocean* (Learner's Book, Session 3.4, Activity 1); Track 17; Worksheet 6.1; dictionaries/online spelling tools

Description: Initially, pairs should skim read the poem to get the main idea. Ask: *What is the poem describing? What is the poem's mood?* If they are unsure of the meaning of any of the poem's words and they cannot work them out from the context, suggest they use a dictionary or an online spelling tool. Remind them to note any words they look up in their word list in their learning journals.

Having got an idea of the poem's theme, learners practise reading the poem aloud in pairs, in a manner of their choice. Remind them that they must not only speak clearly and fluently but also interpret the poem's mood and theme. After a few minutes of discussion followed by practice, each pair performs the poem for another pair. Remind the listening pairs that their role is to appreciate the performance as well as to offer suggestions for possible improvement.

> **Differentiation ideas:** Use a mixture of pairings of more and less confident learners to allow you to focus attention on pairs who may need more support.

> **Assessment ideas:** Assess learners' answers to see how well they listen for information and understanding.

Answers:
1 a In the first stanza, the poem describes the ocean, in wild stormy weather, when the tide is coming in. In the second stanza, it describes what is left behind when the tide goes out and the storm dies down.
   b–d Learners' own answers.

2 Analyse the poem (25 minutes)

Learning intention: To explore a poem's theme, mood, structure and features

Resources: Learner's Book, Session 3.4, Activity 2; *Right Here Was the Ocean* (Learner's Book, Session 3.4); Track 17; dictionaries/online spelling tools

Description: Learners answer a range of lower- and higher-order questions to help them analyse and interpret the poem. The questions, as well as their earlier reading, prepare them to write a paragraph to summarise their analysis of the poem and its features, giving their personal response. Share your response to the poem as a model.

Some learners may find it helpful to plan their paragraph using a mind map or other planning tool. After writing, learners check their own paragraphs carefully to correct any errors before writing it out neatly and legibly. When partners give each other feedback, they should review both content and how the paragraph was written.

As a final discussion point, learners should discuss whether a poem or a descriptive paragraph is a more effective way to describe something – in this case the ocean. Both can be effective but a poem tends to be more figurative, conjuring up images that could

be different for each reader. For some learners, however, poems can be harder to understand. It depends on what they like to read. Listen to their reasoning carefully and then share your own ideas.

> **Differentiation ideas:** Support less confident learners by discussing what they will include in their paragraphs before they start writing. Some learners can prepare a mind map or answers in note form rather than a paragraph. Encourage more confident learners to work individually rather than in pairs to answer the questions in their notebooks.

> **Assessment ideas:** Use learners' paragraphs analysing the poem to assess their understanding of theme, structure and features as well as poetic techniques.

Answers:
2 a Two sentences – one for each stanza.
   b Learners' own answers, but they should note that the ocean is rough and stormy.
   c It is likely to be stormy, windy weather.
   d The repetition of the present participles (–*ing* words) reflects the idea of the water repeatedly crashing against the rocks.
   e The ocean – given human emotions, (*angry, petulant*) the moon – given human characteristics (*reticent, modest*) and having a friend, the rocks – with parched tongues sticking out.
   f The moon.
   g The tide has gone out, exposing the rocks and barren shoreline, although the moon is still reflected in the remaining puddles of water.
   h–k Learners' own answers.

Plenary idea

Share your paragraph (5 minutes)

Resources: Learners' paragraphs analysing the poem from Activity 2

Description: Invite volunteers to share their paragraphs with the class.

Allow learners to ask questions if there is time and discuss whether everyone agrees with the analysis or what they would say differently.

> **Assessment ideas:** Learners can assess the paragraphs by comparing the analysis with their own and through discussion. This will also allow you to see how much

agreement there is or whether more work needs to be done in any area of poem analysis.

<table>
<tr><td>CROSS-CURRICULAR LINKS</td></tr>
</table>

Geography: Gather reference material on seas and tides, erosion and weather patterns.

Homework ideas

Learners can complete the Workbook activities for Session 3.4 to consolidate their understanding of personification. Learners can swap books and mark each other's work, discussing any differences.

Answers for Workbook

1 Personification means using <u>human</u> qualities or actions to describe a <u>non</u>-living object. The word *personification* is a clue because it contains the word <u>person</u>. Personify is a <u>verb</u> meaning to describe something as if it were a person. So, rather than saying: *The moon is a crescent shape tonight*, say: *The <u>moon</u> is just peeping out tonight.*

2 Using a human word to describe an object makes a poetic <u>image</u> more vivid. It can also tell you how the <u>narrator</u> of the poem feels about the object. For example, *The moon <u>shyly</u> watched me*, shows

sympathy with the moon; whereas, *The moon barely <u>noticed</u> me* does not show sympathy. Poems can also be written in <u>first</u> person as if the object has <u>feelings</u> like a person.

3

Z	R	S	T	A	N	Z	A	T	R	Z	A	O	H
N	S	O	A	H	R	T	I	H	A	P	L	N	S
M	M	T	I	H	Y	T	Y	O	N	R	L	O	E
A	E	P	Y	R	R	M	A	M	O	E	I	M	H
O	S	X	P	E	E	A	L	Y	I	S	T	A	R
Y	H	H	I	A	N	N	E	T	S	E	T	T	E
M	E	A	A	R	S	A	I	E	I	N	R	O	A
R	N	Y	M	R	H	O	T	C	T	R	A	P	R
S	I	M	I	L	E	O	R	S	E	O	T	O	L
I	R	N	P	T	I	Y	R	S	P	I	I	E	M
E	C	N	A	N	O	S	S	A	E	H	O	I	N
M	S	R	T	Y	T	E	M	S	R	A	N	A	O
A	D	Y	A	L	P	D	R	O	W	S	P	O	N
M	O	H	A	E	I	N	O	T	A	E	T	Z	Z

3.5 Explore figurative language

LEARNING PLAN

Learning objectives		Learning intentions	Success criteria
Main focus	**Also covered**		
6Rv.04, 6Rv.06, 6Ri.07, 6Ri.11, 6Ra.02, 6Wv.02, 6Wv.04, 6Wv.05, 6Wp.04	6Ri.02, 6Ri.06, 6Ri.08, 6Ri.10, 6Ri.13, 6Ri.14, 6Ri.15, 6Ra.01, 6Wc.01, 6SLm.01, 6SLp.01, 6SLr.01	• Read a poem. • Explore figurative language. • Practise writing figurative language.	• Learners can read a poem with appreciation and understanding. • Learners can identify and appreciate figurative language. • Learners can write different types of figurative language.

LANGUAGE SUPPORT

Learners are still working with figurative language but looking at extended metaphors and other features. The language of the poem is not difficult, but it is very evocative and some learners may need help to appreciate the imagery that is not explicit.

Starter idea

Extend a metaphor (5 minutes)

Resources: Learner's Book, Session 3.5: Getting started

Description: Learners revise what a metaphor is together giving each other examples.

Share examples as a class before discussing what an extended metaphor could be and how it would work in a poem.

Main teaching ideas

1 Extended metaphors (25 minutes)

Learning intention: To identify figurative language and its impact on understanding beyond the literal

Resources: *The Storm* (Learner's Book, Session 3.5, Activity 1); Track 18; Worksheet 6.1

Description: Read through the Language focus box in the Learner's Book with learners and discuss extended metaphors.

Once you feel they have understood the concept, organise learners into small groups to read the poem *The Storm*. Explain that it contains an extended metaphor and allow them to find it rather than point it out.

Learners can also revise other figurative techniques encountered in previous stages and sessions by identifying them in the poem.

Having looked at the figurative techniques, encourage learners to focus on the imagery created and how it tells the story in the poem more vividly than any literal depiction. They will know the poem is about a storm from its title but encourage them to look at the imagery to see how it creates the effect of stormy conditions.

When they add the poem to their learning journals, suggest they include examples from the poem of figurative techniques as a reminder for later work as well as giving their opinion of the poem.

> **Differentiation ideas:** Organise groups that contain a mixture of more and less confident readers to read and discuss the poem so that learners can support each other. Encourage more confident learners to write the answers in their notebooks.

> **Assessment ideas:** Use learners' answers to this activity to informally assess how well they identify figurative language.

Answers:
1. a Learners read the poem.
   b Extended metaphor: Without warning a snake of black | cloud rises in the sky. | It hisses as it runs and spreads its hood. Personification: The shout of the demon, the storm rattling an iron chain in its teeth, the mountain lifting its trunk or the lake roaring Simile: The lake roars like a wild beast.
   c • It is likely that storm clouds have covered the moon blocking its light.
      • The shout is likely thunder.
      • The storm: The rattling of an iron chain in its teeth – this gives the impression of huge noise, screeching wind and rattling.
      • Lightning: The mountain suddenly lifts its trunk to the heavens – suddenly there is light and it can be seen.
      • Possible answer for the lake roaring: Water is crashing about in the wild wind and rain.
   d Learners' own answers.

2 Practise figurative language (20 minutes)

Learning intention: To write figurative language for effect

Resources: Learner's Book, Session 3.5, Activity 2; Workbook, Session 3.5; thesauruses

Description: Source images to stimulate learners' thinking about possible topics for the exercise.

Allow learners to choose their own topic if they are excited about a different one.

Demonstrate choosing one of the topics to get learners started and then encourage learners to share what they create with a partner and to give each other ideas. Keep it a lively session and go around encouraging learners and making suggestions.

If they find it difficult to create an extended metaphor, remind them of their answers in Activity 1 to show how to group images around a theme and use the activities in Workbook Session 3.5 for consolidation if there is time in class. Give the example of 'life being like a river', flowing up and down, overcoming obstacles, dark and stormy at times and sparkling, gurgling and frolicking at others. Focus on word choice as well as images and have thesauruses handy.

Learners can evaluate and enjoy each other's poems in a group at the end, saying what they enjoyed and adding images if they can.

> **Differentiation ideas:** Support learners by providing a starter image for the topic of their choice to help them build an extended metaphor.

> **Assessment ideas:** Use learners' poems to assess how well they can create images using extended metaphors.

Answers:
2   a–d   Learners' own answers.

Plenary idea

Build class poems (5 minutes)

Resources: Learners' poems from Session 3.5

Description: Ask learners to group themselves by topic and to put together their short poems around the same topic to make longer poems.

Listen to each group's 'topic poem'.

> **Assessment ideas:** Groups can give feedback on the topic poems, suggesting a different order of stanzas or selecting their favourite images.

CROSS-CURRICULAR LINKS

Geography: Gather information on weather conditions, particularly storms. Review the Beaufort wind scale.

Homework ideas

Learners can complete the Workbook activities for Session 3.5 to consolidate their understanding of extended metaphors, if these have not been completed in class. Explain that a motorway is the same as a highway, if motorway is not the common word in your region.

Answers for Workbook

1   a   The tide of life ebbs and flows. It sings when life is good. It cries when times are bad.

     b   Learners' own answers.

2–3   Learners' own answers.

3.6 Write your own poem

LEARNING PLAN

Learning objectives		Learning intentions	Success criteria
Main focus	**Also covered**	• Re-read a favourite poem.	• Learners can choose and re-read a favourite poem from the unit.
6Wv.02, 6Wv.04, 6Wv.05, 6Wc.01, 6Wp.03, 6Wp.04, 6SLm.01, 6SLm.04, 6SLp.01, 6SLp.03, 6SLp.04, 6SLr.01	6Rv.03, 6Rv.04, 6Rv.06, 6Rs.02, 6Ri.02, 6Ra.02, 6Ww.07, 6Wv.06, 6Wp.01, 6Wp.05, 6SLm.05, 6SLp.02	• Use it as a model for writing a poem. • Perform a poem.	• Learners can analyse it to use as a model for writing their own poem. • Learners can perform their poem for an audience.

LANGUAGE SUPPORT

The focus of Session 3.6 is writing using figurative language and vivid imagery. Some learners may need support to develop their ideas using figurative language. Have thesauruses available for more interesting word choices but be prepared to spend a significant amount of time helping learners develop their imagery.

Note that *mushairas* are traditional poetry recitals in Pakistan and India – both of which are countries where poetry is popular and widespread.

Common misconception

Misconception	How to identify	How to overcome
Poetry has to include some rhyme.	Review the poems in Unit 3 and ask which ones had rhyme as a feature.	While not preventing learners from using rhyme as a poetic technique (as it can be very effective and evocative), the poems in Unit 3 should show that rhyme need not be the overriding feature. Word choice, vivid description and figurative language are all powerful storytellers.

Starter idea

Share your favourite poem (5 minutes)

Learning intention: To express a personal response to a poem

Resources: Learner's Book, Session 3.6: Getting started; the five poems from this unit

Description: Organise learners into groups to discuss the poems they have read in the unit.

They should say what they enjoyed about the different poems and which was their favourite. Encourage them to tell each other why.

Main teaching ideas

1 Write a poem (30 minutes)

Learning intention: To write a poem including figurative language techniques

Resources: Learner's Book, Session 3.6, Activity 1; Worksheet 6.9; learners' favourite poems from the unit

Description: Once learners have chosen their favourite poem from the unit, ask them to make notes of the poem's key features and techniques, such as personification or number of stanzas.

They can write their own poem on the same theme, following a similar approach. If they would like to choose their own topic, allow it but still ask them to follow a similar approach.

Hand out Worksheet 6.9 Writing assessment sheet to guide learners in their writing. Negotiate success criteria with them. You can use these to differentiate the activity.

While they are using the poem as a model, emphasise that they can add in extra figurative language techniques, especially repetition, alliteration, onomatopoeia and shape, e.g. long and short line lengths.

Encourage quiet time to allow learners to get on with planning (making mind maps, lists of images, etc.) and writing their first draft. Remind them that they do not have to worry about getting everything perfect as they will have time to edit and improve.

Learners should read their drafts in small groups to get feedback and suggestions from others. If learners are reluctant, allow them to read to you.

Allow further quiet time for learners to edit and improve their poems. They can choose whether to write them out by hand in neat, legible handwriting and use dictionaries and thesauruses, or write them out online using online editing tools.

> **Differentiation ideas:** Support less confident learners by allowing them to write their poem in pairs or to write a more limited version of their favourite poem – e.g. just one stanza, fewer lines or focusing on one figurative technique.

> **Assessment ideas:** Use Worksheet 6.9 to assess learners' poems adding some of your own criteria.

Answers:
1   a–e   Learners' own answers.

2 Perform at a *mushaira* (15 minutes)

Learning intention: To perform a poem with expression and style

Resources: Learner's Book, Session 3.6, Activity 2; learners' powms from Activity 1; cushions and drapes (if possible)

Description: Allow learners time to plan how to perform their poems. Some may prefer to do a straight reading just with expression, other may prefer a more creative approach to increase the impact.

Focus on the imagery and impact each poem has on listeners, and how it promotes understanding and empathy beyond the literal. Some learners may want another learner to work with them to create different voice effects.

Once they have planned and written some performance notes for themselves, give learners practice time – either alone to make sure they are fluent or with a partner to get feedback on their performance.

Set up *mushaira* groups or organise the performances as a class. Rearrange the classroom and provide cushions and drapes, if possible, to create atmosphere, and enjoy the performances.

> **Differentiation ideas:** Support less confident learners so that they do not feel the pressure of a big performance by creating larger and smaller groups for the *mushairas*.

Answers:
2   a–c   Learners' own answers.

Plenary idea

Hear my poem (5 minutes)

Resources: Learners' poems from Activity 1

Description: If learners have worked in groups for the poetry performances in Activity 2, invite one or two learners to share their poems with the whole class. Ask them first to explain which poem it was modelled on and which techniques they used before reading it out.

Invite feedback from the rest of the class.

> **Assessment ideas:** Learners can assess how well the poem follows the model and give credit for any additional figurative techniques used.

Homework ideas

Learners can complete the Workbook activities for Session 3.6 to extend their figurative language writing in a poem. Invite learners to share their writing process as well as the resulting poem.

Answers for Workbook

1–3 Learners' own answers.

CHECK YOUR PROGRESS

1 a Giving human actions, characteristics and feelings to non-living objects or ideas.

   b Learners' own answers.

2 a over, never, it is, ever, it was.

   b To change the rhythm and flow of the line or to create a different sound effect.

3 a It compares one thing to another using *like* or *as*.

   b Learners' own answers.

4 a It compares one thing to another directly by saying one thing is another thing.

   b Learners' own answers.

5 a An extended metaphor continues the image of one thing as another thing beyond one image across several lines of poetry.

   b Learners' own answers.

PROJECT GUIDANCE

Gather as many poetry anthologies and suitable online sites as possible. Also ask learners to bring in poetry books from home and encourage them to go to their local libraries. They can also ask their families if they have any poems they can share.

Group project: Learners choose a poem to perform and film as a group. They should assign clear roles in the planning and executing, and preferably all take part in the performance. They should consider costumes, lighting, vocal effects and music as well as the quality of the performance. They can perform their poems live and share the recordings with other classes.

Pair project: Learners can choose a poem with any type of figurative language – but they must be able to identify it. They then think creatively about how to illustrate the poem to enhance the imagery. They could consider a multimedia presentation rather than straight illustration.

Solo project: Learners can browse anthologies to look for poems with figurative language. They can find all the techniques in one poem or separate poems. Invite them to read them out to the class in a reading time.

> 4 Back to the future

Unit plan

Session	Approximate number of learning hours	Outline of learning content	Resources
4.1 Looking into the future	1	Skim read an extract. Scan an extract for details. Make predictions.	Learner's Book Session 4.1 Workbook Session 4.1
4.2 Step into their shoes	1	Empathise with characters. Make inferences from the text. Explore a golden thread.	Learner's Book Session 4.2 Workbook Session 4.2 ⬇ Worksheet 6.1
4.3 Useful punctuation and grammar tips	1	Explore dashes, commas and brackets in parenthesis. Explore the use of colons. Investigate quantifiers.	Learner's Book Session 4.3 Workbook Session 4.3
4.4 Begin planning a longer story	1	Explore chapters. Plan a chapter story. Write a draft of Chapter 1.	Learner's Book Session 4.4 Workbook Session 4.4 ⬇ Worksheet 6.2 ⬇ Worksheet 6.5 ⬇ Worksheet 6.18 ⬇ Language worksheet 4A
4.5 Going back and looking into the future	1	Explore science fiction. Read an extract. Make predictions.	Learner's Book Session 4.5 Workbook Session 4.5
4.6 Working with voices and moods	1	Explore the active and passive voice. Investigate the conditional mood.	Learner's Book Session 4.6 Workbook Session 4.6 ⬇ Differentiated worksheets 4A–C
4.7 Working with chapters, paragraphs and connectives	1	Explore paragraphs. Investigate and use connectives.	Learner's Book Session 4.7 Workbook Session 4.7

Session	Approximate number of learning hours	Outline of learning content	Resources
4.8 Write paragraphs describing fictional surroundings	1	Plan Chapter 2. Write Chapter 2. Edit and improve Chapter 2.	Learner's Book Session 4.8 Workbook Session 4.8 ⤓ Worksheet 6.18 ⤓ Language worksheet 4B
4.9 Going forward in time	1	Read and perform an extract. Write an entry.	Learner's Book Session 4.9 Workbook Session 4.9 ⤓ Worksheet 6.19
4.10 Spelling, punctuation and grammar	1	Piece together the details. Explore writing techniques. Investigate spelling rules.	Learner's Book Session 4.10 Workbook Session 4.10
4.11 Finish your story	1	Complete a science-fiction story. Get feedback from a partner. Make improvements.	Learner's Book Session 4.11 Workbook Session 4.11 ⤓ Worksheet 6.6
4.12 Take part in a *Readaloudathon*	1	Read stories in a group. Summarise them to another group. Identify the golden threads.	Learner's Book Session 4.12 Workbook Session 4.12
Cross-unit resources			
Learner's Book Check your progress Learner's Book Projects End-of-unit 4 test			

BACKGROUND KNOWLEDGE

Science fiction as a genre is often credited to the French writer, Jules Verne (1828–1905). His many adventure novels about space and underwater travel at the time were published before such things were common and he is often known as the 'father' of science fiction. Science fiction is often associated with space travel, which with modern developments may seem to be less and less part of the future. Inventions that would have been considered incredible 120 years ago may seem quite common today. For example, when *The Hitchhiker's Guide to the Galaxy* was written, the Guide was a futuristic invention. The idea that you could ask a device about anything and get an almost instantaneous answer is no longer so incredible with the internet and smartphones. Nonetheless, the story itself remains clearly in the science-fiction genre and is a classic of the genre.

TEACHING SKILLS FOCUS

Differentiation

No class of learners will ever be entirely homogenous as learners will exhibit different abilities, different learning strategies, different confidence levels and different levels of concentration. The teacher's role in striving for inclusive education primarily depends on awareness of individual learners' strengths and challenges. Grouping learners by ability for activities to target support more easily is a well-tried and tested option for differentiation but it is insufficient as a tool on its own.

Identifying learners' barriers to more successful learning is the first step to finding strategies to support each learner individually. Differentiation is not just about supporting those who struggle; it is also about knowing how to extend and stimulate learners who finish work quickly or easily. Behaviour-wise, bored and frustrated learners for whom the pace is too slow are every bit as problematic as learners who struggle to grasp concepts or to concentrate.

This unit provides many options for creative differentiation especially linked to the extended writing that takes place over the unit. Learners are required to write a four-chapter science-fiction story, stimulated by three different texts and various writing activities. An obvious differentiation would be by outcome, with some learners being encouraged to write more chapters and therefore a more complex story with more developed characters, setting and plot line. An alternative approach could be to restrict the writing to four chapters but to require some learners to write in more depth and detail in each chapter than other learners.

In other areas, group work provides opportunities for mixed-ability and more confident groups, both in reading, discussion, writing and performing. Allowing learners to write in pairs rather than individually enables learners to support each other before requiring support from the teacher. What might be a mixed-ability group for reading or writing can become a different mixed-ability group for performance, for example.

Encouraging learners to evaluate each other's work enables learners to learn from each other and to improve their work in more depth, focusing on areas such as characterisation, plot and setting as well as the more obvious areas related to standard English, punctuation and spelling.

Make sure that learners have easy access to dictionaries and thesauruses so they can be more independent and use more personal strategies in working out unfamiliar words. Enable them to form the habit of using a thesaurus to choose more precise and descriptive words for all writing – even the factual writing they do when compiling an entry for the *Vogon Constructor Fleets*.

Finally, use their learning journals (Worksheet 6.1) as another tool for differentiation. Encourage more able learners to include more in their journals, such as writing techniques they would like to use again, interesting words, extracts from texts to use as models for writing, words that are challenging to spell and, above all, commentary on their reading life, such as the books they enjoy, books they have been encouraged to read that they would not necessarily have chosen themselves and the characters they like and why.

Cambridge Reading Adventures

Meltdown by Peter Millet (Level 4 Voyagers) is a story set in a futuristic world, which ties in usefully with Unit 4's science-fiction theme.

4.1 Looking into the future

LEARNING PLAN

Learning objectives		Learning intentions	Success criteria
Main focus	**Also covered**	• Skim read for the main idea.	• Learners can skim read a text to get the main idea.
6Rv.01, 6Rg.08, 6Ri.06, 6Ri.09, 6Ri.10, 6Ri.14, 6Wv.02, 6SLm.03, 6SLg.02	6Rv.02, 6Rv.04, 6Rg.01, 6Ri.02, 6Ri.11, 6Ra.01, 6Ra.02, 6Wg.08, 6Wc.06, 6Wp.05, 6SLg.03, 6SLg.04, 6SLp.01	• Scan an extract for detail. • Make predictions.	• Learners can scan a text to find detail to answer questions. • Learners can use clues in the text to make predictions.

LANGUAGE SUPPORT

The extract contains American spellings. Discuss the basic differences between US and UK spelling, and identify which is more common in your region. The session focuses on the use of words and word origins, as well as the different impact created by one synonym rather than another. It also focuses on words with multiple meanings and choosing the most appropriate one for the context.

Keep a wall chart of other words you encounter across all subjects that have more than one meaning and discuss not only the different meanings but also any differences in word class to activate learners' awareness of the importance of using words appropriately in context.

Starter idea

Going to Mars (5 minutes)

Resources: Learner's Book, Session 4.1: Getting started

Description: While the Mars One mission does not appear to be going ahead, many people applied despite knowing they would not return. Survey learners to find out how many would be interested in such a mission and invite reasons.

Pairs or small groups can then brainstorm a list of what they would need to start a colony on a new planet. Share ideas with the class and build a list of essentials on the board.

Discuss how the idea of a voyage to Mars 50 years ago would have seemed impossible, whereas now people going to Mars is being considered.

Main teaching ideas

1 Imagine and read about the future (20 minutes)

Learning intention: To skim read and scan an extract for detail to answer questions

Resources: *The Green Book* Part 1 (Learner's Book, Session 4.1, Activity 1); Track 19

Description: Start with a fun discussion about what learners think the future will be like and what new inventions they can imagine.

The Green Book follows a group of colonists forced to leave a dying Earth. Pattie, the youngest, takes with her a blank journal which proves to be the 'golden thread' that runs through the novel. She writes an account of their experiences, which turns out to be the novel itself: the first lines of her journal are identical to the opening of Chapter 1 – linking the end to the beginning.

Use the audio of *The Green Book,* Part 1 (Track 19).

Remind learners to scan when looking for details of what the characters take with them (e.g. axe, saw, file) to determine where they might be going. Guide learners to pick up clues: *What might that be for? What makes you think that?*

Encourage learners to empathise with the characters and imagine how they would feel being faced with leaving everything they have ever known to go to an unknown future. Ask: *What would you take with you?*

Remind learners to take turns in discussion – even only in pairs and to listen carefully to each other's ideas. Encourage them to build on each other's ideas rather than just stick to their own point of view.

> **Differentiation ideas:** Organise mixed confidence groups to skim read and scan the text for detail, to allow learners to support each other in drawing inferences from the text.

Differentiate the activity further by joining selected groups to discuss how they perceive the characters to be feeling and how they would feel themselves. Use targeted questions, prefaced by some of your own reactions.

> **Assessment ideas:** Check knowledge of use italics and ellipses in texts through discussion.

Answers:
1   a   Learners' own answers.
    b   Learners' own answers but should suggest something about going to another planet and taking very little with them: tools, clothing, iron rations, a book and two personal items each.
    c   Learners' own answers but should include that there is no mention of items to take like smartphones, tablets or computers, so it was probably written before these things were invented. The mention of the slide-projector and photographs tell us that the text is dated.
    d   Father's words about the light on the planet getting colder and bluer for years.
    e   They look as if they had gone 'brownish with age' when in reality they are normal, but the world's light has changed.
    f   Learners' own answers but should include a little about whether they are boys or girls and their possible ages and that their mother has died. They were excited and disturbed about going and taking so little.
    g   Learners' own answers.

2   What can you find out? (20 minutes)

Learning intention: To scan the text for detail

Resources: Learner's Book, Session 4.1, Activity 2; *The Green Book* Part 1 (Learner's Book, Session 4.1); Track 19; dictionaries and thesauruses

Description: Learners scan for detail and make inferences from clues about the journey. The words *voyager* and *rations* imply a long journey where there may not be much food. Revisit the ellipsis technique by asking why the extract in Activity 2 ends in an ellipsis and what the drama is. In this case it is the big reveal of the golden thread – that the green book is in fact Patti's journal – the story of their voyage and adventures. It is how the story started in the extract in Unit 4.1. Discuss what other effects could be achieved by a book or story ending on an ellipsis – for example, it could imply another book in the series.

Learners must select the correct meaning of the word *file* for the context. Discuss that many words have multiple meanings (homographs) as well as different shades of meaning. Ask for other examples, such as *fair, right* and *type*. Discuss that words with the same spelling but multiple meanings are homonyms (in fact, both homophones and homographs are homonyms). Encourage learners to look up the words in their dictionaries, thesauruses or online word resources.

In pairs, learners scan the text for the italicised words and identify their purpose.

Build on what learners found out about ellipses to allow the reader to fill in missing thoughts or actions for dramatic effect in Unit 1 in *East*. Ask a volunteer to explain the effect the writer was trying to achieve with the ellipsis in line 11 of the extract. Explain that often describing exactly what is going on is less dramatic and effective than a speaker trailing off, allowing the reader to imagine what is going on - in this case the drama and danger attached to the light getting bluer and colder such that the children don't even remember how it used to be - the dramatic situation that sparked the voyage to a new planet. Invite volunteers to think of sentences ending in an ellipsis to create drama or suspense, for example: She watched petrified as the door slowly opened... or Jake started to speak, "If only we hadn't..." but it was already too late. However, explain to learners that it loses its effect if over-used - like all writing techniques and features.

Encourage learners to make predictions, not as guesses, but using clues from the text. Invite pairs to share their predictions with the class before writing their paragraphs. Make sure learners check their work carefully before finalising.

Spelling link: Remind learners that nouns ending in *is* usually take the plural form *es* – *ellipsis/ellipses*. Invite other examples, *oasis, crisis, hypothesis*. Elicit whether learners associate this spelling with the origin of the words in Latin/Greek. Ask: *Why do you think the spelling works this way?* There are more activities on unusual plurals in the Spelling section at the back of the Learner's Book.

> **Differentiation ideas:** Support less confident readers by pairing them with more confident readers. Consider reading the extract and working through the initial activities with an extended group before returning to class discussion. Challenge more confident learners by encouraging them to write independently.

> **Assessment ideas:** Learners could write their answers in their notebooks after discussion to assess their ability to scan the detail and understand words in context.

Answers:
2 a • The root noun is *voyage*.
      • The definition should imply that they are going on a very long way.
      • Likely synonyms: *journey, trip, expedition, cruise, tour, flight, passage, excursion, jaunt*. Likely to suggest that the word implies a long journey or that it will be by ship or in space.
   b • Learners' own answers for rations.
      • Iron rations are medicine people take to ensure they have enough iron for their bodies to be healthy.
      • Pattie thinks it means eating iron – the metal.
   c *A small tool with a rough edge to make a surface smooth*, because it is mentioned with a selection of other tools.
   d • Italics: *one or two* – for emphasis; *only* – for emphasis, *A Dictionary of Intermediate Technology* – title of the book, *The Oxford Complete Shakespeare* – title of the book.
      • The ellipsis creates a pause for effect to show that Father is looking back and remembering.
   e Learners' own answers.

Plenary idea

What did you predict? (5 minutes)

Resources: Learners' paragraphs from Activity 2

Description: Invite learners or pairs to read out their paragraphs. Ask: *What clues did you use? Are there any other clues?*

Discuss as a class the evidence in the extract – including use of words such as *voyage* and *rations*. At the end, model how to make an informed prediction as opposed to a guess.

> **Assessment ideas:** Learners can assess each other's use of evidence to inform their predictions and make further suggestions where appropriate.

> ### CROSS-CURRICULAR LINKS

> **Science:** Gather books and research on space travel, the solar system and astronomy.

Homework ideas

Learners can complete the Workbook activities for Session 4.1, focusing on word origins. Go through the answers in class, making sure that in Activity 2 learners are able to pronounce each of the words correctly to identify which notice board they belong on.

Learners can look in newspapers for articles about space travel and research.

Answers for Workbook

1 a–b Learners' own answers.

2 a *–et*
   b 'THEY' Notice board:
      ballet   bouquet   buffet
      crochet   croquet   duvet
      sachet   sorbet

      'EDIT' Notice board:
      banquet   basket   carpet
      closet   cornet   racket   trumpet

3–4 Learners' own answers.

5 soprano – the highest type of female singing voice
   orchestra – a large group of musicians playing many different instruments together and led by a conductor
   solo – a single performer
   piano – a musical instrument with keys and strings
   opera – a musical play in which most of the words are sung
   alto – the lowest female voice or the highest male voice
   allegro – lively, at a brisk pace
   tempo – a musical term for time (the timing or beat of the music)

6 *o* and *a*.

7 Learners' own answers.

8 Possible answers: pasta   mozzarella   al dente
au gratin   béchamel   biscotti   broccoli
canapé   cappuccino   flambée   fondue   gelato
macaroni   pepperoni   purée   salami   sauté

4.2 Step into their shoes

LEARNING PLAN

Learning objectives		Learning intentions	Success criteria
Main focus	**Also covered**	• Empathise with characters.	• Learners can empathise with the different characters.
6Ri.02, 6Ri.03, 6Ri.06, 6Ri.09, 6Ri.10, 6Ri.14, 6Ra.02, 6SLm.02, 6SLp.03	6Rs.01, 6Rs.03, 6Ri.11, 6Ri.16, 6Ra.03, 6Wp.01, 6Wp.02, 6SLm.01, 6SLm.05	• Make plausible inferences. • Explore a golden thread.	• Learners can use evidence to make plausible inferences. • Learners can discuss how a golden thread works.

LANGUAGE SUPPORT

The session builds on the extract in the previous session and so learners should feel confident with the vocabulary needed to work through the activities, supported by additional glossary words.

Starter idea

Preparing for space (5 minutes)

Resources: Learner's Book, Session 4.2: Getting started

Description: Partners discuss, based on prior knowledge, what it would be like to prepare to go on a mission into space. Start off their conversations with a few ideas of your own about how to prepare, like getting fit, having your hair cut and deciding what to take. Ask learners to share their ideas, especially what they might be thinking about and what they would miss. Be sensitive to learners who may be fearful of not returning from the mission or something going wrong.

Main teaching ideas

1 Empathise with the characters (25 minutes)

Learning intention: To empathise with characters

Resources: *The Green Book* Part 2 (Learner's Book, Session 4.2, Activity 1); Track 20

Description: Explain that the characters are embarking on a no-return voyage to settle on another planet, not knowing what they will find, except that it should support human life. They name the planet *Shine*.

The aim of the activity is to encourage empathy with the characters and for learners to consider their own responses to a similar situation. In pairs, they make a short speech outlining the books they would take. Be strict about timing but insist that learners make notes of key words and phrases to help them practise what to say. Their speech should include the book title, author, genre and reason they chose it. Organise groups to give speeches to each other to save time. Conduct a survey to see if there are any popular choices.

Explain *commonplace book* – an old-fashioned term for a personal journal. Discuss Pattie's choice. Ask: *Would any of you choose a blank journal rather than your original choice?*

> **Differentiation ideas:** Support learners who find it difficult to infer meaning beyond the literal work are either in a group overseen by you by placing them with a group of more confident learners. There is no need to pair learners specifically for their short presentations about their book choices for a similar voyage. Provide a frame for pairs of learners to help them build their speech, e.g. *I would take three books which are … I chose them because, first … second … and third …*

> **Assessment ideas:** Use learners' short presentations to assess ability to empathise with the depicted scenario and to explain reasons for their choices.

Answers:
1   a   Learners' own answers, likely to suggest that Father thinks he will need practical skills at their destination.
    b   Learners' own answers.
    c   Learners' own answers, may suggest they think it is silly to choose a book with nothing to read in it.
    d and e   Learners' own answers.

🎧 21   2   A golden thread (20 minutes)

Learning intention: To explore how a book's end links back to the beginning

Resources: *The Green Book* Part 3 (Learner's Book, Session 4.1, Activity 2); Track 21; Worksheet 6.1

Description: Discuss with learners what *making it huge with listening* (in *The Green Book* Part 3) means and discuss examples of when this situation might be encountered. Remind them that figurative language appears in novels as well as poems A 'golden thread' is a recurring theme running through a piece of writing. In this case, it is *The Green Book,* also the novel's title.

When Pattie's choice of book is first introduced, it is not obvious that it will become the unifying thread in the story. Even at the end, the link between the story Pattie wrote in her journal and the novel is not explicitly stated. Learners must infer the link from the clue when Father starts to read out Pattie's book.

Consider reading the whole novel with, or to, the class. Establish if the book was written in first or third person.

Learners should comment on the golden thread technique in their learning journals (Worksheet 6.1) and note ideas for golden thread objects in a story

of their own. Encourage them to write down uses of ellipses and italics for emphasis. Challenge them to incorporate these techniques into their writing.

> **Differentiation ideas:** Support less confident learners by allowing them to write the answers to the questions in note form, while encouraging more confident learners to write in full sentences in the notebooks. Learners can check their work with a partner.

Answers:
2   a   •   Learners' own answers, but along the lines of making what they hear important to them all.
        •   The description is figurative because the words are not literally huge.
    b   •   The last line is a quotation – lines being read out from the book.
        •   It is the same as the first line of the novel.
    c   Learners' own answers.
    d   The novel is the story Pattie has written in her journal.
    e   Learners' own answers.

Plenary idea

Do you like science fiction? (5 minutes)

Resources: A selection of science-fiction stories

Description: Survey learners to find out what other science-fiction novels or stories they have read, if any. Ask them what features made them science fiction.

Survey learners to find out who would enjoy reading the rest of *The Green Book*.

Explore as a class whether science fiction is a popular genre and whether learners would be interested in reading further novels. Have a selection available in the class library.

> **Assessment ideas:** Assess whether learners are familiar with the genre and whether they can articulate whether they do or do not enjoy the genre and why.

Homework ideas

Learners can complete the Workbook activities for Session 4.2, listing and categorising and then creating spelling patterns. Go through answers in class for Activities 2 and 3 and invite learners to share their answers for Activity 1.

Answers for Workbook

1   Learners' own answers.

2 **a** elegant **b** absent **c** important **d** adolescent **e** magnificent **f** significant **g** tolerant **h** confident **i** ignorant **j** present **k** brilliant **l** dependent

3 **a** accountancy **b** consistency **c** truancy **d** tenancy **e** fluency **f** frequency **g** efficiency **h** buoyancy **i** transparency **j** leniency

4.3 Useful punctuation and grammar tips

LEARNING PLAN

Learning objectives		Learning intentions	Success criteria
Main focus	**Also covered**	• Identify suitable information to be in parenthesis.	• Learners can identify suitable information to be in parenthesis.
6Rg.01, 6Rs.02, 6Wg.06, 6Wg.08	6Ra.02, 6Ww.07, 6Wv.06, 6Ws.02, 6Wc.06, 6Wp.01, 6Wp.05, 6SLm.02, 6SLg.02	• Use colons appropriately. • Practise using quantifiers with countable and uncountable nouns.	• Learners can use colons appropriately. • Learners can practise using quantifiers with countable and uncountable nouns.

LANGUAGE SUPPORT

This session focuses on some of the grammatical and punctuation detail. Explain the term 'in parenthesis'. Learners may be more familiar with the term 'brackets', but since brackets, commas and dashes can all be used in parenthesis, it is useful to differentiate.

In US English, **em dashes** (longer) are often used in place of **en dashes**. No space appears between the *em dash* and the surrounding words, e.g. *The man—the one in the brown coat—is running away.* The em dash is also common in older English texts.

Learners need to draw on prior knowledge working with colons. Essentially, all colons 'introduce' something, such as the words spoken in a playscript, a list or part of a sentence to which to add emphasis.

Learners encountered quantifiers in Stage 5 but the concept may need revising, critically that certain quantifiers cannot be used with singular or with plural nouns – a concept that may be difficult for some learners especially when dealing with countable and uncountable nouns.

Starter idea

Bracket that (5 minutes)

Resources: Learner's Book, Session 4.3: Getting started

Description: Invite a volunteer to explain what brackets are and what they are used for. Build up a class explanation on the board, inviting learners to give examples of when how brackets might be used.

Ask whether they think brackets are more common in fiction or non-fiction writing and why.

Main teaching ideas

1 Using brackets (10 minutes)

Learning intention: To identify suitable information to be in parenthesis

Resources: Learner's Book, Session 4.3, Activity 1; The Green Book Part 1 (Learner's Book, Session 4.1); Track 19

Description: Brackets (parentheses) can easily be over-used, giving too much information in asides that should be inferred. Complete the activity before looking back to see how brackets were used in the *The Green Book* Part 1 (first paragraph).

Remind learners that bracketed information must be surplus to the main sense of the sentence. Dependent clauses cannot stand alone but the main clause should be able to. Workbook Session 4.3 contains further practice, which can be done in class if time, or for homework.

While the Learner's Book explains the different reasons for using brackets, commas and dashes, in reality the difference is often blurred in fiction writing. Nonetheless, it is useful for the learners to understand that there are differences in effect. Ultimately, brackets should be avoided as much as possible and dashes add much more emphasis. Use of commas to include additional information can later be linked to using complex sentences with clauses introduced by *which* and enclosed in commas (descriptive, additional information) as opposed to being introduced by *that* with no commas (definitive and therefore not additional information). The sentence must be able to stand alone without the information enclosed by commas.

Supplementary teacher information: *BCE* stands for *Before the Common Era* and is to be preferred to the Christian-based *BC* (*Before Christ*). Similarly, *CE* stands for *Common Era* in place of the Latin *AD* (*Anno Domini – Year of the Lord*).

While the Learner's Book explains the different reasons for using brackets, commas and dashes, in reality the difference is often blurred in fiction writing. Nonetheless, it is useful for the learners to understand that there are differences in effect. Ultimately, brackets should be avoided as much as possible and dashes add much more emphasis. Use of commas to include additional information can later be linked to using complex sentences with clauses introduced by 'which' and encloses in commas (descriptive, additional information) as opposed to being introduced by 'that' with no commas (definitive and therefore not additional information). The sentence must be able to stand alone without the information enclosed by commas.

> **Differentiation ideas:** Learners can support themselves by writing the answers in their notebooks as well as discussing them and then checking each other's answers, discussing any differences.

> **Assessment ideas:** Assess learners' knowledge of brackets, colons and quantifiers through the class work. Ask learners to write answers in their notebooks if you require a more formal assessment to inform your planning.

Answers:
1 a • The ancient Chinese invented paper during the Han Dynasty (the 2nd century BCE).
      • Istanbul (previously called Constantinople) is in Turkey.
      • The South Pole, the southernmost point on Earth, is on the continent of Antarctica.
      • The camel (or the dromedary) is well adapted for the desert.
      • Cook the onions – gently – until they are soft (not brown).
   b Providing additional information.
   c Paragraph 8: said Joe, <u>our brother</u>, the eldest of us. Paragraph 10: *But what he showed us – a beach, with a blue sea, and the mother* <u>we couldn't remember</u> *lying on a towel, reading a* <u>book</u> *– looked a funny hue...*

2 Using colons (20 minutes)

Learning intention: To use colons appropriately

Resources: Learner's Book, Session 4.3, Activity 2

Description: Learners will have encountered colons previously in playscripts and dialogue. This activity presents contexts in which colons introduce a list that is an entity in itself.

Remind learners that a dialogue script is similar to a playscript. Revise how dialogue is set out with the names on the left followed by a colon and the spoken words on the right. Encourage learners to write the dialogue in the siblings' probably bickering tone.

Remind them that when the dialogue is introduced by a colon in this way, no speech marks are used. After they read their dialogues in pairs or groups, encourage them to make any suitable changes and to rewrite it in the correct format using neat joined-up handwriting.

> **Differentiation ideas:** More confident learners can include 'stage directions' to indicate how words should be spoken, e.g. (*in a bored voice*), using brackets to provide the additional information.

You may decide to introduce the use of colons for creating emphasis only to more confident learners, so as to avoid giving too much information to less confident learners. You could also use the Workbook activities for Session 4.3 on using colons to create emphasis.

Answers:
2   a–b Learners' own answers.
    c   I did not think I would be allowed to take my favourite clothes: a blue cardigan and a striped headscarf.

3   Quantifiers need to agree (10 minutes)

Learning intention: To practise using quantifiers with countable and uncountable nouns

Resources: Learner's Book, Session 4.3, Activity 3

Description: Read through the Language focus box with learners to revise quantifiers. Invite learners to give examples of sentences containing quantifiers.

Ask whether numbers would be considered quantifiers e.g. *three potatoes*. Discuss their answers and explain that numbers give a specific quantity and therefore are not considered quantifiers.

Go through the questions as a class inviting learners to suggest which verb or quantifier is appropriate in each context. Remind learners that *either* and *neither* are considered singular.

> **Differentiation ideas:** Support less confident learners by working with them orally, while encouraging more confident learners to complete the activities in their notebooks.

> **Assessment ideas:** Learners can check that the sentences have quantifiers and verbs that agree.

Answers:
3   a   is; go; is; have; was
    b   fewer; less; Each; Both; Enough

Plenary idea

Use quantifiers (5 minutes)

Resources: A selection of quantifiers on the board

Description: Write a selection of quantifiers on the board and invite learners to invent sentences using the quantifiers in context.

The more familiar they become with using them and matching them to verbs, the more likely learners are to use the correct agreement habitually.

> **CROSS-CURRICULAR LINKS**
>
> Maths: Make comparisons between quantifiers and specific numbers, including words like *couple*, *score* and *dozen* which indicate specific amounts.

Homework ideas

Learners can complete the Workbook activities for Session 4.3 if not completed in class. Discuss their answers in class and invite learners to share their rewritten emails in Activity 2 with the class.

Learners can research words for numbers like *couple, dozen, score, baker's dozen, half a dozen, gross, brace, duo, pair, quartet, quintet, trio,* and *twosome*.

Answers for Workbook

1   a   I take part in two sports, basketball and golf, that require lots of practice.
    b   The learners – who are only in Year 6 – have set up their own business.
    c   The Dead Sea (in fact a hypersaline lake) is one of the world's saltiest bodies of water.
    d   Homework – although I hate doing it – helps me be an independent learner.
    e   My holiday in Greece, my best holiday ever, was almost three years ago.

2   Learners' own answers.

3   a is b are c is d have e was

4   a fewer b less c each d both
    e Enough

4.4 Begin planning a longer story

LEARNING PLAN

Learning objectives		Learning intentions	Success criteria
Main focus	**Also covered**		
6Rs.01, 6Rs.02, 6Rs.03, 6Wv.04, 6Wg.08, 6Ws.02, 6Wc.02, 6SLs.01, 6SLg.02	6Ri.03, 6Wv.01, 6Wv.02, 6Wg.04, 6Wg.04, 6Wp.01, 6SLg.01, 6SLg.04	• Explore chapters. • Plan a chapter story. • Write a draft of Chapter 1.	• Learners can analyse and talk about chapters and why they are used. • Learners can plan a story in chapters with planned writing techniques. • Learners can write a draft of Chapter 1.

LANGUAGE SUPPORT

Learners should be well supported in the vocabulary for writing their first draft as they have been working extensively with extracts from *The Green Book* as a science-fiction model. Ensure learners clearly understand what is meant by an episode so that they can use appropriate vocabulary when discussing the reason for and purpose of chapters, linking them to story stages.

Starter idea

Check the contents (5 minutes)

Resources: Learner's Book, Session 4.4: Getting started; independent readers

Description: Invite learners to explore their independent readers with a partner. Not all will have a contents page and not all will have chapter titles as well as numbers.

Discuss with the class what a contents page is useful for – both finding the page number for the start of each chapter and, if there are chapter titles, getting a taste of what the book contains.

Main teaching ideas

1 Explore chapters (15 minutes)

Learning intention: To explore the purpose of chapters in a novel

Resources: Learner's Book, Session 4.4, Activity 1; selection of fiction and non-fiction books

Description: Talk about how learners have moved on from picture books with no words, to illustrated stories, to chapter books. Consider how each chapter is usually an episode or a mini story in itself. Explain that in the 19th and early 20th century, many novels were serialised in weekly or fortnightly periodicals, e.g. the works of Charles Dickens. The author would build a climax at the end of each episode to encourage readers to buy the next periodical to find out how the story continued, in a similar way to many soaps or ongoing drama series on television.

Invite suggestions for reasons to start a new chapter, e.g. a different setting, series of events or character.

Explore a selection of books to investigate and compare how chapters end. Can learners identify reasons for starting a new chapter in both fiction and non-fiction books? Discuss the fact that non-fiction chapters tend to be content-related with no transition from the previous chapter.

> **Differentiation ideas:** Support less confident learners by allowing them to do their summaries verbally. Challenge more confident learners to do their summaries either in writing, in full sentences or on a mind map using key words only.

Answers:
1 a–b Learners' own answers.

2 Begin planning an extended narrative (30 minutes)

Learning intention: To plan an extended narrative and write a first draft of Chapter 1

Resources: Learner's Book, Session 4.4, Activity 2; Worksheets 6.2, 6.5 and 6.18; Language worksheet 4A; flipchart paper and marker pens

Description: Ask groups to brainstorm ideas. Flipchart paper and marker pens are ideal to encourage free-flowing creative thinking. Appoint a scribe, a timekeeper and a coordinator in each group to ensure everybody gets a chance to speak. Emphasise that brainstorming is not an organised, neat activity and they should not judge any ideas as silly, because one idea leads to another creatively. Set a strict time limit. Let learners know they will be required to summarise their ideas to the class at the end. You can use Worksheet 6.5 My writing process here.

Before the brainstorming, go through the *Readalouadathon* criteria in the Learner's Book, reminding learners about flashbacks and prologues (Unit 1). They will gather input for some areas (e.g. the surprise discovery or describing scenery) later in Unit 4.

Dip in and out of group's brainstorming – especially about the item that could act as a golden thread. It does not have to be a real item – for example it could be a special stone with mysterious powers or even an animal of some kind, real or imagined. The critical issue is for the groups to realise that this item or thing will be something important at various points in the story, especially at the end – it is the golden thread. If some groups struggle to think of ideas, allow them to also use a journal or notebook like Patti's. This will support some learners who will then just have to change the characters and the context for the story they will write throughout the rest of the unit.

Remind them that this is only a plan and that their ideas may change as they write. Remind them of standard story structure so they can begin to plan the problem/challenge/complication, the build-up to the climax and how the object may be part of that.

Explain that stories need to be planned, edited and revised. Authors choose what to write about and how, e.g. sequentially or via flashbacks, choosing narrative person, style and structure. They add different sentence types to maintain flow and interest, colour, e.g. informal language in dialogue, and vivid description. They build suspense, include clues and use punctuation and layout techniques. Remind them especially of how an ellipsis was used in Unit 1 and in Units 4.1 and 4.2 as a way to create drama or suspense. Praise every technique learners plan, use or even discard.

In this unit, learners only plan the story overview and write an attention-grabbing opening chapter The plan is the focus; details may change later on. Learners can use a table, mind map or flowchart. They should plan the paragraphs for the first chapter only. Ask questions as you circulate: *Where is it set? Where are they going? What is the golden thread? Who are the main characters? What are they taking? What is their mood? What is the attention-grabber?* Ask volunteers to share plans.

If possible, let learners write drafts using ICT as they will be working on them for an extended period.

Use Language worksheet 4A to give learners practice at writing effective science-fiction beginnings and endings.

> **Differentiation ideas:** Support less confident earners by allowing them to plan in pairs. Offer suggestions to those who find it difficult to develop their plans into clear, simple stages (chapters).

Encourage learners to develop their own science-fiction story criteria, and challenge more confident writers to plan more than four chapters.

If you are using worksheets, use Worksheet 6.18 My Readaloudathon story to help learners develop their own story and success criteria.

> **Assessment ideas:** Encourage learners to develop success criteria; for example:

- *I contributed ideas to the brainstorming session.*
- *I developed a clear four-chapter plan to follow.*
- *I listed my plans for each chapter.*
- *I included an attention-grabbing sentence.*

Ask learners to choose a couple of personal goals for assessment, e.g. writing in a consistent tense or using a variety of sentence types. You can use Worksheet 6.2 Personal goals here. (If you set personal goals in Unit 1, revisit them here and ask learners to reflect on their progress so far.)

Answers:
2   a–d Learners' own answers.

Plenary idea

Chapter 1 (5 minutes)

Resources: Learners' drafts of Chapter 1 from Activity 2

Description: Invite learners to read aloud their drafts of Chapter 1 to the class. Listen to a selection before allowing class discussion and evaluation. Invite learners to suggest ideas for improvement.

> **Assessment ideas:** Learners can evaluate the drafts of Chapter 1 that they hear. They should assess them against the criteria and try to identify specific writing techniques each learner has included. They can also make suggestions for improvement where appropriate.

CROSS-CURRICULAR LINKS

Science: Gather books and information on different planets, astronomy and astrology.

Homework ideas

Learners can continue their work on Chapter 1 if appropriate.

Learners can complete the Workbook activities for Session 4.4. Go through the answers in class, inviting learners to share their *Contents* pages in 4.

Answers for Workbook

1 a Present tense.

   b Learners' own answers, e.g. *arrives, go, offers, are, looks*.

   c It gives a sense of permanence – a timeless quality.

2 a After four years, their spaceship <u>arrived</u> and <u>touched</u> down. The voyagers <u>explored</u> the strange landscape, <u>tested</u> the water, <u>breathed</u> the air, and <u>found</u> out if they <u>could</u> eat the plants and grow their seeds. The plants <u>were</u> like glass, sharp and shiny like jewels and easily broken. But the lake <u>was</u> more inviting. Pattie, as the youngest traveller, <u>named</u> the planet *Shine*.

   b It makes it sound more like narrative in a book, fixing it as if the events have already happened.

3 a Left to right – row by row: 2, 5, 4, 1, 7, 3, 6.

   b Everyone will be overjoyed when (if) the children are fine; they will realise they will be able to live on the strange, glassy wheat crop. Father will turn the old moth wings into thread to make clothes. Slowly, the people will realise that they will have a future after all. Joe will find Pattie's green book which will now be full of writing. Father will read it out to everybody – it will be the story of the people of Shine.

4 Learners' own answers.

4.5 Going back and looking into the future

LEARNING PLAN

Learning objectives		Learning intentions	Success criteria
Main focus	**Also covered**	• Explore the genre of science fiction.	• Learners can analyse and discuss the science-fiction genre.
6Rv.04, 6Rg.08, 6Rs.02, 6Ri.03, 6Ri.10, 6Ri.14, 6SLs.01	6Rv.01, 6Rv.03, 6Ri.07, 6Ri.08, 6Ri.09, 6Ri.11, 6Wg.08, 6Wc.08, 6SLm.02, 6SLm.03, 6SLg.02, 6SLg.03	• Skim read and scan an extract for detail. • Make predictions.	• Learners can skim read and scan a text for detail. • Learners can make predictions based on clues in the text.

LANGUAGE SUPPORT

Encourage learners to work out what unfamiliar words mean using context and other strategies before consulting a dictionary. Suggest they add any new or unfamiliar words that they have learnt in the text, as well as words they would like to use again, to their learning journals (Worksheet 6.1).

Common misconception

Misconception	How to identify	How to overcome
Science fiction is fiction about science	Having read *The Green* Book, learners have encountered the science-fiction genre, although they have not yet pinned it down as a genre. Ask learners what they think fiction about science would be like.	Use *The Green* Book texts and the text in this session to start comparing features of what makes science fiction. It is not just about science; it is really science that has not yet happened but that perhaps could happen. Emphasise that the texts were written some time ago and so what may have seemed impossible then may seem very possible now.

Starter idea

🎧 22 Find out about early science fiction (10 minutes)

Resources: *Early science-fiction stories* (Learner's Book, Session 4.5: Getting started); Track 22

Description: The audio (Track 22) provides learners with some early history on the science-fiction genre. Play the audio to the learners and then allow time for them to review the questions individually to see what they can remember.

Replay the audio to allow them to listen for missing information to answer the questions. Then allow small groups to discuss the answers rather than writing them in their notebooks.

Audioscript: *Early science-fiction stories*

Speaker 1: While historians of literature argue about the origins of the science-fiction genre, many people believe Mary Shelley's novel *Frankenstein*, published in 1818, was the first truly science-fiction novel. Set in Switzerland, it featured a mad scientist, Victor Frankenstein, who experimented with advanced technology to bring his hideous invention to life. Others suggest another novel by Shelley, *The Last Man*, as the first true science-fiction novel where she writes about a world set in the future that has been almost destroyed by a plague.

Speaker 2: Later in the 19th century, two writers had a big effect on the genre. Jules Verne wrote several extremely popular scientific adventure novels. He is often called the 'father of science fiction' and because he made his living out of his books he was regarded as 'the world's first full-time science-fiction novelist'. The other writer was H. G. Wells, who popularised the idea of time travel in his book *The Time Traveller*, published in 1895. Since then, the genre has gone from strength to strength in both adults' and children's literature alike, with ever more extreme inventions and futuristic worlds being imagined.

Answers:
1 Mary Shelley's *Frankenstein* or *The Last Man*. Some think one, some the other.
2 Jules Verne and H. G. Wells.
3 Jules Verne.
4 The world's first full-time science-fiction novelist.
5 Popularising the idea of time travel – He wrote *The Time Traveller*,.

Answers:
Learners' own answers but should include some of the following:
1 a Science fiction can be regarded as a form of fantasy, but it focuses on the imagined impact of science on society rather than magical or other worldly issues.
  b All of them. Learners' own paragraphs.

Main teaching ideas

1 Talk about science fiction (15 minutes)

Learning intention: To explore the genre of science fiction

Resources: Learner's Book, Session 4.5, Activity 1; a selection of science-fiction novels

Description: Science fiction is a relatively new genre, less than 200 years old. Jules Verne (1828–1905) is often referred to as the 'father of science fiction', being one of the first to write novels concerned with inventions and journeys that would have been considered impossible at the time. He made them seem feasible through his ideas and characterisation.

Be mindful of regional and cultural sensitivities that may be attached to certain science-fiction scenarios. Focus on futuristic inventions and possibilities of space and time travel as opposed to other worlds and species. Use the questions to focus on science-fiction inventions.

Discuss what we consider futuristic and what people in the past may have considered futuristic, which we may not do so now. Share your collection of science-fiction novels and stories, allowing learners to browse and explore the covers, blurbs and content.

When learners write their paragraphs, remind them to use evidence to back up their ideas – putting forward arguments both before and against before coming to a conclusion. Model one scenario yourself before they start.

> **Differentiation ideas:** Organise learners into mixed-confidence groups, as this is a largely discussion-based activity.

Support less confident learners by allowing them to make notes rather than write out a whole paragraph giving their point of view.

> **Assessment ideas:** Informally assess learners' grasp of the genre of science fiction and its key features.

2 Read an extract (25 minutes)

Learning intention: To skim read and scan an extract for detail

Resources: *The Diary of a Space Traveller and Other Stories* and *Satyajit Ray biography* (Learner's Book, Session 4.5, Activity 2); Track 23

Description: Play Track 23 to learn a bit more about the author of the extract *The Diary of a Space Traveller and Other Stories*. The character of Professor Shonku was created over 50 years ago. Enjoy discussing with learners what things would not have been invented when he was first created. Probably the most pervasive inventions not to have been in existence in those days were personal computers, tablets, smart phones and the internet – all of which are very much part of learners' lives today. Encourage them to visualise life without these things.

Remind learners that skimming to get the main idea is not the same as reading for detail. Invite learners to give a one-sentence overview of the extract before they answer the questions.

Learners will need to scan for more detail to answer later questions such as the features that show it is a diary – primarily first-person narrative, informal language, use of the present continuous tense when he says he is writing his diary and the mixture of tenses.

Learners may infer that the extract was written some time ago based on some of the things Professor Shonku takes with him such as a camera or binoculars. It does not seem to be such science fiction to travel to Mars in modern times as unmanned probes have already done so.

Learners may not realise initially that *Bidhushekhar* is a robot. Encourage them to find the details that reveal he is not human.

Discuss with learners why the inverted commas/speech marks are used in the passage, reminding them that they can be used around a word to show that it is not being used literally.

While learners may predict anything as not that many clues have been given, discuss with them that it would not be much of a story if the professor just landed on Mars and everything went smoothly. Therefore, it is likely that some disaster or frightening event will follow, especially since the extract ends with a rhetorical question, building suspense.

> **Differentiation ideas:** Support less confident learners by talking through the answers with selected groups.

For more challenge, learners can write their answers neatly in their notebooks, before swapping with a partner to compare answers.

> **Assessment ideas:** Formalise Activity 2 by getting learners to write the answers in their notebooks. You can then use them to assess their ability to read for appropriate detail to answer questions.

Answers:
2   a   Learners' own answers.
    b   • Science fiction: They are travelling to Mars, the unusual landscape.
        • In the past: The objects he gathers to take with him – no modern equipment.
        • Diary: First-person pronouns. It is like he is talking to himself.
    c   • He is a robot because the professor had to push a button on his shoulder to stop him, and *mind* is in inverted commas when it refers to Bidhushekhar's mind because it is not a real one.
        • Learners' own answers about pulling the handle, but they might consider that the robot is sensing danger and trying to stop them landing on Mars.
    d   • The dash creates suspense leaving readers to suspect that although they do not want to sense trouble, it may be ahead.
        • Other dashes: Para 2 – to add additional information, Para 8 – an aside, Para 9 – explanation.
    e   • *mind:* because it refers to the robot's mind which is not a real one.
        • *rocky:* because they only look like rocks; they are not real rocks as they are not hard.
        • *water:* because it is not like normal water – it is red.
    f   The mood is chatty, curious and calm until the end when suspense builds as the professor starts to question himself and what is around him.
    g   Learners' own answers.

Plenary idea

What happens next? (5 minutes)

Resources: Learners' predictions from Activity 2

Description: Invite learners to share their predictions about what happens next.

Encourage them to notice the building of suspense as the professor wonders why everything is so quiet and the atmosphere eerie. It is clearly building up to some sort of climax and so their predictions should include something dramatic happening.

> **Assessment ideas:** Learners can comment on and evaluate each other's predictions – whether they are realistic, whether they fit with the story and whether they are sufficiently 'science fiction'.

CROSS-CURRICULAR LINKS

Science: Source information about recent scientific activity in relation to the planet Mars.

Homework ideas

Learners can complete the Workbook activities for Session 4.5. Share their answers in class and compare what they have included on their mind maps.

Learners can research the planet Mars and compare it to what the professor found.

Answers for Workbook

1   **a–b**   Learners' own answers.

2   Possible answer: Axel and his uncle see an unusual light filling the cavern.

3   It must be electrical.

4   **a**   *No; the illuminating power of this light, its trembling diffusiveness, its bright, clear whiteness, and its low temperature, showed that it must be of electric origin.*   **b**   cosmic

5   The prefix *sub–* is added to *terra* to make a word meaning 'below earth' 'subterraneus' (Latin) when the suffix *–an* is added.

6   Learners' own answers.

4.6 Working with voices and moods

LEARNING PLAN

Learning objectives		Learning intentions	Success criteria
Main focus	**Also covered**	• Explore and use the active and passive voice.	• Learners can identify and use the active and passive voice appropriately and for effect.
6Rv.04, 6Rg.02, 6Rg.06, 6Wg.03, 6Wg.05	6Rg.03, 6Ri.11, 6Ww.03, 6Ww.05, 6Wg.04, 6SLm.03	• Explore the conditional mood.	• Learners can use the conditional mood accurately and for effect.

LANGUAGE SUPPORT

General English sentence construction leads us to expect a *subject–verb–object* construction, that is, agents perform actions 'actively' (to or on objects). In such constructions, the verb is called an 'active verb' and the subject is the be-er or do-er, e.g. *The boy* (subject) *read two books* (object). Some learners may struggle to achieve active verbs, using passive verb constructions instead. In English, however the active voice is the best voice to write in unless there is a good reason to use the passive voice.

The passive voice has several uses: when the agent is unimportant, when the agent is hidden for a reason, e.g. to create suspense, and when the focus is on the agent having the action done to it rather than doing the action. Writing in the passive voice when the active voice should be used sounds clumsy in English and uses more words than is necessary.

The verb *to be* is always the helping/auxiliary verb used with a past participle and it determines the tense, e.g. *the girl **is** helped by her friend, the girl **was** helped by her friend, the girl **will be** helped by her friend*. The agent in a passive voice sentence becomes the indirect object introduced with *by*, and the direct object of the sentence – if it had been in the active voice – effectively becomes the subject with the action being done to it.

Starter idea

What/who is the focus? (5 minutes)

Resources: Learner's Book, Session 4.6: Getting started

Description: Small groups can discuss the differences between the two sentences for a couple of minutes. Ask directing questions such as: *Who is doing the action? What is the tense? How is the verb formed? Is there a direct or an indirect object? What is the subject? What/who is the focus?*

Discuss learners' ideas as a class, focusing on meaning and where the focus lies in the sentence. Point out that the passive voice sentence is longer in form – it uses more words.

Main teaching ideas

1 Active and passive voice (15 minutes)

Learning intention: To explore the active and passive verb forms

Resources: Learner's Book, Session 4.6, Activity 1; Differentiated worksheet pack

Description: In a passive sentence construction, the direct object effectively becomes the subject, which is acted on by an agent (indirect object). ***Two books*** (subject) *were read by **the boy*** (agent). The passive voice (it is a voice not a mood or a tense) is not incorrect but it changes the focus of the sentence to the books rather than the boy. In general, narrative writing should be in the active voice unless there is a reason for it not to be.

Discuss how the passive verb construction works. Encourage learners to explain. Give them plenty of examples to try orally before doing the activities. Ask who is doing what to whom (or what).

Some common passive verbs (e.g. *was asked, was told*) are followed by an infinitive verb form (e.g. *to walk, to sing*). *He was asked to sing. She was told to sit down.*

Use the Differentiated worksheets 4A–C for more practice on the active and passive.

Supplementary teacher information: Explain briefly, if it arises, that not all verbs can be put into the passive voice. Intransitive verbs cannot be in the passive. For example, *to go* cannot transmit action and so cannot be passive in voice. *I go to school* cannot be turned into *The school was gone to me.*

Spelling link: Encourage learners to remember the familiar spelling rules for regular verbs with the suffix –*ed*, e.g. *y* changes to *i* if –*ed* is added unless the *y* is preceded by *e* or *a* – *carry/carried, obey/obeyed*; consonants after a single, short vowel sound are doubled – *slam/slammed*; verbs ending in *e* drop the *e* before adding –*ed* (or just add *d*) – *smile/smiled.* There are more activities adding suffixes in the Spelling section *at the back* of the Learner's Book.

> **Differentiation ideas:** Support less confident learners by going through parts c and d orally before asking them to write the answers in their books.

> **Assessment ideas:** Suggest that learners write all their answers in their notebooks. Check their sentences to find out whether they have grasped the concepts of active and passive voice.

Answers:
1 a • laughed cried smiled slammed obeyed
   • laughed – the suffix–ed was added, cried – y changed to i, smiled – final e was dropped, slammed – final consonant was doubled before the suffix was added, obeyed – y did not change to i because it was preceded by a vowel.
   • Learners' own examples for each rule.
   • flew, grew, sung, run, thought, brought
   • Learners' own irregular verbs.
   b • passive
   • active

   • passive
   • active
   c • The girl opened the gate.
   • The tree was climbed by Lorcan in two minutes.
   • The class gave the apple to the teacher.
   • The book was read quietly by Malik.
   d • The bag was carried by the porter.
   • The flowers were picked by Babalwa.
   • The nuts were hidden in the tree by the monkeys.
   • The grass was cut by the gardener when it stopped raining.

2 Passive voice and suspense – hidden agent (15 minutes)

Learning intention: To explore the passive voice to create suspense

Resources: Learner's Book, Session 4.6, Activity 2

Description: Common reasons for using the passive voice are to change the focus of the sentence (as practised in Activity 1), if the agent is irrelevant or unimportant (*Gold is mined in South Africa.*) or to build suspense by hiding the agent (*The lid was pushed slowly open from below …*). The third purpose is the most relevant to the learners for story writing, as it can help them build a climax – especially at the end of a chapter – leaving a reader wanting to find out what happens next.

This activity also reveals how clumsy the passive voice can be as a narrative voice which underlines the fact that the passive voice should only be used for a specific reason such as to create suspense or if the agent is irrelevant.

> **Differentiation ideas:** Less confident learners may need to practise internalising the difference between the active and passive voice, although they will probably use both naturally. Additional practice is provided in the Workbook.

Answers:
2 a • The door: To hide the agent and build suspense.
   • Lunch: The agent is irrelevant or unimportant.
   • A parcel: The agent is hidden – either because it is unimportant, or to build suspense – depends on context.
   b Learners' own answers.

c • The voice is passive.
  • It creates suspense because it is unclear who was lifting the subject off the ground and it makes it seem unexpected.
  • Learners' own sentences.
d • A living creature has not yet been seen by me. Was a mistake made in my assumptions?
  • Learners should note that the sentences sound awkward compared to the original.
e • Mostly in the active voice.
  • The active voice flows more smoothly and sounds more natural.

3 If clauses (15 minutes)

Learning intention: To investigate *if* clauses as subordinate clauses

Resources: Learner's Book, Session 4.6, Activity 3

Description: *If* clauses imply that the outcome depends on certain conditions, so it is known as the conditional mood. The conditional mood can be quite complex as it encompasses various degrees of likelihood (zero conditional, first conditional, second conditional and third conditional), but at this stage, keep it simple for learners by talking about how likely an outcome will be resulting from an *if* clause. Some learners find it quite difficult to understand conditionals that are impossible, e.g. *If I had worked harder, I could have (or would have) passed my test.* Explain that the time has passed and so the outcome cannot be changed.

Conditionals are useful for building suspense, especially with an omniscient, third-person narrator who gives clues with foreknowledge of what will happen – *if she had only known, she would never have … * The conditional can also be used in the first person to reflect on possible actions: *If I find out that my father is a secret agent, should I let him know I know?*

Point out that the conditional clause (*if* clause) can come after the main clause without a comma or before it, separated by a comma. Examples: *I will be very happy if I win the race. If I win the race, I will be very happy.*

> **Differentiation ideas:** Support less confident learners by allowing them to discuss parts a and b in a group and respond to parts c and d orally, checking with each other on the effectiveness of their sentences.

Answers:
3 a • Spaceship: always/definite
    • Bus: very likely/definite
    • Back in time: likely to want to but impossible to happen.
  b The *if* clause is the subordinate/dependent clause and the other clause is the main clause in each sentence.
  c–d Learners' own answers.

Plenary idea

If Professor Shonku … (5 minutes)

Resources: Whiteboard

Description: Write on the board *If Professor Shonku …* Invite learners to complete the sentence to create different levels of possibility or likelihood and to create suspense, by either combining it with the passive voice or using an omniscient, third-person narrator.

> **Assessment ideas:** Learners can assess each other's sentences identifying the way suspense has been created as well as whether the sentences are in the active or passive voice. You can also assess how well they have grasped the conditional mood and the active and passive voice.

Homework ideas

Learners can complete the Workbook activities for Session 4.6 if not completed in class. Go through the answers for Activities 1–3 and invite learners to read out their rewriting of the passage in Activity 4, encouraging learners to raise their hand if they spot a verb in the wrong voice.

Answers for Workbook

1 a The first column has the active sentences and the second column the passive sentences.

  b a → iii b → v c → i d → ii e → vi f → iv

2 Possible answers:

  a The family always prepares the food.

  b The coach gave the ball to the best player.

  c The children will decorate the street for the festival.

  d Jules Verne wrote several science-fiction novels.

  e The chef opened the can of tomatoes.

3 Possible answers – phrases and adverbs may appear in different places in the sentences.

   a A warm glowing heat was given off by the sun.

   b The learners' uniforms were checked by the teacher for tidiness.

   c The stick was chewed into pieces by the dog.

   d The boy's wound was gently washed by the nurse.

   e The horses were patted after the race by several riders.

4 A hole was dug by Axel in the sand. The Professor folded his jacket up on a nearby boulder to stay dry. Something hard was struck by Axel's spade, making a metal on metal sound. Quickly the Professor and Axel cleared the hole with their hands. The object was picked up by Axel slowly and carefully. It was stared at by them both, saying nothing at first. Suddenly a faint glow and a low hum were started to be given off by the object …

4.7 Working with chapters, paragraphs and connectives

LEARNING PLAN

Learning objectives		Learning intentions	Success criteria
Main focus	**Also covered**	• Investigate paragraphs.	• Learners can talk about how and why paragraphs are used.
6Rs.01, 6Ws.03	6Rs.02, 6Rs.03, 6Ws.02, 6SLs.01, 6SLg.02, 6SLg.03	• Explore chapters. • Investigate connectives.	• Learners can discuss chapters and their structure. • Learners can investigate and use connectives appropriately.

LANGUAGE SUPPORT

Connectives are not traditional parts of speech in the same way as conjunctions. They encompass a broader range of words and phrases used to connect and link words, phrases, clauses, sentences and even paragraphs.

All connectives have a purpose and while some may be synonyms and interchangeable, others potentially achieve the opposite effect and so would distort the meaning of a sentence if used incorrectly. Some learners may need support in deciding which connective to use and may even need to learn them more formally. Suggest they write connectives they use regularly and their purposes into their learning journals (Worksheet 6.1) for reference.

Starter idea

What does that connective do? (5 minutes)

Resources: Learner's Book, Session 4.7: Getting started

Description: Find out learners' prior knowledge of connectives by getting them to explain to each other what they are and how they are used. Give learners a couple of minutes to compile a list of connectives they use regularly and build a class list on the board.

Encourage learners to give examples of the connectives in use as they suggest them.

Main teaching ideas

1 Paragraphs – one main topic (20 minutes)

Learning intention: To explore paragraphs and chapters as organising devices

Resources: Learner's Book, Session 4.7, Activity 1; *The Diary of a Space Traveller and Other Stories* (Learner's Book, Session 4.5); independent readers

Description: Revise paragraphs and focus on transitions between paragraphs. Discuss differences between fiction and non-fiction paragraphs. Non-fiction paragraph structure is more obvious: topic sentence, supporting sentences to elaborate or provide evidence, a concluding sentence. Fiction paragraph construction is less obvious, but still tends to contain a main idea or episode.

Discuss how paragraphs make text easier to read and visually support units of information, description or ideas, making the content easier to absorb. Paragraph length in fiction is flexible, e.g. a one-line paragraph may emphasise a thought, idea or action. Discuss why authors start new paragraphs: a change of action, focus or scenery and to indicate new character is speaking in dialogue.

Discuss similarities between chapters and paragraphs. Draw out that they are both organising devices to signal a change of direction or the start of a new thought or episode. Chapters group paragraphs; paragraphs group sentences. Chapters, as mini episodes of a larger story, need a beginning, middle and end, encompassing a purpose and a complication/problem/issue, but resolution is often delayed, building suspense in the overall plot. Discuss how authors may use chapter titles to preview what will happen and tantalise the reader, or as organisers for a contents list (especially in non-fiction). Some authors include tag lines, verse, images, quotations or similar at the start of chapters.

Decide whether to do part a as a class or in pairs, based on your general discussion.

Pairs discuss the paragraph structure in their own reading books, noting and comparing reasons with other pairs. Some learners could add reasons for paragraph transition in the writing techniques section of their journals, noting examples from their independent reading.

> **Differentiation ideas:** Support less confident learners by working through some of the questions with small groups, using part a to kickstart them into the next questions.

Answers:
1   a–c Learners' own answers.

2 Using different connectives (20 minutes)

Learning intention: To explore a variety of connectives and their purposes

Resources: Learner's Book, Session 4.7, Activity 2

Description: This activity builds on the previous one by focusing on conjunctions and connectives linking parts of sentences or transitioning between paragraphs. This activity highlights the fact that connectives have different purposes and therefore their meaning is important.

Learners draw a mind map in their notebooks. Explain that some connectives may have differently nuanced meanings, so one might be better than another in a particular context. Variety is another consideration.

Supplementary teacher information: Learners are often taught never to start a sentence with *and* or *but* (coordinating conjunctions). However, fiction authors use both to start sentences on occasion, for effect. While it should not be encouraged, it is not necessarily an indicator of poor writing if handled effectively: it is an example of narrative licence.

> **Differentiation ideas:** Work with a group of less confident learners for parts b and c to ensure they can recognise the connectives and link them to sentence types and time passing. More practice on connectives can be found in the Workbook.

For greater challenge, learners could add other connectives under the headings. They may also need to add further arms to the mind map to accommodate other connectives. They can think of their own, explore their reading books or refer to a list you write on the board. This activity can be ongoing, especially if the work is in their learning journals (Worksheet 6.1).

> **Assessment ideas:** Assess learners' mind maps to check they understand the meaning and purpose of the connectives.

Answers:
2   a   sequencing: *next, later, before, then, finally, until*; comparing: *like, compared with, as*; adding: *and, in addition*; contrasting: *although, unlike, otherwise, however, though, but, except*; cause and effect: *therefore, as a result, because.*
     b   •   Link clauses and sentences in paragraphs: *though, now, but, until, that, as, except*;

- Link paragraphs to each other: *today,*
  then.

c   Learners' own answers (e.g. *next, later,*
then, finally before, until).

d   I went to the market <u>because</u> I needed
vegetables and spices. I went to the market
<u>as</u> I needed vegetables and spices. (I went
to the market <u>and</u> I needed vegetables and
spices. I went to the market <u>before</u> I needed
vegetables and spices.)

Plenary idea

Create a time sequence (5 minutes)

Resources: Whiteboard

Description: Write this series of connectives on the
board: *first, second, next, finally; and, in addition, as
well as, although.*

Challenge learners to come up with a creative narrative
that uses the connectives in order.

> **Assessment ideas:** Learners can vote on the most
creative narrative using the two series of connectives.
They can also add ideas to make the narrative more
imaginative.

Homework ideas

Learners can complete the Workbook activities for
Session 4.7. Go through the answers in class.

Learners can keep an eye out for connectives in other
reading and subjects.

Answers for Workbook

1   **a** before – sequencing;   **b** so – cause and effect /
sequencing;   **c** although – contrasting;
d so – cause and effect; as soon as – sequencing.

2   Learners' own answers.

3   **a** because;   **b** before;   **c** while;   **d** so that;
e although.

4   I wanted to explore the planet **because** I was
interested in how it would compare with Earth.
Before I started, I explained to Prahlad everything
that we would do. **In addition**, I gave him a notepad
and pen to record his observations. **At last**, we were
ready to explore.

First, we tested the ground and the rocks, which
seemed to be quite soft. **Next**, we drank the red
river water **although** not without some nervousness.
Finally, we made sketches of the plants, noting they
were blue **compared to** the green we were used to
on Earth.

4.8 Write paragraphs describing fictional surroundings

LEARNING PLAN

Learning objectives		Learning intentions	Success criteria
Main focus	**Also covered**	• Plan a chapter describing the setting. • Write a draft of the chapter. • Improve the draft based on feedback.	• Learners can plan the details of a chapter to describe a science-fiction setting . • Learners can write a draft of the chapter based on a plan. • Learners can improve the draft based on feedback and proofreading.
6Rs.01, 6Rs.02, 6Ww.07, 6Wv.02, 6Wv.04, 6Wv.06, 6Wg.04, 6Wg.08, 6Ws.02, 6Ws.03, 6Wc.03, 6Wp.04, 6Wp.05	6Rs.03, 6Wg.03, 6Ws.01, 6SLm.03, 6SLp.01		

LANGUAGE SUPPORT

In writing their drafts, learners should be encouraged to use all the writing techniques and word classes they have covered in earlier sessions, including varied use of connectives, sentence variety and length, paragraphing, active and passive voices, the conditional mood and vocabulary to promote imaginative detail. Monitor learners' confidence and support them by discussing their plans.

Common misconception

Misconception	How to identify	How to overcome
Settings are less important than characters.	Ask learners how they knew *The Green Book* and Professor Shonku's diary were science-fiction stories. Draw out that it is as much the setting (if not more) and what the characters find and encounter that make the stories science fiction rather than the characters.	Encourage learners' creativity and imagination when planning a description of the setting. Use questions such as *What do they see? How does it smell? How is it different to what we know?* In the diary, the colours and textures are different, but there are no clues as to whether the planet is inhabited. Ask: *What could the people/beings look like?*

Starter idea

What is it like? (5 minutes)

Resources: Learner's Book, Session 4.8: Getting started; a collection of science-fiction stories

Description: Build learners' excitement about planning Chapter 2 of their story by allowing learners to discuss ideas with a partner. Chapter 2 will describe the science-fiction setting.

Read descriptions of settings from books you have gathered as a stimulus.

Encourage learners to brainstorm, explaining that no idea is too outrageous in a brainstorm, and let them spark ideas off each other, making notes if appropriate.

Main teaching ideas

1 Plan and write descriptive paragraphs (25 minutes)

Learning intention: To plan and write a draft of a chapter to describe a science-fiction setting

Resources: Learner's Book, Session 4.8, Activity 1; Language worksheet 4B; learners' planning tables and drafts of Chapter 1 from Session 4.4

Description: *The Diary of a Space Traveller and Other Stories* extract describes a landscape the reader could never have seen. The author has transformed familiar details into a fantastical science-fiction setting. Science-fiction settings work best if they can be related back to ordinary human experience. For example, a machine that can travel through space or to another planet is an extension of a car, train or plane. The creativity is in visualising those inventions and the unknown surroundings in which the characters then find themselves.

Encourage learners to follow a similar pattern to the extract from *The Diary of a Space Traveller and Other Stories*. In their paragraphs, characters should encounter a new landscape; a vivid description of the initial scenery should be followed by an unusual sight or experience, e.g. drinking the water; they should describe the characters' reactions and then lead into the next chapter which will develop to the story climax.

Allow learners to continue working in their planning groups, in pairs or individually. Remind learners that this is an extension of their original story so they can alter their draft of Chapter 1, if they need to, especially the transition from Chapter 1 to Chapter 2.

Remind learners about suspense-building techniques, such as asides by an omniscient narrator, *if* clauses, use of the ellipsis and use of the passive voice to deliberately hide an agent, although the narrative should be largely in the active voice. Recap connectives and their purposes in joining clauses, sentences and paragraphs for sentence variety.

Use Language worksheet 4B to provide learners with a word bank to help them describe a science-fiction setting. Learners could use the worksheets to guide their descriptive paragraphs.

> **Differentiation ideas:** Support learners in groups, pairs or working alone. Ensure that less confident learners write their own stories even if they discuss the content. If some learners need additional support, consider allowing them to work together on a single story, taking turns to scribe and to dictate.

Answers:
1   a–b Learners' own answers.

2   Edit and improve your draft (20 minutes)

Learning intention: To proofread, edit and improve a draft based on feedback

Resources: Learner's Book, Session 4.8, Activity 2; learners' drafts of Chapter 2 from Activity 1; dictionaries, thesauruses, personal word lists

Description: Once they have finished their drafts, ask learners to review their paragraphs carefully. They can underline words that could be improved and sentences that could be linked by connectives. Remind them to check whether they could use connectives to link paragraphs to create a time sequence.

When they are confident they have improved their drafts, they read their chapter to a partner – using appropriate expression to bring it to life. Partners should offer feedback both on what they like and ideas for improvement.

Learners finalise their chapters based on their partner's feedback. Remind them to use their own lists of collected words to use again.

Remind them that Chapter 2 must follow on from Chapter 1 and if necessary, they should make changes to Chapter 1 and develop the transition into Chapter 2. For example, Chapter 1 could begin inside the spaceship and Chapter 2 could be arriving on the planet or a science-fiction setting.

> **Differentiation ideas:** Support less confident learners by helping them identify words and sentences for improvement.

> **Assessment ideas:** While the overall story will be assessed using the *Readaloudathon* success criteria (or by referring to Worksheet 6.18 My Readaloudathon story), this tranche can be assessed independently based on its own success criteria – some suggested by you to reflect the learning covered over the previous sessions and one or two chosen by the learners as personal writing goals. Some possible success criteria:

- I described the setting and scenery vividly using adjectives, descriptive phrases and interesting vocabulary and figurative comparisons.
- I included some dialogue between the characters.
- I invented and described an unusual sight.
- I included their reaction and clues on how it will affect their new lives.
- I used connectives and suspense-building techniques.

Answers:
2   a–c Learners' own answers.

Plenary idea

Science-fiction settings (5 minutes)

Resources: Learners' drafts of Chapter 2 from Activity 1

Description: Invite volunteers to read out their final drafts of Chapter 2.

Remind learners of the criteria for science-fiction stories and how to create drama and suspense to help them give each other constructive feedback.

> **Assessment ideas:** Learners can evaluate volunteers' chapters. Promote discussion and building on each other's ideas. Add your own ideas where appropriate.

Homework ideas

Learners can complete the Workbook activities for Session 4.8, practising descriptive writing. Invite them to read out the old-fashioned paragraphs they wrote for Activities 2 and 3 in class.

Answers for Workbook

1–3 Learners' own answers.

4.9 Going forward in time

LEARNING PLAN

Learning objectives		Learning intentions	Success criteria
Main focus	**Also covered**		
6Rv.01, 6Ri.02, 6Ri.03, 6Ri.10, 6Ri.14, 6Ra.02, 6Wv.04, 6Ws.04, 6Wc.01, 6Wc.06, 6Wp.03, 6SLm.04, 6SLp.01, 6SLp.02	6Rv.03, 6Rs.02, 6Ri.01, 6Ri.06, 6Ri.07, 6Ri.08, 6Ri.11, 6Ra.03, 6Wv.02, 6SLm.01, 6SLg.01, 6SLp.03, 6SLr.01	• Skim read and respond to an extract. • Perform an extract. • Write an entry for the guide.	• Learners can skim read and respond to an extract. • Learners can perform their part in an extract, with expression and gesture. • Learners can write an entry for the guide in an appropriate format.

LANGUAGE SUPPORT

Encourage learners to try to understand unfamiliar words using the context and other strategies before using the glossary or a dictionary. Arthur sometimes uses an ironic or sarcastic tone which may be challenging for some learners to identify. When discussing how to read the extract aloud, it may be useful to model how Arthur speaks to help learners get the right tone.

Starter idea

When and where would you go? (10 minutes)

Resources: Learner's Book, Session 4.9: Getting started; Worksheet 6.19

Description: Have a class discussion about where learners would visit if they had a time machine. Explain that they can go backwards or forwards in time.

Give learners a minute or two to gather their thoughts before they give a partner a short speech explaining when and where they would visit or whom they would like to meet and why. They can use Worksheet 6.19 My time machine to help them organise their ideas.

Main teaching ideas

24 1 Read and perform an extract (25 minutes)

Learning intention: To read and perform an extract

Resources: *The Hitchhiker's Guide to the Galaxy* (Learner's Book, Session 4.9, Activity 1); Track 24; filming/recording devices

Description: Learners skim read the extract to get the main idea and then get into groups to read aloud. Mixed-ability groups will work well. Encourage learners to talk about how they will read the different parts, considering expression, characterisation and style of speaking.

Learners will find it easier to summarise the events and how the characters reacted after their group reading. The discussion will help them refine their performance, as will using body language to reflect the content of the extract. Let them be creative. If possible, film their performances so they can review and improve their practice.

> **Differentiation ideas:** Read one of the parts with selected groups of less confident learners to show them how to maintain flow and direction.

Organise some learners into groups based on their reading abilities, to allow you to target support when they are practising for their performance.

Play the audio of the extract (Track 24) for selected groups of less confident learners to help them get into the characters.

Challenge more confident learners to summarise the events in their notebooks rather than just orally to each other. Encourage them to write summary sentences in no more than 25 words. Alternatively, they could summarise on a mind map using key words.

〉 **Assessment ideas:** Use learners' dramatic readings to assess how well they convey ideas about characters in different roles and scenarios through deliberate choice of speech, gesture and movement.

Answers:
1   a–d Learners' own answers.

2   Identify features of a science-fiction story and write an entry (25 minutes)

Learning intention: To explore features of genres and text types

Resources: Learner's Book, Session 4.9, Activity 2; *The Hitchhiker's Guide to the Galaxy* (Learner's Book, Session 4.9); Track 24; Worksheet 6.1; examples of internet references (explanations of items)

Description: Revise the features of science fiction, e.g. futuristic settings, science and technology, space travel, time travel and writing as if it could really happen. Discuss which features this extract suggests. Encourage learners to think about what they use when they want to know about something – anywhere. Learners will be familiar with smart phones and tablets as devices to find out almost anything – which is exactly what the *Hitchhiker's Guide* does.

In thinking about whether the story is modern or written some time ago, discuss with learners that science-fiction writers imagine technology that does not exist and write about it. This implies that the book was written some time ago as the author is imagining an amazing invention that you can just type in what you want to know about and it gives you the answer – today, that concept is taken for granted.

Share examples of explanations of different items on the internet (rather than in reference books),

preferably some using organisational devices such as bullets. These will help learners get the idea for writing the entry. Although they are writing fiction, the entry should seem factual as if in a reference book, although they can be as creative as they like with the detail. Remind them to consider layout as well as content. Encourage them to reflect on whether they would normally choose a science-fiction story as a reading choice when they write their entry into their learning journals (Worksheet 6.1). They should compare all three science-fiction texts they have read and conclude whether reading them has changed their ideas about reading the genre.

〉 **Differentiation ideas:** Support less confident learners by allowing them to write the *Vogon Constructor Fleets* entry in pairs.

〉 **Assessment ideas:** Take in learners' entries and assess how well they have used a factual style suitable for a reference book combined with creative ideas.

Answers:
2   a   Possible answers: it includes a spaceship, it is set in the future, it is set in outer space, it involves futuristic gadgets, it involves alien species. Earth has been destroyed.
      b   The internet – accessed via a smart phone, tablet or other device
      c   It is written some time ago because the idea of such a guide is no longer futuristic.
      d–e Learners' own answers.

Plenary idea

Vogon Constructor Fleets (5 minutes)

Resources: Learners' *Vogon Constructor Fleets* entries from Activity 2

Description: Invite volunteers to read out their entries and have fun comparing what learners have written.

As well as reading out their entries, learners should show how they have set out their entry to make it like an official *Hitchhiker's Guide* entry.

〉 **Assessment ideas:** Learners can comment on whether the entries read out sound factual as well as being creative. They can also evaluate whether the layout is suitable for the text type.

History: Source information about the creation of the internet and development of computers, laptops, tablets and smartphones.

Homework ideas

Learners can complete the Workbook activities for Session 4.9, using time connectives and including science-fiction features. Invite learners to exchange Workbooks and the comment on each other's entries as well as any differences in Activity 1.

Answers for Workbook

1 a now; **b** as soon as; **c** first; **d** or; **e** next; **f** so; **g** and; **h** then **i** but.

2–3 Learners' own answers.

4.10 Spelling, punctuation and grammar

LEARNING PLAN

Learning objectives		Learning intentions	Success criteria
Main focus	**Also covered**	• Investigate relevant details.	• Learners can identify relevant details.
6Rg.01, 6Rg.07, 6Rs.02, 6Ri.03, 6Ri.14, 6Ww.02, 6Ww.03, 6Ww.05, 6Wv.03	6Rv.01, 6Rv.02, 6Rg.03, 6Ri.02, 6Wg.08	• Notice writing techniques. • Explore prefixes, suffixes and spelling rules.	• Learners can identify and talk about writing techniques. • Learners can explore prefixes, suffixes and spelling rules.

LANGUAGE SUPPORT

Learners investigate details relating to writing techniques and the science-fiction genre. All have been covered previously but some learners may need support if they cannot remember, for example, the different uses of the apostrophe (to show possession and in contractions).

They also investigate words with similar sounding endings (–er/–or and –ible/–able). Some learners may find these spelling differences challenging especially as there seems to be no obvious reasons for one or another. Even going back and looking at Latin/Greek word origins is not completely reliable as a strategy. In addition, as the suffixes begin with a vowel, other spelling rules also come into play when adding the suffixes, including soft and hard gs and cs, doubling final consonants, changing y to i and dropping the final e.

Starter idea

Looking at suffixes (5 minutes)

Resources: Learner's Book, Session 4.10: Getting started

Description: Remind learners that suffixes are added to the end of words and can be as simple as –s, –ed and –ing as well as suffixes that transform words into another class, e.g. –ful, –less, –ible/–able, –er/–or.

Allow pairs a couple of minutes to think of common suffixes before compiling a list on the board – with examples, pointing out any spelling rules and exceptions.

Main teaching ideas

1 Investigate the detail (25 minutes)

Learning intention: To investigate detailed features of the text type

Resources: Learner's Book, Session 4.10, Activity 1

Description: Learners should scan the text for evidence to support their answers and apply their knowledge, using both recent and prior knowledge of writing – modern and classic.

As this activity is well-suited to an assessment, ask learners to write answers in their notebooks and consider asking them to work alone. Discuss the activity as a challenge for learners to find out how much they know and remember. Set a time limit to encourage focused work.

> **Differentiation ideas:** For extra support, learners could work in pairs for this activity to share their knowledge. Less confident learners could be allowed more time or just write key words.

For more challenge, ask learners to write answers in full sentences.

> **Assessment ideas:** Assess Activity 1 formally as an overview of learners' knowledge of language features in context.

Answers:
1 a Learners' own answers.
   b Emphasis as part of sarcasm, identifying what someone might have said, title of a book, quote from cover of book, title of an entry in the guide
   c It omits an explanation of why he should shade his eyes, leaving Arthur to fill in the missing details and take action.

   d • sub– means 'under'.
      • subconscious, submarine, substandard, subset, subplot, subtotal and learners' own sentences.
      • sub-ether means 'beneath the ether'.
   e Plenty of examples of contractions, e.g. we're and showing possession, e.g. Thumb's.
   f Dialogue and to emphasise a moment.
   g • The narrative person is third-person.
      • The narrative is mainly past tense; dialogue mainly present tense.
      • The writing style can be seen as informal as mostly dialogue.
   h Learners' own answers, e.g. calm.

2 Focus on spelling rules and strategies (20 minutes)

Learning intention: To explore suffixes and spelling rules

Resources: Learner's Book, Session 4.10, Activity 2

Description: Spelling is always important. ICT can help but cannot always interpret words correctly for context, so learners will need to develop their own strategies for reading, writing and internalising spelling before applying their knowledge. They also need to develop listening skills to help them spell words they have heard but not seen.

The activities focus on different ways word sounds can be created. Encourage learners to write words in groups of letter sounds in their notebooks so they can kinaesthetically internalise the sound, sight and feel of the letter groups in the actual words.

> **Differentiation ideas:** Support less confident learners by allowing them to work in pairs or small groups, checking their answers in a dictionary.

Answers:
2 a • terrible, bearable, available, horrible.
      • Learners' own answers.
   b • reason, accept, inflate, believe, forget, regret, justify, rely
      • Spelling rules: final e is dropped, the final consonant is doubled, y changes to i.
      • The e is retained to keep the soft g or c sound.
      • sensible, collapsible, reducible, forcible (drop final e).
      • –ible/–able: capable of being or having, e.g. sensible – capable of having sense.

c • Learners' own agent nouns. *–er* is more common.
• Learners' own answers for decisions.

5

Plenary idea

Let's refresh (5 minutes)

Resources: Learner's Book, Session 4.10, Activity 2

Description: Invite volunteers to give strategies for deciding whether to use the suffix *–ible* or *–able*. Now invite examples to test out the strategies and ask which spelling rules were used each time.

> **Assessment ideas:** Use Activity 2 to see how well learners have made use of spelling rules

Homework ideas

Learners can complete the Workbook activities for Session 4.10. Go through the answers in class. The wordsearch is quite challenging, so try to complete it as a class activity.

Answers for Workbook

1   **a** incredible **b** unsupportable **c** visible
    d fashionable **e** desirable **f** legible **g** sizeable
    h flexible **i** responsible

2   Learners' own answers.

3   **a** actor **b** sailor **c** worker **d** builder
    e tutor **f** dictator **g** editor **h** dancer
    i runner **j** driver **k** inventor **l** survivor

4   Learners' own answers.

H	J	D	P	U	R	N	W	Z	D	J	E	E	I	S
E	L	B	I	T	S	E	G	G	U	S	L	K	N	K
Q	L	J	L	Z	R	E	K	S	B	B	B	F	S	A
S	H	B	Y	A	L	O	T	A	I	D	A	F	P	T
K	W	F	I	B	U	I	N	S	M	R	E	J	E	E
N	R	I	A	T	F	G	R	R	M	A	C	O	C	R
K	U	V	M	I	R	E	H	E	E	P	I	E	T	O
Q	O	F	A	M	V	E	R	A	E	T	G	O	T
L	T	B	N	E	E	V	L	B	V	O	Z	R	C
F	L	Z	R	W	Q	R	I	N	H	L	N	G	U	E
E	Q	E	P	O	R	G	F	G	O	Q	E	N	M	R
C	O	U	N	C	I	L	L	O	R	C	B	L	Q
A	C	P	O	B	R	O	Y	E	V	R	U	S	L	D
M	O	K	L	E	G	I	B	L	E	S	M	L	O	Z
T	R	E	L	L	E	T	W	S	P	D	J	V	T	F

4.11 Finish your story

LEARNING PLAN

Learning objectives		Learning intentions	Success criteria
Main focus	**Also covered**	• Complete science-fiction stories. • Get feedback from a partner. • Make improvements to the overall story.	• Learners can complete at least four chapters of their science-fiction stories. • Learners can discuss their stories with a partner. • Learners can make improvements based on proofreading, editing and feedback.
6Ww.07, 6Wv.02, 6Wv.04, 6Wg.01, 6Wv.01, 6Wg.04, 6Wg.05, 6Wg.08, 6Ws.01, 6Ws.02, 6Ws.03, 6Wc.01, 6Wc.02, 6Wc.03	6Ri.11, 6Ri.15, 6Wv.05, 6Wv.06, 6Wg.02, 6Wp.03		

LANGUAGE SUPPORT

As learners write, dip in and out of their drafts, and discuss the language aspects of their writing, especially with learners who need support.

Starter idea

How is it going so far? (10 minutes)

Resources: Learner's Book, Session 4.11: Getting started; learners' drafts of Chapter 1 from Session 4,4 and Chapter 2 from Session 4.8

Description: Learners should skim over their two chapters, summarise what has happened so far and outline the plan for the next chapters. They should also explain their golden thread themes to each other.

Ask volunteers to share their summaries and plans with the class and invite feedback.

Main teaching ideas

1 Complete your story (25 minutes)

Learning intention: To complete their stories

Resources: Learner's Book, Session 4.11, Activity 1

Description: Learners should know how their story is progressing having both planned it and written Chapters 1 and 2. In this session, learners need to write the final two chapters of the story (or more, if they have time and inspiration). They should follow their plan closely and focus on building suspense for a dramatic climax. Some learners may enjoy trying to end on a cliffhanger.

Allow quiet time for learners to work alone and keep writing. Remind them not to stop to check spellings or structure until they have finished writing at least a paragraph, or preferably their whole story.

In the previous session, learners focused on criteria relating to the first part of the story as well as the overall story. In this session, focus on improving the use of techniques to create suspense, spelling and 'readaloudability', and ensuring the golden thread in the story links the ending to the beginning.

> **Differentiation ideas:** Support less confident learners by allowing them to write in pairs. Talk to learners about their plans. Encourage more confident learners to write more than four chapters or to include more detail.

Answers:
1   Learners' own answers.

2 Get feedback on your draft (20 minutes)

Learning intention: To edit, review, proofread and illustrate stories to finalise them

Resources: Learner's Book, Session 4.11, Activity 2; Worksheet 6.6; dictionaries, thesauruses and online spelling/grammar checking tools

Description: Allow learners about half the lesson to complete the last two chapters and the remainder of the lesson for reviewing, improving and proofreading, working alone or in pairs. If appropriate, model how to give feedback and suggestions for improvement to one or two learners. You can use Worksheet 6.6 Check, check and check again at this point.

Encourage learners to focus on details, asking for example: *Have you used chapter titles that give clues? Have you used different suspense-building techniques to add variety?*

Allow learners, if possible, to choose whether to type their final drafts or to write them out in neat, fluent and legible handwriting, both with illustrations.

> **Differentiation ideas:** Support learners by pairing less confident learners in the review phase to help them identify areas to improve or correct.

Each learner should have written a story of at least four chapters. Encourage more advanced writers to write either more chapters or to develop their four chapters more fully. This will be an individual negotiation with each learner depending on your assessment of their progress so far. Allow learners writing longer stories to complete them at home.

> **Assessment ideas:** Assess the extended narrative using the learners' planning tool and their final version. Although they did not need to stick to every detail of their plan, there should be a significant correlation. You could assess stories in terms of:

- planning
- content and creativity
- structure – chapters, paragraphs, sentences
- dialogue
- suspense-building techniques
- vocabulary and spelling.

Answers:
2 **a–c** Learners' own answers.

Plenary idea

Share the golden thread (5 minutes)

Resources: Learners' stories (Chapters 1–4)

Description: Invite volunteers to explain their golden thread themes to the class – how they started, how they were important in the story and how they linked the end to the beginning.

> **Assessment ideas:** Learners can evaluate the golden thread themes and compare the different examples given.

CROSS-CURRICULAR LINKS

Science: Gather books and information on incredible or futuristic inventions.

Homework ideas

Learners can complete their stories if they are writing more than four chapters or writing in greater depth.

Learners can also complete the Workbook activities for Session 4.11, practising proofreading and writing techniques.

Answers for Workbook

1 The problem is that <u>Earth</u> has been obliterated. It <u>means</u> that you <u>won't</u> be able to go home ever <u>again</u>. But don't <u>worry</u>, the universe is full of <u>fascinating</u> places. You <u>could</u> choose to live <u>anywhere</u>. <u>You'll see</u> – you will <u>hardly miss</u> it after a <u>while</u>.

2 'Where is your courage?' snapped Ford Prefect. 'It's never deserted you before.'

'But look!' screeched a terrified voice.

'That's the Dentrassi!' exclaimed Ford. 'I'd know that ugly appearance anywhere.'

'What's that noise?'

3–4 Learners' own answers.

4.12 Take part in a *Readaloudathon*

LEARNING PLAN

Learning objectives		Learning intentions	Success criteria
Main focus	**Also covered**	• Read stories aloud in a group.	• Learners can read their stories aloud with expression and fluency.
6Ri.07, 6SLm.02, 6SLm.04, 6SLm.05, 6SLp.01, 6SLp.02, 6SLp.03, 6SLr.01	6Rs.02, 6SLm.01, 6SLr.02	• Summarise stories to other groups.	• Learners can summarise another person's story to another group.
		• Identify the golden threads.	• Learners can identify the golden threads.

LANGUAGE SUPPORT

Listen particularly to learners who may need support as they practise reading their stories aloud and assist with pronunciation where appropriate.

Starter idea

How to read aloud expressively (5 minutes)

Resources: Learner's Book, Session 4.12: Getting started

Description: Give partners a few minutes to explain to each other what it means to read aloud expressively. Write a few words on the board to help them get started: *expression, volume, accent, pace, tone, fluency, gesture* and *body language*.

Encourage them to be creative about how to prepare and discuss as a class what strategies could be used, such as highlighting particular areas, underlining and notes to the side.

Main teaching ideas

1 Tell your stories (25 minutes)

Learning intention: To read aloud expressively and fluently

Resources: Learner's Book, Session 4.12, Activity 1; learners' science-fiction stories (Chapters 1–4 or more); copies of the stories (if possible)

Description: Make this session a lively celebration of learners' stories; they deserve the opportunity to show off. If possible, make copies of learners' stories so they can write presentation notes on them, e.g. to highlight different characters' dialogue, or make notes about expression. Allow practice time. Ideally, learners should also have had the opportunity to take their stories home to practise beforehand.

Remind learners that as they read aloud, they may wish to make minor changes to enhance flow. Create three to four story groups so learners can present to each other. Listen in to stories being read aloud and give words of praise and encouragement. Allow time for discussion of the stories if possible.

> **Differentiation ideas:** Support any learners who are reluctant to read their own stories aloud to a group, by offering them the option of having another learner read their story for them. Allow more confident learners to recruit other learners to read their stories aloud in parts, such as narrator and characters.

> **Assessment ideas:** Use the reading aloud sessions to informally assess how fluently they read with expression.

Answers:
1   a–b Learners' own answers.

2   Summarise the stories (20 minutes)

Learning intention: To summarise the stories, identifying the golden thread

Resources: Learner's Book, Session 4.12, Activity 2

Description: Learners should choose a representative from their group once they have listened to all the stories to summarise the stories to other groups, highlighting the golden thread in each.

Listeners should try to identify the golden thread from the person summarising, who will tell them if they were correct.

> **Differentiation ideas:** Two representatives can go from some groups to summarise stories to another group to support each other if they forget anything.

> **Assessment ideas:** Assess learners' summaries of each other's stories to see how well they grasp the key points and whether they can identify the golden threads linking to the stories' themes.

Answers:
2   a–b Learners' own answers.

Plenary idea

Let's hear a summary (5–10 minutes)

Description: Invite learners who summarised their own group's stories to choose their favourite from the other groups and to summarise it for the class.

Invite the class to identify the golden threads.

> **Assessment ideas:** Survey learners to find out which story is their favourite and which they considered fulfilled the original criteria the best.

Homework ideas

Learners can complete the Workbook activities for Session 4.12. Invite learners to read out their answers for Activity 1 in class.

Learners can practise their reading at home and then hold a storytelling session for their families.

Answers for Workbook

1   Possible answers:

   a   The enormous Vogon grabbed at Arthur.

   b   Ford and Arthur raced back as fast as they could.

   c   Although travelling in space is exciting, not everyone would enjoy it.

   d   Arthur was aghast and scared to see the Vogon.

   e   The panicked friends gripped on to the useful *Hitchhiker's Guide*.

2   Arthur decided to give Ford a <u>peace</u> of his mind. 'Of <u>coarse</u> you <u>wood</u> say this is normal but <u>its</u> <u>knot</u>. <u>Nun</u> of the things that have happened are normal. You are <u>sew</u> <u>shore</u> that <u>won</u> of these Vogons won't find us. I don't <u>no</u> how <u>ewe</u> can <u>bee</u> <u>sow</u> confident. As far as I am concerned, we <u>knead</u> to get out of <u>hear</u> in the next <u>our</u> if we don't want to get <u>court</u>. At the moment, we are just a <u>pear</u> of sitting ducks waiting to be <u>maid</u> into mincemeat by <u>sum</u> <u>grate</u>, green, alien beast. <u>Witch</u> door did you say is the <u>whey</u> out?'

3   Arthur decided to give Ford a **piece** of his mind. 'Of **course** you **would** say this is normal but **it's not**. **None** of the things that have happened are normal. You are **so sure** that **one** of these Vogons won't find us. I don't **know** how **you** can **be so** confident. As far as I am concerned, we **need** to get out of **here** in the next **hour** if we don't want to get **caught**. At the moment, we are just a **pair** of sitting ducks waiting to be **made** into mincemeat by **some great**, green, alien beast. **Which** door did you say is the **way** out?'

CHECK YOUR PROGRESS

1 Learners' own answers but it should involve an object or theme that runs throughout an entire story.

2 a Kolkata, <u>previously known as Calcutta</u>, is where Satyajit Ray was born.

   b Mars (the red planet) is the closest plant to Earth.

   c We ate jelly – my favourite is mango – on my birthday.

3 NB word order may differ slightly

   a Strange moth-like creatures covered the glassy trees.

   b A tiny blue-leaved plant was picked from the red river by Professor Shonku.

4 a impossible   b possible   c certain

5 a changeable, flexible, forcible, believable.

   b changeable – keep the *e* to keep the soft *g* sound; forcible – drop the final *e* as the soft *c* sound is kept because the suffix *ible* begins with *i*; believable – drop the final *e*.

PROJECT GUIDANCE

Group project: learners put together an illustrated display of the solar system. Allow free choice of how to present the solar system but encourage creativity, with models, slideshows and video clips. Discuss including suitable music to accompany their words and images, e.g. *The Planets* 1914–1916, by composer Gustav Holst. If it is a different teacher, liaise with the art teacher or department so that learners can paint their planets or even make models of the entire solar system, preferably according to scale and distance from the sun. Learners can present their solar systems to the class or even to another class. Encourage each person to have a chance to speak in the presentations.

Pair project: learners research a planet each. Negotiate which planet they will research so that you have a good spread of the different planets in the solar system. Once they have completed their research, pairs can compare the information they have gathered about their planets. Encourage a question and answer format. Having discovered what each person has found out, encourage them to identify whether they would like to find out any additional information on either of the planets so that they have comparable information on each.

Solo project: learners research a planet and make notes to help them prepare a two-minute presentation on their chosen planet. Allow free choice of material and sources to research. Remind learners that they have only time to make three good points in a short presentation. Encourage them to have three sections to their notes and to add detail underneath. Discuss what sort of information would be interesting to include, such as size, number of moons and distance from the sun, composition.

>5 The facts of the matter

Unit plan

Session	Approximate number of learning hours	Outline of learning content	Resources
5.1 Poles apart	0.5+	Discuss and compare information. Identify facts and opinions. Use connectives effectively.	Learner's Book Session 5.1 Workbook Session 5.1
5.2 A news report	0.5+	Explore a news report. Identify the purpose, audience, language and layout. Recognise how ideas are organised and linked in a text.	Learner's Book Session 5.2 Workbook Session 5.2 ⬇ Worksheet 6.3 ⬇ Worksheet 6.4 ⬇ Worksheet 6.10
5.3 Support a view	0.5+	Explore a scientific explanation. Distinguish between facts and opinions. Extend a discussion.	Learner's Book Session 5.3 Workbook Session 5.3
5.4 Express possibility	0.5+	Explain the difference between a phrase and a clause. Revise complex sentences. Use the *if* clause to express possibility.	Learner's Book Session 5.4 Workbook Session 5.4
5.5 Keep it formal	0.5+	Identify formal, standard English. Use pronouns for effect. Use the active or passive voice for effect.	Learner's Book Session 5.5 Workbook Session 5.5

Session	Approximate number of learning hours	Outline of learning content	Resources
5.6 A balanced report	0.5+	Read and analyse a balanced report. Discuss meaning in a text. Identify the features of a balanced report.	Learner's Book Session 5.6 Workbook Session 5.6 ⬇ Worksheet 6.3 ⬇ Worksheet 6.4
5.7 Language techniques	0.5+	Explore the use of connectives and verb forms in balanced views. Understand the link between the purpose and language of a text.	Learner's Book Session 5.7 Workbook Session 5.7
5.8 and 5.9 Present a balanced view	1.5	List criteria of a balanced report. Plan and edit a report. Present a report.	Learner's Book Session 5.8 and 5.9 Workbook Session 5.8 and 5.9 ⬇ Differentiated worksheets 5A–C ⬇ Worksheet 6.5 ⬇ Worksheet 6.6 ⬇ Worksheet 6.9 ⬇ Worksheet 6.20 ⬇ Worksheet 6.21
5.10 A strong viewpoint	0.5+	Read for meaning. Identify persuasive language. Find synonyms that sound more or less persuasive.	Learner's Book Session 5.10 Workbook Session 5.10 ⬇ Worksheet 6.4
5.11 Pick a side	0.5+	Express a viewpoint. Share it with others. Discuss other viewpoints.	Learner's Book Session 5.11 Workbook Session 5.11 ⬇ Language worksheet 5A
5.12 Have a class debate	0.5+	Listen to and analyse a speech. Prepare a persuasive speech. Have a class debate.	Learner's Book Session 5.12 Workbook Session 5.12 ⬇ Worksheet 6.8 ⬇ Worksheet 6.10 ⬇ Worksheet 6.22

Cross-unit resources
Learner's Book Check your progress
Learner's Book Projects
Unit 5 Language worksheets
Mid-point test
End-of-unit 5 test

BACKGROUND KNOWLEDGE

Many learning opportunities and text types can be found on the topic of climate change and the environment, with many viewpoints and personal experiences to be shared. You can use this topic to demonstrate to learners that while facts may be the same, opinions can differ. You can also use the topic to explore balanced and persuasive language techniques.

Begin with a news report that gives information in a rational way yet still aims to persuade the reader with facts and figures. Compare this to a balanced report that presents both sides of an issue in an objective way without aiming to persuade. This is a good way to introduce balanced arguments – where both sides are presented before you can pick a side. Then move on to show how a persuasive speech supports only one side of an argument and, finally, how to argue one side of an argument in a debate.

In this unit, you will take the learners beyond the basic structure of the text to explore the language at a deeper level. In news reports, for example, explain that journalistic commentary can be more or less objective in presenting the facts to the reader.

While your learners are familiar with persuasion texts (since they are exposed to them on a daily basis) you might find introducing balanced text and writing more challenging. It requires learners to think beyond concrete ideas to more abstract ideas as they aim to understand another view or way of seeing something. Look out for learners who struggle with these abstract concepts, particularly some learners who will benefit from the extra support suggested in each lesson.

TEACHING SKILLS FOCUS

Assessment for learning

Assessment is not simply about finding out where the learner is in terms of the benchmark, it is also understanding where the learning is going and how to get there. With this in mind, teachers can be effective in planning lessons and adjusting them to meet the needs of the learners. It is a dynamic, organic process based on ongoing feedback facilitated by the teacher to ensure learners do not get left behind. Feedback is managed in various ways – sometimes formal but often informal observations of learners' written and verbal responses. In this unit, try implementing some of the following ideas to assist the assessment process and promote learning.

- Read, display or write out the learning intentions at the start of each session so learners know exactly what they are aiming at and where they are going before they begin.

- Set baseline questions before you introduce a topic or text. The starter ideas at the beginning of each session aim to check where the learners are with their understanding. This will inform and guide you on how much background knowledge or revision is needed before moving on.

- Use opportunities provided in each session for regular feedback during lessons and at the end of a task. This may be a self- or peer-check, or a teacher check. Use the 'How am I doing?' and 'How are we doing?' questions to help learners assess their understanding and progress.

- The Differentiated worksheet pack helps learners to identify their level of ability then choose and use each level to practise and build their skills.

- For learners who need extra support, use the Vocabulary development and Skills development worksheets to build their skills in these areas before they move on.

- Aim to make feedback a positive part of the lesson that provides constructive ways to improve.

- Monitor self- and peer-assessment. Display some rules for 'How to give feedback' that reminds everyone to be helpful, patient and encouraging so the learners feel confident in moving forward.

5.1 Poles apart

LEARNING PLAN

Learning objectives		Learning intentions	Success criteria
Main focus	**Also covered**	• Discuss and compare information.	• Learners can describe and compare two places.
6Ws.03, 6SLm.03	6Ri.10, 6Ri.12, 6Rv.02, 6Wv.03, 6Wv.05	• Identify facts and opinions.	• Learners can explain the difference between facts and opinions.
		• Use connectives effectively.	• Learners can write sentences using connectives to express comparisons.

LANGUAGE SUPPORT

The names Arctic and Antarctic are a good opportunity to revise word origins, prefixes and root words. Learners will benefit from exploring other words with the prefixes *ant* or *anti* and observe how the meaning is transformed (clockwise – *anti*clockwise).

Connectives do more than simply join sentences or paragraphs. Some have a specific role like comparing things. Comparing and contrasting connectives include: *but, instead of, alternatively, in contrast, whereas, on the other hand, unlike, otherwise, likewise, similarly, equally, as with, in the same way, like.*

Some connectives work in pairs to compare or contrast. When using paired (or correlative) connectives, ensure the verbs agree: Both places *has/have* snow and ice. Neither A nor B *is/are* an option.

Common misconception

Misconception	How to identify	How to overcome
Opinions are based on facts	Write the following sentence starters on the board and invite learners to complete them: *I think … I like … I believe ….* Ask: *Are all these statements based on facts?*	List examples of opinions and do research to find out if they are based on facts, e.g. *I don't like ice because it's hard. I'd love to visit Antarctica but it's too expensive.*
All words that begin with *ant* or *anti* have a root with *ant* or *anti* as the prefix.	Display these words and ask the learners to identify the root word: *antenna, anthem, antic, antibiotic.*	Use dictionaries to explore the meanings of words that begin with *ant* or *anti* and identify those with prefixes.

Starter idea

Facts and opinions (10 minutes)

Resources: Learner's Book, Session 5.1: Getting started; a display of pictures of different places (if possible)

Description: Ask learners to describe their favourite type of climate. Ask: *Do you prefer hot or cold places? Do you enjoy wind or rain? Do you prefer sunny days or cloudy days?* Write the words *fact* and *opinion* on the board. Ask learners to explain the difference. Look out for learners who struggle to recognise the difference between facts and opinions. Session 5.2 will provide further examples and support. As learners discuss, remind them to take turns to speak and to listen actively when others speak.

Main teaching ideas

1 Describe the similarities and differences (10 minutes)

Learning intentions: To use facts, opinions and figurative language to describe and compare two places; to revise prefixes

Resources: Learner's Book, Session 5.1, Activity 1; a display of pictures of different places (if possible)

Description: Learners work in pairs to compare the pictures of the North and South Poles. The pictures provide visual information while learners can add their own facts and opinions. They read the statements about the pictures and say if they are facts or opinions. Discuss which pictures give clues to support these facts. Explore the prefix *ant/anti* and the meaning of Arctic, Antarctic and Antarctica. The word *Arctic* comes from the Greek word *arktos*, meaning 'bear' – referring to the Great Bear constellation. Antarctic has the prefix *ant* (*anti*), meaning 'opposite' or against. So Antarctic means 'opposite to the north'.

Discuss figurative expressions and their impact on the reader. Ask: *Can we use figurative expressions in non-fiction texts?* (yes) *Do they express facts or opinions?* (They can relate to facts or support them; they are used to create an image in the readers' mind.) Consider other possible figurative expressions that relate to the pictures in the Learner's Book or pictures you might have on display.

Spelling link: Some prefixes – like *ant*/*anti* – make words mean the opposite. Explore other prefixes that do this, e.g. *non, dis, in, im, ir, il* and *un.* Use the Spelling spreads at the back of the Learner's Book for extra practice.

> **Differentiation ideas:** Support learners by revising spelling rules for adding prefixes and suffixes to root words. Revise facts and opinions.

Challenge more confident learners by exploring figurative expressions that support facts. Use on-screen tools to research the North and South Poles. Make travel posters for the classroom using facts and figurative language.

> **Assessment ideas:** Observe and listen as learners work together and discuss in groups. Check they know the difference between facts and opinions and can give examples of both relating to the pictures, e.g. *There is snow in both pictures. It looks freezing. I don't like snow.* (fact) (fact) (opinion)

Answers:
1 a Learners identify anything they see in each picture.
  b They are all facts because they can be proved.
  c It is figurative. They are very different, yet they look the same.
  d Accept any reasonable answers such as 'as dry as a bone' or 'as white as snow'.
  e It depends on the purpose of the text. Information texts use mostly facts while creative texts use figurative language however both can be included in information texts.

2 Use connectives to compare and contrast (25 minutes)

Learning intention: To use connectives to link ideas and to use language with increasing clarity and detail

Resources: Learner's Book, Session 5.1, Activity 2

Description: Learners read and discuss the statements in Activity 1b and identify the connective in each sentence. Ask volunteers to explain the specific role of these connectives. (To link ideas, to compare/contrast.) Discuss using other connectives to replace the ones in the statements but keep the meaning the same.

Learners work in pairs then share their ideas with the class. This is good for developing their vocabulary and using language to convey ideas and opinions.

Move on to connectives that work together to link ideas of equal importance. These connectives can also be used to compare and contrast ideas. Demonstrate using the example provided then invite the learners to complete the sentences on their own. Once learners have practised comparing ideas, invite them to write their own sentences.

> **Differentiation ideas:** Encourage less confident learners to write five or more of their own sentences, according to the time available. For more challenge, learners can complete more sentence examples using different connectives to compare and link ideas.

> **Assessment ideas:** Read and assess learners' written answers on connectives using the answers provided. Learners can also check each other's sentences to show how well they can use connectives to describe and compare.

Answers:
2 a • The connectives *and, while whereas, but, however, although* are used to contrast and compare ideas.
    • Yes. Accept any reasonable examples: *One is the Arctic and/while/but/however the other is the Antarctic.*
  b • (whether/or)
    • (both/and or neither/nor)
    • (neither/nor)
    • (either/or)
    • (Not only/but also)
  c Learners' own sentences using facts, opinions, figurative language and connectives.

Plenary idea

Peer check (5 minutes)

Resources: Learners' answers and own sentences

Description: Learners swap and mark each other's work using the answers provided. They read their own sentences aloud to each other.

> **Assessment ideas:** Learners offer ways to improve and then do corrections.

Homework ideas

Learners complete the Workbook activities for Session 5.1. Additionally, they could source non-fiction books or magazines (about the environment) and bring them to school to share.

Answers for Workbook

1   Accept any reasonable answers. For example:

   a   but

   b   whereas

   c   Although

   d   while

   e   however

   f   on the other hand

2   Learners' own ideas.

3   Learners' own paragraphs.

5.2 A news report

LEARNING PLAN

Learning objectives		Learning intentions	Success criteria
Main focus	**Also covered**	• Explore a news report. • Identify the purpose, audience, language and layout. • Recognise how ideas are organised and linked in a text.	• Learners can answer questions to explain a report. • Learners can describe the purpose, audience, language and layout of a report. • Learners can identify how information is organised and linked.
6Rs.02, 6Ri.05, 6Ri.07	6Ri.06, 6Wp.02, 6SLm.03, 6SLp.01		

LANGUAGE SUPPORT

A news report is a type of persuasive text because it is generally one-sided. Journalist commentary is usually persuasive, aiming to impact the reader and express a specific viewpoint. A news report may be more or less objective, depending on the purpose. This nuance might be tricky for the learners to grasp, especially for some learners who need concrete rules and guidelines to support their reading and writing skills.

The report talks about climate change using Celsius (C). For temperature in Fahrenheit (F), you can use these figures: $2°C = 3.6°F$, $1.5°C = 2.7°F$, $1°C = 1.8°F$, $0.5°C = 0.9°F$

The report in this unit is taken from the NewsForKids website. Sites like this are helpful because news is presented in a way that is accessible and interesting, and has background and contextual references.

Common misconception

Misconception	How to identify	How to overcome
All headlines are persuasive	Write the headline on the board: *Report Gives Strong Climate Change Warning.* Ask: *Is this headline mainly informative or persuasive?* (Mainly informative.) *Can a headline be both?* (Yes.)	Find examples of other headlines. Display them and, together, analyse them to decide if they are more or less persuasive.

Starter idea

What do you know about climate change? (5 minutes)

Resources: Learner's Book, Session 5.2: Getting started

Description: Discuss the purpose of news reports. Ask: Do they report facts only? What viewpoint do they give? Are they persuasive? Learners then work in pairs to describe climate change in their own words. They share answers with the class and discuss. Remind learners to take turns to speak and listen patiently when others give their views.

Invite them to provide facts and opinions on the topic. Find out if and how they have been personally affected by climate change and share experiences.

Main teaching ideas

1 Explore the contents of a news report (20 minutes)

Learning intention: To understand, explore and summarise explicit meanings in a text

Resources: *Report Gives Strong Climate Change Warning* (Learner's Book, Session 5.2, Activity 1); Track 25; Worksheets 6.3 and 6.4

Description: Invite learners to skim the text titled 'Report Gives Strong Climate Change Warning' to get a general idea of what type of text it is and what it is about. (It is actually a news report about a report on climate change.) Remind learners that a paragraph deals with one idea or topic. It usually has a topic sentence and supporting details. Connectives link ideas and help paragraphs to flow from each other.

Use Worksheet 6.3 Reading strategies to recall useful reading strategies. Read the report in detail. Identify and discuss unfamiliar words. Use them in other sentences.

Read (and explain if necessary) the first four questions before the learners answer the questions independently in their books.

Learners use mind maps or other forms of note-taking to summarise the information. Their summary should reflect how the information is organised and linked. This is good for practising note-taking skills in all other subjects.

Complete the Workbook activities if there is time in class.

Learners add this text to Worksheet 6.4 Features of fiction and non-fiction texts listing the features of this text type. They can also include this example in their learning journals.

Spelling link: Remind learners that *affect* is usually a verb and *effect* is usually a noun. These words sound similar but are used differently – e.g. *How does it affect you?* and *What is the effect of climate change?* (However, *effect* can be used as a verb – e.g. *to effect change.*)

> **Differentiation ideas:** For extra support, learners could practise summarising using notes in other subjects. Challenge more confident learners by exploring the topic further. Research climate change. Choose an aspect and create a digital presentation or poster to tell people about climate change.

> **Assessment ideas:** Check learners' mind maps. Assess how well they can organise information and summarise explicit meaning drawn from more than one point in a text.

Answers:

1   a   Any reasonable answers based on the text.
        Example answers:
        • Human activity creates air pollution
          which affects the air temperature around
          the Earth.
        • Five effects: melting ice in the Polar
          regions, heat waves, dry periods/
          drought, wildfires, record rains, strong
          hurricanes …
        • Governments could replace fossil fuel
          energy with solar, wind and water power,
          reduce travel, plant more trees …
        • Ordinary citizens can eat less meat,
          reduce travel, use less electricity, reuse
          and recycle.
     b   Learners' own notes.

2 Discuss the purpose, audience, language and layout of the news report (20 minutes)

Learning intention: To identify, discuss and compare the purposes and key features of different non-fiction text types

Resources: Learner's Book, Session 5.2, Activity 2; *Report Gives Strong Climate Change Warning* (Learner's Book, Session 5.2); Track 25; Worksheet 6.10

Description: Write the words *purpose*, *audience*, *language*, *layout* on the board. Invite learners to explain what they mean and how they link and relate to any text. Then ask learners learners to analyse the text. (Track 25 supports this.) They should check the date (October 2018), the details about who wrote the article (NewsForKids) and where it appeared (on the internet). Ask: *Is it still relevant?* (Yes.) *Who is it for?* (Kids/children/ learners.) *What is the purpose of a news site for kids?* (To tell real news in a way that is appropriate and interesting to kids.)

Consider how the text is set out and the language used. Discuss register and style – how formal or informal a text sounds and why some texts are more formal than others. Ask: *Would the text have the same effect/impact if it used slang or informal language? Is the layout appealing?*

Invite learners to skim the text for facts and opinions. They will notice there are only facts.

Skim for figurative language. Ask: *Why are there no opinions or figurative language?* (It is a formal, factual news report, so personal opinions and creative language are not included.) Highlight examples where the writer has avoided personal expressions, e.g. *Climate change is such a big problem* … Ask: *What other more expressive ways are there to say this?* Discuss how this article uses facts and information to support and promote a specific view.

Learners take turns to read aloud, using appropriate expression, tone and style. This is good for practising basic reading skills and developing confidence.

Complete the Workbook activities for Session 5.2 if there is time in class.

> **Differentiation ideas:** Support learners by encouraging small groups choose a local news report, and help them to rewrite it 'for kids'.

Encourage more confident learners to start a 'news for kids' newspaper in your class. Supervise learners as they use the NewsForKids website for ideas.

> **Assessment ideas:** Invite learners to read aloud. Assess clarity, confidence, expression and tone. You can use Worksheet 6.10 Reading, speaking or performing assessment sheet to guide you.

Answers:

2   a   The news report aims to inform the public
        about details of a report on climate change.
        The news report is aimed at young people.
        (The actual report on climate change is
        aimed at governments and the public.)
     b   formal, factual, direct, rational, informative
        also convincing and persuasive.
     c   Layout features include: a headline,
        paragraphs, introduction, diagrams, web
        page information with bold used for
        emphasis … The layout is formal, organised
        with short paragraphs for easy reading. The
        layout fits the purpose of delivering news
        and information to young readers.
     d   Facts only, no figurative language because
        its purpose is to inform, not to be creative.
     e   Formal expression and clear.
     f   Learners add the text to their learning
        journal (Worksheet 6.1).

Plenary idea

Read aloud – be formal (5 minutes)

Description: Invite learners to read a news report aloud. They can use the text in the Learner's Book or another one they find. Reflect on expression and style. Remind learners to use similar expression to a news broadcast. Discuss how it will sound (formal/serious).

> **Assessment ideas:** Learners listen to each other reading and offer ways to improve. Peers can use a 1–5 rating scale to assess different aspects of reading aloud: volume, pace, expression, confidence, expression. Learners respond to the 'How am I doing?' questions in this session.

CROSS-CURRICULAR LINKS

Geography, Current Affairs and PSHE: Explore climate change issues in along with responsible habits and things everyone can change to make a difference.

Homework ideas

Learners complete the Workbook activities for Session 5.2 to practise analysing other news reports. They make a poster on 'What you can do' (as a family/community) to display at home. They could also research climate change, then prepare a speech and present it in class or in assembly.

Answers for Workbook

1–4 Learners' own work

5.3 Support a view

LEARNING PLAN

Learning objectives		Learning intentions	Success criteria
Main focus	**Also covered**	• Explore a scientific explanation.	• Learners can explore and order an explanation.
6SLm.02	6Ri.04, 6Ri.05, 6Ri.06, 6Ri.07, 6Ri.12, 6Wp.02, 6Wc.06, 6SLm.03, 6SLg.02, 6SLg.03, 6SLg.04	• Distinguish between facts and opinions. • Extend a discussion.	• Learners know the difference between facts and opinions. • Learners can extend a discussion by building on their own and others' ideas.

LANGUAGE SUPPORT

Learners use facts from a scientific explanation to support a viewpoint. The scientific explanation on climate change is different to the news report on climate change in Session 5.2. It differs in purpose and layout. However, it is the type of information that could be included a report. Explanation texts are often factual, chronological, formal, precise and written in sections that flow together.

Common misconception

Misconception	How to identify	How to overcome
You do not need facts to support a viewpoint.	Write the following on the board: *Climate change is a hoax.* Ask: *Is this statement complete without facts? Do you need facts to support it?*	Discuss the reasons why a viewpoint should be based on facts.

Starter idea

Share ideas (5 minutes)

Resources: Learner's Book, Session 5.3: Getting started

Description: Learners work in small groups to explain the science of climate change. This will give you a good idea of where their understanding lies before they read the scientific explanation text. Each group lists facts to support what they think. Share ideas with the class. Ask: *Was this difficult to do? Why?* Discuss why it is important to be able to back up a view with facts.

Main teaching ideas

1 Read a scientific explanation and discuss the facts (20 minutes)

Learning intention: To explore non-fiction texts and summarise explicit meanings drawn from more than one point in a text

Resources: Learner's Book, Session 5.3, Activity 1; Workbook, Session 5.3

Description: Learners read the text silently. Then, in pairs, they check the order. Together, they read the text aloud together in the correct order. Discuss the importance of getting the order right. Ask: *What would help to show the correct sequence?* (Different layout, numbers or letters.) Learners retell the information to their partners to check their understanding. Using facts from the text and their own opinions on the topic, learners discuss the questions in the Learner's Book. Walk around as they discuss to hear their responses. Have a class feedback session to share ideas.

Invite learners to summarise the information and add it to their notes from the previous session. They should choose a format that helps to show the sequence. This is good to help learners to decide when it is helpful to take notes, how to record them and decide if the order is important.

Complete the Workbook activities for Session 5.3 if there is time in class.

> **Differentiation ideas:** Support learners by encouraging them to practise making notes in other subjects using key words. Working with them, sequence another process such as the water cycle or steps in a recipe.

Challenge more confident learners by asking them to compare the purpose and structure of chronological and non-chronological text types (e.g. posters).

> **Assessment ideas:** Check learners' understanding and spelling of vocabulary from the text.

Answers:

1   a   The correct order for the information is:
- Carbon dioxide (CO_2) is part of the atmosphere. Some CO_2 is created naturally but some comes from fumes of cars, aeroplanes and the generation of electricity.
- As CO_2 collects in the atmosphere it acts like a blanket over the Earth: heat cannot escape and so the Earth heats up.
- Excess heat is absorbed by the ocean and distributed. This helps regulate the temperature.
- The extra heat causes the water temperature to rise. The warmer waters melt the ice in the Polar regions, raising sea levels.

   b–d   Learners' own work.

2 Extend a discussion by considering both sides (20 minutes)

Learning intention: To show consideration of another point of view and extend a discussion by building on own and others' ideas

Resources: Learner's Book, Session 5.3, Activity 2

Description: Write the following on the board: *Agree to disagree*. Find out how learners feel when someone disagrees with them. Ask: Do *you get upset? Do you take it personally? Do you want them to agree? Do you try to force them to change to your way of thinking?*

Learners read the statements in Activity 2 and write their own responses to say why they agree and disagree. This helps learners see that there are both sides to any issue.

Once they have written their responses, they should work in small groups to have a discussion and share their ideas. They won't agree on everything. This teaches them to agree to disagree. Remind learners to encourage each other to take turns to speak and to listen to others, even if they disagree.

Use the Speaking tip to remind learners to structure what they say to make it easier for others to follow.

> **Differentiation ideas:** Support learners by listening, as a class, to a debate on climate change or watch a documentary. These can be easily sourced online. Challenge more confident learners by asking them to independently research an individual or group doing positive things towards helping the environment. They could make a poster or presentation.

> **Assessment ideas:** Listen as learners organise the text to assess their ability to order information and summarise it. Assess their ability to hold a discussion by taking turns to speak, showing consideration for another view and building on their own and others' ideas.

Answers:

3   Learners' own work and discussion.

Plenary idea

Group report back (5 minutes)

Description: Invite groups to summarise (for the class) the main points of their discussion, and to note which points everyone agreed on and those they disagreed on.

Invite learners to reflect on areas that caused disagreement. Ask: *Did you disagree over the facts or the opinions?*

> **Assessment ideas:** Learners listen to each group's report back and decide which groups communicated well. Share ideas on ways to improve communication.

CROSS-CURRICULAR LINKS

History: Find out about events or people in history that have made an impact to the topic of climate change.

Homework ideas

Complete the Workbook activities for Session 5.3, if not completed in class. Learners could also read more on the topic. They can each choose something they would like to change or do differently to help climate change and keep a diary to record their efforts.

Answers for Workbook

1   Learners' own rules.

2   A fact can be proved; an opinion is what someone thinks or believes.

3   Example answers
   a   Animal habitats are destroyed by climate change.
   b   Deforestation is destroying all our forests.
   c   Climate change affects everyone.
   d   Animals suffer due to human activity.
   e   The Earth is being destroyed.

4   Learners' own opinions.

5.4 Express possibility

LEARNING PLAN

Learning objectives		Learning intentions	Success criteria
Main focus	**Also covered**	• Explain the difference between a phrase and a clause.	• Learners can explain the difference between a phrase and clause.
6SLm.03	6Rg.02, 6Wg.03, 6Wg.04	• Revise complex sentences.	• Learners can identify the main clause in a complex sentence.
		• Use conditional clauses to express possibility.	• Learners can construct sentences expressing possibility.

LANGUAGE SUPPORT

A phrase is a group of words acting together without a finite verb. It doesn't make sense on its own. A clause is a group of words acting together with a finite verb. It can be a full sentence and makes sense on its own.

A simple sentence has one clause. A compound sentences has more than one independent or main clause of equal importance. The clauses are joined by a coordinating conjunction (*for, and, nor, but, or, yet, so*).

A complex sentence has one main (or independent) clause plus one or more subordinate (dependent) clauses.

A conditional clause is a subordinate (dependent) clause. It expresses the likelihood of something happening, depending on whether or not a particular condition is met. The word *if* is commonly used.

Common misconception

Misconception	How to identify	How to overcome
A conditional clause can also be a main clause.	Write sentences on the board and break them up to show two clauses: *The flowers will grow / if it rains.* Ask: *Which clause can stand on its own? Can the conditional clause (if clause) stand on its own?* (No.)	Provide further examples. Learners complete Activities 3 and 4 in the Workbook.

Starter idea

What do you know? (5 minutes)

Resources: Learner's Book, Session 5.4: Getting started; dictionaries

Description: Give learners the chance to share what they know about phrases and clauses and simple, compound and complex sentences. Look out for incorrect answers. Clear up any misconceptions.

Write the words *subordinate*, *dependent* and *conditional* on the board. Ask: *What do these words have in common? How is this type of clause different to a main clause?* Look out for any learners who struggle to keep up with revising these concepts. Make time to recap and explain the information again.

Main teaching ideas

1 Identify the main clause (20 minutes)

Learning intention: To understand a complex sentence and identify the main clause and other clauses

Resources: Learner's Book, Session 5.1, Activity 1; Workbook, Session 5.4, Activities 3 and 4

Description: Read the sentences together and decide if they are simple or complex sentences. Ask learners how they would create simple sentences from them. (Use only the main clause.)

Ask learners to give their own examples of complex sentences with a main clause. Learners work in pairs to practise – one gives the main clause and the other adds another clause.

Learners work independently to write out each sentence in their books and underline the main clause. Share answers.

> **Differentiation ideas:** For support, supervise learners in groups as they complete the Workbook activities to revise sentence structure.

Challenge more confident learners to use their readers to find other examples of complex sentences then write their own complex sentences.

> **Assessment ideas:** Listen as learners express their understanding of the language terms *phrase* and *clause*; *simple*, *compound* and *complex* sentences. Look out for learners who do not understand the difference and provide extra support before continuing with the lesson. Check that learners can identify the main clause in the sentences provided.

Answers:
1 a   They are all complex sentences because they have at least one subordinate clause.
   b   The main clause in each sentence:
   • If the temperature goes up 1°C instead of just 0.5°C, <u>things will get worse</u>.
   • <u>The world will reach this temperature in about 12 years</u> unless all countries work together.
   • In order to reach the goal, <u>the world must move to energy that does not give off CO$_2$</u>.

   • While the big decisions are made by governments, <u>ordinary citizens can make a difference</u>.
   • <u>Ice in the Polar Regions melts</u> when water temperatures rise.

2 Use conditional clauses to express possibility (20 minutes)

Resources: Learner's Book, Session 5.4, Activity 2

Learning intentions: To introduce the *if* clause; to use punctuation effectively to clarify meaning in complex sentences

Description: Write the following sentences on the board: *If you make a mistake, you can redo your work. You can read a book if you finish your work quickly.* Ask: *How can you tell these are complex sentences?* (They have more than one clause.) *Can you swap the order of the sentences?* (yes) *What common connective do they have?* (if) *Do you notice any differences in punctuation?* (There is a comma after the conditional *if* clause when it begins the sentence.)

Read the Language focus box together and use further examples to clarify and explain.

Learners complete the written activities individually. Assess their progress by checking their answers. Offer support and further examples if necessary. Complete the Workbook activities in class if there is time.

> **Differentiation ideas:** With supervision, learners practise writing conditional sentences using if clauses. Learners could complete the Workbook activities for Session 5.4 independently for greater challenge.

Answers:
2 a   Accept any reasonable answers. For example:
   • If everyone uses less fuel, there will be less air pollution.
   • When ice in the Polar Regions melts, sea levels rise.
   • In order to reduce car fumes, we must use public transport.
   • As long as factories pollute the air, the Earth will heat up.
   • If all the plankton in the sea dies, sea life will die.

b Example answers:
• There will be less air pollution if everyone uses less fuel.
• Sea levels rise when ice in the Polar Regions melts.
• We must use public transport in order to reduce car fumes.
• The Earth will heat up as long as factories pollute the air.
• Sea life will die if all the plankton in the sea dies.

Plenary idea

Teach it – practise it (5 minutes)

Description: In pairs or small groups, learners teach each other the concepts learnt in this session. They can use the information in the Language focus box and their example sentences. Invite learners to reflect on how helpful this is. Ask: *How did you enjoy teaching others? Did you learn anything new? Did it help you to understand the concepts better? Did you find anything confusing?*

> **Assessment ideas:** Learners rate each other based on how well the information was communicated. Invite them to use a rating of 0–5 or symbols like 'happy face' or 'confused face'. They also review the 'How am I doing?' questions at the end of the session.

Homework ideas

Learners use readers, magazines or newspapers to read and identify complex sentences and conditional sentences with conditional clauses. Invite them to look out for cause and effect examples at home and write their own conditional sentences.

Answers for Workbook

1   a   A simple sentence: A basic sentence with one independent (or main) clause.

    b   A compound sentence: A sentence that has at least two independent (or main) clauses that have related ideas. The independent clauses are joined by a coordinating conjunction (*for, and, nor, but, or, yet, so*).

    c   A complex sentence: A sentence that has an independent (or main) clause and at least one dependent (or subordinate) clause. In a complex sentence, the independent clause shares the main information, and the dependent clause(s) provide details.

    d   A main clause: A clause that can stand alone as a sentence, containing a subject and a finite verb.

    e   A subordinate (dependent) clause, also called a subordinate clause or conditional clause. A clause, usually introduced by a connective, that forms part of and is dependent on a main clause.

2   a   Complex.
    b   Simple / Compound.
    c   Complex.
    d   Simple.
    e   Compound.

3   a   If it stops raining, the match will resume.
    b   You can go out to play unless it rains.
    c   When it snows, it will be cold.
    d   As long as you take an umbrella, you can go outside.
    e   We can go on holiday, provided you are well.
    f   If they all take their jackets, they will be warm.

4   Learners' own sentences.

5.5 Keep it formal

LEARNING PLAN

Learning objectives		Learning intentions	Success criteria
Main focus	**Also covered**	• Identify formal, standard English.	• Learners can change sentences to be more formal.
6Wg.05, 6Wg.08, 6SLm.03	6Rv.04, 6Rg.03, 6Rg.05	• Use pronouns for effect.	• Learners can change sentences from personal to impersonal.
		• Use the active or passive voice for effect.	• Learners can identify and use active and passive voice for effect.

LANGUAGE SUPPORT

Standard English is the uniform, established and widely accepted form of English spoken, written and understood by home-language speakers. It is associated with formal schooling and official texts and publications. Standard English is a formal version of the English language excluding local colloquialisms and jargon.

Pronouns can be replaced by articles (*a*, *an*, *the*) to make a text or speech sound more formal. *Her car uses a lot of fuel* can be replaced by

The car uses a lot of fuel to sound less personal.

A sentence can have the same meaning but a different voice. The active voice is used more in standard English. It is more direct, clear and shorter, so you can get your point across more easily. The passive voice is indirect and uses more words. It also changes the focus of the sentence. However, the passive voice is useful for making general statements, especially where the agent (or doer) is unimportant.

Common misconception

Misconception	How to identify	How to overcome
The active voice is better than the passive voice.	Write the following examples on the board and compare them: *The girl wrote an excellent essay.* *An excellent essay was written by the girl.* Ask: *One is better than the other.* (No – the voice depends on the purpose of the sentence and the focus of the sentence – the girl or the essay.)	Find examples of the active and passive voice in various texts. Complete Activity 4 in the Workbook.

Starter idea

What is standard English? (5 minutes)

Resources: Learner's Book, Session 5.5: Getting started

Description: Learners discuss what standard English means to them. Remind them that standard English is a uniform accepted form of English. It is especially used in formal texts and speech in order to avoid colloquial expressions, contractions and personal pronouns.

Discuss the reasons for having a standard that is uniform and useful.

Learners give examples of the kinds of informal language they use. Discuss what makes language informal and what makes it formal. Ask: *Why do we need to learn to use formal language?*

Main teaching ideas

1 Explore standard English used in formal texts (20 minutes)

Learning intentions: To identify word classes; to use the conventions of standard English appropriately in writing

Resources: Learner's Book, Session 5.5, Activity 1; Workbook, Session 5.5

Description: Ensure all learners can identify pronouns as a word class and understand their purpose. Also revise articles – *a*, *an*, *the*.

Learners write sentences in their books. Afterwards, in groups, they share their answers and discuss how the style changes when the pronouns are removed.

Complete the Workbook activities for Session 5.5 if there is time in class.

> **Differentiation ideas:** Support learners by revising, as a class, the different types of pronouns (e.g. personal, possessive, reflexive, demonstrative, relative), and check learners' understanding.

Indepdendently, more confident learners could revise informal language techniques such as contractions and colloquialisms. Ask learners to rewrite sentences like these to remove the contractions: *It's become a problem that they'll have to solve; If you're concerned about what's happening, you'll need to get involved; It'll take time to improve the situation but that's to be expected.*

> **Assessment ideas:** Use the answers provided to assess their written work and their understanding

and language skills. Assess their understanding of standard English: Ask yourself: *Do learners understand what it means to use standard English? Can they change sentences to be more formal?*

Answers:

1 a Accept any of the following: *the planet, a/ the report, a/the idea, the/an investigation, the/a local transport system*

   b Learners' own sentences.

2 Use active and passive forms for effect (20 minutes)

Learning intentions: To show awareness of the impact of a writer's choice of sentence structure; to use active and passive verb forms within sentences

Resources: Learner's Book, Session 5.5, Activity 2; Workbook, Session 5.5

Description: Read together the Language focus box. Discuss the content and explain further using other examples. Check the learners' understanding by asking questions and provide further support if necessary, particularly for learners who may not have grasped the sentence construction.

Ask: *In the passive voice, why is the 'doer' sometimes hidden?* (To make a general statement, imply something or leave various options open for consideration.)

Read the task and use the example provided to remind learners to identify the verb and the tense before attempting to change the voice. To keep the tense, the verb may change. Passive verbs are formed using the verb *to be* (*be, being, been, am, is, are, was* and *were*). Do examples together then allow the learners to complete the activity on their own.

Learners write their own sentences to demonstrate their ability to change from the active to passive voice.

Complete the Workbook activities for Session 5.5 if not already done alongside Activity 1.

> **Differentiation ideas:** Organise group or paired work to help learners needing extra support.

Challenge learners by encouraging them to practise the passive voice, using a different agent each time showing different degrees of generalisation, e.g. *The situation can be improved; The situation can be improved by concerned citizens; The situation can be improved by anyone who would like to get involved.* Learners write the following sentence three times with a different agent each time: *Less electricity must be used.*

〉 **Assessment ideas:** Assess learners' understanding of active and passive forms: Can they write sentences in the active or passive voice to create a different effect? Can learners explain the difference between active and passive voice? Can they identify the action and agent – even if the agent is hidden?

Answers:
2   a   active, active, active, active, passive
     b   •   The reporter reads the news.
         •   Scientists wrote the report.
         •   He printed the entire booklet.
         •   The teacher answered the students' questions.
         •   The report will be read by many.
     c   •   The news is read by the reporter.
         •   The report was written by scientists.
         •   The entire booklet was printed by him.
         •   The students' questions were answered by the teacher.
         •   Many will read the report.
     d   Learners' own sentences.

Plenary idea

Check your answers (5 minutes)

Description: Learners swap books and mark each other's work. Provide the answers. Invite learners to reflect on their errors and to make corrections.

〉 **Assessment ideas:** Learners give each other a mark to show how many they got right. Allow time for them to do corrections. Review the 'How am I doing?' questions at the end of the session.

Homework ideas

Learners use their readers to find examples of active and passive forms. They practise using standard English at home and complete the Workbook activities for Session 5.5 if not completed in class.

Answers for Workbook

1   usual, standard, informal, impersonal, first, should not

2   a   the report   b   the planet
     c   a/the teacher/an
     d   the environment   e   a/the solution, a bicycle.

3   I am, I have, I had, I will, we are, we have, we would, we will, they are, they have, they had/would, they will, have not, must not, could not, would not, cannot, will not, do not, would have, should have.

4   a   [Active] Responsibility must be taken by individuals.
     b   [Passive] Everyone must complete the homework on climate change.
     c   [Active] A survey will be conducted by the learners.
     d   [Passive] You must implement a plan.
     e   [Active] The area must be cleaned up by the council before it becomes a problem.
     f   [Passive] The class must complete the report.

5.6 A balanced report

LEARNING PLAN

Learning objectives		Learning intentions	Success criteria
Main focus	**Also covered**	• Read and analyse a balanced report.	• Learners can read and analyse a balanced report.
6Ri.06, 6Ri.07, 6Ri.13, 6Ri.14, 6Wp.02	6Rs.02, 6Rs.03, 6Ri.04, 6Ri.05, 6SLp.01	• Explore and discuss meaning in a text.	• Learners can discuss meaning in a text.
		• Identify the language and layout features of a text.	• Learners can identify the features of a balanced report.

LANGUAGE SUPPORT

A balanced report or argument provides a balanced view of an issue, usually in a formal format. It presents two sides, gives pros and cons, and raises points for and against the topic. There should be an introduction, paragraphs for each point and a conclusion. In the conclusion, a balanced report may leave readers to decide for themselves; alternatively, a balanced argument might choose a side based on the evidence provided.

Starter idea

Explore vocabulary (5 minutes)

Resources: Learner's Book, Session 5.6: Getting started; dictionaries and thesauruses

Description: Write the words *balanced* and *objective* on the board. Learners use dictionaries to look up definitions for the words. Use thesauruses to find synonyms. Write some examples on the board.

Discuss the different meanings. Invite learners to make up sentences using these words in context.

Explore the difference between a 'balanced report' (a report that gives factual information about a topic) and a 'balanced argument' (an argument gives opinions, sometimes based on facts).

Main teaching ideas

1 Read and analyse the information of a balanced report (20 minutes)

Learning intentions: To read and explore non-fiction text types; to summarise explicit meanings drawn from more than one point in a text

Resources: *Is it time to ban cars from city centres?* (Learner's Book, Session 5.6, Activity 1); Track 26

Description: Write the statement *What do you think?* on the board. Remind learners that a balanced report gives the facts and different opinions on a topic so the reader can decide how they feel about something.

In small groups, learners read the text 'Is it time to ban cars from the city centres?' (Track 26). They discuss the questions and share ideas. Have a class report back to find out their views on the issue.

Discuss the value of note-taking (to clarify meaning and organise ideas) and when and how it is helpful to take notes. Invite learners to practise using the format they prefer.

Individually, learners summarise the information in a way that shows both points of view. Learners must choose how to take notes to show the two sides of the argument. They can use a table with two columns, or a Venn diagram or any other suitable format they prefer.

This is good groundwork for the later sessions when learners will take a side in a debate.

> Differentiation ideas: Discuss the issue in supported groups. Have groups speaking 'for' and 'against' the idea to ban cars.

Challenge learners by asking them to present a speech on how to stop air pollution. Find other texts on the issue of air pollution and share them with the class.

> **Assessment ideas:** Check learners can summarise and make notes using key words. Assess how well they can analyse the text. Ask: *Can you identify the features? Can you describe the purpose, audience, language and layout of the text?*

Answers:
1 a • air pollution, everyone
       • people will use their cars less/people will rely more on public transport/less traffic will reduce emissions
       • cities will have to upgrade public transport including safety, make it affordable and reliable…
       • Learners' own views.
   b Learners' own summary using key words.

---

2   Explore the features of a balanced report (20 minutes)

Learning intentions: To identify, discuss and compare the purposes and features of non-fiction text types; to read aloud with accuracy and increasing confidence and style

Resources: Learner's Book, Session 5.6, Activity 2; *Is it time to ban cars from city centres?* (Learner's Book, Session 5.6); Track 26; Workbook, Session 5.6; Worksheets 6.1 and 6.4

Play the audio of the text (Track 26) for the learners to hear the tone and formal expression used.

Description: In their groups, learners practise reading aloud, using appropriate expression, style and tone. They discuss the structure, language and features of the text. Invite them to compare the text to the news report text in Session 5.2, Activity 1. Ask: *What is similar and what is different? Which one is more balanced? Does the balanced report have a different impact? How is the purpose of each one different?* This is good for comparing audience, purpose, language and layout.

Learners list the features they notice like – e.g. *It has a heading and sections, the introduction states the issue, each point is supported with reasons/facts evidence, paragraphs link and flow together with connectives, the conclusion summarises both sides, the language is formal and it uses standard English.*

Learners add this text to their learning journals (Worksheet 6.1) and list some of the features. They can also add this text to Worksheet 6.4 Features of fiction and non-fiction texts. Complete the Workbook activities for Session 5.6 if there is time in class.

> **Differentiation ideas:** In groups, encourage learners to practise comparing texts in terms of purpose, audience, language and layout.

For challenge, ask learners to work in pairs to make a list of other important issues that need attention. They should list points for and against them.

> **Assessment ideas:** Use the text to assess learners' reading aloud. Check for volume, pace, expression and confidence. Assess their reading comprehension using the answers provided.

Answers:
2 a Learners read aloud.
   b Purpose: To provide information and opposing opinions on a current topic. Audience: As many people as possible. Language: Formal and objective. Layout: A heading, linking paragraphs, introduction and conclusion.
   c A balanced report aims to present both sides of a topic and allow the reader to choose a side; a news report aims to inform about an event – usually from one perspective so it can be persuasive.
   d Learners add to their learning journals.

Plenary ideas

Check the features (5 minutes)

Description: Learners share their answers with each other and give examples from the text of the features listed in their checklist.

> **Assessment ideas:** Learners review the 'How are we doing?' questions at the end of the session and rate their performance and confidence in each area.

Homework ideas

Learners look out for examples of balanced texts beyond the classroom – in magazines, newspapers or posters they see on their way to school. This will help them become aware of balanced versus persuasive texts.

Answers for Workbook

1   Any reasonable features such as: heading, introduction, conclusion, points for and against, formal standard English, impersonal language …

2   Example answers:

   a   Action may be needed to reduce air pollution created by the traffic on our roads.

   b   Two sides. Cars should be banned from city centres. Cars should not be banned from city centres.

   c   • ban: forbid, prohibit

      • significant: notable, noteworthy, key

   • emissions: discharge, production or outflow (of gas or radiation fumes)

   • mode: way or manner

   d   Learners' own answers supported with reasons. For example: It is relevant to those with cars or who travel to cities because they will have to change the way they travel. It is relevant to governments and leaders because they must make the rules. It is relevant to everyone because we all live with the effects of air pollution.

   e   Learners' own answers.

3   Learners summarise using key words and headings.

5.7 Language techniques

LEARNING PLAN			
Learning objectives		**Learning intentions**	**Success criteria**
Main focus	**Also covered**	• Explore the use of connectives and verb forms in balanced views. • Use modal verbs. • Understand the link between the purpose and language of a text.	• Learners can identify and use connectives. • Learners can use modal verbs for effect. • Learners can link the purpose and language of a text.
6Wg.08, 6Ws.03	6Rg.08, 6Rs.03		

LANGUAGE SUPPORT	
Connectives do different jobs. Connectives are used to link sentences and paragraphs clearly and smoothly but also to introduce opposite ideas or points in a balanced report or argument, emphasise a point or link similar views. The connectives *if, when, as long as, unless, provided/providing* are often included in conditional sentences to indicate possibility.	Modal verbs also indicate possibility – modals are covered in year 5. Revise modals of possibility (*can, could, will, would, may, might, should*) and some rules: Modal verbs are helping verbs that do not have a tense of their own but are used with other verbs to form the tense. For example: *She would/could/might/may have finished the report if she had/was given/had been given more time.* *When you press the pedal, the car will/should/ could go faster.*

Common misconception

Misconception	How to identify	How to overcome
Conditional sentences always use *if* clauses.	Display and compare the following examples: **If** you are ready, we *can/could/should* chat. **When** you are ready, we *can/could/should* chat.	Use examples to show learners different ways to write conditional sentences. Complete the Workbook activities.

Starter idea

Make the link (5 minutes)

Resources: Learner's Book, Session 5.7: Getting started; *Is it time to ban cars from city centres?* (Learner's Book, Session 5.6); Track 26

Description: Write the word *connective* on the board. Ask*: What is the base word?* (connect) *What does it tell you about the purpose of these words?* (they link/connect sentences/paragraphs/ideas)

Learners work with a partner. They skim the text 'Is it time to ban cars from city centres?' from Session 5.6, Activity 1 and find examples of connectives. Together, share and compare answers.

Discuss the different ways to use connectives in a text – particularly a formal text like this one. Accept various answers such as: *connectives show the order*, *start a paragraph, link ideas, create flow* and so on.

Look out for learners struggling to identify connectives. Provide further support as needed.

Main teaching ideas

1 Use connectives to combine or connect ideas for effect and clarity (20 minutes)

Learning intention: To use a range of connectives to link paragraphs and sections clearly and cohesively and to explore and recognise how ideas are organised and linked cohesively across a text

Resources: Learner's Book, Session 5.7, Activity 1; *Is it time to ban cars from city centres?* (Learner's Book, Session 5.6); Track 26

Description: Write the following tip on the board: *We use connectives to link sentences and paragraphs. We also use connectives to introduce new ideas or link points in a balanced report or argument.*

Together, start a list of possible connectives. Invite learners to add to the list when they come across other examples of useful connectives.

Using the text 'Is it time to ban cars from city centres?', learners work together to find specific examples of connectives that perform certain functions like presenting a balanced view. Share and discuss ideas and answers.

Individually, learners rewrite the sentences using appropriate connectives. Remind them that there may be more than one appropriate connective for some sentences.

> **Differentiation ideas:** Support less confident learners by allowing them to work in pairs, to practise using connectives to link simple sentences. Challenge learners to make a poster that explains the purpose of various connectives used in non-fiction texts.

> **Assessment ideas:** Check the learners can identify and use connectives in a text in various ways – not simply joining sentences but to make a point or show opposing points.

Answers:
1 a • On the other hand,
  • in addition/furthermore,
  • for example,
  • therefore/hence,
  • Over the past few decades/on the other hand/while
  b Accept any correct/reasonable answers. Some can have more than one. For example:
  • Some believe cars are essential *however/although/on the other hand/*while others say they are a luxury.
  • Electricity is essential *therefore* everyone should have it.

- Children can be part of the solution *although/however/since/while* they are young.
  c Learners' own sentences.

---

2 Practise using modal verbs (20 minutes)

Learning intention: To explore and discuss grammatical features in a range of texts and use the conventions of standard English appropriately in writing, e.g. verb forms

Resources: Learner's Book, Session 5.7, Activity 2; *Is it time to ban cars from city centres?* (Learner's Book, Session 5.6); Track 26

Description: Ask learners to identify the main tense in the text 'Is it time to ban cars from city centres?' (It is mainly present tense, with some past and future tense.) As a class, discuss the purpose of the different tenses in the balanced report and give examples. Learners work together to identify specific sentences in the past, present and future tense.

Review conditional sentences (see the Writing tip in Session 5.6, Activity 1) and identify the modal verbs used to express possibility. Invite learners to give their own examples using: *may, might, could …*

Learners skim the text for examples of modal verbs and the verbs they go with. Remind them that conditional verbs have no tense but work with other verbs to form the tense.

Independently, learners rewrite the sentences and underline the modal verbs, highlight the verbs they go with and identify the tense (or combination of tenses) in the sentence.

> **Differentiation ideas:** As a class or in supported groups, review tenses, conditionals and modals.

For extra challenge, learners could work in pairs to write sentences to express levels of possibility. Examples could include: *Air pollution causes health issues.* ⟶ *Air pollution could/may/will cause health issues*; *Rising temperatures create climate changes.* ⟶ *Rising temperatures will/might create climate changes.*

> **Assessment ideas:** Assess learners' ability to write complex sentences using modal verbs.

Answers:
2 a Mainly the present and also future.
   b Accept any of the following: may be needed, would reduce, could create, would need, may object, could achieve, could be made.
   c • might take (present)
      • would be (future)
      • could have (past)
      • will use (future)
      • can explain (present)
      • might have (past)
   d Learners' own sentences.

Plenary idea

It might be right (5 minutes)

Description: Learners swap work and mark each other's sentences. Invite them to reflect on the impact of modal verbs in a balanced report like the one in Session 5.6.

> **Assessment ideas:** Various answers can be accepted. Discuss and share ideas and possible answers.

Homework ideas

Learners complete the Workbook activities for Session 5.7 if they have not been completed in class. Additionally, they search their readers for further examples of sentences with modals of possibility.

Answers for Workbook

1 a might – change
   b can – drive
   c could – eat
   d should – make
   e might – find
   f would – enjoy
2 Learners' own sentences for the following:
   a should …   b might …   c may …
   d ought …   e would …

3 Example sentences:

a Animals <u>could</u> become extinct if we don't protect them.

b Unless we all pay attention, the global problems <u>will</u> increase daily.

c Young people <u>may</u> have the solution to the problem so leaders should listen to them.

d Leaders <u>could</u> make a difference but they don't always do what they should.

e Children <u>might</u> lead the way when it comes to finding a solution.

5.8 and 5.9 Present a balanced view

LEARNING PLAN

Learning objectives		Learning intentions	Success criteria
Main focus	**Also covered**	• List criteria for a balanced report.	• Learners can list criteria for writing a balanced report.
6Wc.08, 6SLr.02, 6SLg.02	6Ws.01, 6Ws.02, 6Ws.03, 6Ws.04, 6Wp.05 6Wp.05, 6Wc.02, 6Wc.06, 6Wc.07, 6Wp.01, 6SLp.01	• Plan and edit a report. • Present a report.	• Learners can plan and edit a report. • Learners can present a report.

LANGUAGE SUPPORT

In this session, learners can choose to write a balanced report or a balanced argument. The difference between them is in the conclusion. A balanced report presents all aspects of an issue, summarises both sides then leaves the readers to make up their own minds. A balanced argument presents all aspects of an issue then picks one side to support, based on the evidence.

At this stage of the writing process, learners should be ready to incorporate all the language skills learnt so far. Their writing should show a good level of formal, standard English and include examples of facts, different sentence types, connectives used to link ideas, correct use of conditionals and the active and passive voice used for effect.

Common misconception

Misconception	How to identify	How to overcome
An argument is always one-sided.	Ask: *What is an argument?* Gather responses. Ask: *Can an argument be balanced?* (yes)	Use dictionaries to find meanings of the terms *argue* and *argument*. Explain how an argument is balanced when both sides are presented before one side is chosen. Use the Differentiated worksheet pack to develop the skill of forming a balanced argument.

Starter idea

Just checking (5 minutes)

Resources: Learner's Book, Session 5.8 and 5.9: Getting started

Description: Learners discuss the importance of gaining a balanced view of something and also the purpose of a balanced report in specific situations or circumstances. Invite their ideas and remind learners to show consideration for every idea. Learners work in pairs to create a list of criteria they think are important when writing a balanced report. Share ideas with the class. Write some of their criteria on the board to use later in the lesson.

Main teaching ideas

1 Plan a balanced report or argument (40 minutes)

Learning intention: To use effective planning to inform the content and structure of extended writing and develop writing for a purpose

Resources: Learner's Book, Session 5.8 and 5.9, Activity 1; Worksheets 6.20 and 6.21; Differentiated worksheet pack; dictionaries and thesauruses

Description: Discuss and stimulate ideas for topics. They can be real or imaginary. Use the topics in the Learner's Book and add other topics that are relevant to your learners and school, and list them on the board.

Once learners have chosen a topic, remind them to consider: purpose – audience – language – layout. They can work in groups to discuss this and make notes.

Learners use Worksheet 6.20 Plan a balanced report to write a first draft with the criteria in mind. To assist in this writing process, particularly for some learners, offer learners Differentiated worksheets 5A–C to complete this task at different levels.

Learners edit their work using checklists, dictionaries and thesauruses to encourage good vocabulary and spelling. Then they check each other's work, offering ways to improve.

> **Differentiation ideas:** Support learners by pairing them with a partner, to help each other use onscreen tools to plan and check their work. Challenge more confident learners to work individually.

Challenge: Learners work individually.

Answers:
1 a–c   Learners' own answers.

2 Edit and present (40 minutes)

Learning intentions: To write balanced arguments, developing points logically and convincingly; to develop an idea across an extended piece of writing

Resources: Learner's Book, Session 5.8 and 5.7, Activity 2; Workbook, Session 5.8 and 5.9; Worksheet 6.6; dictionaries and online editing tools

Description: Provide dictionaries or onscreen tools for learners to edit their own work. An editing checklist (e.g. Worksheet 6.6 Check, check and check again!) will remind them what to look out for.

When they are ready, learners can write (or type) their reports neatly. At this stage, learners should be managing to write neatly, using an acceptable font size and at a good pace. However, some learners might still struggle in this area and using a keyboard might be a skill they can manage better. Although neat handwriting continues to be a good skill to have, consider giving learners a choice.

Complete the Workbook activities for Session 5.8 and 5.9.

> **Differentiation ideas:** Provide a template to assist those needing help to organise their reports into paragraphs and sections. Encourage more confident learners to work on their own.

> **Assessment ideas:** Assess learners' final report using Worksheet 6.21 Balanced report assessment sheet or a list of your own criteria. Check for correct spelling and punctuation. Ask: *Does the report have the correct purpose, audience, language and layout?*

Use Differentiated worksheets 5A–C to build each skill level and guide their balanced report writing.

Answers:
2 a–d   Learners' own work.

Plenary idea

Listen up (5 minutes)

Description: Discuss the expression, tone and style appropriate to reading this text type aloud. Learners take turns to read their reports in front of the class.

> **Assessment ideas:** Invite learners to reflect on which report sounded the most authentic.

Homework ideas

Learners watch or listen to a news or magazine programme and identify the point of view. They then decide if it is balanced.

Answers for Workbook

1–4 Learners' own work.

5.10 A strong viewpoint

LEARNING PLAN

Learning objectives		Learning intentions	Success criteria
Main focus	**Also covered**	• Read for meaning.	• Learners can read for meaning.
6Ri.06, 6Ri.08	6Rv.01, 6Rv.03, 6Rv.04, 6Rv.05, 6Ri.10, 6Ri.14, 6Ri.16, 6Ra.02, 6Ra.04, 6Wv.05, 6Wv.06, 6SLp.01	• Identify persuasive language. • Find synonyms that sound more or less persuasive.	• Learners can identify persuasive language. • Learners can find synonyms that sound more or less persuasive.

LANGUAGE SUPPORT

Now that learners can identify both sides of an issue and express various views in a balanced text, they must learn to choose a side and support a personal view using facts, opinions and persuasive language. Use words like *emotive* or *biased* to extend their vocabulary and to describe views that are one-sided.

Common misconception

Misconception	How to identify	How to overcome
Persuasive writing techniques are always obvious.	Display words of different intensity: *struggle – strive* *sick – contagious* Discuss how words can mean the same but have a different effect. The effect is not always obvious to the reader.	Use these words in sentences. Complete the Vocabulary development worksheet on suitable synonyms.

Starter idea

Viewpoint (5 minutes)

Resources: Learner's Book, Session 5.10: Getting started

Description: Discuss different techniques used by writers to express themselves. Writers may choose more or less intense vocabulary, give a personal or impersonal point of view, use figurative language and choose facts to support a particular view. If possible, show examples of these different types of texts.

Consider how easy or difficult it is to identify a writer's viewpoint. Even a factual text can be one-sided if it only provides facts to support one side of an issue.

Ask: *Do we all react in the same way? Does a text have the same effect on everyone? Why is context important?* (This can be the situation, condition, historic setting of the reader and/or writer.)

> **Assessment ideas:** Listen and observe as learners discuss in groups. Check that learners are able to take turns and consider other views.

Main teaching ideas

1 Explore a news article with a strong view (20 minutes)

Learning intentions: To explore explicit and implicit meaning; to support answers to questions with reference to, or quotations from, one or more points in a text

Resources: *The shrinking world of penguins* (Learner's Book, Session 5.10, Activity 1); Track 27; Worksheet 6.4; dictionaries; examples of visual images that may or may not be literal

Description: Introduce the text 'The shrinking world of penguins' (Track 27) by asking learners to skim for the main idea. Then study the photograph and ask learners to describe what they see and how they think it relates to/supports the text.

Discuss how photographs can look real and factual but may not always be so – especially in this digital age of photo-shopping. Ask learners to explain why the photograph works well in the context of the article and why it can be a literal image (penguins floating on a piece of ice) but also a figurative image (penguins threatened by a shrinking environment).

Check learners can identify the facts *and* opinions in the text. Ask: *Does the article include facts or opinions or both?* (both) *What impact does this have?*

(to persuade the reader) *Is this article balanced or persuasive?* (persuasive) *How can you tell?* (It includes facts but uses persuasive language to give the facts.)

Learners discuss the questions in pairs or small groups and report back to the class. This is good for encouraging discussion and building on ideas from each other.

If time permits, learners write answers to the questions in their notebooks, using dictionaries if needed. This is good for practising comprehension skills.

Learners add this text to Worksheet 6.4 Features of fiction and non-fiction texts, listing the features of this text type. They can also include this example in their learning journals.

> **Differentiation ideas:** Help learners with their understanding of bias by finding examples to share and discuss. For extra challenge, learners could write a definition of bias and find examples they can share.

> **Assessment ideas:** Assess learners' comprehension skills using the questions and answers provided. Assess their reading aloud of the text using good pace, fluency and expression.

Answers:

1. a The article explains how climate change is affecting penguins in Antarctica.
   b The photograph shows a group of penguins huddled together on a small, floating piece of ice. The picture is figurative – it is an image of the problem.
   c Accept any three facts.
   d Created by humans.
   e global sentinels – guardians of the earth; alien animals – animals that aren't meant to be in that environment; guano mining – collecting seabird excrement for fertiliser
   f Since everyone loves penguins and hates to see them suffer, people are becoming more concerned about the problem and willing to be involved.
   g The writer feels upset and angry; Learners' own reponses to the issue.
   h The text in the online news article (Session 5.2) is factual (no emotive language); the text in the report is balanced and this news article is emotive and persuasive.

2 Explore the language of persuasion (20 minutes)

Learning intentions: To comment on a writer's choice of language, demonstrating awareness of the impact on the reader; to deduce the meanings of unfamiliar phrases from their context

Resources: Learner's Book, Session 5.10, Activity 2; *The shrinking world of penguins* (Learner's Book, Session 5.10); Track 27; Workbook, Session 5.10; dictionaries and thesauruses

Description: Write the words *balanced* and *persuasive* on the board. Ask learners to describe the difference between a balanced and a persuasive text. (A balanced text gives the reader all sides of an issue but a persuasive text supports one side of an issue and aims to convince the reader to agree.)

In pairs, learners explore the emotive language and vocabulary in the text 'The shrinking world of penguins' guided by the questions in the Learner's Book. Individually, learners write the answers in their notebooks using dictionaries and a thesaurus to assist.

Complete the Workbook activities for Session 5.10

> **Differentiation ideas:** Encourage less confident learners to work in pairs to find other interesting figurative expressions to describe places or animals. Challenge more confident learners to work independently on this.

> **Assessment ideas:** Assess learners' ability to identify persuasive language and write sentences that are more or less persuasive by changing the vocabulary.

Answers:

2 a Any of the following: *tuxedoed seabirds, melting beneath their feet, global warming strikes hard, best allies in the fight, global sentinels.*

b Partners – allies, growing – mounting, a lot of – a host of, irregular – capricious, guardians – sentinels

c • Penguins are <u>falling prey</u> to climate change.

• Their homeland is melting <u>beneath their feet</u>.

• These <u>elegant</u> creatures are <u>global sentinels</u>.

• Penguins <u>cope</u> with a <u>host of problems</u>.

• I've never met <u>a person who didn't love penguins</u>.

d Learners' own sentences.

e Learners record in the learning journal (Worksheet 6.1).

Plenary idea

Share and discuss answers (5 minutes)

Description: Learners share and discuss their answers with the class.

> **Assessment ideas:** Learners use the 'How am I doing?' questions at the end of the session to review and rate their understanding and performance.

CROSS-CURRICULAR LINKS

History: Consider examples in history of bias text and persuasive speech.

Homework ideas

Learners watch documentaries or films that relate to the topic then write a paragraph expressing their point of view on the topic.

Answers for Workbook

1 Example answers: synonyms: practical, sensible, realistic, responsible, reasonable, rational, logical, sound, sober, no-nonsense, pragmatic, level-headed

Antonyms: partial, biased, distorted, jaundiced, lopsided, one-sided, predisposed, prejudiced, slanted and unfair

2 Any reasonable answers.

Example answers:

(1) hit – (2) strike – (3) beat – (4) attack

(1) helper – (2) partner – (3) ally – (4) collaborator

(1) tussle – (2) argue – (3) fight – (4) battle

(1) fine – (2) stylish – (3) chic – (4) elegant

3 Learners' own sentences.

5.11 Pick a side

LEARNING PLAN

Learning objectives		Learning intentions	Success criteria
Main focus	**Also covered**	• Express a viewpoint. • Share it with others. • Discuss other viewpoints.	• Learners can express a viewpoint. • Learners can share a view and discuss it with others. • Learners can listen to others.
6Wc.06, 6Wc.07, 6SLg.04	6Wv.02, 6Wv.06, 6SLg.02, 6SLg.03		

LANGUAGE SUPPORT

Personal views are constantly expressed on news programmes, social media, posters and advertisements. Personal views can be positive or negative, damaging or encouraging. Learners should be able to identify the pros and cons of expressing a personal view and draw up a set of rules to guide them when they express themselves. This should include encouraging others to take turns in a discussion.

Starter idea

In other words … (5 minutes)

Resources: Learner's Book, Session 5.11: Getting started; thesauruses

Description: Write the words *Express yourself* on the board and have a short discussion about what this means. These days, it is popular for people to express themselves on social platforms, which is often done without any planning. Ask: *What are the dangers of expressing yourself without thinking about it first. Why is it good to take time to check your texts before sending?* In small groups or with a partner, learners discuss guidelines on how best to express themselves using various platforms.

Main teaching ideas

1 Write a persuasive paragraph on a topic you feel strongly about (20 minutes)

Learning intentions: To develop writing for a purpose; to use words and phrases to express a viewpoint

Resources: Learner's Book, Session 5.11, Activity 1; Language worksheet 5A; dictionaries and thesauruses

Description: Prepare learners by explaining that it is time for them to pick one side of an issue. Read the topic options aloud and invite the learners to choose the one that they feel most passionate about.

Use Language worksheet 5A to demonstrate how to support a view and how to write a persuasive text. You can read and discuss this worksheet or get the learners to complete it, according to how much support they need.

Learners write a short persuasive text to support their view on the topic. Include a good opening and conclusions, strong vocabulary and persuasive language. Encourage learners to come up with two or three points with facts to support their view.

Learners check their own work. Ask: *Does it say how you feel in a way that aims to inform others? Have you used appropriate language that will persuade others, not upset them?*

> **Differentiation ideas:** In supported groups, ask learners to write a short or long paragraph according to their pace and ability.

More confident learners can take another point of view and write a second paragraph.

> **Assessment ideas:** Assess learners' persuasive paragraphs using the criteria provided in Activity 1 of this session.

Answers:
1   **a–d** Learners' own work.

2   Share your views and consider others' views (20 minutes)

Learning intention: To show consideration of another point of view; to extend a discussion by building on own and others' ideas

Description: In groups of three or four, learners read out their paragraphs. While listening, learners make notes and write questions to discuss afterwards. Once all the views are aired, learners share ideas, consider other views and build on what they think. Remind learners to encourage each other to take turns in a discussion.

> **Differentiation idea:** Support learners by having a class discussion in which you analyse text messages and messages posted on social media.

Challenge more confident learners by asking: Wh*at language is used? What is the message? Is it polite? Is it appropriate?*

> **Assessment ideas:** Observe as learners discuss and share their views. Ask yourself: *Are they able to listen and take turns?* Observe how well learners encourage each other to take turns.

Answers:
2   **a–b** Learners' discussion.

Plenary idea

Wrap it up (5 minutes)

Description: Groups write a short conclusion to summarise their views and share them with the class. Invite learners to reflect on why it is important to consider different views and how this can have a positive effect on how you understand something. Ask: *Can another view make you change your view?*

> **Assessment ideas:** Learners review the 'How am I doing?' questions at the end of the session and rate their performance.

Homework ideas

Learners complete the Workbook activities for Session 5.11.

Answers for Workbook

1–3 Learners' own written work.

5.12   Have a class debate

LEARNING PLAN			
Learning objectives		**Learning intentions**	**Success criteria**
Main focus	**Also covered**		
6Ws.01, 6Ws.02, 6Ws.03, 6Ws.04, 6SLm.01, 6SLm.02, 6SLm.03, 6SLs.01, 6SLp.03, 6SLr.01	6Ri.10, 6Wc.06, 6Wc.07, 6SLm.04, 6SLm.05, 6SLg.01, 6SLg.02	• Listen to a speech and analyse it. • Prepare a persuasive speech. • Have a class debate.	• Learners can listen to a speech and identify the features. • Learners can prepare a persuasive speech. • Learners can take part in a class debate.

LANGUAGE SUPPORT

A debate is a type of formal argument or discussion. A debate involves two or more individuals who put forward opposing points to an audience so the audience can choose which side is most convincing.

A debate can be conducted in various ways. You can adapt the format of a debate to suit your class and your learners according to their ability, the time you have and the size of your classroom.

Starter idea

Listen and analyse (5 minutes)

Resources: *Let's curb global warming together* (Learner's Book, Session 5.12: Getting started); Track 28

Description: Active listening is an important skill to develop in each lesson and in every discussion. Track 28. Learners listen and take notes on the following: the speaker's viewpoint, facts and opinions, and persuasive language. They identify and discuss various features of this persuasive speech – e.g. ask them to find:

- the title: *Let's curb global warming together*
- the introduction: first paragraph
- three convincing points: paragraphs 2, 3, 4
- the conclusion: Paragraph 5
- connectives to order or link paragraphs or make a point: The first step; Last, but not least; clearly

> **Assessment ideas:** Learners listen to the audio. Assess their ability to listen for detail and meaning as they identify specific language features in the speech.

Audioscript: *Let's curb global warming together*

Global warming is a global issue. This means we are all in it together. Humans have caused the problem, and we need to help solve it. Everyone must do their bit to heal our ailing Earth.

The first step is to take stock of how much litter you create. Try this experiment: for one week collect all your rubbish in a bag. Multiply that by the number of people in your class. You will be shocked. Clearly it's time to cut down on waste.

Following this, analyse your rubbish. Are you guilty of throwing away plastic? It is time to cut down on buying plastic goods if all you do is throw them away. Tonnes of non-degradable plastic is discarded daily – consequently poisoning and cluttering up our environment. Earth is the only home we have. Let's look after it.

Last, but not least, we must take reusing seriously. Have you started reusing plastic bags, bottles and even drinking straws? It may seem insignificant – but imagine if eight billion people reused these small items! That's a BIG deal!

Clearly we can ALL make a difference. There's NO excuse. As a wise person once said: 'Every little bit helps. Start today and be part of the global solution.

Answers:

1 Viewpoint: The speaker believes humans can/should solve global warming. Key points: track your waste, analyse it, reuse it. A fact: Global warming is a global issue. An opinion: Everyone must do their bit. Introduction: first paragraph. Conclusion: final paragraph. Persuasive language examples: *You will be shocked. Are you guilty? That's a BIG deal!*

2 This is an example of a persuasive speech because it only provides one viewpoint and aims to convince the audience to agree.

Main teaching ideas

1 Choose a topic to debate and prepare an argument (20 minutes)

Learning intentions: To develop writing for a specified audience, using appropriate content and language; to develop writing for a purpose using appropriate language and features

Resources: Learner's Book, Session 5.12, Activity 1; Worksheets 6.8 and 6.22; space for group work; a list of other interesting topics for learners to choose

Description: Organise the class into groups according to class size. If you choose to debate just one topic as a class, you can divide the class into two large groups – those 'for' and those 'against' the topic. Alternatively, if you choose to debate two or three topics, there could be two groups allocated to each topic – one group to argue 'for' and the other group to argue 'against'.

Choose a topic from those provided or any other topics relevant to your learners. Groups choose a point of view to support and list facts and opinions to support this view. Use Worksheet 6.22 Present a persuasive speech to guide the process. Each group writes a short speech.

This is good for working together in a limited time. You can use Worksheet 6.8 Group work to remind the learners to stick to roles, responsibilities and rules.

> **Differentiation ideas:** For support, talk about one or more topics as a class – according to the time you have.

For challenge, create two groups (for and against) each topic. Invite more confident learners to talk to the class about their points of view.

> **Assessment ideas:** Learners use Worksheet 6.22 Present a persuasive speech to guide and plan their speech.

Answers:
1   **a–d** Learners' own written work.

2   Have a class debate (20 minutes)

Learning intentions: To structure information to aid the listener's understanding of the main and subsidiary points; to use language to convey ideas and opinions, with increasing clarity and detail

Resources: Learner's Book, Session 5.12, Activity 2; Worksheets 6.10 and 6.22

Description: Use the diagram in the Learner's Book to show how to organise the class for the debate with teams facing the audience.

Learners choose a spokesperson (or two) to represent their group on a team (for or against).

Give each spokesperson a chance to stand and deliver the speech (written by the group) while the audience listens and takes notes and prepares questions.

Afterwards, provide time for learners to ask questions, clarify points made and share opinions. Encourage learners to use words to convey opinions such as '*I think …*', '*In my opinion …*', '*I believe …*'. This is good for expressing personal views and opinions clearly and confidently.

> **Differentiation ideas:** Organise a debate to give all learners a chance to speak about a less difficult

topic. Encourage only positive feedback for points of view expressed. Challenge learners who are more confident to speak to select more contentious topics.

> **Assessment ideas:** Assess their ability to speak in front of an audience with confidence using language to convey their ideas and opinions. You can use Worksheet 6.10 Reading, speaking or performing assessment sheet to guide this.

Answers:
2   **a–d** Learners' own speeches.

Plenary idea

Give feedback (5 minutes)

Description: Invite learners to reflect on what makes a good speech. Ask: *Is it the speaker or the speech, or both?* Learners give feedback on which groups made the most convincing speech.

> **Assessment ideas:** Learners vote to choose the best argument.

Homework ideas

Learners look out for good topics to debate and bring these ideas to school to start a 'Let's debate' display board in class. They also complete the Workbook activities for Session 5.12 to practise presenting an argument.

Answers for Workbook

1   A debate is a formal discussion in a public meeting about a subject on which people have different views.

Rules can include: one person speaks at a time; listen carefully; consider the other person's view; be persuasive but be polite; don't get personal; focus on the facts; don't talk for too long …

2   Example answers:

a   It is a global issue which humans have caused and humans should solve.

b   Everyone must be involved to solve the problem. Assess your rubbish, analyse it and reuse it.

c   Learners' own responses.

d   The first step, following this, last, but not least, clearly

e   Accept any reasonable examples.

3   Learners' own work.

CHECK YOUR PROGRESS

1   a   I don't love snow <u>however/although/in spite of this</u> I'd love to visit Antarctica.

   b   The Artic is very cold <u>however/while/on the other hand</u> the equator is very hot.

   c   I'd like to visit <u>either/neither</u> the Arctic <u>or/nor</u> the Antarctic.

   d   It is <u>neither</u> here <u>nor</u> there.

2   Accept any reasonable opinions that are opposite.

Animals in danger of extinction should be kept in zoos.	
I agree because they must be protected.	I disagree because it's unnatural and cruel.

3   Accept any correct answers: It presents both (or all) sides; It gives facts to support each side; It uses impersonal language; It links and compares points using connectives …

4   a   When I'm an adult, <u>I'd like to be part of a climate change campaign</u>.

   b   <u>You can join our campaign today</u> if you are interested in climate change.

5   a   *You <u>could</u> be a part of the solution if you join us.*

   b   *If she goes for a walk, she <u>might</u> take her brother.*

6   Accept slight variations: unsafe, risky, threatening, dangerous, hazardous.

PROJECT GUIDANCE

Group project: Learners organise a performance to highlight awareness of environmental issues. Brainstorm ideas as a class (so you can manage these), then invite groups to develop an idea – according to their capacity and ability. They can write stories to read to younger children, research poems and read them aloud in front of a large audience (this can include parents and/or teachers). Alternatively they can write and perform songs or choral verse to perform in assembly.

Pair project: Learners choose an area of interest that is affected by climate change. It could be the sea, a country or a specific area. Encourage learners to choose an area that is topical and has recently been in the news so they can find information easily and make their presentation relevant to their classmates. The learners should gather the information, summarise it and present it to the class (or the school) using a multimedia option of their choice.

Solo project: Learners make a poster (warning people) about the causes and effects of climate change, using some of the language techniques and ideas covered in this unit. Invite learners to brainstorm thoughts and ideas on the content and to consider the audience, purpose, language and layout of the poster. Provide thesauruses for learners to explore synonyms to sound persuasive. Encourage learners to come up with a catchy slogan and to make their poster look and sound appealing. Afterwards, display them around the school.

>6 Poetry at play

Unit plan

Session	Approximate number of learning hours	Outline of learning content	Resources
6.1 Poetic licence	0.5+	Explore a poem. Understand poetic licence. Identify the point of view.	Learner's Book Session 6.1 Workbook Session 6.1 ⬇ Worksheet 6.10 ⬇ Language worksheet 6A
6.2 A string of words	0.5+	Read a shape poem. Explore figurative language. Write a shape poem.	Learner's Book Session 6.2 Workbook Session 6.2 ⬇ Worksheet 6.9 ⬇ Language worksheet 6B
6.3 Patterns and shapes	0.5+	Explore cinquain poems. Compare poems. Write a poem together.	Learner's Book Session 6.3 Workbook Session 6.3
6.4 Follow the rules	0.5+	Plan ideas and vocabulary. Explore word classes. Proofread and present.	Learner's Book Session 6.4 Workbook Session 6.4 ⬇ Language worksheet 6A
6.5 Laugh with limericks	0.5+	Read aloud. Explore features of limericks. Perform in groups.	Learner's Book Session 6.5 Workbook Session 6.5 ⬇ Worksheet 6.23 ⬇ Worksheet 6.24

Topic	Approximate number of learning hours	Outline of learning content	Resources
6.6 Play with words	0.5+	Plan limericks. Check and edit. Present and read aloud.	Learner's Book Session 6.6 Workbook Session 6.6 ⬇ Worksheet 6.10
Cross-unit resources			
Learner's Book Check your progress			
Learner's Book Projects			
Unit 6 Differentiated worksheet pack			
End-of-unit 6 test			

BACKGROUND KNOWLEDGE

Learners are generally familiar with the many rules that guide their reading, writing and speaking. Introduce poetic licence as the freedom to ignore or change the rules of writing to create an effect or make a point. Some poems break the rules to express a point while others follow strict rules and a specific format. Point out that breaking language rules should be done with a specific outcome in mind.

There are a number of poetic formats that are fun and useful to teach your learners. A cinquain is a five-lined poem originally developed more than 100 years ago by the American poet Adelaide Crapsey. She was inspired by the Japanese haiku. According to traditional cinquain, each line has a specific syllable count of 2-4-6-8-2. The aim is to describe a moment or event and create a vivid image that tells a story. These poems may use the technique of run-on sentences or enjambment. More modern forms of cinquain focus on word count (1-2-3-4-1) with rules for each line. For example, the first line is the subject of the topic and is usually a noun, the second line describes it using adjectives, the third line shows action using verbs and the fourth line describes a feeling or emotion. The last line links to the first line with a synonym or term used to sum it up. Commas separate the words and each line begins with a capital.

A limerick is a five-lined humorous poem with a characteristic rhythm and rhyme (AABBA). Limericks were around in the 1700s but Edward Lear, famous for developing nonsense poetry, popularised them. He wrote over 200 limericks. Limerick Day, celebrated in May, honours Edward Lear's 12 May 1812 birthday.

TEACHING SKILLS FOCUS

Skills for life

In our fast-changing world, the classroom should offer opportunities for learners to build skills that will enable them to continue to grow, adapt and learn in various situations. This unit provides many opportunities for learners to collaborate, communicate and be creative as they engage

CONTINUED

with different poems and use language to express themselves. Finding enjoyment in reading and writing poetry will help to develop their skills. Try the following ideas in your classroom.

- Display poems for learners to read, enjoy and discuss.
- Form a poetry group that learners can join and participate in during and/or after class.
- Invite a local poet to the school to teach a poetry lesson and inspire the learners.
- Expose learners to different types of poems that challenge their language and vocabulary.
- Invite learners to share their favourite poems – to read them aloud or perform them.
- Work in groups to perform choral verse – even the shortest poems can be performed.

- Borrow poetry books from the library and let learners take home a different one each day.
- Celebrate 'poetry day' in your school. Involve the learners in organising various activities. They can work in groups, organise a timetable of events, prepare a choral verse performance and so on.
- Invite learners to take part in an Eisteddfod (a music and poetry competition).
- Choose poems for another age group and read poetry to younger learners in the school.
- Encourage learners to start a poetry magazine which should include articles of interest, poems by famous poets, classic and modern poems and their own poems.
- Guide learners as they give each other feedback – ensure it is positive and constructive.

6.1 Poetic licence

LEARNING PLAN

Learning objectives		Learning intentions	Success criteria
Main focus	**Also covered**	• Explore a poem. • Understand poetic licence. • Identify point of view.	• Learners can explore the features of a poem. • Learners can explain poetic licence. • Learners can identify a writer's point of view.
6Rv.04, 6Ri.02, 6Ri.11	6Rg.01, 6Rs.02, 6Ri.15, 6Ri.16, 6Ri.17, 6Ra.01, 6Ra.02, 6Ww.04, 6Wg.03, 6Wg.08, 6SLs.01, 6SLp.01		

LANGUAGE SUPPORT

Reading poetry involves interpretation. Some learners may need guidance to grasp implicit meanings of a text – meaning that is not obvious.

The visual impact is what readers see when they look at a poem and interpret it. Visual impact is created by the punctuation, format and font. Auditory impact is how the poem sounds when read aloud. It is in part created by the punctuation and font (size or boldness) to show expression.

The term *voice* refers to *the speaker* used by a writer to tell a story or describe an event or an emotion. The voice in the poem is not always the voice of the writer. The writer may use the voice to say things that express how other people, animals or objects may see or experience something.

Common misconceptions

Misconception	How to identify	How to overcome
All poems have rules and structure.	Learners skim the poem 'According to my Mood' and notice that it has no specific structure, poor punctuation and incorrect spelling.	Explain the use of poetic licence. Expose learners to different types of poems – those with structure and rhyme and those without.

Starter idea

Poetry rules (5 minutes)

Resources: Learner's Book, Session 6.1: Getting started

Description: Write the words 'Poetry writing rules' on the board. Ask learners to list any rules they think guide poetry. Ask learners to explain what 'poetic licence' means. Write answers on the board then look up the meaning to answers. Deal with misconceptions that poems must have a structure and rhyme.

Main teaching ideas

29 1 Read a poem and talk about poetic licence (20 minutes)

Learning intention: To explore the language, features and theme of a poem, understand poetic licence and read aloud

Resources: *According to my Mood* (Learner's Book, Session 6.1, Activity 1); Track 29; Workbook, Session 6.1; Language worksheet 6A

Description: Learners skim the poem and express their initial thoughts and observations. Write on the board what they notice – e.g. incorrect spelling and punctuation. Find out what they think about this. Ask: *Is it written like this for a reason or is it an error? Why?*

In pairs, learners take turns to read *According to my Mood* aloud. Afterwards discuss whether this was different from reading other poems or prose. Ask: Does the exaggerated punctuation and incorrect spelling make it easier or more difficult to read? Discuss their reasons. Guide the discussion.

Take turns to read the poem aloud to the class or play Track 29. Ask: *Does the verbal expression add to the message of the poem? Is it better to read the poem or hear it?* Explain the terms visual and auditory. Talk about how the poem uses both for effect.

Ask learners to describe the poem in their own words and compare it to other poems in terms of theme and structure. Share thoughts and opinions.

If necessary, revise colons, semi-colons, ellipses and parenthesis. Learners use Language worksheet 6A to write the poem using correct punctuation and spelling. Talk about how the message is the same but with less impact.

Learners add to their learning journals and explain the use of poetic licence in poetry.

Spelling link: Identify words spelt incorrectly in the poem. Point out the use of *rong* and *write*. Link this to silent letters and homophones. Learners make a list of words often confused and record them in their learning journals.

> **Differentiation ideas:** Support learners by looking, as a class, for other poems with a similar theme to read aloud and enjoy. Challenge more confident learners to work individually to complete the Workbook activities for Session 6.1.

> **Assessment ideas:** Observe learners' discussions. Look out for misconceptions to discuss and overcome. Listen as learners read aloud. Assess expression, pace and fluency. Check learners can use correct punctuation and spelling.

Answers:
Accept any reasonable interpretation of the poem.
1 a It has a heading and lines like a poem but the punctuation marks are over-used and incorrect, words are spelt incorrectly and the font style is inconsistent.
  b Learners read aloud and comment on how easy or tricky it was to read. Own answers.
  c Learners' own answers, for example: Hearing the poem makes it fun/expresses the mood of the writer/gives the words more impact …
  d Accept various answers, for example: the poem is very different to other poems in terms of the theme, the language and the

punctuation. Learners can describe it as: humorous, personal, informal, unusual, exaggerated and/or rebellious – giving their own reasons and examples.

e   The effect is both visual and auditory. The way it looks and sounds adds impact to the message.

f   Accept reasonable answers like: The poem will look different with everything correct and proper. It may sound different with less expression. The message would not change but will have less impact.

g   Learners add to their learning journals and explain the use of poetic licence.

2 Explore the voice and viewpoint (20 minutes)

Learning intentions: To identify the voice of a poem; to read a biography to understand the writer's point of view

Resources: *Benjamin Zephania* (Learner's Book, Session 6.1, Activity 23); Track 30; Workbook, Session 6.1

Description: On the board, write the words *writer*, *speaker*, *narrator* and *voice*. Discuss these terms and how they relate to poetry.

Read the title of the poem (*According to my Mood*) and the first line. Learners identify the attitude of the speaker in the poem. Ask: *Do you think the voice in the poem is that of the poet? Could he be speaking for others? Who?* (Those who struggle to write and feel frustrated with all the rules of writing.)

Together, read the biography and discuss the poet's background, interests and audience. Ask: *Who does the poet want to reach and what does he aim to achieve through his poetry?* (To make poetry interesting and accessible to everyone – especially to those who struggle to read and write.) Ask volunteers to explain the poem's message. Learners listen and share ideas.

> **Differentiation ideas:** In pairs or small groups, learners complete the Workbook activities. Encourage learners to research the poet and find other poems written by him.

For more challenge, learners could rewrite the poem as a paragraph (with multi-clause sentences) using punctuation effectively to clarify meaning.

Answers:

2 a Accept various answers such as: *the speaker feels frustrated, rebellious, impatient, selfish, angry …*

b Example answer: The speaker feels hindered, stifled, frustrated with language rules and is eager to express himself despite/without the rules. The speaker may be expressing this on behalf of others.

c He wants to inspire young people and those who might not feel very good at writing or reading. He uses an informal style and imperfect language and punctuation to appeal to young readers and those who can't read or struggle to understand poetry. He wants everyone to enjoy poetry no matter how good or bad they are at it.

Plenary idea

Feel the mood (5 minutes)

Resources: Worksheet 6.10

Description: Invite learners to reflect on different emotions that inspire poetry such as love poems or poems that deal with anger or loss. Make a class list of moods. Learners read aloud *According to my Mood* with expression. Invite feedback and suggestions on ways to improve.

> **Assessment ideas:** Use a rating system or symbols to show how well the learners read in these areas: expression, tone, pace and fluency or use Worksheet 6.10 Reading, speaking or performing assessment to assess them.

CROSS-CURRICULAR LINKS

Geography: Use a map to find out where Jamaica is and get information about the country and culture.

PHSE: Discuss ways of handling emotions.

Homework ideas

Learners find out more about Benjamin Zephaniah from his own website and search for some of his poems online.

Answers for Workbook

1 Any similar answer to: The freedom to change or break the rules of conventional language.

2 a commas, semicolons, full stops, brackets, hyphens, colons, question marks, inverted commas, apostrophes, exclamation mark.

  b No, to make a visual impact, to support the message.

  c frustrated, rebellious, mischievous.

d Answers may vary but should include full sentences and correct punctuation, e.g. *One day, I'm going to pick up all the commas, semicolons and full stops I've ever used. I'm going to roll them up with all the brackets, hyphens, colons, question marks, inverted commas and apostrophes. Then I'll throw them all out again as one big exclamation mark!* (There is less impact when written correctly.)

3 Learners' own research and answers.

6.2 A string of words

LEARNING PLAN

Learning objectives		Learning intentions	Success criteria
Main focus	**Also covered**	• Read a shape poem.	• Learners can read a shape poem.
6Rs.02, 6Ri.02, 6Rv.05, 6Wv.04, 6Wv.05, 6Wc.01	6Rv.04, 6Rv.06, 6Ri.15, 6Ra.01, 6Rv.06, 6Ww.04, 6Wp.03, 6Wp.04, 6Wp.05, 6SLg.02, 6SLp.01	• Use figurative language. • Write a shape poem.	• Learners can use figurative language. • Learners can write a shape poem.

LANGUAGE SUPPORT

Review the following with your learners.

A shape poem is a poem where the lines take on a shape or form or pattern, usually linked to the subject of the poem. The shape will often give the reader a clue to what the poem is about.

Commonly confused words include words like homophones (words that sound the same but have different meanings, e.g. there, their) and homonyms

(words that look the same and may sound the same but have multiple meanings, e.g. book).

There are different types of rhyme, e.g. internal rhyme (a word part way through a line rhymes with the end word of the same line), end rhyme (rhyming words occur at the ends of lines), half rhyme (words have a similar but not identical sound) and full rhyme (words rhyme exactly).

Common misconceptions

Misconception	How to identify	How to overcome
Homophones, homonyms and homographs are all the same thing.	Write the words on the board. Ask learners to say what they mean. Look up the meanings.	Find examples of each. Make class posters and invite learners to add their examples.

Starter idea

Who needs rules? (5 minutes)

Resources: Learner's Book, Session 6.2: Getting started

Description: Have a short discussion on why we need rules for writing. Ask: *Are there different rules for different text types? Is it easy or difficult to follow the rules? Are the rules the same for narrative and poetry?* Ask learners to explain the difference between an error and poetic licence.

Main teaching ideas

1 Read a poem with words that have been strung together for a certain effect (10 minutes)

Learning intention: To explore the writer's choice of language and explain how figurative language creates imagery

Resources: *Amaized* (Learner's Book, Session 6.2, Activity 1); Track 31; Workbook, Session 6.2; Language worksheet 6B; dictionaries; images of maize crops and different mazes

Description: Display an image of a maize plant. Ask learners to identify it and say what word they use for it – maize or corn? Explain that it is called different things in different contexts. Find out if they know how or where it grows and what it's useful for.

Silently, learners read the poem *Amaized*. Afterwards, ask what they noticed about the direction of the lines and the words. Invite responses.

Read the poem aloud or play the audio (Track 30) and ask learners to identify words that look or sound the same but have a different meaning. Write them on the board – *maize, maze, days, daze, wind*. Learners look them up and discuss their meanings. You can also include the other words from the poem that have homophones: *through/threw, here/hear, know/no*.

Use Language worksheet 6B to practise commonly confused words.

Discuss the figurative image created by the way the poem is visually structured – the words are written in lines to represent rows of maize but also the path of a maze. Ask: *How does the language and structure take the reader beyond the literal?*

Read the Language focus box in the Learner's Book and add to the examples provided. Start a class list (or poster) of words easily confused and invite learners to add to it as they discover other words.

Learners complete the questions in their books.

Spelling link: Explore word origins. Homograph comes from ancient Greek *homo*, meaning 'same' and *graph* meaning 'something written'. Homographs are spelt/written the same way, but do not always sound the same, e.g. *read* (present tense)/*read* (past tense); whereas homophones (*homo/same* and *phone/sound*) sound the same but may not be spelt the same, e.g. *sight/site*. Learners add examples to their learning journals.

> **Differentiation ideas:** Support less confident learners by allowing them to work in pairs or small groups to complete the Workbook activities or Language worksheet 6B. They could also make a list or create a class poster of homophones and other words that are easily confused.

Challenge more confident learners to find other examples of word play in a range of poems.

Answers:
1 a The words are written in columns or rows, they read from top to bottom then bottom to top – not left to right as in conventional texts.
  b The theme is about playing and having fun outside – playing in a crop of maize.
  c The structure and the words used are playful. The poem is arranged to imitate the rows of maize in a crop.
  d Example answers:
   • daze, days and maize, maze
   • The road winds through the country. The wind blows the leaves.
   • The word 'amazed' means to be surprised or astonished. Since the speaker is walking in a crop of maize, the spelling of the title has changed to match it.
   • A crop of maize is compared to a maze.

2 Work in groups to create a string poem using creative words and images (30 minutes)

Learning intention: To develop creative writing and use figurative language to evoke an imaginative response from the reader

Resources: Learner's Book, Session 6.2, Activity 2; Worksheet 6.9; examples of different shape poems (if possible); poster paper and marker pens

Description: Invite learners to explore the different types of shape poems on display or use onscreen tools to research others. Ask: *Are there any rules to writing shape poetry?*

Explain the idea of a string poem – words and phrases put together to form a string of words that can be arranged in a shape to represent something – e.g. a flock of birds flying in formation might look like a 'V' or a bowl of spaghetti might look like worms.

Read the example of the washing machine in the Learner's Book to show the use of images, synonyms, comparisons and other figurative language techniques.

Learners can work in groups or on their own. They should choose a topic from the ideas box or they may come up with their own idea for a topic. They can use Worksheet 6.9 Writing assessment sheet to help plan and assess their writing.

Remind learners to show consideration for different views when working together. Once they have brainstormed, they should choose their favourite ideas and plan the structure of the poem. Afterwards they check and edit it.

Hand out poster paper and marker pens. Encourage learners to use the full page with text/images/shapes large enough to be seen on display.

> **Differentiation ideas:** In small groups, encourage learners to research, explore and/or write shape poems for extra support.

For more challenge, invite individuals to read their poems then answer questions about them.

> **Assessment ideas:** Check learners' written answers to both activities to assess their understanding of the poem. Observe as the learners work together and note those who struggle to participate actively.

Answers:
2   Learners' own work.

Plenary idea

String it out (5 minutes)

Description: Invite learners to reflect on what they enjoyed about this activity and what they found challenging. Display their final work and encourage positive feedback.

> **Assessment ideas:** Learners check each other's work and decide if the poem:

- looks interesting and has a specific shape that represents something
- strings together interesting, creative words and phrases
- uses punctuation to show expression
- creates a visual and auditory effect
- uses figurative language techniques.

Homework ideas

Learners write shape poems inspired by things in their home, their room or the area around them.

Answers for Workbook

1   Learners' own words.
2   Learners add to the following:

dead	meat	great	threat	heard
bed	suite	straight	debt	bird

3   Learners' own explanations for the following, or similar examples:

by	buy	bye
to	too	two
their	there	they're
we're	wear	where
very	fairy	vary
saw	sore	soar

4   Learners' own sentences.
Example:
I heard a dog bark.
The dead tree lost its bark.

6.3 Patterns and shapes

LEARNING PLAN

Learning objectives		Learning intentions	Success criteria
Main focus	**Also covered**	• Explore features of a cinquain poem.	• Learners can explore features of a cinquain.
6Rg.08, 6Rs.02, 6Wv.04, 6Wv.02, 6Wc.01, 6SLs.01	6Rv.03, 6Rv.06, 6Rg.05, 6Ri.02, 6Ra.02, 6Wv.06, 6Wc.02, 6Ws.04	• Compare poems. • Write a poem together.	• Learners can compare poems with different features. • Learners can write a cinquain poem with a partner.

LANGUAGE SUPPORT

Remind learners that a word class is a part of speech. It refers to a group of words of similar form or function like nouns, verbs or adjectives.

A cinquain is a five-lined poem with a specific number of words or syllables on each line –
depending on which format you use. *Cinq* comes from the French word meaning 'five'.

A syllable is a single vowel sound in a word. Syllables can be made up of one or more letters.

Starter idea

Explain the name (5 minutes)

Resources: Learner's Book, Session 6.3: Getting started; dictionaries

Description: Invite learners to use their dictionaries to look up the meanings of *cinquain* and *cinq*. Share answers. Some dictionaries also give the pronunciation. Share ideas. The way to pronounce it is 'sin-cane'. Ask if anyone has read or written these poems before and invite them to share experiences. Ask: *Is there only one way to write a cinquain poem?* Look out for misconceptions and explain you will deal with these during the session.

Main teaching ideas

1 Work together to identify the theme and structure of poems (20 minutes)

Learning intentions: To read aloud with accuracy and expression; to identify the theme and structure of cinquain poems

Resources: *Going fishing, Detention and Cinquains explained* (Learner's Book, Session 6.3, Activity 1); Tracks 32 and 33; Workbook, Session 6.3

Description: In pairs, learners read the poems aloud to each other. Compare and identify what looks and sounds the same about them. Discuss what each poem is about and how the poems capture a moment, or thought or feeling. Learners should notice that the words and lines form a diamond shape, or *diamante*. Ask which poem they enjoy the most and why. Share ideas.

Encourage active listening in every lesson. Remind learners that to listen carefully they must practice focusing on what is being said. Listen to Track 33 *Cinquains explained*. Learners will discover that there are two main ways to write a cinquain – the original cinquain has a specific syllable count; the more modern version has a specific word count and word class allocation. Learners discuss the questions in the Learner's Book. Play the audio again if necessary.

Look out for those needing more support and use the Workbook activities for Session 6.3 to support them. Highlight the punctuation in the poems – each line begins with a capital letter, commas separate the words on lines 2 and 3, end punctuation is not essential. Learners use this information and understanding to analyse the poems provided and answer the questions. They can write the answers in their notebooks for you to check.

> **Differentiation ideas:** Support learners to research and understand rules for counting syllables. In pairs or small groups they write the rules into their notebooks or make a poster, then complete the Workbook activities. Encourage more confident learners to revise word classes then try to explain them to a partner or small group. Invite them to read aloud both types of cinquain – word count and syllable count.

> **Assessment ideas:** Listen to learners reading aloud and identify those who need support using expression. Check their written answers to assess their ability to analyse the poems and identify the features. Use the audio to assess their listening skills. Ask: *How much information did you remember?*

Audioscript: *Cinquains explained*

Speaker 1: A cinquain is a simple, five-lined poem developed by the American poet Adelaide Crapsey over a hundred years ago. She was inspired by the simplicity of Japanese haiku. According to traditional cinquain, each line has a syllable count of 2-4-6-8-2. The aim is to capture a moment, tell a story and describe a mood with a few, well-chosen words that may or may not rhyme. Cinquains are easy and fun to write.

Speaker 2: A more modern form of cinquain poetry focuses on the word count of 1-2-3-4-1 words per line. The first line identifies the topic and is usually a noun. The second line describes the topic using vivid adjectives. The third line shows action using –ing verbs and the fourth line is a phrase that describes a feeling or emotion. The last line links to the first line with a synonym or term that sums it up. Commas are used to separate the adjectives and verbs. Each line begins with a capital letter. Most lines have no end punctuation. Although there are more rules in this format, the aim is the same: to capture a moment and a mood – just like painting a picture.

Answers:

1 a • Accept any reasonable answers: fishing – having fun and detention – being punished.
   • Example answers: Both are short and concise, capture a moment or feeling, have five lines with long and short ones, have titles, use describing words and verbs …
   • symmetrical shape, a diamond or diamante.
   • Learners' own answers.
   b • Syllable count or word count.
   • American poet, Adelaide Crapsey – inspired by Japanese haiku.
   • The word count cinquain has more rules concerning word class and punctuation.
   c • There is no syllable pattern.
   • 1,2,3,4,1
   • 1 – noun, 2 – adjectives, 3 – verbs
   • They are all -*ing* verbs
   • An emotion or feeling.
   • They connect – either a synonym or an idea.
   • Example: every line begins with a capital letter, commas between the adjectives and nouns, no end punctuation necessary. Ellipsis included in both poems – indicates a pause, a moment of reflection

---

2 **In pairs, create a cinquain (20 minutes)**   34

Learning intentions: To identify different word classes; to explore synonyms; to develop creative writing

Resources: *Popcorn* (Learner's Book, Session 6.3, Activity 2); Track 34

Description: Write the word *cinquain* on the board (or you may still have it on the board from earlier). Invite learners to name three rules that apply to these poems. (Five lines: three long and two short; describes a moment or event or feeling; the first and last line connect with the topic.)

Read the poem *Popcorn* together. Invite learners to give ideas for a different title like *Perfect snack* or *Snack time*. Write ideas on the board. In pairs, using thesauruses, learners replace words in the poem with their own words. Remind them to stick to the correct word count and word class for each line.

> **Differentiation ideas:** In small mixed groups, learners rewrite all the cinquain examples using their own words for extra support.

Working individually, more confident learners change these word-count cinquains into syllable-count cinquains of 2-4-6-8-2 syllables per line.

⟩ **Assessment ideas:** Observe and check as they work together to create a cinquain. Look out for those needing support.

Answers:

2 a–b Learners' own answers.

Plenary idea

Cinquain sequence (5 minutes)

Resources: Learners' poems from this session

Description: Learners share their poems with the class. Invite constructive feedback and discuss ways to improve. Invite learners to reflect on things they found easy or difficult. Ask: *Have you captured a moment or feeling using effective words and images?*

⟩ **Assessment ideas:** Learners use a rating system or symbols to indicate which poems they enjoyed the most or which poems they think worked out the best. Discuss why and ways to improve.

CROSS-CURRICULAR LINKS

PHSE: Discuss emotions and discuss why poems are a useful way to describe feelings. Learners could look for some examples.

Homework ideas

Learners illustrate the cinquain poem examples in this session. Then they rewrite them using own words and images.

Answers for Workbook

1 Accept any of the following:

A – Has five lines with 1-2-3-4-1 words on each line.	B – Has five lines with 2-4-6-8-2 syllables
Line 1 and line 5: one word, links to the title	Line 1 and line 5: two syllables, links to the title
Line 2: two adjectives separated by commas	Line 2: four syllables
Line 3: has *-ing* verbs separated by commas	Line 3: six syllables
Line 4: a four-word phrase	Line 4: eight syllables

2

Nouns (common and abstract)	Adjectives (comparative and superlative)	Verbs	Adverbs
creation	creative	create	creatively
imagination	imaginative	imagine	imaginatively
attraction	attractive	attract	attractively
obedience	obedient	obey	obediently
love	loving	love	lovingly
softness	soft	soften	softly
success	successful	succeed	successfully
breath	breathless	breathe	breathlessly

3 Learners' own answers.

6.4 Follow the rules

LEARNING PLAN

Learning objectives		Learning intentions	Success criteria
Main focus	**Also covered**	• Plan ideas and explore vocabulary. • Explore word classes. • Proofread and present.	• Learners can plan ideas and explore vocabulary. • Learners can use word classes effectively. • Learners can proofread their work and present it neatly.
6Rg.08, 6Wv.04, 6Wc.01, 6Wc.06	6Rg.05, 6Rs.02, 6Wv.02, 6Ws.04, 6Wv.05, 6Wv.06, 6Wc.02, 6Wp.03, 6Wp.04, 6Wp.05		

LANGUAGE SUPPORT

By Year 6, learners should be familiar with syllables but you may need to revise the following rules: every syllable is a vowel sound – if a word has one vowel it is not divided; separate prefixes and suffixes from the root; separate double consonants; if words end with -ckle divide before the le; the silent e is not counted; if the vowel is in the middle of a word, split the word after the vowel before the consonant wa/ter.

Common misconceptions

Misconception	How to identify	How to overcome
The syllable count is always obvious.	Write these examples on the board and ask learners to count the syllables: *blessed or blesséd, o'er or over* Ask: *Is the syllable count always clear?* *Might a poet choose a syllable count to fit their poem?* (Yes.)	Read other examples of poems where the syllable count could be different.

Starter idea

Create criteria (5 minutes)

Resources: Learner's Book, Session 6.4: Getting started

Description: In pairs, learners come up with five criteria to use for assessing a (word count) cinquain poem. Look out for learners needing help and guide them to ensure they have included the following: five lines; 1-2-3-4-1 words per line; first line and last line connect; second line has adjectives; third line has -ing verbs; fourth line is a four-word phrase describing a feeling or emotion.

Main teaching ideas

1 Gather ideas and organise your thoughts (20 minutes)

Learning intentions: To develop creative writing in a range of poems; to use vocabulary carefully to develop imaginative detail

Resources: Learner's Book, Session 6.4, Activity 1; Language worksheet 6A; thesauruses

Description: Use part a of Language worksheet 6A. Write some ideas on the board for things learners can write about. Invite their ideas.

Working on their own, learners choose an idea then list words and phrases related to their topic. Invite them to describe how they feel about the topic.

Learners use thesauruses or onscreen tools to find different words to describe things and experiment with different word combinations. They write their poems and share them with each other. Then they check each other's poems using the criteria they listed in the Starter activity and discuss ways to improve. Remind learners to show consideration for another point of view as they try to help each other improve.

> **Differentiation ideas:** In pairs or small groups, learners write a list of criteria for a syllable-count cinquain poem for extra support.

Working individually, more confident learners plan a syllable-count cinquain.

> **Assessment ideas:** Observe learners as they use a thesaurus to brainstorm vocabulary and create images. Walk around as they plan their poems, assisting and checking that they use the guidelines provided.

Answers:
1   a–e   Learners' own creative work.

2   Edit and present your poem (20 minutes)

Learning intention: To check and edit a first draft then present a poem

Resources: Learner's Book, Session 6.4, Activity 2; Workbook, Session 6.4; Language worksheet 6A

Description: Learners check their poems against the criteria listed in the Starter activities. Invite them to make further improvements, particularly to word

choice. Suggest they use their own list of interesting words as a resource.

Learners write their poems on poster paper or key it in online and print it – one poem placed in the middle of the page for effect. If time permits, let them illustrate their own poem or a peer's poem.

Complete the Workbook activities for Session 6.4.

> **Differentiation ideas:** Learners can use Language worksheet 6A for support in writing a syllable-count cinquain poem.

For greater challenge, learners could edit and present different cinquain poems – as many as they can manage. They can use Language worksheet 6A to guide their independent work.

> **Assessment ideas:** Assess learners' final written work according to the criteria on the board (as discussed in the Starter idea).

Answers:
2   a–c   Learners' own work.

Plenary idea

High five (5 minutes)

Resources: Learners' poems from in Activity 2

Description: Learners share their poems with each other. Then they reflect on which poems were the most effective, giving their reasons.

> **Assessment ideas:** Learners use the criteria discussed to assess each other's poems.

Homework ideas

Learners choose one topic and write two cinquain poems – a word count and a syllable count version.

Answers for Workbook

1–3 Learners' own work.

6.5 Laugh with limericks

LEARNING PLAN

Learning objectives		Learning intentions	Success criteria
Main focus	**Also covered**	• Read aloud with expression.	• Learners can read aloud with expression.
6Rs.02	6Rv.04, 6Rv.06, 6Rg.03, 6SLp.01, 6Ww.07	• Explore features of limericks. • Perform in groups.	• Learners can identify features of a limerick. • Learners can perform a poem in groups.

LANGUAGE SUPPORT

Most learners may need extra support in grasping rhythm (sound pattern) in poetry as it is not an obvious thing. Poetic metre is the rhythm or pattern of beats in a verse. It is a poetic device that expresses a sound pattern according to stressed and unstressed syllables in each line.

A syllable is a vowel sound that makes the *a, e, i, o, u* or *y*. The number of times you hear a vowel in a word is the number of syllables there are. When two or more syllables are next to each other, the number of syllables depends on the number of sounds they make. 'Hour' is one sound. A silent vowel does not count as a syllable.

Starter idea

Hear the beat (5 minutes)

Resources: Learner's Book, Session 6.5: Getting started

Description: Lead a class discussion. Invite learners to demonstrate the beat or rhythm in a song or poem. Ask: *Does the beat go according to the number of words or syllables?* (It is a combination of stressed, unstressed and extended syllables.) Compare songs and poems. Ask: *Can a poem have a beat?* (Yes, but not all poems have a beat/rhythm/metre.) Write words on the board and clap the syllables. Ask: *Is a syllable also the beat?* (No, a syllable is a vowel sound in a word; a beat is created by following a pattern of stressed and/or unstressed syllables.)

Main teaching ideas

1 Enjoy limericks (20 minutes)

Learning intention: To read aloud and identify features of a limerick

Resources: Four limericks (Learner's Book, Session 6.5, Activity 1); Tracks 35, 36, 37 and 38; Worksheets 6.23 and 6.24

Description: Invite learners to read the four limericks aloud and share their initial responses. Provide poetry books with further examples of limericks to small groups of learners to read and enjoy and so they can begin to identify common features. In pairs, learners answer the questions in the Learner's Book, giving examples to support each answer. They make up their own rules for limericks then, together, read the Language focus box to compare to their own rules. They make corrections where necessary.

Spelling link: *Metre* (UK spelling) and *meter* (US spelling) are easily confused words. Both refer to the rhythm but can also mean a unit of measurement. Learners make a list of other UK/US spelling words and add them to their learning journals.

> Differentiation ideas: In pairs or small groups, learners research when and where limericks originated. They also explore limericks by Edward

Lear. Challenge more confident learners to speak to the class about what they have found out.

> **Assessment ideas:** Learners compile a list of 'limerick rules' to use for checking limericks – including their own. Assess if learners can describe the features of a limerick. Use Worksheet 6.23 Plan a limerick and Worksheet 6.24 Limerick assessment to guide you.

Answers:
1   a   Five lines, lines 1, 2, 5 are longer; lines 3, 4 are shorter

    b   AABBA

    c   humour, nonsense, fun, light-hearted

    d   Various types of word play example rhyme, palindrome, tongue-twisters…

    e   Learners' own rules based on the information.

2   **Work together to practise the rhythm of a limerick, then perform it (20 minutes)**

Learning intention: To work together to perform a poem using expression

Resources: Learner's Book, Session 6.5, Activity 2; a range of limericks

Description: Organise small groups of learners. Allow time for learners to practise reading and performing the limericks. Learners perform the poems in front of the class. This is good for collaborating and building confidence.

> **Differentiation ideas:** Support learners, in small groups and with supervision, by allowing them to record audio or videos of their performance. In larger groups, which can be more challenging but will extend group work skills, learners record audio or video of their performance.

Answers:
2   a–c   Learners' own work.

Plenary idea

Do you 'like' your limerick? (5 minutes)

Resources: Learner's Book, Session 6.5, Activity 2

Description: As learners practise, invite them to reflect on their performance and consider ways to improve.

> **Assessment ideas:** Learners choose their favourite limerick performance and say why they like it.

CROSS-CURRICULAR LINKS

Geography: Learners identify places on a map mentioned in some limericks, like 'Glenelg', and discover that there is actually the city of Limerick.

Homework ideas

Learners complete the Workbook activities for Session 6.5. Then they do some further research on other types of nonsense poems.

Answers for Workbook

N	R	Q	E	H	W	Z	W	N	T	Z	I	T	Z	B
H	T	X	Z	U	G	E	S	Q	M	M	A	H	I	F
F	L	O	W	E	R	U	I	I	C	D	S	Y	H	L
I	G	M	P	X	T	O	R	X	W	K	M	H	N
I	N	U	E	A	E	R	Y	D	T	H	C	E	G	S
H	F	P	G	R	A	I	O	V	Z	E	I	X	U	M
F	D	R	A	A	F	E	J	S	N	Y	T	O	O	Y
I	E	R	W	T	H	E	W	E	D	O	S	Q	R	I
E	A	A	R	D	X	O	R	L	O	X	U	R	V	R
I	Y	A	F	O	Z	P	U	F	A	I	R	G	Z	Y
H	E	E	Q	O	A	O	T	R	J	Q	N	W	H	E
H	G	S	G	W	H	K	E	R	O	S	A	G	K	T
L	I	M	E	S	N	N	Q	P	Q	S	Y	P	G	L
R	E	E	T	S	Q	O	T	R	A	P	I	Q	T	V
X	Z	B	P	R	P	W	B	T	F	E	D	B	B	N

1 agree – sea; dough – know; fair – rare; flower – hour; heart – part; lime – thyme; nought – sort; puff – rough; saw – sore; should – wood; six – sticks; The following rhyming words are included in the word search as extension: away – whey, – true, pie –, steer – weir

2 There was an Old Man with a beard
Who said, "It is just as I feared!
Two Owls and a Hen,
Four Larks and a Wren,
Have all built their nests in my beard!"

3 Learners' own research.

6.6 Play with words

LEARNING PLAN

Learning objectives		Learning intentions	Success criteria
Main focus	**Also covered**	• Plan limericks.	• Learners can plan limericks.
6Rs.02, 6Ra.01, 6Wv.04, 6Wc.01, 6Wc.07	6Wv.05, 6Ws.04, 6Wc.02, 6Wp.03, 6Wp.04, 6Wp.05, 6SLp.01, 6SLp.03, 6SLm.05	• Check and edit. • Present and read aloud.	• Learners can check and edit their work. • Learners can present their work with confidence.

LANGUAGE SUPPORT

Word play is a popular technique used in limericks and other rhymes and nonsense verse to create humour. It is not always easy for learners to grasp word play. It requires a subtle understanding of language and vocabulary. Revise various techniques.

Homophones and homonyms are words that look or sound the same but have different meanings. Poets can also invent their own 'nonsense' words or create new words like portmanteau words – words that combine two words to make a new word as when 'lunch' and 'breakfast' become 'brunch'.

Starter idea

Rhymes and patterns (5 minutes)

Resources: Learner's Book, Session 6.6: Getting started

Description: In pairs, learners share ideas on how to write a limerick. Check for those who might need guidance or further assistance. Write examples of rhyming patterns on the board and invite learners to demonstrate them: AABB, ABCB, AABA as revision.

Main teaching ideas

1 With a partner, make up a limerick (20 minutes)

Learning intention: To collaborate to write a limerick

Resources: Learner's Book, Session 6.6, Activity 1; Worksheet 6.23; dictionaries and thesauruses

Description: In pairs, learners brainstorm topics for a limerick, choose one topic, then note phrases and words connected to the topic. Invite learners to choose imaginary people, objects and places to avoid being personal or hurtful. They can make up nonsense words and names.

Learners decide how to start their limerick using the examples provided, then write the first line. Learners use Worksheet 6.23 Plan a limerick to guide and check their writing. As a class share the limericks.

> Differentiation ideas: Support less confident learners by allowing them to work in pairs or small groups to complete the Workbook activities for Session 6.6.

Challenge more confident learners to work in large groups to plan and write limericks for a particular audience. For example, they could write about characters from nursery rhymes or folk tales for younger children to enjoy.

Answers:
1   a–e   Learners' own work.

2 Write your own limericks (20 minutes)

Learning intention: To plan, edit and present limericks

Resources: Learner's Book, Session 6.6, Activity 2; Worksheets 6.23 and 6.24 an atlas or map; thesauruses

Description: Learners work on their own using Worksheet 6.23 to help them plan a limerick. Provide ideas for topics, an atlas or map of the world to inspire ideas of different places and a thesaurus to enrich vocabulary.

In pairs, learners read their poems aloud to check and edit each other's work, offering ways to improve. They key in their poems and print them out or write them neatly. Whichever they choose, the work should be well presented. Learners practise performing their poems with expression and rhythm.

> Differentiation ideas: With support, learners can work in pairs or small groups to write one poem. Working individually or in pairs, more confident learners can be encouraged to write more than one poem.

> Assessment ideas: Observe paired work and assess how well individual learners participate. Learners use Worksheet 6.24 Limerick assessment to help assess their work.

Answers:
2   a–d   Learners' own work.

Plenary idea

Share your poems (5 minutes)

Resources: Worksheet 6.10; learners' own poems

Description: Learners read their poems aloud then participate in positive feedback.

> **Assessment ideas:** Use Worksheet 6.10 Reading, speaking or performing assessment to assess learners' reading with expression. Learners choose their favourite limericks and explain what makes them good.

Homework ideas

Learners write more limericks, inspired by the people they know or live with and the places they visit. Then complete the Workbook activities for Session 6.6.

Answers for Workbook

Learners' own limericks.

CHECK YOUR PROGRESS

1   Accept any reasonable answer like poetic licence is the freedom a writer has to change conventional language, spelling and punctuation rules.

2   Accept any variations of the following answers.

    a   Visual impact (what you see) is created by the size and shape of the poem. The shape is created by the direction of words and/or the lines, the size and/or boldness of the font.

    b   Auditory impact (what you hear) is created by how the reader reads the poem. The reader follows the punctuation clues for expression and spelling clues for pronunciation. Font size and boldness can also add to the expression.

3   Accept any similar answers for the word origins of

    a   Cinquain – *cinq* comes from the French (or Latin) word meaning 'five'. It is a five-line poem.

    b   Homophone – *homo* comes from the Latin word meaning 'the same' and *phone* meaning 'to hear'. Homophones are words that sound the same but have a different meaning.

4   Learners give the word classes and write their own sentence: imagine – verb; imagination – noun; imaginary – adjective.

5   Accept any reasonable sentences that show the correct use of the words:

    They will <u>write</u> a letter to express their <u>right</u> to attend a religious <u>rite</u> with the family. <u>They're</u> going to have a celebration over <u>there</u> to honour <u>their</u> grandmother.

PROJECT GUIDANCE

Group project: Learners discuss and plan a school event to celebrate 'Poetry is Fun Day'. Learners make a list of activities and draw up a timetable to show when, where and how each activity will take place during the school day. Activities might include poetry recitations, choral verse, dress-up, a film, a trip to the library and/or a talk by a local writer or poet. Groups will give a short presentation to advertise the event, including a poster or flyer to persuade everyone to join in the fun.

Pair project: Learners research two poets mentioned in this unit. They summarise the information using a mind map or a fact file then use the information to write two paragraphs, in their own words, about each poet. Learners include a poem by each poet as an example of their writing style. Learners display the information neatly in their books or as posters around the class.

Solo project: Learners research different types of poems to find explanations, origins and examples of each. They summarise the information in a comparison table describing and comparing poems according to their features. These can be displayed in the class and used as a reference when reading or writing poetry.

>7 A different medium

Unit plan

Session	Approximate number of learning hours	Outline of learning content	Resources
7.1 A multimedia novel	1	Skim read and scan a multimedia extract. Rewrite dialogue. Answer questions.	Learner's Book Session 7.1 Workbook Session 7.1
7.2 Language matters	1	Discuss narrative. Investigate connectives. Explore sentences and paragraphs.	Learner's Book Session 7.2 Workbook Session 7.2
7.3 and 7.4 Plan and write an illustrated episode	1.5	Plan an episode. Write a draft of an episode. Revise and improve writing.	Learner's Book Session 7.3 and 7.4 Workbook Session 7.3 and 7.4 ⬇ Worksheet 6.9 ⬇ Worksheet 6.25
7.5 Introducing manga	1	Explore a manga cover. Scan and interpret a manga extract. Answer questions.	Learner's Book Session 7.5 Workbook Session 7.5
7.6 Shion	1	Plan a character profile. Write three paragraphs about Shion. Edit and improve writing.	Learner's Book Session 7.6 Workbook Session 7.6
7.7 Medium matters	1	Rewrite the manga extract. Give a presentation on different media.	Learner's Book Session 7.7 Workbook Session 7.7 ⬇ Worksheet 6.10

Session	Approximate number of learning hours	Outline of learning content	Resources
7.8 All the world's a stage	1	Write about a famous playwright. Explore the layout and structure of plays.	Learner's Book Session 7.8 Workbook Session 7.8
7.9 What has changed?	1	Read a play extract. Predict what words mean. Explore how language changes.	Learner's Book Session 7.9 Workbook Session 7.9
7.10 Using language	1	Explore a plain words version. Investigate figurative language. Work with colons and semicolons.	Learner's Book Session 7.10 Workbook Session 7.10 ⬇ Worksheet 6.26
7.11 Shakespeare alive	1	Explore a modern version of Shakespeare. Compare it to the original version.	Learner's Book Session 7.11 Workbook Session 7.11 ⬇ Worksheet 6.27
7.12 Write your own playscript	1	Plan a playscript. Write a playscript. Present a playscript in a group.	Learner's Book Session 7.12 Workbook Session 7.12 ⬇ Worksheet 6.28

Cross-unit resources
Learner's Book Check your progress Learner's Book Projects Unit 7 Language worksheets Unit 7 Differentiated worksheet pack End-of-unit 7 test

BACKGROUND KNOWLEDGE

Many of the texts in this unit have multimedia elements – a novel with illustrations and a cartoon strip prologue, Japanese manga and a manga graphic novel version of a Shakespeare play. Learners today are proficient at dealing with multimedia platforms – potentially being more conversant with multimedia than a pure text-based option. While they may not have encountered a Japanese manga graphic novel, learners may well be familiar with some of the anime based on manga characters, such as Pokémon and Dragonball Z.

Manga has a long history in Japan and the medium is not confined to children or young adults. People of all ages read manga across a wide range of subjects, from adventure and fiction to business, history and science. It is an interesting discussion point for learners to consider – does a graphic component enhance their enjoyment, their understanding or both? The manga version of *Twelfth Night* in the unit has not been written from back to front and right to left as in a traditional manga, but it does retain the characteristics of manga artwork and style. There are many other graphic novel versions of Shakespeare plays that are not done in the manga style, but it is easy to see the appeal for this age group.

TEACHING SKILLS FOCUS

Active learning

Active learning focuses on how learners learn as much as what they learn. The aim is for learners to understand how they learn and thus take responsibility for more of their learning and become independent and confident learners.

This unit provides plentiful opportunities for promoting active learning in your classroom. In a concrete form, active learning is encouraged by the worksheets that focus learners on their process leading to a final outcome. Throughout the unit learners are encouraged to reflect and self-assess, and to think about what they found hard or challenging and what they could have improved to ensure a better learning process in future.

Learners are encouraged to increase their vocabulary and improve their word choice using a range of tools, from dictionaries, thesauruses and online tools to their own compiled list of words. Improving and focusing on words in the context of writing helps learners reflect on how they are achieving characterisation, imaginative detail and authenticity. Listening to others allows learners to compare their choices and outcomes, instilling an embedded urge for self-improvement.

While some learners will need more support to reflect on how they learn and how they could improve their learning, all learners benefit from regular discussion and questioning by you as the teacher and by each other.

Use the activity when they write a new episode for *Flora and Ulysses* to include a cartoon sequence to encourage learners not just to reflect on what they want to include in the episode but how they want to present it and how to achieve a similar, quirky style. Dip in and out of learners' work praising good word choices, for example, but also talking about how they chose, what they reflected on and their decision-making criteria.

Above all, you need to strive to create a classroom where process is appreciated as much as the end product. If learners are not always able to finish their work completely, praise their work in progress and discuss how they could perhaps have worked faster and what they could change or do differently next time.

7.1 A multimedia novel

LEARNING PLAN

Learning objectives		Learning intentions	Success criteria
Main focus	**Also covered**	• Skim read and scan a multimedia extract for detail. • Rewrite dialogue. • Answer questions on the text.	• Learners can skim read for the main idea and scan a text for detail. • Learners can rewrite dialogue with accompanying narrative. • Learners can answer questions based on a text using evidence.
6Rv.01, 6Rv.02, 6Ri.06, 6Ri.07, 6Ri.09, 6Ri.10, 6Ra.02, 6Wg.02, 6SLm.04, 6SLp.01, 6SLp.02	6Rv.03, 6Ri.02, 6Ri.08, 6Ri.13, 6Ri.14, 6Ra.01, 6Ra.03, 6Wv.02, 6Wv.04, 6Wv.06 6Wc.01, 6SLm.01, 6SLm.03		

LANGUAGE SUPPORT

This session requires learners to scan for detail and use different strategies to understand unfamiliar phrases and words, as well as to use context to decide on the correct meaning of words. Learners must also use common word roots to infer meaning. It would be helpful to demonstrate an online etymological dictionary to show the word origin of *incandescent* to help them understand what the word *Incandesto* implies about the superhero. Remind learners that inferring meaning is not the same as guessing, they must search for clues to guide their thinking.

Starter idea

What does multimedia mean? (5 minutes)

Resources: Learner's Book, Session 7.1: Getting started

Description: Learners are likely to be familiar with *multimedia* content through television, computers, tablets and smartphones but they may not be familiar with the term itself. Allow time for learners to break down the word into its component parts – *multi* and *media* – and use their knowledge of word roots to help understand the term. Discuss their ideas as a class. List different multimedia formats on the board, then ask which ones they think relate to writing.

Main teaching ideas

1 Read a multimedia novel (15 minutes)

Learning intention: To skim read and summarise

Resources: *Flora and Ulysses: The Illuminated Adventures* (Learner's Book, Session 7.1, Activity 1); Track 39

Description: Kate DiCamillo's novel centres on the adventures of Flora (a young girl who enjoys reading superhero comics rather than the 'quality' literature her mother would like her to read) and Ulysses (the squirrel who acquires superhero attributes after being sucked up by the neighbour's vacuum cleaner). The novel's narrative is interspersed with comic book sequences, full-page illustrations and other unusual narrative features. It contains madcap adventures and unlikely scenarios, plus plenty of humour and wordplay.

The beginning of the novel is a comic book format prologue that outlines events leading up to what Flora sees out of her window – a vacuum cleaner dragging her neighbour round the garden, about to vacuum up a squirrel. The cartoon sequence foreshadows later events through the name of the vacuum cleaner and what Ulysses represents; the comic book Flora is reading foreshadows the squirrel acquiring superpowers.

Learners should read the cartoon sequence before you tell them about the novel so they have a chance to interpret the events and infer how the characters feel from the visual aspect of the cartoon as well as the dialogue, e.g. the husband's gestures explaining the vacuum cleaner; the huge instruction manual; the husband excitedly listing its magnificent qualities, juxtaposed with the mother's deadpan reaction and expression when confronted with its capacity (not a very exciting birthday present for her!); her exasperation with her husband's enthusiasm; and their shocked expressions when the cleaner gets going and whizzes off into the garden.

Play Track 36 to give learners an opportunity to hear the cartoon sequence dialogue in contrast to the narrative section of Chapter One.

The narrative part is what learners might expect at the beginning of a novel, setting the scene and introducing the main character.

Discuss the book's format and get a feel for it by reading the cartoon sequence aloud. Encourage learners to role-play the characters as much as possible when reading aloud, mirroring the characters' actions.

Learners' summary of the cartoon sequence can be oral or written – either way, they summarise it to each other orally before writing two or three sentences summarising the action.

At the end, encourage them to predict what could have started with a vacuum cleaner. There are few clues so they can use their imagination.

> **Differentiation ideas:** Support less confident learners by working with selected pairs to help them identify the key points before they summarise the extract.

Challenge more confident learners to work individually to identify the key points, or they can support some of the selected pairs.

Answers:
1   a–c Learners' own answers.
    d   Prologue because it is linked to the story rather than explaining how the book came to be written.
    e   Learners' own answers.

2 Practise your narrative and dialogue skills (15 minutes)

Learning intention: To punctuate dialogue accurately

Resources: Learner's Book, Session 7.1, Activity 2; thesauruses

Description: Learners write out the cartoon dialogue in narrative form. Focus on the punctuation and creative alternatives to *said*, using characters' actions and expressions to decide. Learners could use *said* with an adverb, but an expressive verb would be better.

Ask a volunteer to explain the difference between first- and third-person narrative. The sequence naturally lends itself to third person. If learners struggle to start, ask them to describe what they see: *Mr Tickham (Donald) proudly launched into singing, "Happy birthday to youuuuuu!" as he dragged in an enormous contraption.* This will also help them write in the past tense for the connecting narrative.

Encourage learners to add some of the alternative verbs to *said* to their word list in their learning journals (Worksheet 6.1).

> **Differentiation ideas:** Support less confident learners by allowing them to write in pairs to provide each other with support. Also allow them to use *said* in their draft. Sit with them in small groups and encourage them to choose more descriptive alternatives from the box or using a thesaurus and to add them to their work.

Ask more confident learners to write a more detailed narrative to accompany the dialogue in Activity 2.

> **Assessment ideas:** Activity 2 could be used for assessing accuracy in dialogue punctuation and creativity at choosing precise words.

Answers:
2   a   Learners' own answers but with the cartoon bubbles inside the speech marks.

3 Answer questions on the text (20 minutes)

Learning intention: To scan for detail to answer questions

Resources: Learner's Book, Session 7.1, Activity 3

Description: This activity encourages learners to focus on the details and select precise words. It helps them note, infer, predict and gather clues about Flora's character. Learners are looking for a combination of explicit and implicit meaning.

Pairs should discuss the questions briefly before writing answers. Check they remember (from Unit 4) that speech marks can indicate a quotation as well as dialogue, and that the exact words being quoted (what someone said or wrote) are enclosed.

Spelling link: The title of Chapter One is *A Natural-Born Cynic*. Point out the adjective *natural-born* and ask what word class it is. Learners should see it as an adjective, but discuss that *natural* and *born* are both words in their own right; when they come together, the compound adjective acquires a meaning of its own derived from both words. Encourage learners to come up with other compound adjectives they can think of (e.g. *light-hearted*, *well-meaning*, *free-range*). Explore how many have a hyphen and how many have become a single word – e.g. *handwritten*, *everyday*, *online*, *multimedia* – although *multimedia* is still sometimes written with a hyphen.

Remind learners that compound adjectives are not necessarily fixed but can be created by the author to fit context – e.g. *she built a four-foot table*; *It is a light-blue dress* (note different meaning from a *light, blue dress* – i.e. a blue dress that weighs very little).

› **Differentiation ideas:** Support less confident learners by allowing them to answer only selected questions, and to jot down notes for the answers so they can focus on content.

Encourage more confident learners to write in their learning journals about the novel and multimedia format, together with how well they think it works and how they might be able to use it in a story. Learners can say whether they would enjoy the rest of the book.

› **Assessment ideas:** Activity 3 could be assessed for understanding and ability to infer characterisation and interpret clues in the text to predict elements of the story.

Answers:

3 a Learners' own answers.

   b • Because she is introduced in the opening scene and is the focus.
      • She is reading a comic book.

   c It implies that Flora was born believing that people are not always sincere – her character is suited to that way of thinking. It refers to Flora.

   d • "*work to turn her face away from the idiotic high jinks of comics and towards the bright light of true literature.*" The words from the contract are enclosed in speech marks (quotation marks) to indicate the words are being quoted.

      • It means she should read improving literature rather than waste her time on childish comics. Flora's mother made her sign it because she doesn't approve of her reading comics.
      • She is not obeying the contract because she is reading a comic.

   e Learners' own answers.

   f Accept sensible answers as aspects of all three meanings are contained in the title.

   g • It has capital letters. The person is introduced indicating a name or at least a title.

      • *Incandescent*: 1 producing a bright light from a heated filament or other part; 2 (literary) extremely bright. The meaning indicates he is probably a superhero who glows brightly in some way.

   h Learners' own answers. Encourage reasons.

   i The squirrel – it would not have been introduced and called after the vacuum cleaner if it was not a main character.

   j Learners' own answers.

Plenary idea

What did you think? (5 minutes)

Resources: Learners' answers to the questions in Activity 3

Description: Organise learners into groups to compare answers. Encourage them to discuss any differences and come up with a group answer to share with the class. If there is time, share answers as a class.

› **Assessment ideas:** Learners assess each other's work and, through discussion, iron out any differences and take in different points of view.

CROSS-CURRICULAR LINKS

Science: Find reference books and resources about squirrels, plus information on how vacuum cleaners work.

Homework ideas

Learners could sketch a superhero character and think up 'heroic' names. Then they complete the Workbook activities for Session 7.1. You could share ideas and answers in class.

Answers for Workbook

1   Accept all sensible answers. Possible answers:
    a smashed; **b** glanced; **c** stashed;
    d glared; **e** wandered

2   Possible examples: darted, bolted, bounded,
    dashed, ambled, marched, meandered, plodded,
    slinked, sprinted, strutted, toddled, traipsed, raced,
    gallivanted, strode, scrambled, hurtled, hurried,
    trekked, wandered, wafted, gadded, flounced

3   Possible answers: saw – spied; pulled – dragged; new
    – birthday; powerful – vigorous; suck up – swallow;
    small – tiny; let out a cry – squealed/shrieked; went
    – rushed; took – grabbed; pulled – yanked; looked
    carefully – peered; get – extract/rescue;
    frightened – terrified; looked up – gazed.

7.2 Language matters

LEARNING PLAN				
Learning objectives		**Learning intentions**	**Success criteria**	
Main focus	**Also covered**	• Discuss narrative.	• Learners can discuss different features of narrative.	
6Rv.04, 6Rg.03, 6Rg.07, 6Rg.08, 6Rs.02, 6Ri.03, 6Ri.11, 6Ri.17, 6Ra.02, 6SLm.02, 6SLm.03, 6SLg.03, 6SLp.03, 6Ws.03	6Rg.02, 6Ri.02, 6Ri.13, 6Ri.14, 6Ra.03, 6Wg.03, 6Wg.04, 6Wg.08, 6SLm.05, 6SLg.01, 6SLr.01, 6Wc.08, 6SLm.01, 6SLg.04	• Investigate connectives. • Explore sentences and paragraphs.	• Learners can investigate using connectives according to purpose. • Learners can explore paragraphs and different sentence types and their effect in writing.	

LANGUAGE SUPPORT

Learners investigate connectives according to their purpose – whether to link sentences or paragraphs. Learners may need to practise using connectives correctly as it is easy to select the wrong one – especially for some learners. While some are synonymous, others can have the opposite effect. Remind learners that connectives can be conjunctions or adverbs and they can comprise more than one word.

Learners do need to differentiate between complex and compound sentences. The Learner's Book uses the term *dependent* clause. If your learners are more familiar with the term *subordinate* clause, explain that they are the same thing but help learners to see that dependent clauses cannot stand alone – they *depend* on the main clause for sense. Familiarise them with the FANBOYS mnemonic (For-And-Nor-But-Or-Yet-So), as it may help them to identify compound sentences more easily. Point out that coordinating conjunctions – those used in compound sentences – are rarely used to link paragraphs, whereas ones used in complex sentences often also introduce new paragraphs linking them to earlier ones – especially when using time connectives.

Common misconceptions

Misconception	How to identify	How to overcome
Complex sentences have one main clause and one dependent clause.	Write a complex sentence on the board with one dependent clause and ask learners if it could be extended.	Show learners how a sentence can be extended by adding more dependent clauses. (Note: a sentence could be a compound, complex sentence but keep it simple.) Use the activities in 3 to assist.

Starter idea

Paragraphs (5 minutes)

Resources: Learner's Book, Session 7.2: Getting started

Description: Allow partners time to revise the reasons for starting new paragraphs: new action/event, new speaker, new place, new topic, new character.

Discuss ideas as a class and remind learners that fiction writers often start new paragraphs for effect – e.g. to emphasise something; attract the reader's attention; and create a particular sense of flow or lack of flow to mirror content in writing. Reasons like this would appear primarily in fiction writing, as would starting a new paragraph when a new speaker begins in dialogue.

Main teaching ideas

1 Narrative style (25 minutes)

Learning intention: To compare and discuss different features and styles of the genre

Resources: Learner's Book, Session 7.2, Activity 1

Description: In groups, learners use the words in the box to help learners articulate their response to the narrative style. They can choose more than one adjective.

Ask learners to give their impressions of whether the styles in the comic strip and the narrative are similar. Although one is mainly dialogue, both are quirky and humorous in style. Learners may find it hard to imitate the style, but they can note in their learning journals elements that make it quirky.

Can learners explain how they identify if it is third-person narrative? Ask: *Does the narrator appear to be objective or sympathetic to one of the characters?*

(It may not be obvious to learners that the narrator is partisan to Flora.) *Does the narrator seem sympathetic to the mother? Why/why not?* (She is made to appear slightly absurd through the wording of the contract, as much as getting her daughter to sign one in the first place over something so extraordinary.)

Limit discussion time. Ask where learners think the author's (as opposed to the narrator's) sympathies lie. Do they think author and narrator in this case are aligned – authors do become fond of characters?

Finally, groups discuss the mixed format and send a spokesperson to summarise their opinions, backed by examples from the extract, to another group.

The questions take learners through the process of forming an opinion based on reasons. Listing points for and against is always helpful for making up one's mind in an informed manner rather than rushing in to say what you 'feel'. Each group should appoint a scribe to list their ideas of pros and cons (reasons for and against) and a spokesperson. Limit time for this part of the activity to about five minutes to ensure learners stay on task. Organise envoys to report to another group.

Groups listen to the envoy and ask questions. They compare ideas. If time, the envoys can report any differences of opinion to the original group. End with a class vote on whether learners would enjoy reading more books like this, giving reasons.

If you have a copy of the novel, you could share its epilogue. It is titled *Squirrel Poetry* and is an example of Ulysses' poetry. Learners can look up *epilogue* in the Book talk feature in the Toolkit at the end of the Learner's Book.

> **Differentiation ideas:** Encourage mixed groups to help less confident learners write their summary of their opinions of the mixed format in their notebooks.

For extra challenge, encourage learners to take a balanced approach weighing up points for and against before giving an opinion.

Answers:

1 a–b Learners' own answers.

c Third person. No *I/we/us* pronouns in the narrative.

d • Flora – mother made to seem absurd over the contract and its wording.
   • Flora is in the title and so she is obviously the main character rather than the mother; the narrator is more likely to sympathise with a main character.
   • Learners' own answers.

e Learners' own answers.

2 Connectives have meaning (15 minutes)

Learning intention: To explore connectives and their purposes

Resources: Learner's Book, Session 7.2, Activity 2

Description: The incorrect connective in writing can give completely the wrong effect. Learners need to be familiar with different ways of achieving similar effects with different connectives. This activity forces their attention on the purpose of each connective – i.e. linking meaning to purpose. Learners have to use the context to help them establish the meaning/purpose, then apply the knowledge in their own sentences and paragraphs. Ask learners to invent sentences orally to get them started.

The Toolkit at the back of the Learner's Book has a table of connectives and their purpose which learners can use to check their ideas. Be strict about learners using appropriate connectives in their writing whether linking clauses, sentences or paragraphs.

> **Differentiation ideas:** Support less confident learners by limiting and/or selecting connectives for their sentences.

Challenge more confident learners by discussing the purpose of the connective first and then let them work individually to write a sentence using it correctly. Invite some learners to read their sentences to the class.

> **Assessment ideas:** Assess learners' understanding of the purpose of connectives in Activity 2 – especially through the sentences they write.

Answers:

2 a to contrast; to add information; to show cause and effect; to show purpose/give a reason; to provide an example.

b Learners' own answers.

3 Focus on paragraphs and sentences (10 minutes)

Learning intention: To explore multi-clause sentences and paragraphs

Resources: Learner's Book, Session 7.2, Activity 3

Description: This activity builds on paragraphs and transitions, addressed in earlier units. Paragraphing tends to be more flexible in fiction than in non-fiction (excepting texts like advertising, posters, instructions and emotive writing).

Learners apply their knowledge of sentence structure including simple sentences, the difference between coordinating and subordinating conjunctions/connectives, and compound/complex sentences. The short statements of fact add variety to the unusual style.

> **Differentiation ideas:** Support groups/pairs of learners in identifying the connectives and then consult the Language focus box to help decide on the type of multi-clause sentence.

More confident learners can work alone then share their work.

> **Assessment ideas:** Assess learners' knowledge of paragraph and sentence structure.

Answers:

3 a [1] Introducing Flora. [2] Flora's mother starts speaking. [3] Flora replies. [4] Her mother responds. [5] Explains the contract mentioned in the dialogue. [5] Emphasises the absurdity of the contract/her mother. [6] Emphasises how absurd her mother is with the contract. [7] Gives more detail about the mother. [8]–[10] Short factual statements.

b Starting a new paragraph when a new speaker begins speaking.

c Compound – use of *and* to connect the main clauses.

d Learners' own answers – three short factual statements emphasise the quirky style of writing and the characters.

e • Complex – *so that* is the connective – implying cause and effect.

• They have the effect of a list – a list of features.

Plenary idea

How does it end? (5 minutes)

Resources: Learner's Book Session 7.2, Activity 3

Description: Give learners a minute to reflect on how the cartoon strip ends. Invite a volunteer to talk about how it ends. (It is three sentences/phrases.)

Ask about the effect of these three short sentences. (The final one being a single word. It is quirky and humorous and breaks several rules of sentences as fiction writers often do. The first one begins with *and*. The second is a phrase rather than a sentence and the last one is a word – adding emphasis.)

Discuss who might be saying those words. Having read the extract, learners might be able to suggest that it is Flora at the start of telling her story, although the main story is written in third-person narrative.

> **Assessment ideas:** Learners can assess how effective they think the ending of the cartoon sequence is and how well it leads into the main story. They can give a vote with slips of paper with a number of 1 to 5 on it, with 5 showing the most positive vote.

CROSS-CURRICULAR LINKS

Science: Find reference books and resources about squirrels and information on how vacuum cleaners work.

Homework ideas

Learners can complete the Workbook activities for Session 7.2 on connectives, multi-clause sentences and paragraphs. Work through the answers in class next lesson.

Answers for Workbook

1 **a** but; **b** or; **c** so; **d** yet; **e** for.

2 **a** unless – complex; **b** so – compound; **c** because – complex; **d** but – compound; **e** when – complex.

3 Sensible answers from: change in time, person, topic or place – or a new speaker.

4 **a** simple; **b** compound; **c** complex; **d** compound; **e** complex; **f** simple.

7.3 and 7.4 Plan and write an illustrated episode

LEARNING PLAN

Learning objectives		Learning intentions	Success criteria
Main focus	**Also covered**	• Plan a new episode.	• Learners can use a planning table to plan a new episode.
6Rg.07, 6Ww.07, 6Wv.04, 6Wg.02, 6Wg.04, 6Wg.08, 6Wc.02, 6Wc.03, 6Wp.03, 6Wp.04, 6Wp.05	6Rs.02, 6Ri.02, 6Ww.06, 6Wv.06, 6Ws.02, 6Wc.01, 6Wp.01, 6SLm.01, 6SLp.01, 6SLp.02, 6SLr.01, 6SLr.02	• Write a new episode. • Revise and improve an episode.	• Learners can write a new episode according to a plan. • Learners can revise, improve and proofread their episodes.

Learners need to focus on their language in this writing activity to mimic the style in Chapter 1 of *Flora and Ulysses*. Point out that it is a combination of techniques: word choice, sentence structure and length, paragraph diversity, use of standard English or departure from it for effect, accurate use of punctuation as well as content. Point out the techniques used in the extract so learners can see it as a model.

Starter idea

Brainstorm Ulysses' unusual abilities (5 minutes)

Resources: Learner's Book, Session 7.3 and 7.4: Getting started

Description: Give learners a few minutes to think together what the squirrel's, Ulysses', unusual abilities might be. Remind them that brainstorming is free thinking. No idea is too absurd. Share their ideas as a class and vote on the most interesting, unusual ability.

Main teaching ideas

1 Plan a chapter (45 minutes)

Learning intention: To plan a new chapter to paragraph level

Resources: Learner's Book, Session 7.3 and 7.4, Activity 1; Worksheets 6.1 and 6.25

Description: Planning is an important part of writing even if the final product does not exactly match the original plan. It should guide the writing process but not be so rigid as to prevent unfolding creativity. Storyboards and ICT presentation slides can be helpful to capture a few words and images to inspire more ideas. Encourage learners to include images and sketches in their brainstorming session, using their learning journal (Worksheet 6.1) if appropriate. Worksheet 6.25 Plan and write a chapter may be useful here.

Learners could write their ideas on a series of sticky notes and put them together on a board or large piece of paper. Similar ideas can be grouped. This allows quieter learners a stronger voice.

Encourage planning at paragraph as well as plot level. Learners are writing another chapter to follow on from the extract. They can be as creative as they like during brainstorming but then do more detailed planning per paragraph. The example chapter in the Learner's Book follows standard story structure.

Learners could include ideas for writing techniques and images per paragraph, and some ideas to bring dialogue to life.

Half the time should be dedicated to planning. Discuss the criteria in Activity 2 at the planning stage. However, the criteria, if applied too strictly during planning, can be restrictive, so use your judgement to consider what would most benefit your learners.

Review learners' plans before you allow them to start writing. Talk about the details of their planning by asking questions: *What made you think of that? How will …? What happens after …?* and so on.

> **Differentiation ideas:** Support less confident learners by providing more detail about the storyline to help with ideas for the planning storyboard/table at paragraph level. It will take the pressure off the 'ideas' side of the writing process and allow them to focus on writing. Part of the planning includes choosing which bit to turn into a comic-book sequence. Any part they plan to have with dialogue (and potentially exclamation marks) might make a suitable section to become the cartoon comic-book segment. Work with learners to help them decide.

Challenge more confident learners to do the detailed paragraph planning in pairs or groups but encourage others to do their own planning after the initial brainstorm. Let them know they can use their own ideas if they prefer, rather than following the guidelines provided in the Learner's Book.

> **Assessment ideas:** Make informal notes about how well learners have planned their overall story structure for the chapter, appropriate content, characterisation and style, plot and writing techniques.

Answers:

1   a–b   Learners' own answers.

2 Write and illustrate the chapter (45 minutes)

Learning intention: To write and edit a new chapter following the same style and format

Resources: Learner's Book, Session 7.3 and 7.4, Activity 2; Worksheets 6.9 and 6.25

Description: Writing should be done in a concentrated burst – at least a first draft. Consider silent working time. Remind learners they do not need to address every concern as it comes up. They should simply make a note of a question and move on. Developing extended concentration periods is important whether writing by hand or on a computer. Remind them not to correct spelling or grammar while they are working; this will interrupt flow and concentration. Corrections can be made at the end.

Encourage learners to review their first draft in terms of the criteria in Worksheet 6.25 Plan and write a chapter as a framework to help them review and edit. Alternatively, they can review with a talk partner. Partners may also be the most fruitful stimulus for thinking about how to present their chapter creatively.

Some learners will have strong ideas of their own and may not welcome peer feedback. Discuss the benefits without negating the original work; learners do not have to act on all feedback.

The chapter can be finalised with or without ICT but encourage creativity. Learners could consider audio clips for dialogue, 3D illustrations and any other creative layout or technique. Hand-drawn images can be scanned into narrative.

Proofreading should be undertaken alone; it should be a habit rather than something learners have to be reminded to do. They should learn to proofread in two ways: first, for flow and coherence; second, for grammar, spelling and punctuation.

Display the chapters as appropriate, some on a wall display; others on a smart board/software presentation display. Celebrate learners' achievements and allow them to read them out to each other.

> **Differentiation ideas:** Allow for different levels of content and editing quality depending on ability. Some learners may be better able to develop their comic book sequence; others may be better at narrative and dialogue. Check and provide support where needed. Encourage some learners to do their whole chapter in a pair or small group.

> **Assessment ideas:** Assess learners' chapters on a number of levels. Use Worksheet 6.25 if appropriate, or negotiate success criteria of your own using Worksheet 6.9 Writing assessment sheet. The main aim is to assess the entire writing process from planning to plot interest, characterisation, dialogue, writing technique, format diversity and attention to detail – a final assessment of learners' narrative fiction writing skills for the year.

Answers:

2   a–e   Learners' own writing.

Plenary idea

Did we do it? (5–10 minutes)

Resources: Learners' chapters from Activity 2

Description: Learners read out their chapters – with or without a partner for dialogue – to a group.

> **Assessment ideas:** Give the group the criteria from Activity 2 or Worksheet 6.25 Plan and write a chapter and allow them to assess each other's chapters according to the criteria.

Homework ideas

Learners can do the Workbook activities for Session 7.3 and 7.4. Invite them to share their planning, cartoon and introductory paragraphs with the class.

Answers for Workbook

1–3 Learners' own work.

7.5 Introducing manga

LEARNING PLAN

Learning objectives		Learning intentions	Success criteria
Main focus	**Also covered**	• Explore a manga cover.	• Learners can identify relevant features of a manga cover.
6Rs.02, 6Ri.02, 6Ri.03, 6Ri.10, 6Ri.11, 6Ri.14, 6SLs.01, 6SLr.02	6Ri.06, 6Ri.07, 6Ri.08, 6Ri.13, 6Ra.02, 6Ra.03, 6SLm.03, 6SLg.03	• Interpret a manga extract. • Answer questions.	• Learners can interpret the visual clues in a manga extract. • Learners can answer questions using evidence from the text.

LANGUAGE SUPPORT

While learners will be familiar with the comic book format, some of the vocabulary may be unfamiliar. Use the listening activity (Track 40) as well as Activity 1 to familiarise learners with the vocabulary and context of manga.

Encourage learners to use Book Talk, which is located at the end of the Learner's Book, to remind them of relevant book terminology.

Common misconceptions

Misconception	How to identify	How to overcome
Manga are the same as any other comic book.	Use the cover and extract to ask learners what they notice is different to other comic books.	If possible, find other examples of manga to identify similarities and differences to other comic books learners may be more familiar with in your region.

Starter idea

Listen to find out about manga (10 minutes)

Resources: *Learning about manga* (Learner's Book, Session 7.5: Getting started); Track 40

Description: Read through the questions with learners, then play the audio and allow learners to jot down notes as answers. Give learners a couple of minutes to compare notes with a partner before playing the audio once more for learners to listen for any missing information.

Choose whether to ask learners to write their answers in their notebooks or just to discuss answers as a class.

Audioscript: *Learning about manga*

Speaker 1: Manga comics or graphic novels are very popular in Japan; both adults and children read them. They follow a style that was created in the late 19th century and are usually in the style of black and white line drawings as it makes them quicker to write and cheaper to print. Many believe, however, that the very first manga in Japan appeared in the 12th and 13th century, in drawings of frogs and rabbits titled *Choju-giga* (Scrolls of Frolicking Animals) produced by several artists.

Speaker 2: Manga come in lots of genres, from action-adventure to science fiction, historical stories and even business. Traditionally, manga stories flow from top to bottom, from right to left and from back to front, although outside of Japan, publishers sometimes print them in the more usual order to make them more familiar to read. Manga characters – people and animals alike – are often characterised by over large eyes. Many popular manga characters evolve into anime, characters that appear in animated versions of the comic books.

Answers:
1   Japanese comic books/graphic novels.
2   Adults and children.
3   12th and 13th centuries.
4   Top to bottom, right to left, back to front.
5   Anime.

Main teaching ideas

1   Investigate manga (20 minutes)

Learning intention: To use visual clues and detail to answer questions

Resources: *No. 6, Volume One* (Learner's Book, Session 7.5, Activity 1); Track 41

Description: In Japan, the manga format incorporates a wide range of fiction and non-fiction topics, including business books. The style is distinctive, with angular drawings and bubbles, usually black and white although more now appear in colour. Traditional Japanese manga read from back to front and from right to left as in other Japanese script. Occasionally, international versions reverse this to make it more familiar to other markets.

To find the answers to Activity 1, learners need to use their visual literacy skills together with their prior knowledge of how stories are structured. In particular, they must work out from the book cover and blurb (Track 41) that the book is approached from back to front; however, like other novels, it is divided into chapters and follows a similar structure. It is also part

of a series. Ask learners to predict what an afterword would be and compare it with a foreword. Forewords tend to be more common in non-fiction and play a different role from prefaces and prologues.

Encourage learners to express their opinions on whether the book sounds exciting and link it to the genre. Find out if they generally enjoy adventure/action books.

> **Differentiation ideas:** Support less confident learners by allowing them to write their answers in note form and then discuss them with a partner.

Answers:
1   a   No.6; It is the first – because it is numbered Volume One; *Shion* (an elite student living in a privileged area of the city, just 12 years old; he helps *Rat* – a fugitive of the typhoon and the security services; his decision to help causes him problems); *Rat* – an underprivileged fugitive from the storm and the city's security services, someone who brings chaos and trouble.
    b   It opens up with the front and back transposed compared with their reading books. It suggests the book may be read from back to front.
    c   Very little tells you it is a graphic novel/comic book/manga. The blurb makes it sound like an adventure story, and illustrations look futuristic (science fiction).
    d–f   Learners' own answers.

2   The story through a cartoon strip (20 minutes)

Learning intention: To interpret narrative, commenting on the impact of multimedia

Resources: Learner's Book, Session 7.5, Activity 2

Description: Allow learners to work in small groups. To help learners work out the order, the frames in the extract have been numbered, although they wouldn't be numbered in the book itself. Most learners will be familiar with standard cartoon strip features such as speech bubbles, small bits of narrative and so on. This extract uses perspective to contextualise what Shion is doing and where he is standing.

Learners should work in pairs or small groups to interpret features in the extract – e.g. to differentiate between general narrative, Shion as the narrator and his mother speaking (different-shaped bubbles).

Learners need to infer information and use visual clues to understand what is implicit as well as explicit – e.g. the feature-lacking faces in frame 6.

Check learners know the word *typhoon*. Do an activity ordering names of storms of different strengths. Information on the Beaufort Wind Scale would also be relevant.

> **Differentiation ideas:** Encourage the formation of mixed groups of more and less confident learners to help support visual literacy skills for those who need it. Ask more confident learners either to work individually or give support to those learners who need it.

> **Assessment ideas:** This activity can be used as an assessment both of learners' visual literacy skills and their understanding of the cues and features of the medium.

Answers:

2 a The frames are read from right to left rather than vice versa, which would be usual for an English novel or comic book.

b The different-shaped text boxes help the reader to interpret whether it is narrative or dialogue and who is speaking. The shape of the boxes even indicates whether it is general narrative or first-person narrative.

c Frames 3, 5 and 6 contain narrative by Shion – the first-person narrative is in straightforward rectangular style whereas the general narrative has the jagged corners.

d • Shion's mother is not in the same room – you cannot see her, and her dialogue is in an irregular shape unlike Shion's – which must indicate something.
   • She is speaking loudly/urgently/shouting, which you can tell because of the exclamation marks.
   • She would not be heard from out of the room if she spoke softly (inference); she is concerned by the danger posed by the typhoon.
   • Shion calls her 'Mother', which implies a more formal relationship or register than Mum, Mummy, Mom, Mommy, Ma, etc.

e Shion is reacting to the sound of his mother calling, looking back 'towards' the sound's source.

f He is smaller in frame 2 because the focus is on what he is doing rather than on his expression. To give the wider perspective,

Shion is depicted as smaller and so more distant having moved further into the room to look out of the window.

g The faces show no eyes and downward curving mouths, implying that everybody has the same reactions and emotions – almost that they are robotic rather than having an individual personalities. Accept any sensible answers.

Plenary idea

What sort of world does it sound like? (5 minutes)

Description: Have a class discussion on what it might be like to live where Shion does. Invite volunteers to make suggestions based on the visual clues in the text and what the narrative says. Discuss whether it seems like a good place to live and how it is different from where learners live.

Ask what the narrative in frame 5 means (that people as well as animals and the environment are managed).

> **Assessment ideas:** Give learners time to reflect on how much they can learn from the visual and textual clues, and assess how well they are able to build an understanding of the story's setting.

> ### CROSS-CURRICULAR LINKS
>
> **Geography:** Gather reference books on Japan to provide background context.
>
> **Science:** Gather information on typhoons and where they occur in the world. Provide information on the Beaufort Wind Scale to show how dangerous typhoons can be.

Homework ideas

Learners can do the Workbook activities for Session 7.5 to familiarise themselves with manga features and answer questions. Go through the answers in class, inviting learners to share their opinions.

Answers for Workbook

1 Order may vary. Accept sensible variations. Judge how many are appropriate to note for each learner.

Front cover
- Title – to identify the book.
- Picture/illustration – to give an impression of plot/main idea (to attract reader).

- Volume number – to say which book it is in the series.
- Author name – to say who wrote the story.
- Art – to say who drew the artwork in the manga novel.
- Punctuation to show surprise and mystery.

2 **Spine**
- Title – to be able to identify book when in a shelf.
- Author's name.

Back cover
- Blurb – a taste of the plot to attract readers to the book.
- Mini review – to indicate how good the book is to read.
- Background illustrations – to give a flavour of the book.
- Content list – to give an idea of the book's organisation.
- Page numbers – to show where each part of the book or chapter begins.

3 a They indicate surprise and mystery.
  b Back to front.
  c It creates suspense and encourages the reader to want to read the story inside.
  d Mystery, action – adventure based on what is in a box that has been found.
  e Learners' own answers, but something along the lines of the boy finds out how to open the box.
  f Two pages.
  g Learners' own answers, but maybe something about how the box got to the beach.
  h Learners' own answers.

7.6 Shion

LEARNING PLAN

Learning objectives		Learning intentions	Success criteria
Main focus	**Also covered**	• Plan a character profile. • Write three paragraphs about a character. • Edit and improve writing.	• Learners can plan a character profile drawn from the texts. • Learners can write three paragraphs, two descriptive and one opinion-based. • Learners can edit and improve their writing based on proofreading and feedback.
6Ri.07, 6Ri.08, 6Ri.10, 6Ri.13, 6Ww.07, 6Wv.02, 6Wv.06, 6Wg.08, 6Wc.03, 6Wp.04, 6Wp.05	6Ri.11, 6Ri.14, 6Wg.04, 6Ws.03, 6Wc.06, 6SLm.03, 6SLg.02, 6SLg.03		

LANGUAGE SUPPORT

Remind learners of the difference between descriptive and opinion-based writing, particularly in relation to the use of connectives. In order to back up their opinion with evidence and build a balanced argument, connectives such as *however,* *although, because, therefore, on the other hand, since* and so on will be particularly useful. Write them on the board while learners write their paragraphs to remind them to use them.

Starter idea

How to build a character profile (5 minutes)

Resources: Learner's Book, Session 7.6: Getting started

Description: Learners have drawn up character profiles in greater or lesser detail in other units and stages, so give them a few minutes to draw on their prior knowledge and list what a reader would want to know about a character in a book.

Share their ideas as a class and discuss how the writer can provide that information – try to elicit that it is not always by telling the reader directly but by letting the reader infer things through what a character says and does.

Main teaching ideas

1 Plan a character profile of Shion (15 minutes)

Learning intention: To build a character profile based on two texts

Resources: Learner's Book, Session 7.6, Activity 1; manga book cover from Session 7.5

Description: This activity will require at least one-third of the session for planning, one-third for writing and one-third for revising. Set limited criteria, potentially different ones for different groups.

Questions are the best way to find out information – either from others or oneself – because they are a focusing device. If appropriate, have a class discussion on questions in the mind map about Shion and to elicit some more from the class. Encourage partners to share their mind map with another pair to compare their answers and discuss any differences.

Lead a class discussion on how the writer and illustrator have given information about Shion. (Much of it is visual interpretation rather than text description, for example.) Invite suggestions as to whether it seems in or out of character for Shion to help Rat and ask for learners' reasons for their views. They will have to use both explicit and implicit information to answer.

> **Differentiation ideas:** Organise learners into groups of more and less confident learners so they can support each other, especially as one might be stronger at interpreting the text and another stronger at interpreting the visual clues.

Answers:

1 a–b   Learners' own answers.

2 Write about Shion (30 minutes)

Learning intention: To write three paragraphs – two descriptive and one opinion-based

Resources: Learner's Book, Session 7.6, Activity 2; manga book cover from Session 7.5; learners' mind map profiles from Activity 1

Description: Discuss what learners will write as the topic sentence for each of their three paragraphs: *Shion lives in … He … . He helped Rat because …* Learners must provide examples from the text to support their responses. Encourage linking connectives to transition between ideas or paragraphs. Time/order connectives are not appropriate because the information is content-dependent rather than sequential.

Learners edit and review their work according to the paragraph checklist in the Learner's Book and give each other feedback using the checklist. They should review their own work first as a comparison with what a partner suggests. Ask volunteers to share the feedback they received and what they have decided to change to show that everyone can review and improve their work.

Spelling link: Remind learners that checking and editing spelling as well as grammar is as much part of the writing process as the first draft. By now learners should be aware of some of their challenges in spelling and have worked out strategies to assist them when writing by hand or on a computer. Encourage learners to use their learning journals to record useful strategies and root words, letter patterns suffixes and regular spelling rules for adding suffixes. Remind learners to use dictionaries as well as their own word lists or an online tool if they are using ICT.

> **Differentiation ideas:** Support less confident learners by allowing them to work in pairs to share the writing of the paragraphs.

Encourage more confident learners to act as a reviewing partner for selected learners to help them identify areas for improvement.

> **Assessment ideas:** Formally assess the paragraphs as an example of learners' ability to produce an extended piece of writing several paragraphs long, that has coherence and links to the same theme.

Answers:
2   a–c   Learners' own answers.

Plenary idea

Share your writing (5 minutes)

Resources: Learners' paragraphs about Shion

Description: Invite volunteers to read out their three paragraphs about Shion. Compare learners' ideas and build a resource of information on the board about Shion and his motivation.

> Assessment ideas: Learners can assess paragraphs for use of connectives to build an argument in the third paragraph.

Homework ideas

Learners can complete the Workbook activities for Session 7.6 on building a character profile and planning events for different chapters. Share answers as a class and use their ideas to build a class outline of events for the story.

Answers for Workbook

1–3 Learners' own answers.

7.7 Medium matters

LEARNING PLAN

Learning objectives		Learning intentions	Success criteria
Main focus	**Also covered**	• Rewrite the manga extract. • Plan and give a presentation.	• Learners can rewrite the manga extract in novel format. • Learners can plan and give a presentation on their opinion on different media.
6Rg.07, 6Ra.02, 6Wg.02, 6Wg.04, 6Wg.08, 6Ws.02, 6Wp.03, 6SLm.01, 6SLm.03	6Rs.01, 6Rs.02, 6Ri.02, 6Wc.06, 6Wp.01, 6Wp.04, 6Wp.05, 6SLm.02, 6SLm.05, 6SLg.03		

LANGUAGE SUPPORT

Learners may need to be reminded of the key features of standard narrative and dialogue format in novels. While the manga extract has snippets of narrative to accompany the dialogue, learners will need to 'fill in the gaps' using their imagination to create a flowing narrative with dialogue as if in a book. Remind learners of the key features of standard English for narrative and how the language may be more colloquial in the dialogue.

Starter idea

What do you enjoy about multimedia? (5 minutes)

Resources: Learner's Book, Session 7.7: Getting started

Description: Partners should discuss what they like or do not like about multimedia aspects of books. They have so far encountered a multimedia novel with illustrations and cartoon strips, and a fully graphic novel/manga comic book.

Have a class plenary on the pros and cons of the different aspects of multimedia, as not all learners will enjoy the full graphic novel/manga format and may prefer a more text-based format. Encourage them to express a personal response to the different styles and ways of presenting themes and storylines, as well as the role multimedia plays.

Main teaching ideas

1 Plan and rewrite an extract with a prologue, narrative and dialogue (30 minutes)

Learning intention: To write appropriately punctuated and narrated dialogue

Resources: Learner's Book, Session 7.7, Activity 1; *No. 6, Volume One* (Learner's Book, Session 7.5); Track 41

Description: The No. 6 story from Session 7.5, Activity 1 was created in fully visual format. To explore how much difference format/medium can make, learners rewrite the manga extract in standard narrative format. Building on their knowledge of prologues from Unit 1 and the *Flora and Ulysses* text in Session 7.1, encourage them to separate the extract into prologue and narrative/dialogue. They should discuss their plan before writing.

Emphasise that learners should expand on the text in the extract – e.g. the first frame contains key points rather than linked sentences that have flow and coherence. Remind them that the prologue can have a different narrative voice from the main story – e.g. third person for the prologue and first person for the main story, with Shion as the narrator.

As the content is largely provided, learners should focus on the quality of their language, grammar, punctuation and spelling – especially punctuating dialogue correctly and choosing interesting verbs.

Editing and revising should be the primary focus of the activity.

The activity should either be written in presentation, joined-up handwriting, or typed on a word processor using appropriate font style and size, layout, and properly spell-checked.

Provide time at the end for learners to compare their writing and how they have interpreted the extract and discuss any differences.

> **Differentiation ideas:** Support less confident learners by allowing them to write in pairs to cut down on the amount of writing required, e.g. one doing the prologue and one the main story narrative and dialogue.

Challenge more confident learners by encouraging them to add descriptive detail to the extract as well as including more complex sentences and vocabulary.

> **Assessment ideas:** Use the rewrite as a record of how well the learners can interpret the extract into standard format, with a focus on the grammar, punctuation, structure and flow.

Answers:
1   a–b   Learners' own answers.

2 Analyse different media (15 minutes)

Learning intention: To have a group discussion

Resources: Learner's Book Session 7.7, Activity 2; Worksheets 6.1 and 6.10; manga cover from Session 7.5

Description: Encourage learners to think and reflect individually on what they have read so far in the unit and their own reading experiences. Encourage them to make notes of their views in their learning journals (Worksheet 6.1) so they know what to talk about when they move into groups.

Organise the learners into groups. You can choose mixed ability or ability groups according to your class's needs and where you want to target support. Remind groups about how to listen to each other attentively before adding their own opinions and building a group view – taking turns and building on each other's ideas. Remind them also that it is fine to disagree or have different opinions because there is no right or wrong – it is about personal preference. Explain that learners should structure their ideas carefully, using examples to back up their opinions. Encourage learners to ask each other questions to extend the discussion.

Spelling link: Revise unusual plurals. Learners have already encountered a range of unusual plurals. The word *media* stemming from *medium* is a good opportunity to briefly revise unusual plurals. Make a list on the board categorising unusual plurals, e.g. *um* to *a* (*medium–media; stadium–stadia*); *us* to *i* (*radius–radii, syllabus–syllabi, fungus–fungi, nucleus–nuclei*); *is* to *es* (*crisis–crises, oasis–oases, analysis – analyses*) and even words that appear not to have a plural form that is different to the singular form: certain animals, e.g. buck, deer, giraffe and words that are always plural (*trousers, scissors*).

There are more activities on unusual plurals in the Spelling section at the end of the Learner's Book.

> **Differentiation ideas:** While it is important for all learners to be able to speak confidently in a group, not everyone is equally confident. Help less confident learners to prepare and organise their ideas. Challenge more confident learners to present their opinions to the class.

> **Assessment ideas:** Assess learners listening and response skills either informally or formally using Worksheet 6.10 Reading, speaking or performing assessment sheet as you move around the groups listening to their views, questions and responses. Ask questions of your own to help you assess.

Answers:
2   a–b   Learners' own answers.

> **Assessment ideas:** Learners can either use the assessment sheets from Worksheet 6.10 Reading, speaking or performing assessment sheet, or assess the presentations on one or two criteria that you write on the board – e.g. Speaks clearly and presents points in a logical way or Gives a personal opinion *backed up by evidence.*

CROSS-CURRICULAR LINKS

All subjects: Gather textbooks and reference books from a wide range of subjects and encourage learners to discuss the multimedia aspects they notice – e.g. diagrams in Science or Maths, or photographs or illustrations in Science and Geography.

Homework ideas

Learners can complete the Workbook activities for Session 7.7 to give them more practice at working in different media. Allow them to compare their interpretations with each other and notice any differences.

Invite learners to share ideas about a recent book they have read and its suitability for graphic novel format.

Answers for Workbook

1–3 Learners' own answers.

Plenary idea

Present to the class (5 minutes)

Resources: Worksheet 6.10

Description: Invite one or two volunteers to share their views with the class. Allow time for questions at the end of the informal presentations to make them more interactive.

7.8 All the world's a stage

LEARNING PLAN

Learning objectives		Learning intentions	Success criteria
Main focus	**Also covered**	• Write about a famous playwright.	• Learners can use a fact file to write a summary paragraph.
6Rs.02, 6Ri.02, 6Ri.03, 6SLs.01, 6SLg.04	6Rv.01, 6Ri.07, 6Ra.01, 6Wv.01, 6Wg.08, 6Wc.06, 6SLm.03	• Explore the layout and structure of plays.	• Learners can talk about how plays are structured and laid out using appropriate vocabulary.

LANGUAGE SUPPORT

Learners may find some of the language in the extract challenging as much of it is not in common usage today and some of the sentence structures would be unusual in modern English. Encourage learners to try to work out the main idea of what is being said rather than worrying about what each word means. In Session 7.10, Activity 1 they will focus on meaning with a plain language version.

Common misconceptions

Misconception	How to identify	How to overcome
Shakespeare is difficult to understand.	Encourage the class to discuss what they think Viola and the Captain are discussing. Encourage them to use all the clues from the scene and the characters to the content. Help them to look for familiar words and to infer the general idea.	Working with little bits of Shakespeare can be fun for learners – it is like decoding a puzzle. Help learners focus on what they can decode before discussing more challenging words and phrases to help them infer meaning.

Starter idea

What playwrights and plays do you know? (5 minutes)

Resources: Learner's Book, Session 7.8: Getting started

Description: Give learners time to jot down a list of all plays they have seen or read – especially on school outings – and any of the playwrights they can remember or have also heard of. Share ideas as a class and build a list on the board – where possible assigning playwrights to plays. Encourage learners to summarise what they remember about the plays they noted down.

Main teaching ideas

1 Talk about Shakespeare (25 minutes)

Learning intention: To discuss and summarise the life and times of a classic playwright

Resources: *William Shakespeare* (Learner's Book, Session 7.8, Activity 1); Track 42

Description: Shakespeare is often viewed with trepidation but remembering that Shakespeare wrote for all sorts of people is reassuring. Emphasise that he wrote plays to be laughed at and cried over for educated and uneducated people. The language may at times seem difficult to us but people at the time would have understood it and they would find ours equally challenging.

Remind learners to start their summary paragraphs with a topic sentence to enlarge on aspects of Shakespeare's life in the next sentences and conclude with a thought about his enduring importance after 400 years. They can work with a partner.

Remind learners there was no electricity in Shakespeare's time, so there were no computers, printers or scanners. Every play was handwritten and few were ever printed. Most people could not read so there was no market for books. Actors would have learnt their parts quickly from one or two handwritten copies of the script and through rehearsals. Playscripts were fiercely protected as the property of the particular acting company. Plays were a major form of entertainment in the absence of television, cinemas, etc.

> **Differentiation ideas:** Support less confident learners by providing a more extensive frame for their paragraph.

Encourage more confident learners to work individually to find out more about the time in which Shakespeare lived, and add their findings into their paragraphs.

Answers:
1 a Learners' own answers.
    b Learners' own answers.
    c By hand; maybe only a single copy – very few anyway.
    d Largely through rehearsal and memorising them by listening and repetition.

2 Understand a play's story structure and special features (20 minutes)

Learning intention: To discuss the features of playscripts

Resources: *Twelfth Night* (Learner's Book, Session 7.8, Activity 2); Track 43

Description: Plays, like stories, have a format, structure and layout that helps people know what to expect. Partners explain similarities and differences in how plays and novels are set out, e.g. plays are completely dialogue, but novels tend to contain both narrative and dialogue. Point out the different

vocabulary – e.g. *scenes* and *acts* rather than *chapters*. If possible, have a wide selection of other playscripts for learners to look at and compare.

Check understanding of the term *standard English*. Do learners consider Shakespeare's English to be standard English or not? (It was in his day.) Before approaching the content of the *Twelfth Night* extract, learners study its layout and format. Give a bit of context by explaining the basic background to the play.

As ever, when learners talk in a group, remind them to take turns, listen to each other respectfully and to encourage each other's ideas to build a discussion rather than everyone just saying their piece without really listening to others.

Twelfth Night is a comedy. Viola and her twin brother, Sebastian, are shipwrecked off the coast of Illyria and separated. Each believes the other has drowned. Viola disguises herself as a man and, under the name of Cesario, gets a job as a servant for Duke Orsino. Sebastian later turns up and is mistaken for Cesario. Lots of confusion follows around the mistaken identity of Sebastian and Cesario (Viola), before eventually all is revealed, and brother and sister are reunited, having found the people they love.

> **Differentiation ideas:** Support less confident learners by allowing them to work in small groups to focus on just layout and features. Target your support where needed.

> **Assessment ideas:** It is more important to ensure that learners understand the main idea and can talk about the structure and layout.

Answers:
2 a–b Learners' own answers.

Plenary idea

Talk about features (5 minutes)

Resources: A selection of playscripts

Description: Invite volunteers to list the key features of playscripts. Write them on the board. Now invite comparisons with ordinary novels. Ask: *How are they similar or different?*

> **Assessment ideas:** Assess how well learners can identify the salient features and compare features with different genres and formats.

Geography: Illyria is the ancient name for the coast on the Adriatic Sea, which takes in parts of modern Serbia, Slovenia, Bosnia, Albania, Croatia and Montenegro. Source maps and reference books relating to these areas.

Homework ideas

Learners can complete the Workbook activities for Session 7.8. Go through the answers for 1 and 2 in class. Learners can swap with a partner and compare what they have done in 3.

Answers for Workbook

1   **a** playwright; **b** know; **c** wrote; **d** There; **e** four; **f** two; **g** see; **h** pairs; **i** which; **j** feet.

2   **a** has; **b** enjoys; **c** was; **d** is; **e** appears.

3   **a** Learners' own stage directions – script as below.

Viola: (*looking thoughtful*) Who is Olivia?

Captain: She is the daughter of a count. The count died and left her to be looked after by her brother. But would you know it – he also died shortly after … (*shaking his head*)

Viola: What a sad thing! Does she favour the Duke Orsino's suit?

Captain: No one knows my good lady, for she will see no man admitted to her house so much is she grieving the death of her poor brother.

Viola: Well … (*folding her arms*)

b Learners' own answers.

7.9 What has changed?

LEARNING PLAN

Learning objectives		Learning intentions	Success criteria
Main focus	**Also covered**	• Read a play extract.	• Learners can read a play extract with old-fashioned language.
6Rv.01, 6Rv.04, 6Rg.08, 6SLs.01, 6SLr.02 6SLm.03	6Rv.02, 6Rv.03, 6Ri.02, 6Ri.06, 6Ri.13, 6Ra.01, 6Ra.02, 6SLm.02, 6SLm.05, 6SLp.01, 6SLp.02, 6SLg.03	• Predict what words and phrases mean. • Explore how language and communication changes.	• Learners can predict the meaning of unfamiliar or old-fashioned language. • Learners can discuss how language and communication has changed over time.

LANGUAGE SUPPORT

Shakespeare's language is challenging. If necessary, consult a plain language version of the play in advance to ensure you understand the language fully. Learners will work with a plain language extract in the next session. Encourage a range of strategies to help deduce the meaning of unfamiliar words and phrases such as using context, looking for prefixes and suffixes, and focusing on word roots, origins and families. The word order will also sound unfamiliar to a modern ear and will possibly make the language and register seem more formal when in reality it is an everyday conversation between Viola and a sea captain.

Starter idea

Is English always the same? (5 minutes)

Resources: Learner's Book, Session 7.9: Getting started

Description: Give learners a chance to discuss whether they think English is the same the world over. Encourage them to think about people they know who come from elsewhere and also speak English.

When you come together, focus on all aspects – different words and expressions, accents, different idioms and colloquialisms, spelling. If you have a smartboard, show them all the different versions of English that can be used as an editing language. Discuss what the differences could be.

End by asking whether they think people have always spoken English in the same way. Discuss historical films which reflect people speaking from different eras.

Main teaching ideas

1 Language is not fixed – old-fashioned English (20 minutes)

Learning intention: To deduce meanings of unfamiliar words and phrases that have changed over time

Resources: Learner's Book, Session 7.1, Activity 1; dictionaries

Description: Many words have been adopted into the English language from other languages. For example, *buffet* is a French word with a distinct meaning in English different from its French origin. Every region has its unique 'Englishisms'. Some of these will be considered colloquial although, over time, they may acquire more formal status.

As learners focus on the challenging text, dip in and out of their discussions about unfamiliar words and expressions, guiding them where you can with useful decoding strategies.

Model how to read the text aloud before learners do so themselves in pairs. This will help with expression and pronunciation, which can also help them deduce meaning.

> **Differentiation ideas:** Consider reading the extract with a group of less confident learners so they are not intimidated by the unusual words. Encourage a strong sense of sound and word attack skills – some long words can be very expressive and therefore

very satisfying. Make sure that learners' guesses at meaning and pronunciation are not said to be 'wrong'; instead, take a consultative approach and give guidance.

> **Assessment ideas:** Establish whether learners are confident about approaching unfamiliar language and regard it as a challenge rather than too difficult.

Answers:
1   a–c   Learners' own answers.

2 Focus on the detail (20 minutes)

Learning intention: To explore how language and communication differs over time

Resources: Learner's Book, Session 7.9, Activity 2; selection of archaic words (e.g. *afore, anon, betwixt, coxcomb, forsooth, gudgeon, life, malapert, mummer, prithee, rapscallion, thither*)

Description: Versions of Shakespeare's plays may differ marginally in terms of spelling and punctuation. Different manuscripts were not always identical. Discuss that spellings were not as fixed as they are now; Shakespeare himself appeared to write his own name using a number of different spellings. Compare this with the different ways the same name may be spelt in different places, cultures or even generations. If possible, give examples of names common to your region with varied spellings – e.g. *Catherine, Katherine, Katharine, Catharine, Kathryn.*

Explain the meaning of archaic words. Explain that once they would have been used commonly but have fallen into disuse or rare use over time. Demonstrate, if possible, using a dictionary definition that shows the usage as *archaic*.

Discuss other places they may have come across old-fashioned language such as in religious texts or prayers, hymns and poetry. Point out that although Shakespeare's plays were not necessarily in verse, the rhythm and scansion were important and words could be shortened by removing a vowel sound with an omission apostrophe or even lengthened with an accent, e.g. on the *e* in an *ed* suffix to over-pronounce the syllable which might otherwise be unstressed. Remind learners of the meaning of register and ask e.g. of different contexts for using formal and informal register.

Spelling link: Discuss that spelling has not always been fixed and even now varies between regions, e.g. UK and US English. Use historical evidence – e.g. how Shakespeare spelt his name in different ways depending on what he was signing: *Willm Shakp, William Shaksper* (the *e* indicates a shortening), *Wm Shakspe*. He even signed his will in three different ways: the last sheet has *William Shakspere, Willm Shakspere* and lastly *By me William Shakspeare*. There is no written record of him ever spelling his name as we do: *William Shakespeare*.

⟩ **Differentiation ideas:** Support less confident learners by allowing them to work in pairs or small groups.

Encourage more confident students to work individually and/or help others needing support.

⟩ **Assessment ideas:** Assess how learners reflect on variations in speech and their use of standard English.

Answers:

2 a To indicate the final syllable is unstressed; *Do you know?*; *it was* – it begins with the apostrophe because the first letter (i) has been dropped to form the contraction.

   b thou and thy.

   c *s*

   d Learners' own answers.

Plenary idea

What does it mean? (10 minutes)

Resources: *Twelfth Night* (Learner's Book, Session 7.8); Track 43

Description: Invite volunteers to choose bits of the extract from *Twelfth Night* to say in more modern English. Invite comments and give ideas of your own at the end. Remember there is no 'right' answer as things can be phrased in many different ways.

⟩ **Assessment ideas:** Learners can assess each other's ideas by checking whether they make sense in the overall context of the extract or by focusing on specific words or phrases.

History: Source information on Shakespearean England and similar times in your region.

Homework ideas

Learners can complete the Workbook activities for Session 7.9 to explore further archaic and Shakespearean language. Go through the answers to Activities 1 and 3 in class, and invite volunteers to read out their Shakespearean phrases from Activity 2.

Answers for Workbook

1

2 a adjective, adjective (compound), noun

   b Learners' own answers.

3 a Because they are exclamations.

   b They are compound adjectives; Learners' own answers.

   c Learners' own answers.

7.10 Using language

LEARNING PLAN

Learning objectives		Learning intentions	Success criteria
Main focus	**Also covered**	• Explore a plain words version.	• Learners can read and understand a plain words version of a Shakespeare extract.
6Rv.01, 6Rv.04, 6Rg.01, 6Ri.06, 6SLm.03, 6SLr.02	6Rv.02, 6Rv.06 6Ri.02, 6Ri.07, 6Ri.13, 6Ra.01, 6Ra.02, 6Ww.03, 6Wv.03, 6Wv.04, 6SLm.01, 6SLm.05, 6SLp.01	• Identify and appreciate figurative language. • Work with colons and semicolons.	• Learners can identify and appreciate the effect of figurative language. • Learners can work with colons and semicolons appropriately.

LANGUAGE SUPPORT

Remind learners of the different types of figurative language they might come across in prose or plays as well as poetry (alliteration, metaphor, simile, idioms). Discuss why writers would choose to use figurative language in prose or plays, demonstrating the power of the imagery and how readers can develop their own mind pictures, even more than with more literal descriptive writing.

Common misconceptions

Misconception	How to identify	How to overcome
Figurative language is only in poetry.	Discuss different types of figurative language and ask learners where they would be likely to encounter them and why figurative language is used (for effect).	Encourage learners to look out for figurative language in their independent readers. Use *Twelfth Night* to show that writers use figurative language in any context where they wish to take understanding beyond the literal – either through mind pictures or effects. Explain, however, that Shakespeare was also a poet and that much of his writing has a pattern of syllables in lines like some poetry.

Starter idea

Simile or metaphor? (5 minutes)

Resources: Learner's Book, Session 7.10: Getting started; examples of similes and metaphors

Description: Learners must draw on their prior knowledge to remember the difference between similes and metaphors. They explain to each other and agree on how each type of figurative language works. Then they demonstrate this by giving each other examples.

As a class, discuss why writers use figurative language and what effect they are trying to achieve – understanding and imagery beyond the literal.

Main teaching ideas

1 Using figurative language (25 minutes)

Learning intention: To compare different versions of a text

Resources: *Two versions of Twelfth Night* (Learner's Book, Session 7.10, Activity 1); Track 44; Worksheet 6.26

Description: Compare the meaning of the plain words version of Shakespeare's text from *Twelfth Night* with the original words (Track 44). Use Worksheet 6.26 Plain Shakespeare for a plain language version of the entire extract from Session 7.8. Ask which version learners prefer. Some may prefer the version that is easier to understand; others may prefer the sound of the original words spoken aloud. Discuss why the plain words version is easier to understand.

Discuss the different effects of the two versions and which one appears more modern. Encourage reasons for learners' views and discuss how language and communication has changed over time – level of formality, style of speaking, sentence construction and word order, different words and phrases.

Remind learners about figurative language and discuss where they most often find it. Discuss how a play can appear like poetry, especially in Shakespeare when the dialogue is like a poem – new lines starting with a capital letter for reasons other than being a new paragraph.

Explain to learners that *Arion* was a poet and musician in Greek myth who was saved from drowning by a dolphin. Remind learners when they start their plain words version to refer to the glossary beneath the original *Twelfth Night* extract

to remind them what *Elysium* is and explain that *Illyria* is a place. Emphasise that they should aim for their plain words version to sound and flow like modern speaking.

> **Differentiation ideas:** Encourage more confident learners to try writing a plain version of other parts of the extract.

> **Assessment ideas:** Informally assess learners' recall of figurative language and whether they can identify a simile in a text.

Answers:
1 a Learners' own answers.
  b *... like Arion on the dolphin's back.*
     Learners' own answers but something along the lines of it conjures up an image of Viola's brother potentially being saved by holding onto the mast in the same way as Arion was saved by the dolphin. It also gives Viola hope that perhaps her brother is saved and not drowned.
  c Learners' own answers but something similar to:
     What should I do here in Illyria? My brother is in heaven. But perhaps he hasn't drowned after all: what do you think sailors?
  d *by*
  e *by chance or perhaps.*

2 Using colons and semicolons (20 minutes)

Learning intention: To explore colons and semicolons

Resources: Learner's Book, Session 7.10, Activity 2

Description: Recap the layout of a playscript with a colon to introduce each speaker. Remind learners that colons introduce things: in a playscript, the speaker. A colon can also introduce part of a sentence for emphasis. Discuss part a as a class, taking suggestions and deciding which versions add emphasis to which part of the sentence. A simple way to explain the semicolon is that it creates a break between clauses (main or subordinate), either before a connective or where the break needs more than a comma but less than a full stop, particularly to set up a contrast. It can also be used to avoid ambiguity in lists.

> **Differentiation ideas:** Support less confident learners by allowing them to rely on straightforward sentence construction with commas and full stops. They may also need extra time with colon and semicolon activities. More practice is provided in the Workbook.

> **Assessment ideas:** Ask learners to write the answers to Activity 2 in their notebooks and formally assess their work to ascertain whether more work needs to be done to consolidate working with colons and semicolons.

Answers:

2 a Example answers:

- Jeremiah has only one thing on his mind: soccer.
- Achim tasted strong flavours in the drink: mint and lemon.

b To introduce each new speaker so that actors know their parts.

c Accept sensible answers. It introduces and emphasises her asking the sailors about her brother.

d
- The crossword winners were D. Davids, class 6C; R. Rutti, class 6B; and B. Dedryver, class 6F.
- My mother believes in sensible exercise; namely, walking and running.
- François is a talented singer; he has won a gold medal.

e The semicolon joins two closely related main clauses without a connective – in this case to explain why he knows the area well.

f Learners' own answers.

Plenary idea

Consolidate colons and semicolons (5 minutes)

Description: Revise and consolidate learners' work on colons and semicolons. Invite comments and questions from class and ask them to give their own examples of how to use the colon. Follow up by inviting volunteers to join sentences with semicolons.

> **Assessment ideas:** Assess learners, examples of how to use colons and semicolons and help by indicating whether they are correct.

CROSS-CURRICULAR LINKS

All subjects: Encourage learners to be aware of how colons and semicolons are used in a variety of references and textbooks. An example would be that many people write the time in a 24-hour format using a colon to separate the hours from the minutes (13:25).

Homework ideas

Learners can complete the Workbook activities for Session 7.10 to practise working with colons and semicolons. Work through their answers in class.

Answers for Workbook

1 a The hall was silent; only the distant whispering behind scenes could be heard.

b The play was a great success; all the actors remembered their lines perfectly.

c In summer it is warm and dry; in winter it is cold and wet.

d The athletes were exhausted; it was a long, gruelling race.

e Lindiwe's mother is a lawyer; my mother is a doctor.

2 The winners of the local art competition were Jo Ackerman, Rustenberg Junior School; Vuyiswa Doo, Bergvliet Primary School; Willem van Biljon, Greenway Junior School; and Rose Makwenda, Timour Hall Primary School.

3 a This is what will be in your geography test: continents, oceans, seas, the equator, the tropics of Capricorn and Cancer, and capital cities.

b I can't believe where we are going on holiday: Hawaii!

c The principal said: "Please sit down."

d Ingredients: tomatoes, lettuce leaves, cucumber, radishes and spring onions.

e **Mother:** Remember not to open the window in this storm.

Shion: I wish I could open the window just a little bit …

7.11 Shakespeare alive

LEARNING PLAN

Learning objectives		Learning intentions	Success criteria
Main focus	**Also covered**	• Explore a manga version of Shakespeare.	• Learners can notice and discuss features of a manga version.
6Ri.02, 6Ri.03, 6Ra.02, 6Wg.08, 6Wc.08, 6Wp.04, 6SLg.03	6Rv.01, 6Rv.04, 6Ri.13, 6Ra.01, 6Ra.03, 6Ww.06, 6Ww.07, 6Wv.01, 6Ws.03, 6Wc.06, 6Wp.01, 6Wp.02, 6Wp.05, 6SLm.02, 6SLm.03, 6SLs.01, 6SLg.02, 6SLr.02	• Compare it to the original playscript. • Write an opinion paragraph.	• Learners can compare it with the original text, noting similarities and differences. • Learners can write a paragraph comparing the features and giving their opinion.

LANGUAGE SUPPORT

The manga version of *Twelfth Night* abbreviates the original text but keeps the original words. Learners should be familiar with the Shakespearean words by now having worked on it in previous sessions and having seen the plain words version

(Session 7.10, Activity 1). Be aware, however, that some learners may need to be reminded as you read the extract of what some of the words and phrases mean.

Starter idea

Shakespeare modernised (5–10 minutes)

Resources: Learner's Book, Session 7.11: Getting started

Description: Discuss when Shakespeare wrote his plays (400 years ago) and ask learners whether they think they would find the play very old-fashioned to watch. What if the actors wore more familiar clothes? This activity asks them to imagine setting a play in a different place or time.

Although the play is based on specific events, it reflects situations across the world and over time where people have been lost or displaced after boat journeys. Learners may feel that because the play is about specific events, it would be best set in times gone by but consider with them how it could be updated to be made into a modern context or a film. An example could be that Viola and her brother could have been

on a family holiday where the boat ran into trouble or experienced unexpected bad weather.

Main teaching ideas

1 Read a manga version of Shakespeare (20 minutes)

Learning intention: To explore the contribution of visual elements to a text

Resources: Learner's Book, Session 7.11, Activity 1

Description: Some learners may not have been to the theatre but may have experienced a school production. Talk about the excitement and courage of actors who perform in front of a live audience. Acknowledge that learners often encounter the film version of a book or a play long before they encounter a written version. Discuss how this might affect their response to the original text.

Graphic novels are an exciting genre for reinterpreting literature of all kinds. They help bring to life stories that learners may find hard to visualise – e.g. classic novels as well as Shakespeare's plays. They are similar to comic books in format and may be produced in different versions – e.g. original text, hybrid original/plain English text or even an abbreviated version. The extract is a hybrid, retaining the flavour of Shakespeare's language but abbreviating it a bit. If possible, show learners examples of both classic books and plays in graphic format.

Read the manga extract as a class, either with you taking one part to help model expression – the text should be largely familiar from the previous sessions – or selecting two confident readers (for Viola and the Captain). Encourage broad discussion about what genre the learners would call it. Do they still consider it a play?

> **Differentiation ideas:** Work at class level, bringing out learners who are less confident at expressing their views.

Invite more confident learners to individually express their views, inviting questions afterwards.

Answers:
1   a   Learners' own answers.
    b   • It is manga/comic book/graphic novel format.
        • It is mostly dialogue like the playscript, but the speaking appears in speech bubbles. The graphic novel obviously has illustrations, which the playscript does not, so learners can visualise the characters, their clothing, the setting and the shipwreck. It also has the large eyes that reflect manga characters. Learners probably find it easier to understand and visualise.
        • Learners' own answers.
    c   • The words have largely been retained but some have been omitted – to make it easier to read.
        • The original words keep the flavour, rhythm and sound of the original play. Learners give their own reasons as to

which version they prefer – original or plain words.
    • Learners' own answers but they should see them as less necessary because they can already visualise what the characters are doing and their expressions.

---

2   Write an opinion paragraph comparing versions (25 minutes)

Learning intention: To write an opinion paragraph following discussion

Resources: Learner's Book, Session 7.1, Activity 2; Worksheets 6.1 and 6.27

Description: Organise learners into groups to discuss the first two questions. Suggest that they make notes as they discuss to help them prepare to write their paragraphs. Remind them of different ways to make notes.

Once they have finished discussing, make sure learners have some quiet time to reflect on their notes and plan their paragraph before writing it. Remind them to open with a topic sentence and to use appropriate connectives, especially relating to comparison and contrast. They explored connectives and their purposes in Session 7.2, should revision be required. Learners must end with their preference but, as always, they should substantiate with reasons.

You can also use Worksheet 6.27 Write an opinion paragraph while learners are writing for assessment to guide them on how the paragraph might be assessed. They should swap paragraphs with a partner for evaluation and feedback. Worksheet 6.27 should help them be more reflective about their writing and how they can improve it based on feedback and proofreading. Learners should use their own word lists and dictionaries or online tools for checking.

Learners should then make notes on the different versions of *Twelfth Night* in their learning journals (Worksheet 6.1) together with their personal response.

> **Differentiation ideas:** Support less confident learners by allowing them to work in pairs to write the opinion paragraph. Alternatively, work with small groups after their discussion to help them pin down the key points they will make before embarking on writing their paragraphs.

> **Assessment ideas:** Assess learners' opinion paragraphs as a record of how well they can compare features of the two formats and articulate their own preferences. The assessment can be both content-based and technical, focusing on their sentence construction, spelling, vocabulary and flow.

Answers:
2   a–d   Learners' own answers.

Plenary idea

Share your ideas (5 minutes)

Resources: Learners' paragraphs from Activity 2

Description: Survey learners to find out who preferred which version of *Twelfth Night*. Invite volunteers from each preference to read out their paragraphs so that learners can ask questions and hear a range of opinions.

> **Assessment ideas:** Learners can use the criteria in Worksheet 6.27 to assess the paragraphs.

Homework ideas

Learners can complete the Workbook activities for Session 7.11, working with a graphic format for a playscript. They can swap their Workbook answers in class and compare what they have done. Invite learners to share their cartoon sequences for the next instalment.

Answers for Workbook

1   Labels: frame 1 – thought bubble; frame 2 – two speech bubbles and narrative; frames 3 and 4 – sound effects; frame 5 – three speech bubbles, emphasis in capitals and exclamation marks, ellipsis; advert/note to read next week.

2   Accept any Roman numerals for Act and Scene numbers.

Atticus: (*thinking to himself*) I wish I could open this box. I know I got it from the junk dealer but I was so drawn to it …

A year later, Atticus is still puzzling over his box. He never let's it out of his sight.

Name: Oh! Atticus I wish you'd let me try.

Atticus: But I've tried everything.

A crashing, squeaking and banging sound occurs. Atticus and Name look shocked and nervous. (Be flexible about how they write this out.)

Atticus: What did we do?

Name: Nothing, nothing! Ooooh!

Atticus: Wait! LOOK …

Read next week's instalments to find out what Atticus has seen.

3   Learners' own answers.

7.12 Write your own playscript

LEARNING PLAN

Learning objectives		Learning intentions	Success criteria
Main focus	**Also covered**	• Plan an original playscript.	• Learners can use a storyboard to plan an original playscript.
6Ra.04, 6Wv.04, 6Wv.05, 6Wc.01, 6Wc.05, 6Wp.03, 6Wp.04, 6SLm.04, 6SLp.02	6Rs.02, 6Ri.02, 6Ri.03, 6Ri.13, 6Ww.06, 6Ww.07, 6Wv.06, 6Wg.04, 6Wc.02, 6Wp.02, 6Wp.05, 6SLm.05, 6SLp.01	• Write and improve an original playscript. • Present a playscript.	• Learners can write and improve an original playscript including stage directions and production notes. • Learners can present a playscript in a group.

LANGUAGE SUPPORT

Remind learners they should include old-fashioned language and phrases as well as some figurative language. Help them decide whether to use similes, metaphors or even alliteration. You could write some words and phrases on the board as cues such as archaic contractions or pronouns like *'twas, 'tis, thy, thou* and so on.

Starter idea

Pros and cons (5 minutes)

Resources: Learner's Book, Session 7.12: Getting started

Description: Discuss as a class whether audiences now or in Shakespeare's time would have reacted differently to the play. Encourage them to think about the context and whether it would be familiar, and the language and register. Broaden the discussion to whether it would be read and understood differently in different parts of the world. It is a European setting, albeit imaginary. Would it have been difficult for audiences in other parts of the world to understand in Shakespeare's day? Would it be different now?

Main teaching ideas

1 Plan your script (25 minutes)

Learning intention: To plan and write an original playscript

Resources: Learner's Book, Session 7.12, Activity 1; Worksheet 6.28; play texts in a variety of formats, own word lists

Description: Explain that learners are going to write their own original playscripts. Encourage them to use their own ideas and creativity, but if that's problematic they can continue the *Twelfth Night* playscript – as they imagine it might continue. The storyboard in the Learner's Book models how to use the storyboard for planning using *Twelfth Night* characters. Encourage learners to use their own lists of interesting words and to incorporate some old-fashioned language such as archaic contractions or pronouns. They could even change word order to sound more like Shakespeare.

Remind learners they will need to include scene setting and stage directions where necessary and that at the end they will write production notes. Encourage learners to use a setting familiar to them if they are writing their own play rather than continuing *Twelfth Night*.

When Learners write their first drafts, they should set it out like a traditional playscript even if they choose a different format for the final version.

This will help them see how they must tell the story through the dialogue.

Allow time for learners to swap their drafts with a partner, who should read it out then give feedback, which learners can use to improve their work in Activity 2. They can use Worksheet 6.28 Plan, write and present a playscript to guide their writing.

> **Differentiation ideas:** Support less confident learners by allowing them to write in pairs or even small groups so that each learner writes only one character's dialogue after they have discussed what will happen.

Answers:
1   a–d   Learners' own answers.

2 Finalise and present your playscript (20 minutes)

Learning intention: To improve, finalise and present an original playscript

Resources: Learner's Book, Session 7.12, Activity 2; Worksheet 6.28; planning and first draft from Activity 1; dictionaries and thesauruses

Description: Based on partner feedback, learners should improve their drafts in terms of either content or language. They should also carefully proofread their own work, highlighting words they need to check for spelling using a range of strategies, a dictionary or online tool. They should look to improve word choice, including old-fashioned language and even word order, to make the dialogue sound more authentic for the time in which it is set.

When learners compile their final versions, they can choose to write it out in traditional playscript format either using ICT or in neat legible handwriting, or they can present it in manga/graphic format. The latter choice may take more time, so you could allow them to complete their writing for homework.

Having finalised their scripts, learners can return to their planning and include production notes to accompany the scene to make it possible to stage the play. Remind them this would include scenery, costumes, props, music or sound effects and so on.

Learners should use Worksheet 6.28 Plan, write and present a playscript to guide their writing to make sure they fulfil the required criteria.

Organise learners into groups according to how many characters are in their playscript to practise reading the scene aloud. Learners can be part of more than one group, depending on how many characters are required. Groups can present to one or more other groups. At the end of each scene, encourage audience feedback on what they enjoyed and what could have been improved, focusing on the presentation.

> **Differentiation ideas:** Support less confident learners by allowing them to omit old-fashioned language and write their playscript in a plain words version.

Encourage confident learners to write a more complex scene, possibly with more characters or more action.

> **Assessment ideas:** Use Worksheet 6.28 to formally assess learners' playscripts for a selection of these success criteria:

- *content, vocabulary and originality*
- *layout and format*
- *spelling, grammar and punctuation*
- *stage directions and production notes*
- *presentation of the playscript.*

Answers:
2   a–d   Learners' own answers.

Plenary idea

Present to the class (5–10 minutes)

Resources: Learners' playscripts with additional copies for all characters (if possible)

Description: Invite volunteer groups who would like to present to the class one of the playscripts they have practised. One learner from each group should act as a spokesperson to introduce the scene, explain when it is set and what the production notes say about putting on a successful performance.

After the introduction, learners enact the scene, using as much body language and expression as possible to get into character.

> **Assessment ideas:** The class can rate each performance. The group performing can have a chance to say what they would improve next time.

Homework ideas

Learners can complete the Workbook activities for Session 7.12. Give them the opportunity to read out their playscript in class or to get together with other learners to do so.

Additionally, they can finish writing their playscript from Activity 2 if they need more time.

Answers for Workbook

1–3 Learners' own answers.

CHECK YOUR PROGRESS

1   a contrast; **b** adding information; **c** cause and effect / show purpose.

2   A *foreword* comes at the beginning of the book, is written by someone other than the author and tells readers why they should read it. An *afterword* comes after the main text and reflects on aspects of the book such as changes in the new edition or mentions recent events that are relevant to the book.

3   Learners' own answers, but should include the following: speaker's name to the left separated from the dialogue by a colon; act and scene numbers; scene setting at the start; stage directions where necessary; no dialogue punctuation.

4   a it is; it was; ashamed; blamed.

   b increases, distresses, escapes.

5   a Marvin felt strongly: both hurt and upset.

   b Imtiaz has a new hobby; she is writing a book.

PROJECT GUIDANCE

Group project: Learners choose one of Shakespeare's plays to research. If necessary, offer them a limited choice of plays to choose from as some of his plays do contain murder and violence. Learners should choose one or two scenes from the play to explain to and perform for the class. Guide learners towards websites which offer plain language versions of Shakespeare's plays – there are many. Their presentation can involve a computer presentation or hardcopy notes, as well as what each learner says, but it must include a dramatic presentation of their chosen scenes. Group work is an important part of the project; encourage learners to assign roles to each person clearly to ensure they do not duplicate work.

Pair project: Learners can research the times Shakespeare lived in – Elizabethan England. They can decide what each person is going to research – e.g. fashion, food, England's rulers, everyday life. They should decide between them how to present their research, on the computer as a presentation or even on card as a project board.

Solo project: Learners research William Shakespeare and his life and works. In advance, source suitable research material and websites, and remind learners to take notes rather than copy out whole chunks and then to choose an imaginative way to draw up an engaging character profile.

>8 Make it happen

Unit plan

Session	Approximate number of learning hours	Outline of learning content	Resources
8.1 Weight up waste	0.5+	Have a group discussion. Explore prefixes. Build vocabulary.	Learner's Book Session 8.1 Workbook Session 8.1 ⤓ Language worksheet 8B
8.2 An article to startle	1	Read aloud. Explore the content of an article. Explore the audience and purpose of an article.	Learner's Book Session 8.2 Workbook Session 8.2 ⤓ Worksheet 6.3 ⤓ Worksheet 6.4 ⤓ Worksheet 6.7 ⤓ Worksheet 6.16
8.3 Language and features	0.5+	Identify text types and their features. Revise narrative voice. Write sentences using relative pronouns.	Learner's Book Session 8.3 Workbook Session 8.3 ⤓ Worksheet 6.16 ⤓ Differentiated worksheets 8A–C
8.4 Punctuation with purpose	0.5+	Identify punctuation in a text. Use punctuation to clarify meaning. Read aloud with accuracy.	Learner's Book Session 8.4 Workbook Session 8.4 ⤓ Language worksheet 8A
8.5 Follow instructions	1	Identify organisational features of instructions. Explore command verbs. Explore quantifiers.	Learner's Book Session 8.5 Workbook Session 8.5
8.6 Clauses to clarify	0.5+	Revise the *if* clause. Use connectives effectively. Give instructions with complex sentences.	Learner's Book Session 8.6 Workbook Session 8.6

Session	Approximate number of learning hours	Outline of learning content	Resources
8.7 Make something	1	Gather ideas for what to make and words to use. Plan and edit a first draft. Present work neatly.	Learner's Book Session 8.7 Workbook Session 8.7 ⬇ Worksheet 6.29
8.8 Demonstrate	0.5+	Prepare a presentation and identify criteria for a good speech. Give a demonstration. Evaluate own and others' talk.	Learner's Book Session 8.8 Workbook Session 8.8 ⬇ Worksheet 6.10
8.9 Facts and opinions about recycling	1	Analyse the impact of a text. Consider pros and cons. Write a short balanced argument.	Learner's Book Session 8.9 Workbook Session 8.9 ⬇ Worksheet 6.20 ⬇ Worksheet 6.21 ⬇ Language worksheet 5A
8.10 Summarise	0.5+	Decide when and how to make notes. Locate and use relevant information. Distinguish between facts and opinions. Use key words to summarise.	Learner's Book Session 8.10 Workbook Session 8.10
8.11 and 8.12 Create a magazine article	1.5	Work in groups and take on roles. Use skills learnt to plan and write a magazine article. Proofread and evaluate own and others' work.	Learner's Book Session 8.11 and 8.12 Workbook Session 8.11 and 8.12 ⬇ Worksheet 6.4 ⬇ Worksheet 6.6 ⬇ Worksheet 6.8 ⬇ Worksheet 6.9 ⬇ Worksheet 6.30 ⬇ Language worksheet 8B
Cross-unit resources			
Learner's Book Check your progress Learner's Book Projects End-of-unit 8 test			

BACKGROUND KNOWLEDGE

As you prepare for this section, collect examples of different magazines – e.g. environmental, sports or craft magazines – aimed at different audiences. Also look out for relevant and appropriate news reports on environmental issues and instructional texts linked to different recycling ideas.

In this final non-fiction unit, you will have the opportunity to revise some of the text types and features covered throughout the year. You will also introduce the learners to text types with persuasive elements they might not have considered before. For example, a magazine article and a set of instructions are both examples of persuasive texts because they present a one-sided view and aim to get the reader to respond in a particular way. As you expose learners to different texts, remind them to analyse and compare texts in terms of their purpose, audience, language and layout. This can be applied to any other texts they come across – your learners can use the extra resources you have on display to practise this skill. Use the Language focus boxes throughout this unit but also refer to the other language skills learnt throughout the year. All this knowledge will help to fully prepare your learners to create their own magazine article using group work skills to demonstrate their ability to cooperate.

TEACHING SKILLS FOCUS

Questioning and feedback

To maximise learning and assessment opportunities in your class, remember that good, well-planned questions are an essential tool to stimulate the learner's thinking, guide their output, provide feedback and give you an idea of how to tailor your lessons. Questioning and feedback will also help you fill in any gaps. Here are some ideas for different types of questions to use in this unit.

Diagnostic questions

- Ask quick, one-word-answer questions before a new section to find out how much learners remember. For example, ask: *Does a prefix go at the beginning or end of a root word? Is a magazine article a fiction or non-fiction text type? Are brackets the only way to show parenthesis?*

- Use true/false statements after explaining a concept to check their understanding, e.g. *A text can be extremely or mildly persuasive depending on its purpose. (True.) We can use commas in texts to list items and also as parenthesis. (True.) A complex sentence has at least one dependent clause. (False.)*

- Ask Yes/No-type questions during your lesson to keep track of those who need extra support: *Did you understand the vocabulary? Can you read aloud with fluency? Are you ready to move on?*

- Use the How am I doing? and How are we doing? questions during each session to check their understanding and find out how well they grasped concepts and skills covered in the section before moving on.

Hinge point questions

At the end of a session, ask *What did we learn today?* to check learners have understood key concepts. Use the Check your progress questions at the end of the unit to check if any learners need extra support in any area.

CONTINUED

Discussion questions

- Learners work out a spelling or language rule for themselves before you tell them, e.g. ask how and why the meaning of words change when you add a prefix or suffix.

- Use 'Why do you think …?' questions to stimulate and check their reasoning: *Why do you think different magazines have different audiences? Why do you think instructions use short, simple sentences? Why do you think waste is a good topic for a magazine article?*

- Create an area in your classroom with examples of waste items that would normally go into the rubbish bin and ask *What could you make with this waste?*

- Regularly ask learners to explore the pros and cons such as: recycling, magazines (vs. online articles), working in groups, etc.

- Organise discussions and/or debates on: ways to solve the problems of waste production and disposal, the issues of sea pollution and the effects on fishing, banning industry, etc.

- Learners gather and discuss their own waste behaviour by keeping a waste diary or a personal record of what and how much waste they produce. Use the information in other subjects like Maths to draw graphs or Geography to plot the journey of a rubbish truck.

8.1 Weigh up waste

LEARNING PLAN

Learning objectives		Learning intentions	Success criteria
Main focus	**Also covered**	• Have a group discussion.	• Learners can discuss and build on a topic.
6Rv.02, 6Ri.04, 6Wv.03	6Ww.03, 6Ww.07, 6SLg.02, 6SLg.03, 6SLg.04	• Explore prefixes. • Build vocabulary.	• Learners can explain how prefixes transform meaning. • Learners can use dictionaries to build their vocabulary.

LANGUAGE SUPPORT

Write new and difficult words relating to the topic on the board before the lesson begins. Begin the lesson by introducing these words and explaining them. Help learners who need extra support in the discussion activity.

Explore the words *generate* and *novel* as base words with multiple meanings. Use dictionaries to check meanings and their derivatives. Use thesauruses to find synonyms.

Use the words *recycle* and *reuse* to explore the prefix re-, which generally means *to repeat* but with slight variations – see Common misconceptions. Use the Workbook activities and Spelling spreads to explore other prefixes that transform the meaning of words.

Common misconceptions

Misconception	How to identify	How to overcome
re– means repeat.	Write *example words on the board:* *recycle, reverse, remain, repel, regenerate* Ask: *Is the meaning of re- exactly the same in each word?*	Use dictionaries to find out what *re–* means in different words: once more (as in *recycle*); to go back (as in *reverse*); behind or after (as in *remain*); a negative force (as in *repel* or *recant*); bring back to life (as in *regenerate*).
re– at the start of a word is always a prefix.	Display these words: *reach, rent, rebel* Ask: *Do these words have a prefix?* (No.)	Use dictionaries to explore words that begin *re–* and find out which ones have prefixes.

Starter idea

The what and where of waste (5 minutes)

Resources: Learner's Book, Session 8.1: Getting started; dictionaries; notebooks

Description: Learners work in pairs or small groups. They discuss the questions in the Learner's Book and make notes to help them report to the class. Use this to identify learners' awareness of their own waste and where it goes.

List on the board any new or interesting words the learners use in the discussion.

Main teaching ideas

1 Have a group discussion on ways to reuse your waste (20 minutes)

Learning intention: To extend a discussion by building on ideas and taking turns to speak

Resources: Learner's Book, Session 8.1, Activity 1; Workbook, Session 8.1; pictures or posters of waste

Description: Use the photographs as inspiration for the discussion on using waste to make things. Not everyone will agree this is a good idea. Some may not like the look of a recycled object and some may question its safety or just not like the idea. Some may feel it takes too much time or money to recycle waste and is not as convenient as going to the shops.

Remind learners of their work in Unit 5 on balanced arguments and why it is important to look at the pros and cons of a topic. Learners take turns to express their thoughts and make notes of the pros and cons of recycling waste to make things. They share their ideas with the class.

> **Differentiation ideas:** Support less confident learners by allowing them to work in pairs or small groups to complete the Workbook activities, giving them an opportunity to conduct a survey on waste. Encourage learners to begin a display board and ask others for suggestions of items that have been recycled. They make posters on good ideas for recycling and using waste.

> **Assessment ideas:** Observe as learners take part in discussions. Assess their ability to cooperate and work together, take turns in a discussion and show consideration for other views.

Answers:
1 a–e Learners' own answers.

2 Use a prefix to change the meaning of root words (20 minutes)

Learning intention: To transform meaning with prefixes and explore how to add prefixes to root words

Resources: Learner's Book, Session 8.1, Activity 2; Language worksheet 8B; dictionaries

Description: Have a class discussion to recall root words and prefixes. Revise words with or without the *re–* prefix to help learners identify root words. Use dictionaries to support this activity.

Remind learners that a prefix changes the meaning of the word. Show examples and ask learners to explain how the meaning changes: <u>un</u>kind – the prefix makes the term negative; <u>re</u>invent – the prefix shows repetition; <u>pro</u>active – the prefix indicates support ...

Read the list of verbs in the Learner's Book. Add the prefix *re–* to each verb and discuss the subtle differences in meaning of this prefix. Deal with any misconceptions as indicated earlier.

Learners use dictionaries to explore other words with the prefix *re–*. They can also list other words that begin with *re–* but not as a prefix. Learners record their findings in a table as shown in the Learner's Book which can be copied into their learning journals. This is good for revising spelling and building vocabulary.

Complete the Workbook activities for Session 8.1, if not already completed during Activity 1, and also the Spelling spread activities at the back of the Learner's Book.

Spelling link: Some words need a hyphen after the prefix to avoid ambiguity (*re-count* and *recount* are not the same). Use a hyphen before a vowel: *re-elect*; *anti-aircraft*; *pro-active*. The prefixes *ex* and *self* are usually followed by a hyphen.

> **Differentiation ideas:** Support small groups of less confident learners by exploring other prefixes and how they transform meaning. Use a similar table to the one in the Learner's Book to make notes.

Encourage more confident learners to use dictionaries to explore root words, word meanings, origins, word class and derivations for words such as: *generate – regenerate – generation – regeneration*. Differentiate the activity further by asking learners to explore words that use a hyphen after the prefix, e.g. *re-elect*.

> **Assessment ideas:** Check learners' written work and assess their understanding of root words, prefixes and how they transform the meaning of a word.

Answers:
2 a   reuse, recharge, restart, recycle, react, regain
   b   to use again, to charge up, reverse, to use again but in another way, to act in response to something, to get back
   c   Learners' own words.

Plenary idea

Prepare to help (5 minutes)

Description: Learners share their answers and help to check each other's work. Discuss corrections and invite learners to reflect on how this helps them improve their spelling.

> **Assessment ideas:** Learners use the words to test each other and check each other's spelling skills. Learners review the *How are we doing?* questions at the end of the session and rate their performance.

Homework ideas

Learners complete the waste survey in the Workbook to find out and record how much waste they generate at home. Learners complete Language worksheet 8B (a crossword) to extend their vocabulary, which they will find useful in this unit.

Answers for Workbook

1   Learners' own work.

2   **a** displease, mistake, misunderstand; **b** ungrateful, nontoxic, unclean; **c** unreliable, unimportant, inexpensive; **d** impatient, illegal, impossible; **e** disuse, decompose, depart

3   **a**   recount: retell a story; re-count: count something again

   b   repress: to stop something; re-press: to iron something again

   c   recover: to get better; re-cover: to cover something again

   d   refuse: *v.* to be unwilling or *n.* rubbish ; re-fuse: to fit another fuse

   e   resort: a place to go on holiday; re-sort: to sort out something again.

8.2 An article to startle

LEARNING PLAN

Learning objectives		Learning intentions	Success criteria
Main focus	**Also covered**	• Read aloud.	• Learners can read aloud with expression and confidence.
6Ri.04, 6Ri.05	6Rs.03, 6Ri.06, 6Ri.12, 6Ri.13, 6Ri.14, 6Wv.01, 6Ww.07, 6SLp.01	• Explore the content. • Explore the audience and purpose of an article.	• Learners can discuss explicit meaning and technical vocabulary. • Learners can describe the audience and purpose of a magazine article.

LANGUAGE SUPPORT

Some technical terms relate to the topic of waste and ocean pollution. Some of the words are explained in the Glossary at the end of the Learner's Book. If there are other tricky words, ask learners to work out the meaning in the context of the article. They should attempt this before using a dictionary. This is particularly useful for learners to learn how to approach any text and use the context to find the meaning of tricky words.

The connection between audience and purpose is key to why any text is written. It affects the language and the layout. This understanding will help learners to be better readers and writers.

Starter idea

Pleasure or purpose (5 minutes)

Resources: Learner's Book, Session 8.2: Getting started: examples of magazines and newspapers

Description: Learners identify different types of magazines and newspapers. Identify the audience – some are for children, some are for adults, some are for a specific interest group … Deal with misconceptions that magazines are only for fun. Ask: *Which magazines do you enjoy?*

Discuss and compare the features of a magazine and newspaper. Learners will notice that both use headlines, facts, opinions and persuasion but magazine articles deal with issues over a period of time, not just daily or weekly news. Use this opportunity to revise features of news articles.

Main teaching ideas

1 Read aloud the article, then discuss the content (30 minutes)

Learning intention: To read aloud and explore explicit meanings, answering questions with reference to the text

Resources: *Ocean pollution – the silent killer* (Learner's Book, Session 8.2, Activity 1); Track 45; Workbook, Session 8.2; Worksheets 6.1, 6.3, 6.4 and 6.7

Description: Skim the text titled *Ocean Pollution – The Silent Killer*. Ask learners to name some of the obvious features. Ask: *Does it look like something you might enjoy reading? Is it appealing? How do you choose what to read?*

Read the article together. Invite pairs or individuals to read different sections aloud. Discuss the tone and how much expression is required when reading this type of non-fiction text. Ask: *Is there a difference reading non-fiction and fiction texts? Does expression still count? Does it sound more or less formal and expressive?* (Fiction texts usually require more expression when reading aloud; some non-fiction texts should sound formal and serious.)

Discuss the questions and/or let the learners write the answers in their notebooks. These questions are good for checking the learners' understanding of explicit meanings and vocabulary. Complete the Workbook activities for Session 8.2 using another magazine article, if there is time in class.

Learners add the magazine text to their learning journal (Worksheet 6.1) with notes. Alternatively they can use Worksheet 6.4 Features of fiction and non-fiction texts or Worksheet 6.7 Analysing non-fiction texts.

> **Differentiation ideas:** As a class, support learners by reading and analysing explicit meaning in other magazine articles like the one in the Workbook activity. Offer further specific explanations where you think they are needed. Use Worksheets 6.3, 6.4 and 6.7 to practise reading skills and analysing features of various text types.

Invite learners to answer basic questions such as: *Who and what is the article about? Where and when did it take place? How and why …? Is it past or present? Are there any tricky or technical words to learn?*

> **Assessment ideas:** Learners read the text aloud. Assess their unprepared or prepared reading skills. Check for fluency, pace, volume and tone.

Answers:
1 a Pollution is killing marine life without us realising because we don't see or hear it happening.
  b Large collections of ocean plastic drawn together by ocean currents and winds. There are five major oceanic gyres with smaller ones off Alaska and Antarctica.
  c Accept any reasonable facts and opinions.
  d Should plastic be banned? Learners choose any side.
  e–f Learners' own answers.

2 Explore the audience, purpose, language and layout (15 minutes)

Learning intention: To explore how ideas are organised and linked, and identify the purpose and audience of the article

Resources: Learner's Book, Session 8.2, Activity 2

Description: Ask learners to explain what makes them interested in reading a text. Check they understand that different magazines are aimed at different audiences. Deal with misconceptions that they are all for the same purpose and audience. Even newspapers have different audiences – use the opportunity to bring in different types of newspapers and review work done in Unit 2.

Together, read the Language focus box. Use the scale to discuss how persuasive different texts are and why. Consider the magazine article. It aims to persuade the reader to be more aware of the issue and take action as seen in the heading 'So … What can YOU do to help?'

The questions in this section deal with implicit meaning – clues that must be interpreted. Discuss the questions together then let the learners answer in their notebooks. Learners can work in pairs to support each other and develop their ideas.

Use the Workbook activities for Session 8.2 to explore and analyse another magazine article, if the Workbook has not already been completed.

> **Differentiation ideas:** Keep a display of magazines and newspapers in the class. Invite learners to bring articles to school on the topic. Allow everyone to browse these. Challenge more confident learners to explore the topic further and to find out more.

> **Assessment ideas:** Learners answer the questions orally or in their books. Assess their comprehension skills and ability to interpret explicit meanings.

Answers:
2 a Appeals to young readers because it is colourful, easy to read, not too much detail, has interesting bits and pieces …
  b Both. Learners' own examples.
  c Headings, sections, questions, photos, maps, bullets, numbers all draw the reader in and make it appealing and easy to read.
  d Short, for younger readers to enjoy. They are linked and flow together – using some connectives.

e   The headings are written as questions to make the readers think about the information provided.

f   Accept any reasonable answer with reasons like: Around 6 as it is persuasive but not obviously so because the language is factual rather than descriptive or figurative (as in an advertisement).

Plenary idea

Waste not, want not (5 minutes)

Description: Report back so learners can compare answers. Invite them to reflect on how well they answered the questions.

> **Assessment ideas:** Learners work through the *How am I doing?* questions and give themselves a rating.

Homework ideas

Learners can carry out a magazine survey at home or with their friends to find out who reads what and why. They record their findings, which can be shared in a class discussion.

Answers for Workbook

1   Example answers:

   a   The founder of soleRebels Footwear.

   b   To make shoes/create jobs.

   c   2004 in Africa.

d   For showing leadership and business skills.

e   By using local skills, natural resources and business opportunities.

f   Accept any reasonable answer based on the text.

2   a   Purpose: to inform. Audience: entrepreneurs or young people interested in business or social projects. Language: friendly but formal, factual and biographical. Format: heading and paragraphs/sections.

   b   Both. Factual because it gives facts and persuasive because it aims to impress the reader.

   c   A heading and short paragraphs is appealing to readers because it looks interesting and easy to read.

   d   It is a play on the word 'sole/soul'. It draws the reader in and links the shoes to the reader's soul or heart – representing love and meaning.

   e   Accept any reasonable answer based on the text.

3   Learners' own notes can include:

Similarities: persuasive language, includes facts and opinions, has an interesting headline, includes quotations, uses third-person narrative, is divided into paragraphs …

Differences: a newspaper provides daily news, it is printed daily, has a specific news format that includes facts in the first paragraph, usually provides only the most recent part of a story; a magazine provides weekly or monthly real-life stories that may or may not be recent, sometimes uses the second-person narrative 'you' to speak directly to the reader …

8.3 Language and features

LEARNING PLAN			
Learning objectives		**Learning intentions**	**Success criteria**
Main focus	**Also covered**	• Identify text types and their features.	• Learners can identify different text types and their features.
6Rg.04, 6Ri.05, 6Ri.16	6Rg.08, 6Rs.02, 6Ri.01, 6Wg.07, 6SLs.01	• Explain fiction and non-fiction texts. • Write sentences using relative pronouns.	• Learners can explain the difference between a fiction and non-fiction text. • Learners can write sentences using relative pronouns.

LANGUAGE SUPPORT

Relative pronouns are also covered in Unit 5 which has a Language focus box.

A relative pronoun joins sentence parts by referring to the noun (*She is the person <u>who</u> inspired me; <u>That</u> is the house I grew up in; You can have the packet <u>which</u> has the most sweets.*)

The most common relative pronouns are *who, whose, which* and *that*. *Whom* is less common – it is the object form of *who* (*Sam is the boy <u>whom (object)</u> I sit next to. I sit next to Sam <u>who (subject)</u> is a boy.*)

In informal speech, the relative pronoun is sometimes left out: *This is the book ~~that~~ I bought.*

That and *which* can be interchangeable but it is usual to use *that* in a defining clause and *which* in non-defining clauses. This means *that* provides essential information, *which* provides non-essential information.

For further support, search online for 'relative pronouns' in the Cambridge Dictionary.

Common misconception

Misconception	How to identify	How to overcome
Relative pronouns are only used in formal writing and speech.	Write the following sentence on the board and ask the learners to identify the relative pronoun: *I'd like the vanilla ice cream which is my favourite flavour.* Ask: *Can this be formal or informal?* (both)	Use other examples to practise combining sentences with relative pronouns. Complete the Workbook activity.

Starter idea

Classify books (5 minutes)

Resources: Learner's Book, Session 8.3: Getting started; a variety of fiction and non-fiction books and magazines and newspapers

Description: Check learners understand the meaning of *classification* from the root *classify*. Write the words *fiction* and *non-fiction* on the board. Check that learners understand the difference between them. Ask learners to name some further ways to classify books in these main categories. (For example, fiction – adventure, romance, sci-fi, drama; non-fiction –biography, autobiography, history, geography, language, psychology.)

Ask learners which sections they enjoy the most and why. Invite personal responses.

> **Assessment ideas:** Check learners understand how books are classified beyond the 'fiction' and 'non-fiction' classification – e.g. bookstores usually have a magazine section.

Main teaching ideas

1 Compare different text types in the magazine article (20 minutes)

Learning intention: To compare the purposes and features of different non-fiction text types within a text

Resources: Learner's Book, Session 8.3, Activity 1; *Ocean pollution – the silent killer* (Learner's Book, Session 8.2); Track 45; Worksheet 6.16

Description: Once learners can recognise fiction and non-fiction texts, the next step is to identify different text types within a text (refer back to the ocean pollution article in Session 8.2).

Begin by classifying the magazine article as a non-fiction article on waste. Then invite learners to look for different text types within the article. They compare the layout, the narrative voice (first, second or third), the tense and the persuasive techniques.

This is good for recalling text types, particularly the ones covered in this text book and revising features of non-fiction text types.

> **Differentiation ideas:** Support learners by using Worksheet 6.16 Plan a biography to guide their planning and writing.

Review the different text types covered in the Learner's Book. Learners draw a table in their learning journals, list the texts, then analyse them as they did in the lesson.

As a class, review figurative language in persuasive texts. Encourage more confident learners to identify the figurative language used in the ocean pollution article and say what it is: *the silent killer* (metaphor), *miracle worker* (metaphor), *the ocean is keeping nature and mankind in harmony* (personification).

> **Assessment ideas:** Various text types appear in the magazine article. Assess the learners' understanding of these. Can they identify features of each? This is important groundwork for the final writing activity in this unit.

Answers:

1   a   Accept any reasonable examples and features.
   * Informative: The questions and answers give information using formal, factual language.
   * Biographical: Short inserts about what different people are doing using third-person pronouns.
   * Instructional: Explanations included using second person narrative.
   * Persuasive: Main text aims to win the reader over with figurative images like 'silent killer'.
   * Balanced: Insert with 'yes' and 'no' options using personal and persuasive language.

2   Revise relative pronouns (20 minutes)

Learning intention: To explore relative pronouns and use them to introduce additional details

Resources: Learner's Book, Session 8.3, Activity 2; Differentiated worksheet pack

Description: Recall relative pronouns. Read the writing tip and turn to the Language focus box in Unit 2, Sessions 2.6 and 2.7 for extra support. Revise further tips using the input in the language support for this session.

Work further examples on the board – ask learners to combine sentence parts with relative pronouns – e.g. *This is the pen. I bought this pen at the shop.* (This is the pen that I bought at the shop.) *I have a friend. My friend lives next door.* (I have a friend who lives next door.) *This is my teacher. My teacher's birthday is today.* (This is my teacher whose birthday is today.)

Learners find sentences in the ocean pollution article that use different relative pronouns. (There is as least one of each in the text.) Organise learners into pairs for extra support, particularly those who may be struggling

> **Differentiation ideas:** Encourage learners to complete one or more levels of the Differentiated worksheet pack on relative pronouns. Then they write sentences using information from the magazine text to demonstrate each type of relative pronoun.

Explore the rules for using *which* and *that*. Explore the rules for using *whom*. Invite confident learners to explain to the class. Then ask learners to make a poster that explains the rules of relative pronouns.

Answers:

2   a   Accept any answers example:
   Dan Edwards is a surfer, diver and marine biologist who decided to tackle the problem.

   Two surfers, Andrew Cooper and Alex Schulze, whose holiday came to an end at the sight of rubbish in the sea, founded 4Ocean.

   Spekboom, also known as Elephant's Food, absorbs carbon emissions like no other plant, which makes it a miracle worker!

   Our oceans are made up of networks of currents that move around the Earth.

b • I know the person *who* collects the rubbish.
  • I support an organisation *that* makes bracelets from sea plastic.
  • This is the boat *that* took us out.
  • The family *whose* car broke down, needs help.
  • He tried to save a seal *that* was injured.
  • To *whom* would you like this gift delivered?

Plenary idea

Relatively speaking (5 minutes)

Description: Learners check and assess each other's sentences. Then they make any corrections.

Homework ideas

Learners complete the Workbook activities for Session 8.3. They could also make observations on household plastic waste then write further sentences using relative clauses such as: *This is the plastic that (which) we throw away every day. There is a lot of food we buy (that) which is packed in plastic.*

Answers for Workbook

1 a That is the bicycle I would like to buy.
  b This is the teacher with whom you must go.
  c These are the volunteers who want to help us.
  d The two girls, whose names were on the list, did not arrive.
  e Is this the question which/that you do not understand?

2 a To whom would you like the flowers delivered?
  b To whom were you speaking?
  c From whom did the parcel come?
  d To whom did you send the letter?
  e To whom does the honour go?

3 Accept any similar answers:
  a 'Whom' is the object form of 'who' (Sam is the boy whom (object) I sit next to. I sit next to Sam who (subject) is a boy.
  b 'That' or 'which' can be interchangeable but it is usual in a defining clause to use that and to use which in non-defining clauses. So 'that' provides essential information, 'which' provides non-essential information.

8.4 Punctuation with purpose

LEARNING PLAN			
Learning objectives		**Learning intentions**	**Success criteria**
Main focus	**Also covered**	• Identify punctuation in a text.	• Learners can identify and explain the purpose of various punctuation marks.
6Rg.01, 6Wg.01	6Rg.02, 6Wg.02, 6Wg.03, 6SLp.01	• Use punctuation to clarify meaning.	• Learners can write sentences using punctuation to clarify meaning.
		• Read aloud with accuracy.	• Learners can read aloud using punctuation to assist.

LANGUAGE SUPPORT

In Unit 4, learners learnt that pairs of brackets, dashes or commas enclose a word or words to separate it/them from the main sentence to show an explanation or additional information or an aside or afterthought. In Unit 7, learners learnt that a colon introduces: a speaker, dialogue, a list, an idea or an explanation and is useful for adding emphasis to a sentence. They also learnt that a semicolon creates a break that is more than a comma but less than a full stop. It adds variety by joining short sentences and it separates list items where a comma may cause confusion. In this unit, learners revise ways that commas, dashes and brackets are used to clarify meaning and clear up ambiguity – when more than one meaning could be inferred from a sentence without the punctuation.

Compound words can be nouns or adjectives. These words can be written in three ways: as open compounds (as two words, e.g. *ice cream*), closed compounds (joined, e.g. *doorknob*), or hyphenated compounds (two words joined by a hyphen, e.g. *long-term*). Sometimes, more than two words can form a compound (e.g. *mother-in-law*). In most cases, a compound adjective is hyphenated if placed before the noun it modifies, but not if placed after the noun.

Common misconceptions

Misconception	How to identify	How to overcome
Parenthesis is only brackets	Ask: *What punctuation marks are used to show parenthesis?* (Commas, dashes, brackets.) Write the following on the board and invite learners to show parenthesis using the different punctuation marks: *I went to visit my friend with a broken arm in hospital.* Accept various answers: *I went to visit my friend (with a broken arm) in hospital.* *I went to visit my friend – with a broken arm – in hospital.* *I went to visit my friend, with a broken arm, in hospital.*	Learners practise using parenthesis with further examples. Learners find examples in their readers to share and discuss. Complete Language worksheet 8A Skills development: Developing punctuation skills

Starter idea

Make sense (5 minutes)

Resources: Learner's Book, Session 8.4: Getting started

Description: Learners use their readers or magazines to find examples where punctuation is used to clarify meaning. They read a short passage to a partner using the punctuation to guide their expression and pace. Clarify any misunderstandings about punctuation in their selected passages.

Main teaching ideas

1 Identify and explain the purpose of specific punctuation (20 minutes)

Learning intention: To read aloud with accuracy and explore the purpose of different punctuation marks in the text

Resources: Learner's Book Session 8.4, Activity 1; Learner's Book Session 8.2, Activity 1

Description: Revise and discuss the purpose of different punctuation marks. Use the information in the language support at the start of this session and the Reading tip in the Learner's Book. Ask learners to work in pairs and read aloud Learner's Book Session 8.2, Activity 1 'Ocean pollution – the silent killer' so it makes sense to the listener.

Using the activities to guide you, analyse specific punctuation in sentences from the magazine article. Clear up misconceptions and work extra examples. Learners complete the activities in their notebooks. Ask: *Do you remember the difference between hyphens and dashes?* (Hyphens are used to connect words. They are not the same as dashes. Hyphens are shorter than dashes. Hyphens are not separated by spaces, dashes are.)

Invite learners to explain the difference between hyphenated nouns and adjectives. Learners find examples in the text then give their own examples or look for more in their readers.

Complete the Workbook activities if there is time in class.

> **Differentiation ideas:** Learners can support each other by practising, in small groups, writing sentences using parenthesis to clarify meaning, sort out ambiguity and provide extra information. Challenge more confident learners to work

independently and write a range of sentences to demonstrate the use of parenthesis.

> **Assessment ideas:** Check learners' ability to use punctuation to clarify meaning in sentences. Use the answers provided to assess their written work. Listen to their reading aloud to assess their use of punctuation to read with expression and meaning.

Answers:
1. a Learners read aloud.
   b • Commas used as parenthesis to add detail.
     • Brackets to clarify and a comma to separate the adverb from the rest of the sentence.
     • A dash to add an aside with emphasis.
     • A colon to introduce an idea.
     • Ellipses to create a pause and present further information.
   c Accept any reasonable answers example
     • The beach is a fun place to go to relax and to fish – if that's what you enjoy.
     • This is, without a doubt, the best beach in the world.
     • We will (all) have to clean up this beach before we can swim.
     • I will be there, if necessary, to clean the beach.
     • Everyone was glad when the factories (polluting the water) closed down.
   d Learners' own sentences.
   e Learners' own answers.

2 Write sentences using commas to clarify (20 minutes)

Learning intention: To use commas, dashes and brackets parenthetically and use punctuation to clarify meaning in complex sentences

Resources: Learner's Book Session 8.4, Activity 2; Learner's Book Session 8.2, Activity 1; Language worksheet 8A Skills development: Developing punctuation skills

Description: Write the following on the board: *Brackets provide extra (sometimes essential) information. Discuss the purpose of the brackets in that sentence.* Read the Reading tip and invite learners to make up other examples where brackets or other punctuation marks clear up ambiguity.

Use Language worksheet 8A Skills development: Developing punctuation skills to practise adding commas for clarity. Learners also complete the sentences from the Learner's Book in their notebooks.

Revise brackets, commas and dashes used for parenthesis. Learners practise how to clarify the meaning in sentences that may be ambiguous.

Complete the Workbook activities if there is time in class.

> **Differentiation ideas:** As a class, revise work on main and dependent clauses, and when to use a comma to separate them.

Invite more confident learners to explain the use of inverted commas and correct punctuation to write sentences with direct speech. Either they or you could give examples on the board.

> **Assessment ideas:** By this stage, learners should be able to go beyond basic punctuation marks used to show expression and different sentence types – full stops, exclamation and question marks. Check they are able to use punctuation to clarify meaning in sentences using colons, semicolons, ellipses, parenthetic commas, dashes and brackets. They should also know how to use commas to separate the main clause and other clauses (subordinate clauses) in a complex sentence and punctuate direct and reported speech accurately.

Answers:

2 a Accept answers such as these.
- *Once filled, it can be used creatively in various ways like building furniture and homes.*
- *From plankton to whales, marine life is affected.*
- *If we do not stop this trend, our planet will perish.*

b
- As far as the eye could see, there was plastic floating on the water.
- Without hesitation, we picked up the plastic on the beach.
- Although the factories pollute the water, they do not care.
- If we don't do something, it will be too late to solve the problem.
- Up to now, there are not enough people involved.

c Learners' own sentences.

Plenary idea

Perfect punctuation (5 minutes)

Description: Learners mark each other's work. Ensure they make corrections, so they learn from their mistakes.

Homework ideas

Learners use their readers to find examples of punctuation used to give clarity.

Answers for Workbook

1

,	comma	…	ellipses
( )	brackets/parenthesis	!	exclamation
-	dash (or hyphen)	?	question mark
:	colon	" "	inverted commas

2 a True

b True

c True

d True.

Learners' own examples.

3 a The teacher wants Inam, Neo, Bekkie, Jo and Di to present their speeches next week.

b To fill in the form, you should print neatly using a black pen without making any mistakes.

c You can have extra time to finish, however, it must be done by tomorrow.

d The book was exciting, interesting, fun and easy to read.

e Since I'd also like to see the film, maybe we should go to see it together.

4 Accept any reasonable variations:

a The class all voted 'yes' to going home early.

b She replied, 'I'd love some more.'

c This ice-cream has delicious, out-of-this-world flavours.

d He received the title of 'Best Young Recycler' of the year.

e I think we (you and I) should redo this work.

f I can join you, if you like, for the clean-up.

5 Learners' own sentences.

8.5 Follow instructions

LEARNING PLAN

Learning objectives		Learning intentions	Success criteria
Main focus	**Also covered**	• Identify organisational features of instructions. • Explore command verbs. • Explore quantifiers.	• Learners can identify organisational features of instructions. • Learners can use command verbs to give instructions. • Learners can use quantifiers with countable and uncountable nouns.
6Rg.08, 6Ri.04, 6Wg.06	6Rv.03, 6Rv.04, 6Rs.03, 6Ri.05, 6Ri.06, 6Wg.08, 6SLp.01		

LANGUAGE SUPPORT

Instructional language is familiar to the learners as it is part of school and family life. The basic organisational features are straightforward yet the potential to develop language skills is key. Instructional language forms a vital part of developing logic, processes and procedures.

The imperative mood is the grammatical form of a command or a request. Imperative verbs (or imperatives) are used to begin a sentence or can stand on their own (Go!). The subject is usually implied (You). At this level, your learners will be more familiar with the terms 'command sentences and verbs'.

Countable nouns (count nouns) are things you can count. They can be singular or plural. You can use *a* or *an* (indefinite article) before them. Uncountable nouns are things we cannot count such as ideas, concepts or substances: e.g. music, art, love, happiness, advice, information, news, furniture, luggage, rice, sugar, butter, water, electricity, gas, power, money, currency … To express an unspecific amount or quantity, we use quantifiers – a measure word. In Unit 4, learners learnt about using quantifiers, e.g. *all, most, many, more, some, none, few, fewer, less, both, no, enough, some, each* and *every*. Some quantifiers are singular, some are plural and some may be either.

Some nouns can be both but with different meanings, e.g. I have <u>more hair</u> than you. There is <u>a hair</u> in my food; I have <u>three lights</u> next to my bed. There is <u>too much light</u> in the room.

Common misconception

Misconception	How to identify	How to overcome
Commands always have a stern tone and an exclamation mark at the end.	Write the following on the board: *Count your blessings.* *Please write neatly.* *Drive carefully and be back soon.* Ask: *What is the tone like? Is an exclamation mark necessary?*	Learners look for other examples of the imperative mood and make a table of different types of commands: a plea, a blessing, a shout or call …

Starter idea

Right this way (5 minutes)

Resources: Learner's Book, Session 8.5: Getting started; instructions and recipes

Description: Learners share experiences of trying to follow instructions (or recipes) that went wrong, were difficult to follow or didn't make sense. Discuss the importance of using clear, correct instructions. Explain that instructions are a type of persuasive text because they tell the reader what to do. Invite learners to find examples using the resources provided.

Main teaching ideas

1 Explore the features of an instructional text (15 minutes)

Learning intention: To explore and recognise how ideas are organised and linked cohesively across a text

Resources: *How to make an ecobrick* (Learner's Book, Session 8.5, Activity 1); Track 46; Workbook, Session 8.5

Description: Learners skim the text *How to make an ecobrick* and identify obvious clues that show it is an instruction. List them on the board. Talk about audience, purpose and layout, and how they are linked to the text type. Discuss how the layout fits the purpose – e.g. the steps are ordered and numbered so readers do not get confused; pictures match the instructions; the language is clear and simple.

Discuss the tone and how instructions generally vary in tone depending on the audience. See the Reading tip on tone.

Check for a defining outcome. Does the text say what the end product should look like, feel like or how to know once the product is finished or ready? This is a good way to extend basic instructions.

Invite learners to discuss in small groups and predict challenges they might encounter. (Cleaning the plastic may not be easy and it uses water; changing your habits; remembering to use the bottle instead of the bin; getting the whole family involved to save their waste.)

Complete the Workbook activities for Session 8.5 if there is time in class.

> **Differentiation ideas:** Prompt and support learners who are having difficulty understanding and recalling the order of the text. Invite more confident learners to explain how they might approach making an ecobrick for themselves.

> **Assessment ideas:** Observe as learners read and discuss the organisational features of the text. Ask: *What type of text is this? How is this text different from other non-fiction texts? How does the layout support the purpose?*

Answers:

1. a The use of organisational features – e.g. headings, sections, numbered steps, simple diagrams to match each step, a list of items needed, symbols to show what can and can't be used. The instructions can be used by anyone but seem to be aimed at primary level because the tone is friendly, the language is simple and the instructions say 'you may need an adult to help you'. Highlight the Reading tip, then ask learners to read aloud using appropriate expression and tone.
   b Accept words like: non-biodegradable, organic matter, decay, compress/compressed
   c headings, numbered steps, diagrams …
   d The conclusion is: If you can squeeze it, it is not complete. Add more waste and compress it further. If you cannot squeeze any part of it, your ecobrick is complete. Well done!
   e Learners' own answers.

2 Make instructions clear and direct to avoid confusion (30 minutes)

Learning intention: To explore and discuss grammatical features in a range of texts

Resources: Learner's Book, Session 8.5, Activity 2; *How to make an ecobrick* (Learner's Book, Session 8.5); Track 46; Workbook, Session 8.5

Description: Discuss and explain the imperative mood and identify command verbs in the text. List them on the board. Learners make up their own command sentences for the text. Share ideas. This is fairly straightforward, as they will previously have covered this in Stage 5, but there is extra practice in the Workbook for this session if needed.

Revise countable and uncountable nouns and the quantifiers that go with them (previously covered in Unit 4). Use the text *How to make an ecobrick* from Activity 1 to discuss and identify examples of countable and uncountable nouns (and nouns that can be both. Say if the noun is singular or plural then identify the quantifier.

Ask learners to draw a table in their notebooks and record these examples. Invite them to add their own examples.

Revise the reminder on when to use the words *less* and *fewer*. Encourage learners to practise when to use these quantifiers before completing the activity.

> **Differentiation ideas:** In supported pairs or groups, learners write more sentences according to the time available and work together on the Workbook activities.

Challenge more confident learners to find examples in other texts of count and non-count nouns and their quantifiers. Working independently, they complete the Workbook activities on countable and uncountable nouns and quantifiers.

> **Assessment ideas:** Check that learners understand the technical and tricky vocabulary using context and clues to work them out (and dictionaries if necessary). Check their written work to assess their sentence construction and use of command verbs and quantifiers.

Answers:

2 a • Step 1 Ensure … Step 2 Cut … Add … Step 3 Use … Do not leave … Step 4 Fill … Step 5 Put … Add … Step 6 Team up … Drop off …

   • Learners' own sentences.

   b Accept any – e.g. countable: ecobricks (plural, a few); uncountable: plastic (singular, more) and/or plastics (plural, some)

   c • Learners own ideas. For example:

Countable nouns	Uncountable nouns	Both
Bottle, ecobrick, stick, spoon, dial, rod, lid	Organic matter, moisture	plastic/s, space/s

   • Learners' own sentences such as: I have made an ecobrick today. I've made some ecobricks today.

   d less plastic, fewer bottles, less waste, fewer straws, less straw, less glass, fewer glasses

Plenary idea

Do you follow? (5 minutes)

Description: Learners read their sentences to each other and suggest ways to improve.

CROSS-CURRICULAR LINKS

History: Explore the necessity and effects of instructions (and rules). Explore how instructions have changed from 100 years ago. Invite examples like how to light an oil lamp. Consider the kinds of instructions we may need in 100 years' time. Write instructions for how to use a time machine in a history class.

Homework ideas

Learners look around their homes for different types of instructions. They could also look in supermarkets or even in their school for examples of different types of instructions. If possible, they bring the instructions to class to display. Learners write instructions for a peer to follow and observe the results.

Answers for Workbook

1 tear, put, add, leave, mix, squeeze, add, store

2 a countable: bowl, container, hands;
   b uncountable: water, flour, pulp, paste, tea;
   c both: paper, egg, glass

3 Learners' own sentences.

8.6 Clauses to clarify

LEARNING PLAN

Learning objectives		Learning intentions	Success criteria
Main focus	**Also covered**	• Revise the *if* clause.	• Learners can identify and use the *if* clause in sentences.
6Rg.02, 6Rg.03, 6Wg.03, 6SLm.03	6Wg.04, 6Wp.04, 6Wp.05	• Use connectives effectively.	• Learners can use connectives to link steps in instructions.
		• Give instructions with complex sentences.	• Learners can write complex sentences with more than one connective.

LANGUAGE SUPPORT

By now, learners should be familiar with simple and multi-clause sentences. They should also remember the difference between compound and complex sentences.

Compound sentences have two or more simple sentences joined by a co-ordinating connective (FANBOYS). Complex sentences have one main (independent) clause and one or more subordinate clauses.

Subordinating connectives join dependent clauses to independent clauses. They are essential in complex sentences that have at least two clauses, with one of the clauses being main (independent) and the other being subordinate (dependent). They are used to express time, cause and effect, reason and result. There are many subordinating connectives, including these common ones: *after, although, as, as soon as, because, before, by the time, even if, even though, every time, if, in case, now that, once, since, so that, than, the first time, unless, until, when, whenever, whether or not, while, why.*

The *if* or conditional clause is used in complex sentences to show possibility.

Common misconceptions

Misconception	How to identify	How to overcome
You can use any connectives to form any multi-clause sentence.	Give examples of a compound and a complex sentence and ask learners to find the main clause in each. Ask learners to look for examples of connectives that do different things.	Remind learners that certain connectives do certain jobs. The connectives *for, and, nor, but, or, yet, and so* (F.A.N.B.O.Y.S) are co-ordinating connectives that link words, phrases or clauses of equal importance in compound sentences. The *if* clause is used to show possibility in complex sentences. Other connectives express time, place, cause and effect and so on.

Continue

Misconception	How to identify	How to overcome
A complex sentence has one connective.	Write the following on the board and ask the learners to identify the connectives: *I will make an ecobrick <u>once</u> I have collected enough plastic <u>and</u> I find a 2L bottle.* or *I will collect all my waste plastic <u>in order to</u> make an ecobrick <u>so that</u> my waste is stored not tossed.*	Practise joining sentences using more than one connective to show sequence. Complete the Workbook activities.

Starter idea

Revise clauses (5 minutes)

Resources: Learner's Book, Session 8.6: Getting started

Description: Learners revise the *if* clause by completing the sentence in five different ways. They also revise conditional clauses and sentences.

Main teaching ideas

1 Use the *if* clause to clarify (15 minutes)

Learning intentions: To identify the main clause and other clauses in a complex sentence; to use correct punctuation

Resources: Learner's Book, Session 8.6, Activity 1; *How to make an ecobrick* (Learner's Book, Session 8.5); Track 46; Workbook, Session 8.6

Description: Learners work in pairs to read the information text *How to make an ecobrick* again and identify the *if* clauses. Remind them to use a comma after the *if* clause that begins a sentence.

Discuss various ways to complete the sentences in the Learner's Book then ask learners to work on their own to write their sentences into their notebooks. In pairs, learners check each other's sentences, offer ways to improve and do corrections.

Complete the Workbook activities for Session 8.6 if there is time in class.

> **Differentiation ideas:** As a class, revise simple, compound and complex sentences. Invite less confident learners to practise writing conditional sentences using other sentence starters.

Challenge more confident learners to find examples of conditional sentences in their readers and in conversations they hear or have. Learners record these in their learning journals.

> **Assessment ideas:** Test prior knowledge to see how much learners remember about simple, compound and complex sentences, clauses and connectives. Use this to guide how to approach the lesson and revise further. Assess learners' ability to write sentences with *if* clauses and subordinating clauses using correct punctuation.

Answers:
1 a If you do not compress it tightly, it will not become solid enough; If you can squeeze it, it is not complete; If you cannot squeeze any part of it, your ecobrick is complete.
    b–d Learners' own sentences.

2 Use more than one connective to link steps and give clarity (25 minutes)

Learning intentions: To use a variety of complex sentences to show sequence or clarity; to use correct punctuation

Resources: Learner's Book, Session 8.6, Activity 2; Workbook, Session 8.6

Description: Discuss the Language focus box. Learners will realise they can use more than one connective in a sentence. Discuss the list of connectives provided and decide which ones show sequence and which provide clarity.

In pairs, learners make up sentences then work independently to write the sentences into their notebooks.

Complete the Workbook activities for Session 8.6 if there is time in class and they have not already been completed during Activity 1.

⟩ **Differentiation ideas:** Support small groups of less confident learners by helping them to write complex sentences using further examples and the Workbook activities. More confident students can work individually on this activity.

Answers:
2   a–e Learners own work.

Plenary idea

It's complex (5 minutes)

Description: In groups, learners check each other's sentences and make adjustments or do corrections if necessary.

Learners read their sentences aloud to the rest of the class.

Homework ideas

Learners use ideas from home or another place they know well to make up complex sentences with conditional and subordinate clauses, e.g. *If I don't do my homework, I can't play a game. My grandma says I can watch TV after I've finished my homework, until she goes to bed.*

Answers for Workbook

1   How to make a planting pot; You need a plastic 2L bottle; To begin, lie the bottle on its side; Cut a 10 cm opening in the 'top' side, and poke holes in the 'bottom' side; Use the opening to fill it with soil; Finally, plant seeds and water the soil; If you water daily, your seeds will grow.

2   **a**   Once the paper has soaked for a few hours, mash it up <u>using your hands</u>.

    b   If you would rather not get your hands dirty, use a blender to mix the pulp <u>into a smooth paste</u>.

    c   If you don't want to wait too long, use hot water <u>instead of warm water</u>.

    d   If it's necessary, add more water <u>to moisten it</u>.

    e   When the pulp is smooth, make a gluey paste <u>by</u> <u>adding flour</u>.

    f   In order to make it last, store it in an air-tight container <u>until you need it</u>.

3   **a**   Ask an adult to help you, if you need to boil water.

    b   If you want to bake a cake, you will need all the ingredients.

    c   You can continue with your art, if you finish your work.

    d   If you want a cooked breakfast, you must boil the eggs.

    e   You must clean up, if you make a mess.

4   Learners' own sentences.

8.7 Make something

LEARNING PLAN

Learning objectives		Learning intentions	Success criteria
Main focus	**Also covered**	• Discuss and share ideas.	• Learners can discuss ideas and explore useful vocabulary.
6Rv.03, 6Ws.01, 6Ws.04, 6Wc.06, 6Wc.07, 6Wp.03	6Wc.02, 6Wp.04, 6Wp.05, 6SLm.03	• Plan and edit a first draft. • Present work neatly.	• Learners can plan and edit a first draft. • Learners can write it out neatly using neat handwriting and layout.

LANGUAGE SUPPORT

Refer back to Language support for Session 8.6. At this stage (Year 6), learners should be able to go beyond simple command sentences. Their instructions should include the imperative mood, but also show their ability to use complex sentences with connectives that show the order and options or advice. Additionally, they should include graphics, be able to vary to the tone and formality, be free of ambiguity and summarise the outcome.

To challenge learners, you could increase the complexity of the topics and the steps involved.

Starter idea

Getting started (5 minutes)

Resources: Learner's Book, Session 8.7: Getting started; magazines or online information with ideas

Description: Learners work together to brainstorm ideas for things to make out of waste. There are many ideas online and in various magazines. Provide some reading material for them to use. Remind learners to choose something simple enough that they can make on their own.

Main teaching ideas

1 Plan instructions to make something from waste materials (25 minutes)

Learning intentions: To use effective planning to inform the content and structure of writing; to evaluate own writing

Resources: Learner's Book, Session 8.7, Activity 1; Workbook, Session 8.7; Worksheet 6.29

Description: Remind learners to order instructions correctly. Once they have chosen a topic, they work individually to plan a set of instructions. Invite learners to go back to the text *How to make an ecobrick* in Session 8.5 to check the layout and language. They should also use the list of things to consider as a guide plus Worksheet 6.29 Guidelines for writing instruction to help them with their writing and editing.

Once they have a first draft, learners check and edit their own work, then make corrections and improvements.

⟩ **Differentiation ideas:** Allow learners to use the Workbook activities to practise the written work. Support less confident learners by allowing them to write the instructions together in small groups.

Vary the complexity of the topic according to how much time you have and how quickly your learners work.

⟩ **Assessment ideas:** Observe as learners work together to discuss ideas and explore vocabulary. Ask: *Can the learners work together? Do they* *give each other a chance to speak? Can they use thesauruses to explore interesting words?* Once learners have a first draft, invite them to check and edit their own and each other's work.

Answers:
1 a–c Learners' own work.

2 Present your ideas (20 minutes)

Learning intention: To evaluate own and others' writing, suggesting improvements for sense, accuracy and content

Resources: Learner's Book, Session 8.7, Activity 2; Worksheet 6.29

Description: Learners write their instructions neatly by hand or use onscreen tools to key it in and lay out. This is good for encouraging awareness of the importance and impact of presentation.

In pairs, learners show their work and read it aloud. Together they take turns to discuss it and give suggestions on what works well and what could improve. Use Worksheet 6.29 Guidelines for writing instructions to guide their discussion. Learners correct and improve their work or, if necessary, redo it.

> **Differentiation ideas:** Invite learners to work in pairs or small groups to complete the Workbook activities, which will help them develop their writing skills.

More confident learners work individually, then discuss and get feedback with partners or in small groups – depending on what works best.

> **Assessment ideas:** Asses their final draft using the list of criteria provided in the Learner's Book (and the plenary session).

Answers:
2 a–e Learners' own work.

Plenary idea

Do what works well (5 minutes)

Description: Learners assist each other in preparing the instructions for the next session. If necessary, learners do corrections or redo the work so it is correct.

> **Assessment ideas:** Use the list in Activity 1 of this session to check and assess their final work. Rate their effort on how well they:

- aimed at a young audience and used a friendly style to keep readers interested
- gave at least five steps in sequence to explain the process
- added a picture or pictures to help clarify
- used organisational features to improve the layout (numbers or bullets or steps)
- used command verbs
- included conditional clauses to add detail
- used punctuation to clarify and make meaning clear
- concluded with a clear idea of what the end product should be like.

Homework ideas

Learners complete the Workbook activities.

Answers for Workbook

1–3 Learners' own work.

8.8 Demonstrate

LEARNING PLAN

Learning objectives		Learning intentions	Success criteria
Main focus	**Also covered**	• Prepare a presentation and identify criteria for a good speech.	• Learners can prepare a speech and identify important criteria to assess it.
6SLm.02, 6SLp.03, 6SLr.01	6Wp.02, 6SLm.01, 6SLm.03, 6SLm.04, 6SLm.05, 6SLp.04, 6SLr.02, 6SLs.01	• Give a demonstration. • Evaluate own and others' talk.	• Learners can give a demonstration. • Learners can evaluate their own and others talk using the criteria.

LANGUAGE SUPPORT

When speaking (and writing), the purpose and audience affects the language and presentation. Before learners prepare their presentations, check they know who the audience is – e.g. it might be a younger class, the whole school or a group of teachers. This will affect language, tone and register and non-verbal communication techniques such as body language and visual props.

Common misconception

Misconception	How to identify	How to overcome
A presentation is the same for any audience.	Discuss different types of audience. Ask: *How would a presentation vary if the audience changed from a group of young children to a panel of senior teachers?*	Learners role-play different types of audience. Learners practise adapting their presentation to suit a different audience each time.

Starter idea

Simple steps (5 minutes)

Resources: Learner's Book, Session 8.8: Getting started

Description: In pairs, learners choose a favourite game or hobby to describe to each other and explain how it works. As one partner speaks, the other listens and takes notes. Afterwards, the listener explains the activity back. This will show the speaker how well they explained and how well the listener understood – good for demonstrating positive communication skills. Discuss the challenges of giving instructions when you have not prepared or do not have visual props.

Main teaching ideas

1 Practise to build confidence (20 minutes)

Learning intention: To show awareness of different audiences and plan an independent presentation

Resources: Learner's Book, Session 8.8, Activity 1; Worksheet 6.10; learners' notes from Session 8.7

Description: Learners use the instructions they wrote in Session 8.7 to give a demonstration. They must choose an audience – their peers, a younger class, an afternoon club or panel of teachers – and consider how this will affect the language and register they use (formal or informal, child-friendly or teacher appropriate talk …). They complete Worksheet 6.10 Reading, speaking or performing assessment sheet.

Remind learners to use speech cards. Ask: *How should you record your notes on speech cards?* (key words) *Why are key words helpful?* (they prompt the speaker.)

Discuss various ways to include visual props. Learners can bring items to school to make the object as they speak, refer to a poster or use a digital slide show. Discuss the importance of managing the visual props as you speak. It should not be distracting for the audience, but a way to help the audience understand what you say.

Remind learners to ensure that their speech is structured to aid the listeners' understanding. This means they should use language appropriate to the audience and order the steps of the instructions correctly so it makes sense.

Discuss important presentation skills and how they should use their voice and body to keep the attention of the audience. Ask: *What effect does it have on the audience if you look at the floor as you speak, or fiddle with your clothes, or if you speak too softly or too slowly or without any expression?*

Remind learners of the dos and don'ts of presenting. Provide time in class and at home for learners to practise their presentation skills.

> **Differentiation ideas:** Support learners by allowing them to work in pairs, making sure both learners have a chance to speak. Help them to choose an object and take turns to present. Vary the complicity and criteria of the presentation according to learners' language ability and confidence. Learners can demonstrate their own recycling object and give a presentation.

Answers:
1 a–d Learners' own work.

2 Present with confidence (20 minutes)

Learning intentions: To deliver an independent presentation confidently; to evaluate own and others' talks

Resources: Learner's Book, Session 8.8, Activity 2; Workbook, Session 8.8; Worksheet 6.10

Description: Together, discuss criteria that learners might use to guide and assess a presentation. List the criteria on the board then ask learners to choose five they think are the most important. Ask: *Are some criteria more important than others or are they all equally important?*

Learners take turns to present and also listen to others' presentations. Encourage them to take notes as they listen so they remember the things they want to discuss afterwards and also to decide which criteria were well covered.

After each presentation (or once all the presentations are done) have a time of feedback to discuss what went well and what could be improved.

> **Differentiation ideas:** Small groups can complete the Workbook activities for Session 8.8 to revise the skills taught in this session and to guide their presentation.

Encourage more confident learners to work individually.

> **Assessment ideas:** Learners use the criteria they develop/choose to guide and assess their own and others' talks. Use Worksheet 6.10 Reading, speaking or performing assessment sheet to support this assessment.

Answers:
2 a–d Learners' own work.

Plenary idea

As easy as 1–2–3 (5 minutes)

Description: Invite learners to reflect on their own and others' talk, using the How are we doing? questions.

> **Assessment ideas:** Invite learners to self-assess and rate how confident they felt on a scale of 0–10; they should also rate how they felt about their overall performance.

Homework ideas

Learners complete the Workbook activities for Session 8.8 to revise and consolidate the skills learnt, if they have not already completed them in class. They practise their presentations in front of a live audience (perhaps at home or at a friend's) to help prepare.

Answers for Workbook

1 Accept any reasonable ideas.

2 X Your voice must be very loud.

✓ Your voice must be clear with a varied tone.

X Keep your eyes open all the time.

✓ Maintain good eye contact with the audience.

X Always stand still.

✓ Use body language effectively.

X Make sure the audience pays attention.

✓ Keep the audience interested with clear, direct instructions.

X Visual props are essential to improve any speech.

✓ Use visual props to support your speech and add impact if necessary.

3 Learners' own work.

8.9 Facts and opinions about recycling

LEARNING PLAN

Learning objectives		Learning intentions	Success criteria
Main focus	Also covered		
6Ra.02	6Rv.04, 6Rs.02, 6Ri.04, 6Ri.05, 6Wc.06m, 6Wc.07, 6Wc.08, 6SLg.03, 6SLg.04, 6SLp.01	• Analyse the impact of a text. • Consider pros and cons. • Write a balanced view.	• Learners can analyse the impact of a text. • Learners can consider the pros and cons of an issue. • Learners can write a balanced view.

LANGUAGE SUPPORT

The visual impact of a text is often age-appropriate and reflects the level of language and content. Remind learners that the layout and language is determined by the audience and purpose.

A good writer chooses the layout and language to suit the readers. The text provided is a poor example – the learners must suggest ways to improve it so it is more appealing to a young reader.

In Unit 5, learners learnt how to write a balanced argument. A balanced argument introduces and states the issue, gives points for and against the issue backed by facts, then concludes by summing up the points for and against and sometimes suggesting a conclusion or the best way forward given different criteria.

Starter idea

What's the appeal? (5 minutes)

Resources: Learner's Book, Session 8.9: Getting started; examples of different text types

Description: Write the following on the board: *text, topics, spacing, colour, pictures, chapters, paragraphs, headings.* Discuss what makes your learners want to read something (a book or a text). Ask: *What draws you in, gets your attention and triggers your interest? Do you prefer large or small text? Long or short chapters and paragraphs? Colourful cartoons or realistic pictures? Hard or soft covers? Sections and headings or chapters? Simple or complex language?*

There are many elements (visual and linguistic) of a text that make it either appealing to different audiences. Show examples of different text types and ask which ones the learners would like to read. Observe if learners go beyond the visual impact of a text to the content and language.

Main teaching ideas

1 Explore the appeal and impact of a text (15 minutes)

Learning intention: To discuss textual features, demonstrating some awareness of the impact on the reader

Resources: *Recycling* (Learner's Book, Session 8.9, Activity 1); Track 47

Description: Learners skim the text. Ask: *Does it look or sound interesting?* (Probably not – the text looks dull and the topic is something they already know about.) *Do you want to read more?* (Probably not unless they think they might learn something new.)

Play the audio of the text (Track 47) as learners follow in their books to gather the details. Discuss their responses to the text. Use the questions provided to discuss how they feel about it. Learners might find it difficult to read without headings and proper spacing and may find the content boring.

In pairs, learners talk about features that could have made the text easier and more interesting to read. Have a class feedback session and list ideas on the board. Revise the meaning of difficult words in the text.

> **Differentiation ideas:** Support less confident learners by allowing them to read silently or aloud in pairs from less familiar (and more complex) non-fiction texts.

Encourage more confident learners to read aloud from more complex texts.

> **Assessment ideas:** Observe as learners discuss the impact of the text, give personal responses and identify the pros and cons.

Answers:
1   a–b Learners' personal responses
     c   Learners' own ideas.

2 Use the information to express a point of view (30 minutes)

Learning intention: To take turns in a discussion and write a balanced argument.

Resources: Learner's Book, Session 8.9, Activity 2; Worksheets 6.20 and 6.21; Language worksheet 5A

Description: Learners identify all the facts in the text. They will notice there are no opinions, although the text is based on the opinion that recycling is important. The text supports one main viewpoint; this makes it a persuasive text although it does not use obviously persuasive language.

Learners consider the pros and the cons of the topic. This is good for getting them to understand that there is always another side. Invite learners to consider a less popular view on the matter – that some people might not want to recycle – and to try to understand their reasons.

Learners use the discussion to write a short, balanced argument presenting both sides of the issues and concluding by taking one side based on the information presented. Use Language worksheet 5A Skills development: Expressing one side of an argument to refresh how to write a balanced argument. Complete the Workbook activities if there is time in class.

> **Differentiation ideas:** Support less confident learners by allowing them to work in pairs or small groups to write an introduction for the text in the Learner's Book.

Challenge more confident learners to choose another topic and write a more detailed balanced argument using facts to support each viewpoint. (Remind learners how to produce a balanced report or arguments as covered in Unit 5.)

> **Assessment ideas:** Use Worksheet 6.20 Plan a balanced report and Worksheet 6.21 Balanced report assessment or Language worksheet 5A to guide and assess their balanced argument.

Answers:
2   a   Accept any facts. There are no/few opinions.
     b   The text promotes recycling.
     c   Accept ideas such as: It is important to manage your personal waste, but it takes a lot of time and effort. Recycling is a way to save and reuse, but recycling can be more expensive for some waste.
     d   Learners' own paragraphs.

Plenary idea

Your view counts (5 minutes)

Description: Invite learners to answer the 'Reflection' questions.

> **Assessment ideas:** Learners rate their ability to make their writing interesting to others and see another point of view.

Homework ideas

Learners complete the Workbook activities.

Answers for Workbook

1   a   <u>bio</u>degrade, <u>re</u>chargeable

    b   manufactur<u>ing</u>, recharge<u>able</u>

c   non-biodegradable, cost-effective, oil-based

d   perhaps even centuries; years ago, however, furthermore …

2   Accept any reasonable facts and opinions.

3   Learners' own answers.

8.10 Summarise

LEARNING PLAN

Learning objectives		Learning intentions	Success criteria
Main focus	**Also covered**	• Locate and use relevant information.	• Learners can locate and use relevant information.
6Ri.07, 6Ws.04, 6SLs.01	6Rs.03, 6Ri.06, 6Wp.02, 6SLg.03, 6SLg.04, 6SLm.02	• Identify facts.	• Learners can find the facts.
		• Use key words to summarise.	• Learners can use key words to summarise.

LANGUAGE SUPPORT

A fact is a statement that can be proved. An opinion is someone's viewpoint that may or may not be based on facts. The information text on recycling is mainly factual but written from the viewpoint that recycling is essential.

Key words are useful when making notes. A key word is a word that is important to the meaning of a sentence or text, usually a noun, verb or adjective. It is a skill to find the right key word that summarises the main idea. Some of your learners may need extra support and practise in identifying key words and phrases.

Starter idea

Take note (5 minutes)

Resources: *From key words to sentences* (Learner's Book, Session 8.10: Getting started); Track 48

Description: Have a discussion on when we need notes, why notes are useful and how to make notes. Invite any ideas, including on-screen versions of note-taking. Then play Track 48.

Invite the learners to make notes as they listen. You may want to play the audio a couple of times to give everyone a chance to gather the details. Afterwards, ask questions that relate to the information in the audio to check how well the learners listened.

Audioscript: *From key words to sentences*

Why do we summarise?

Summarising is a useful skill for a few good reasons. First, when you summarise a text, you have to think about the main ideas and how the text is organised. This helps you understand the content and context of the text. Secondly, when you summarise a text you commit the information to your memory. This is very helpful when it comes to studying. Thirdly, when you summarise a text, you choose key words and phrases only. This means that when you repeat the information, you must add in your own words. In fact, you should aim to repeat the information using mainly your own words as this demonstrates that you truly understand what you have read without copying someone else's words.

How do we summarise?

When we summarise a text, we begin with the main topic. The main topic usually has linking sub-topics or paragraphs. Identify the key words and phrases in each section and group them under headings to show how they link to the main topic. You can use this skeleton of ideas to create your own text. In summarising we move from key words and phrases, to simple sentences and then we add connectives to create a flow in the text. Ultimately, your writing should demonstrate a variety of simple, compound and complex sentences chosen for effect.

Answers:
Reasons to summarise: You focus on the main ideas, you remember the content, you use your own words.

Main teaching ideas

1 Summarise a text using a mind map (40 minutes)

Learning intention: To identify facts and locate and use relevant information from one or more points in a text

Resources: Learner's Book, Session 8.10, Activity 1; Workbook, Session 8.10

Description: Revise note-taking and how to create a mind map. For those needing support, choose a familiar topic – e.g. school – and draw a basic mind map on the board to illustrate how a mind map works.

Read the text again and invite learners to identify the facts and the main sections. Make notes on the board if necessary but leave some for the learners to try.

Learners use this and the diagram in the Learner's Book to create their own mind map of information. Invite the learners to use different colours and shapes according to what makes sense to them.

Afterwards, learners sit in groups and share and compare their notes with each other. Remind learners to take turns, give each other a chance to speak and build on each other's ideas. Check that learners encourage each other to take turns to speak.

> **Differentiation ideas:** Learners can complete the Workbook activities for Session 8.10 to practise note-taking and summarising skills. Challenge learners to discuss the pros and cons of taking notes. (If notes are unclear, they are useless; taking notes is a way to avoid copying someone else's work word for word.)

> **Assessment ideas:** Check learners can distinguish between facts and opinions. Observe how well learners can locate and use information to organise and make notes. Assess their mind maps and how well they can explain the information in the mind map.

Check that learners encourage each other to take turns to speak.

Answers:
1   a–e Learners' own work.

Plenary idea

Share notes (5 minutes)

Description: In groups, learners share their notes and compare them. Discuss similarities and differences. Decide if anything worked particularly well. Then invite learners to reflect on how they did and if their notes made sense and were useful.

> **Assessment ideas:** Learners rate each other's mind maps using criteria such as: *Is organised into sections with headings*; *The organisation makes sense*; *Uses key words and phrases*; *Can be used to discuss the topic*; *Ideas can be added.*

Homework ideas

Away from school, learners practise note-taking using other reference books. Alternatively, they create a poster-size mind map to show their study notes. This might be something they can add to throughout the term or year.

Answers for Workbook

1 Accept various answers within reason – focus should be on important nouns, verbs and adjectives.

a <u>Recycling</u> is something we can all do to help <u>save our environment</u> from further damage.

b It is important that <u>everyone</u> becomes <u>more aware</u> of how to <u>reduce, re-use</u> and <u>recycle</u> their waste.

c It is a <u>challenge</u> to try <u>to re-use any plastic</u> you bring into your home or your workspace.

d Every <u>small act</u> can make a <u>big difference</u> if we all <u>act together</u>.

e <u>Our world</u> will be <u>cleaner</u> and <u>healthier</u> if we all <u>use less</u> and <u>recycle more</u>.

2 Learners' own notes.

3 Learners' own words.

8.11 and 8.12 Create a magazine article

LEARNING PLAN

Learning objectives		Learning intentions	Success criteria
Main focus	**Also covered**	• Work in groups and take on roles.	• Learners can work together.
6Ri.04, 6Ri.05, 6Wg.08, 6Ws.01, 6Ws.02, 6Ws.04, 6Wp.03, 6SLg.01	6Rv.03, 6Wv.01, 6Wv.02, 6Wv.06, 6Wg.04, 6Ws.03, 6Wc.06, 6Wc.07, 6Wp.04, 6Wp.05, 6SLg.02	• Use the skills learnt to plan and write a magazine article. • Proofread and evaluate own and others' work.	• Learners can plan and write a magazine article including various text types. • Learners can proofread and evaluate their own and others' work.

LANGUAGE SUPPORT

The challenge in this writing activity is for learners to use facts and information as a persuasive technique. Learners should include interesting and technical vocabulary to support the topic. Refer to Language worksheet 8B Vocabulary development to revise the meaning and spelling of words that relate to the topic. Encourage learners to use a thesaurus to extend vocabulary and use words that have impact.

Common misconception

Misconception	How to identify	How to overcome
Magazine articles are classified as one text type.	Display various magazines. Ask: *How many different text types can you find?* (Various.) *Are the texts fiction or non-fiction or both?* (Both.)	Use Worksheet 6.4 Features of fiction and non-fiction texts to compare and analyse text types in magazines. Alternatively, learners draw a table in their learning journals and make notes.

Starter idea

Rubbish everywhere (5 minutes)

Resources: Learner's Book, Session 8.11 and 8.12: Getting started; thesauruses

Description: Learners use a thesaurus to look up synonyms such as *litter, trash, waste, debris, garbage, junk, litter …* (Include the phrase: *to throw away – chuck, place, cast, toss, discard …*)

Learners share and compare their words. Discuss the impact of different words and the appropriate context for the following: *Throw your trash in the bin / Please put your rubbish in the bin / Ensure you place your waste in the correct bin.*

Main teaching ideas

1 Work in groups to plan and write a first draft (40 minutes)

Learning intentions: To develop writing for a purpose; to plan and proofread own and others' work

Resources: Learner's Book, Session 8.11 and 12, Activity 1; Workbook, Session 6.11 and 6.12; Worksheets 6.5, 6.6, 6.8, 6.9 and 6.30

Description: Organise groups and ensure learners share responsibilities by fulfilling various group roles. Use Worksheet 6.8 Group work to guide and support this.

Read the Language focus box together then reread the ocean pollution article in Session 8.2 and discuss the audience, purpose, language and layout. Learners use the information in Session 8.9 and their planning from Session 8.10 to create their own magazine article on recycling. Use Worksheet 6.30 Plan an article to guide this planning process. For extra planning support, use Worksheet 6.5 My writing process.

Learners come up with their own ideas for sections they want to include in their magazine article on recycling e.g. 'The Problem' 'The solution' 'What can YOU do?' The why and how of recycling. They should also include pictures and diagrams to make their article visually appealing.

Discuss important writing and presentation skills. Learners plan and write a first draft in their notebooks.

Learners work together to edit each other's work using the checklist in the Learner's Book and/or Worksheet 6.6 Check, check and check again!

> **Differentiation ideas:** Support learners by varying group sizes and individual responsibilities, the length of the written work and the volume of work. Some learners may only manage a short section each while others might manage more.

Encourage all learners to try to work individually on the Workbook activities for Session 6.11 and 6.12 to practise the skills. Be available to help when needed.

> **Assessment ideas:** Assess learners' ability to work in groups (using Worksheet 6.8 Group work).

Use Worksheet 6.9 Writing assessment sheet to encourage self and peer assessment.

Answers:
1 a–f Learners' own work.

2 Present a magazine article (40 minutes)

Learning intention: To use organisational features appropriate to the text type and use the conventions of standard English appropriately in writing

Resources: Learner's Book, Session 8.11 and 8.12, Activity 2

Description: Learners write their sections out neatly using neat handwriting. By now your learners should be aware of the importance of good presentation skills, along with writing neatly and legibly. Also, their writing style should be well developed and presentable. Provide extra support for learners who still struggle in this area.

Finish the Workbook activities if they have not already been completed.

> **Differentiation ideas:** Support learners by allowing small groups to use onscreen tools to design and type the magazine article.

Invite more confident learners to research further information and write other articles about recycling solutions in different parts of the world.

> **Assessment ideas:** In their final written task, check and assess the learners' understanding of:

- the link between audience, purpose, language and layout

- the various text types included in an article (see Session 8.2)

- the use of technical vocabulary and spelling of words.

Answers:
2   a–d Learners' own work.

Plenary idea

Time out (5 minutes)

Resources: Finished articles from this session

Description: Learners present and display their magazine articles for everyone to enjoy. Invite them to reflect on which articles worked well and why.

> **Assessment ideas:** Invite learners to rate the following aspects of each magazine article on a scale of 1–10: presentation, standard English, spelling and punctuation, readability, enjoyment.

Homework ideas

As a term project, encourage learners to create their own magazine away from school among friendship, family or interest groups. This could be for fun, but it also has the potential to be a valuable learning opportunity. Create an area in your classroom to display the magazines at the end of the term.

Answers for Workbook

1–4   Learners' own work.

CHECK YOUR PROGRESS

1   Example answers:

   a   We generate a lot of waste every day. (to make)

   b   Plants degenerate without water, light or air. (decline)

2   The prefix *de-* changes the meaning of the word from positive to negative.

3   a   True;   b   True;   c   False

4   Accept any reasonable answers:

   a   At the end of the day it's up to us – you and me.

   b   We can do this together (or at least we can try).

   c   Two surfers, Matt and Dan, decided to clean up the ocean.

5   Underline the command verbs and highlight the connectives in these instructions.

   While your 2L bottle dries, <u>clean</u> the plastic waste then <u>cut</u> it up into smaller pieces.

   <u>Dry</u> the 2L bottle in order to <u>remove</u> the moisture so that the waste does not rot.

6   Learners' own sentences.

PROJECT GUIDANCE

Group project: Learners prepare a multimedia presentation predicting the state of the Earth in the future (e.g. 2080). The presentation should include opinions and viewpoints based on present facts and evidence that the learners have researched.

Pair project: Learners design a poster for a particular audience and purpose, using appropriate language and layout. The poster should aim to: inform the public of the effects of waste on the environment; encourage people to buy less and use less; warn people of the consequences of too much waste; and give advice on how to change their habits and make a difference.

Solo project: Learners use their note-taking skills to research a current issue and summarise it. Learners can use mind maps or any other form of note-taking to organise their thoughts and ideas. This can be done in their notebooks, on poster paper or using onscreen tools. Afterwards, invite learners to present the information to the class, using their notes to remind them of key points.

>9 A moment in time

Unit plan

Session	Approximate number of learning hours	Outline of learning content	Resources
9.1 When you look at a painting	1	Read a poem. Explore the imagery. Write a paragraph.	Learner's Book Session 9.1 Workbook Session 9.1 ⬇ Differentiated worksheets 9A–C
9.2 Poetic form and features	1	Describe the poem's features. Write a new stanza. Give each other feedback.	Learner's Book Session 9.2 Workbook Session 9.2
9.3 There for a moment	1	Read a fact file. Read and explore a poem. Hold a discussion forum.	Learner's Book Session 9.3 Workbook Session 9.3
9.4 Features for effect	1	Analyse the poem. Compare poetic features of two poems.	Learner's Book Session 9.4 Workbook Session 9.4 ⬇ Worksheet 6.31
9.5 A jewel	1	Read a poem. Explore a flashback. Respond to the poem.	Learner's Book Session 9.5 Workbook Session 9.5
9.6 'Encapsulate' a moment in time	1	Plan a poem according to a frame. Write a first draft. Edit and improve the poem.	Learner's Book Session 9.6 Workbook Session 9.6 ⬇ Worksheet 6.9 ⬇ Worksheet 6.32

Cross-unit resources
Learner's Book Check your progress
Learner's Book Projects
Unit 9 Language worksheets
End-of-unit 9 test
End-of-year test

BACKGROUND KNOWLEDGE

Three poems have been chosen for this unit from around the world that encapsulate a snapshot or a moment in time. Grace Nichols comes from Guyana, Ted Townsend comes from South Africa and Imtiaz Dharker was born in Pakistan but now lives in India, England and Wales. The subject matter of the poems is very different and yet all evoke a sense of the moment – a moment to be held and remembered.

TEACHING SKILLS FOCUS

Skills for life: creativity

Creativity is one of the core skills for life in the 21st century. Amid the drill and mundane activities that often accompany day-to-day life in the classroom, creativity can become a poor relation as it is imaginative, related to self-identity, internal, unpredictable, frequently divergent and often flouts rules, especially when it comes to writing. A poetry unit is therefore an ideal opportunity to promote creativity as poetic licence provides much greater flexibility and latitude, with learners feeling less bound by rules and 'correctness'.

- Use the poem 'When You Look at a Painting' to encourage imagination about how not just eyes but the whole body can respond to a visual stimulus. Encourage learners to create new figurative images, even ones related to touch, hearing, taste and smell as well as vision when they create their new stanza. Be careful not to discourage any creativity by 'correcting' their work.

- Discuss poetic form and compare poems that appear to follow rules and those that are free and more creative in their format. Encourage learners to express personal responses to different types of poems and to appreciate the way poets conjure up images, moods, themes and thoughtfulness.

- Encourage learners to reflect on the stark differences between a fact file and a poem on the same subject and how they can use creativity and memory to evoke the sense of a subject beyond factual detail.

- Use the flashback technique to encourage learners to be creative with memories, real or imagined, associated with a favourite food. Within the framework provided, encourage learners to create images with vivid descriptions and figurative language that evoke the senses and emotions and then to use a creative approach to present their poem.

9.1 When you look at a painting

LEARNING PLAN

Learning objectives		Learning intentions	Success criteria
Main focus	**Also covered**	• Read a poem silently and aloud.	• Learners can read a poem silently and aloud.
6Rv.04, 6Rv.06, 6Rs.02, 6Ri.08, 6Ri.11, 6Ri.14, 6Ri.17, 6Wg.08, 6SLp.01	6Ri.02, 6Ri.06, 6Ri.13, 6Ri.15, 6Ra.01, 6Ra.02, 6Wv.01, 6SLm.01, 6SLm.03, 6SLm.04, 6SLp.02	• Explore the poem's imagery. • Write an opinion paragraph.	• Learners can talk about and appreciate the poem's imagery. • Learners can write a paragraph explaining the poem.

LANGUAGE SUPPORT

The language used in the poem *When You Look at a Painting* is not especially challenging although some learners may find the imagery more difficult to interpret. Support learners through the extended metaphor of the painting as a dance floor with the looker's eyes dancing with the colours, shapes, moods and shades, reflecting the person looking at the painting getting deeply and physically involved in interpreting what is seen.

Starter idea

How do you look at a painting? (5 minutes)

Resources: Learner's Book, Session 9.1: Getting started; postcards or images of paintings

Description: Hand out postcards or images of paintings to pairs or small groups of learners and ask them to describe the painting to each other. Ask learners to consider what they looked at in the painting – the overall image, the shapes, the colours. Share ideas as a class.

Main teaching ideas

49 1 Talk with a partner (20 minutes)

Learning intention: To read and interpret a poem and its theme

Resources: *When You Look at a Painting* (Learner's book, Session 9.1, Activity 1); Track 49

Description: Ask learners to describe a favourite painting to each other. If they cannot think of one, allow them to use an idea from the Starter activity.

Introduce Grace Nichols, the poet. Say where she is from and encourage learners to find out more biographical information about her.

Ask learners to skim read the poem alone to get a feel for it before reading it aloud with a partner. Encourage them to explain to each other what they think the poem is about by imagining themselves looking at a painting in the way the poem suggests. Ask them to compare it to the way they look at a painting and whether it would change what they saw or felt about a painting.

Play the audio of the poem (Track 49) after a few minutes as a further stimulus to partners' discussions.

> **Differentiation ideas:** Support learners by walking around the classroom while they are talking about and reading the poem aloud. Listen into discussions to check learners have understood what the poem is about. Talk to pairs who appear to be struggling to understand the poem to help them onto the right track. Encourage learners with a good understanding of the poem to explain it to others.

Answers:
1   a–c   Learners' own answers.

2   Appreciate the poem through each other's eyes (25 minutes)

Learning intention: To explore imagery and respond to a poem in a paragraph

Resources: Learner's Book, Session 9.1, Activity 2; Differentiated worksheet pack; images of paintings from the Caribbean (if possible)

Description: Learners may find it difficult to decide whether the voice in the poem is the poet's voice or a different narrator's voice. In Unit 3, they read several poems that contained personification where, for example, the river was the narrator. Ask whether they think Grace Nichols believes you should look at a painting in this way to help them associate the narrator in the poem with the poet.

Talk about the imagery in the poem and find out if any learners suggest it is effectively an extended metaphor of the painting as a dancefloor with the looker's eyes and body dancing with the images, shapes, colours and moods in the painting. They came across an extended metaphor in the poem *The Storm* in Unit 3.

If possible, show learners images of paintings from the Caribbean, many of which have vibrant, strong colours and scenes. Discuss whether it would be easier to 'dance' when looking at such paintings than with ones that are faded and paler in colour or even black and white.

Use Differentiated worksheets 9A–C before learners write their paragraphs to provide extra practice at responding to poetry.

After the discussion, learners should be ready to write their paragraphs explaining the theme of the poem and whether they agree with the poet. Remind them to use examples and images from the poem to support their answers.

> **Differentiation ideas:** Support less confident learners by providing them with a frame for writing their paragraph, starting with a topic sentence and interspersing the frame with connectives such as *because*, *as well as*, *therefore* and so on. Invite more confident learners to work with a learner using a frame so they can offer support.

> **Assessment ideas:** Check learners' ability to write a structured paragraph fluently and easily with little guidance from you. Assess whether learners have included all they were asked to include and that sentences are structured appropriately and in standard English.

Answers:
2   a   The poet's voice.
    b–d   Learners' own answers.

Plenary idea

Look at this painting (5 minutes)

Resources: a large image of a painting (abstract or otherwise), preferably from the Caribbean with vibrant colours

Description: Invite volunteers to look at the painting in the way of the poem and to describe what they see. Encourage them to talk about colours, shapes, moods and shades as well as anything else their eyes are drawn to spend time on.

> **Assessment ideas:** Learners comment on each other's descriptions of the painting, adding suggestions of their own to enhance the effect.

CROSS-CURRICULAR LINKS

Geography and Art: Learners look at some reference books about where exactly Guyana and the Caribbean are along with some examples of artwork from the regions.

Homework ideas

Learners can research Guyana and write a fact file.

*   They can choose a favourite painting to write about.
*   They should try to complete Workbook activities for Session 9.1.
*   Go through the answers in class, inviting learners to share what they have found out and their ideas.

Answers for Workbook

1

A	K	J	C	A	K	M	U	E	I	O	C	B	P	N
Y	U	U	A	N	L	X	U	W	E	O	P	O	N	E
O	M	A	N	A	L	L	I	L	C	H	M	I	W	E
M	Q	S	T	I	F	K	I	O	B	E	C	I	M	T
I	U	A	A	R	D	A	N	D	G	E	A	X	A	S
R	A	B	L	U	V	U	V	R	A	C	R	T	L	O
E	T	E	O	D	T	J	A	A	K	N	I	R	D	G
H	K	R	U	V	B	N	L	F	U	U	A	K	Y	N
C	T	R	P	M	A	L	R	F	R	G	X	R	W	A
Q	J	I	E	T	I	U	R	F	E	P	A	R	G	M
R	B	E	E	D	I	V	D	A	N	A	N	A	B	C
V	R	S	O	T	J	A	B	U	T	I	C	A	B	A
E	L	P	P	A	E	N	I	P	M	A	R	U	L	A
B	A	K	I	R	A	M	B	U	T	A	N	H	B	B
S	L	S	B	W	A	P	W	A	P	R	T	E	O	K

2–4 Learners' own answers.

9.2 Poetic form and features

LEARNING PLAN			
Learning objectives		**Learning intentions**	**Success criteria**
Main focus	**Also covered**		
6Rv.04, 6Rv.06, 6Rs.02, 6Wv.02, 6Wv.04, 6Wv.05, 6Wc.01, 6Wp.04	6Ri.02, 6Ri.11, 6Ri.13, 6Ri.15, 6Ra.01, 6Ra.02, 6Wv.06. 6SLm.01, 6SLp.01, 6SLp.02	• Describe a poem's features. • Write a new stanza. • Give each other feedback.	• Learners can identify and talk about a poem's features. • Learners can write a new stanza in the style of a poem. • Learners can give each other feedback and suggestions for improvement.

LANGUAGE SUPPORT

Learners need to use specialised vocabulary to talk appropriately about poems and their structure, features, form and effect. Support learners who need help by reminding them what some of these terms mean, giving examples where possible.

Common misconception

Misconception	How to identify	How to overcome
Rhyming words must end with exactly the same sound or spelling.	Ask learners to give you examples of rhyming words. Put them on the board and compare whether the end spellings are identical or whether the same sound has been made with different letter combinations. Now write on the board two words that nearly rhyme like shade and shape or bright and bought. Ask: *Do these words rhyme?*	Use the poem 'When You Look at a Painting' to bring out the half rhymes at the end of many of the lines. Analyse with learners what creates the half rhyme – the end sound or the final vowel sound. Invite learners to give further examples.

Starter idea

Analysing a poem (5 minutes)

Resources: Learner's Book, Session 9.2: Getting started

Description: Give learners a few minutes to retrieve their prior knowledge of techniques they have used throughout the year to analyse poems – what sorts of features did they look at and talk about? Use learners' discussions to build a class poetry analysis resource on the board, which they will be able to refer to during the lesson's activities.

Main teaching ideas

1 Poems come in many forms (20 minutes)

Learning intention: To analyse a poem's form and features

Resources: Learner's Book, Session 9.2, Activity 1; *When You Look at a Painting* (Learner's Book, Session 9.1) Track 49

Description: Learners work with a partner and begin by re-reading the poem *When You Look at a Painting*. Using what they discussed in the Starter idea and the callout bubbles in the Learner's Book, learners describe to each other the poem's different features and aspects of form. During these discussions, regularly stop the class and invite volunteers to share a feature they have noticed.

Read the Language focus box with learners and discuss the different types of rhymes, asking if they can think of any examples. The poem contains half rhymes (which are also end rhymes), some ordinary end rhymes and one internal rhyme, but it does not have an even rhyming pattern. Expand on rhymes and half rhymes so that learners are clear on these.

Building on the previous session, invite volunteers to explain the extended metaphor in the poem. Remind everybody first that an extended metaphor takes an ordinary metaphor and expands it using different aspects of imagery. The imagery is bound up in the extended metaphor.

Learners may have different ideas about the poem's mood. If they have suggestions beyond the words provided in the box, share them with the class but remind them to give examples to explain their choice.

> **Differentiation ideas:** Gather some learners who need more support into small groups and talk through the questions with them. Invite more confident learners into the groups as support.

> **Assessment ideas:** Take informal notes as you circulate, listening to learners describe the form of the poem to check how well they can describe it using appropriate vocabulary and terminology.

Answers:

1 a Learners' own answers but should include things like three stanzas of six lines each, short even lines, punctuation following sentences (not just a capital at the start of each line), repetition, flowing rhythm – not even. No particular shape, second person narrator in command form.

    b Half rhymes – e.g. *waists, shapes, shades* or *frame* and *plain*; end rhymes – e.g. *in, begin, within,* or *painting, jump in* or *unlock, rocks,* and possibly internal rhyme – e.g. *eyes, shy*.

c The extended metaphor is of the painting as a dancefloor and the eyes and body dancing with the painting's contents/elements.

d No further figurative language.

e Learners' own answers, but likely to be *lively, joyous* or *humorous* – or a choice of their own.

2 Add to the poem (25 minutes)

Learning intention: To write a stanza in the style and form of the poem

Resources: Learner's Book, Session 9.2, Activity 2

Description: Tell learners they will plan and write another six-line stanza for *When You Look at a Painting* to come before the final stanza. They must follow the same format (rhymes, flow, line length and sentences) and continue the extended metaphor of dancing with the painting's elements. If learners are stuck, make some suggestions such as singing and swinging with the characters in the painting, waltzing or pirouetting along the roads or paths, twirling and swaying in and out of trees and flowers, keeping in step. Remind learners they can repeat the 'When you look at a painting …' line.

In small groups, learners should evaluate each other's stanzas, offering ideas – especially around the imagery and rhymes. Allow a few minutes for improvements then ask groups to read the full poem including their new stanzas. Encourage discussion on how they felt it sounded when they read it all aloud.

> **Differentiation ideas:** Support less confident learners by allowing them to work in pairs to brainstorm ideas and support each other to write a stanza. Challenge more confident learners to produce more than one stanza.

> **Assessment ideas:** Assess learners' stanzas. How well have they understood the pattern of the poem? Have they included ideas for the extended metaphor?

Answers:

2 a–c Learners' own answers.

Plenary idea

When you look at a painting (5 minutes)

Resources: Learners' stanzas from this session

Description: Have a class read of *When You Look at a Painting*, adding in each new stanza in turn. You begin with the poem's original two stanzas, then go around the class with each person reading their own stanza, finishing with you reading the final stanza.

> **Assessment ideas:** Talk as a class about how the poem has been changed or enhanced. Then vote for which stanza best fulfilled the criteria and fitted with the poem.

Homework ideas

Learners can complete the Workbook activities for Session 9.2. They can compare answers with a partner in class and discuss any differences.

Answers for Workbook

1 Possible answers:

haiku – set number of lines, stanza, rhyme, syllabification

shape – no form, shape, may have rhyme, rhythm, repetition

limerick – set number of lines, rhyme, rhythm, may have repetition

couplet – rhyme, rhythm, set number of lines

cinquain – set number of lines, syllabification, stanza

free verse – no form

2 Learners' own answers.

3 Possible answers:

a simile – a direct comparison using 'like' or 'as'

b metaphor – a comparison without using 'like' or 'as'

c personification – giving human qualities to an object or idea

d alliteration – repetition of consonant sounds

e onomatopoeia – giving words to sounds

f assonance – repetition of vowel sound.

9.3 There for a moment

LEARNING PLAN

Learning objectives		Learning intentions	Success criteria
Main focus	**Also covered**	• Read a fact file.	• Learners can read and use information from a fact file.
6Ri.02, 6Ri.07, 6Ri.13, 6SLm.01, 6SLm.02, 6SLm.03, 6SLs.01, 6SLg.02, 6SLg.03, 6SLg.04	6Ri.04, 6Ri.05, 6Ri.06, 6Ri.08, 6Ri.11, 6Ri.15, 6Ra.01, 6Ra.02, 6Wp.03, 6SLm.05, 6SLg.01	• Read and explore a poem. • Hold a discussion forum.	• Learners can read and explore a poem and its theme. • Learners can hold a discussion forum, listening and responding to ideas.

LANGUAGE SUPPORT

While the poem contains few challenging words, the language is vivid and, in places, figurative. Some learners may need support to understand the essential 'story' in the poem. Point out when you discuss the narrator's/poet's voice that the poem is written mainly in in second person – directly addressing the reader – with the implied subject *you*.

Starter idea

Animals in Africa (5 minutes)

Resources: Learner's Book, Session 9.3: Getting started; pictures of African animals and habitats

Description: Allow learners to talk to each other about what they know of African animals and their habitats. Provide a range of images to support your sharing of information as a class.

Main teaching ideas

1 Do you know what an impala is? (25 minutes)

Learning intention: To read and explore a poem and its theme

Resources: *Impala fact file* and *Impala* (Learner's Book, Session 9.3, Activity 1); Tracks 50 and 51

Description: The African bush and savannahs contain many varieties of buck (antelope), including impala. Finding out about other species would make good research topics to expand learners' knowledge and to practise reworking notes into a poster, project or fact file (e.g. Thompson's gazelle, eland, kudu, sable, blesbok, bushbuck, springbok, waterbuck, bontebok, steenbok, nyala, gemsbok).

The fact file (Track 50) gives factual, mostly statistical, information about the impala and an image. Reading the poem straight after the fact file will highlight the contrast in how the two authors have described the same animal.

Remind learners to skim over the poem (Track 51) before they read it with a partner. They should agree who will read each part before beginning. Suggest learners close their eyes as they listen to help them respond to the imagery. If the first reading is not very successful or is somewhat stilted, allow time to read it again. Encourage learners to savour the vignettes of the scenery, the spotting of the impala – the impala taking flight and standing for a moment to look back.

The activity encourages learners to focus on how the poet describes a precious moment by telling the story as an observer and participant. Learners should identify the story elements: setting the scene, the build-up, climax and resolution. Encourage them to have a personal response to the part that appeals to them most. Offer your own response as a stimulus.

Bring the discussion back to class level and invite suggestions why the poet chose to write about the impala (e.g. perhaps it is his homeland; maybe he is inspired by wildlife); accept all suggestions. Ask what inspires your learners: anything they enjoy or feel is precious; a person close to them; a role model; or something they love to see or do – sport, wildlife, dancing, eating chocolate, reading, music, being with family. The point is for them to choose something they could encapsulate, to share with others.

Spelling link: Remind learners of nouns, particularly for animals, that do not have a separate plural form (e.g. *buck, deer, antelope, sheep*). Recap that although these common nouns do not have a separate plural form, subject-verb agreement is still important and has to be inferred from the context: *Three sheep are grazing in the field*; *The sheep is grazing*.

These nouns should not be confused with mass/uncountable nouns that do not have a singular or plural form because the number cannot be quantified (e.g. *water, sand, information*). Point out that mass or uncountable nouns take a singular verb despite the mass implying quantity. (*The sand is wet*; *The water is cold*.) There are more activities on words without a plural form and uncountable nouns in the Spelling section at the end of the Learner's Book.

> **Differentiation ideas:** Allow self-choice of partners but be aware of which pairings may need support to understand the story in the poem. Talk with those pairs to ensure they are on the right track and can appreciate the poem.

Ask more confident learners to write a fact file on more than one animal and choose a different way to set it out.

Answers:
1 a Mainly factual information on size, habitat, food and appearance. Learners' own answers.
   b–f Learners' own answers.

2 Have a discussion forum (20 minutes)

Learning intentions: To hold a discussion forum; to record ideas on a poster

Resources: Learner's Book, Session 9.3, Activity 2; images of impala; large coloured card and paper; coloured pens and pencils

Description: Set up a discussion forum that feels different from the usual partner discussions. Create an element of formality with a 'chair' to guide the discussion so that it covers all the questions. Don't be too restrictive about exactly how groups organise themselves but allocate five minutes for them to decide on protocols – e.g. who can speak, when and for how long, whether to raise hands or take turns.

Groups may want to appoint a scribe. Encourage learners to use words, images and ordinary text in their answers as well as text effects (writing size, colour and style). Make sure there is enough time towards the end to put their ideas on the poster – provide images of impala as well as card and paper.

To celebrate their work, write a personal response to each group acknowledging their ideas and poster.

> **Differentiation ideas:** Choose groups carefully for the discussion forum. Make sure each has a confident leader to guide the discussion. Encourage more confident learners to guide and lead groups.

> **Assessment ideas:** Assess learners' ability to work in a group, and to express their ideas fluently and clearly in the discussion forum. Assess learners' ability to listen attentively, ask relevant questions to further the discussion and contribute a personal response.

Answers:
2 Learners' own answers.

Plenary idea

Which did you prefer? (5 minutes)

Description: Talk as a class about the differences between getting information from the fact file and from the poem. Discuss the difference in types of information or knowledge gained and how the knowledge could be used.

Survey the class to find out which one they preferred or whether it would be affected by what they need to use the information for.

> **Assessment ideas:** Assess learners' responses to the different information sources and their overt purposes and how they think each source can be used.

CROSS-CURRICULAR LINKS

Geography: Source reference books and sites on Africa, South Africa, the African bush and impala. Learners could also find out about other animals in the same habitat.

Homework ideas

Learners could research another kind of buck and prepare a fact file on it. They could also complete the Workbook activities for Session 9.3. Invite them to share their research in class.

Answers for Workbook

1–3 Learners' own answers.

9.4 Features for effect

LEARNING PLAN

Learning objectives		Learning intentions	Success criteria
Main focus	**Also covered**	• Analyse a poem.	• Learners can analyse and identify features of a poem.
6Rv.04, 6Rv.06, 6Rg.03, 6Rs.02, 6Ri.03, 6Ri.11, 6Ri.14, 6Ri.17, 6Ra.02, 6Wv.01, 6Wp.03, 6Wp.04	6Ri.06, 6Ri.08, 6Ri.10, 6Ri.13, 6Ri.15, 6Ri.16, 6Ra.01, 6Ws.04, 6Wc.06, 6Wp.02, 6SLm.03, 6SLg.02, 6SLg.03, 6SLp.01	• Compare poetic features of two poems.	• Learners can compare the poetic features of two poems.

LANGUAGE SUPPORT

Learners are working with already familiar vocabulary and should also be familiar with the specialised vocabulary to describe the poems (poetic terms and features). Some learners may need support eliciting any implicit or figurative meaning.

Two new features are introduced: a line that is a complete thought and ends naturally, with a full stop or equivalent – known as an *end-stopped line*; when the meaning of a line of poetry runs over into the next line without any punctuation at the end of the line – known as *enjambment*. While the terms appear in the Language focus box, it is not necessary for the learners to remember the terms (unless they enjoy learning terms) as the activities do not require them to know the terms just to notice the features.

Starter idea

Literal or figurative? (5 minutes)

Resources: Learner's Book, Session 9.4: Getting started; *Impala* (Learner's Book, Session 9.3); Track 51

Description: Give learners time to discuss whether the poem *Impala* from the previous session uses more literal or figurative description. Encourage them to use examples to support their ideas. When you discuss as a class, go through the poem carefully listening to learners' ideas and keep asking for examples.

Main teaching ideas

1 Re-read the poem and discuss answers (25 minutes)

Learning intention: To analyse a poem's features and effect

Resources: Learner's Book, Session 9.4, Activity 1; *Impala* (Learner's Book, Session 9.3); Track 51

Description: This activity focuses attention on the techniques poet Ted Townsend uses in *Impala* to achieve the effect he wants. Pairs should read the questions first, then re-read the poem to find what they are looking for. Remind them of standard comprehension technique: skim to get the main idea; read the questions; re-read with an idea of what to look out for. Suggest learners note this approach in their learning journals.

Learners discuss answers before writing them in their notebooks. Remind them to check the quality of their answers: full sentences, evidence from the text to support their answers, a personal response.

Help learners see the narrator's voice as the poet's voice, directly addressing the reader (second person) – eager to share what he has experienced – the precious moment.

The poem introduces end-stopped lines and enjambment. It is not necessary for learners to remember the terms, but it is useful for them to notice the effect of ideas that end at the end of the line and those that flow on from line to line.

› **Differentiation ideas:** Support less confident learners by allowing them to write notes for their answers rather than full sentences so that they can focus on content. Encourage more confident learners to check their work carefully for spelling, punctuation and grammar errors, using dictionaries where necessary.

Answers:

1   a   Largely second person – the poet is addressing the reader directly using the pronoun 'you'. Some third person.

   b   Although it is the narrator's voice, it seems likely it is also the poet's voice as it appears to be based on a personal experience. Accept all sensible answers.

   c   Present tense. Various examples can be given: *lift, see, are, leaps, soars, stands*. Make sure learners identify finite verbs, as non-finite verbs do not have a tense.

   d   Both lend the immediacy – it makes the reader feel the action is happening as the poem is read and the poet is drawing the reader into the experience.

   e   *Imagine you are the hunter, looking for signs in the wild.* It is both literal and figurative. Literal in that the poet is actually asking the reader to imagine he or she is a hunter, but figurative in that the sight of the hunter means more than exactly what a hunter sees, it also incorporates all his or her knowledge and experience. Accept sensible answers.

   f   Learners' own answers but should reflect something to do with dry, parched, breathless plains and at the end: the impala is frightened and runs away before stopping to look back at what caused the fear.

   g   Stanza 1: Alliteration – with 'panting plains'; metaphor – when you see with the sight of a hunter; some rhyme – trees/breeze; sentences flowing on from one line into the next. Stanza 2: alliteration – dark-ridged and rough | the rich red browns; some rhyme – enough/rough; sentences flowing on from one line into the next. Final stanza: metaphor – soars in fright and streams away.

   h   • Learners' own answers.
       • It is reminiscent of someone actually speaking – the thoughts run on into each other.
       • It draws particular attention to the words in the short lines. It makes them stand out.
       • Not really. Each stanza has its own energy linked to the content – setting the scene, slowly discovering the impala, the impala dashing off before pausing to survey the danger.

   i   • Learners' own answers.
       • The exclamation mark. It draws attention to the sudden discovery that it is an impala.

2 Compare the poetic features (20 minutes)

Learning intention: To compare and discuss poetic features of two poems

Resources: Learner's Book, Session 9.4, Activity 2; Worksheet 6.31

Description: Learners compare the features of the different poem styles. Although a table can seem very formal, it is a useful organisational tool and allows learners to use key words rather than trying to explain in full sentences and paragraphs. A mind map can be used if learners prefer. Together, complete the rhyme line in the table. The features in the box should all end up in the table/mind map. Worksheet 6.31 Comparing poem features may be useful here.

Learners can compare their work with a partner or small group and discuss any differences. They can then add to their own tables or organising tools as necessary.

> **Differentiation ideas:** Support less confident learners by allocating selected features to certain pairs, then group pairs who have discussed different aspects. Allocate more challenging aspects to more confident learners.

> **Assessment ideas:** From learners' tables/mind maps, assess their ability to identify and compare poetic features. You could target questions that require them to refer to their table – e.g. *Which*

poem has the most unusual layout and why? How did Impala use vivid description?

Answers:

2 **a–b** Learners' own answers.

Plenary idea

How did they compare? (5 minutes)

Resources: Learners' tables/mind maps from Activity 2

Description: Invite volunteers to compare the poems for the class using the table or mind map notes. Invite learners to ask questions and give their opinion if it differs.

> **Assessment ideas:** Learners can compare what is explained to what they have written and note down any differences.

Homework ideas

Learners could choose another poem to compare with *Impala* in the same way. They could also do the Workbook activities for Session 9.4. Invite learners to share their ideas in class.

Answers for Workbook

1 Learners' own questions.

2 Learners' own answers.

3 Learners' own answers.

9.5 A jewel

LEARNING PLAN

Learning objectives		Learning intentions	Success criteria
Main focus	**Also covered**	• Read a poem.	• Learners can read and appreciate a poem.
6Rv.04, 6Rv.06, 6Ri.06, 6Ri.07, 6Ri.08, 6Ri.14, 6Ri.15, 6Ri.17, 6Ra.02, 6Ra.04	6Rv.01, 6Rv.03, 6Rs.01, 6Ri.01, 6Ri.02, 6Ri.03, 6Ri.04, 6Ri.10, 6Ri.11, 6Ri.13, 6Ra.01, 6Wc.06, 6SLm.03, 6SLm.04, 6SLp.01, 6SLp.02	• Explore a flashback. • Respond to the poem.	• Learners can identify and understand how a flashback works. • Learners can give a personal response to the poem.

LANGUAGE SUPPORT

Both the listening activity and the poem contain some challenging vocabulary. Ensure learners are able to understand. It may help to write the names from the listening activity on the board so that they are familiar as learners work through the activities.

Common misconception

Misconception	How to identify	How to overcome
Flashbacks appear only in stories and novels.	Ask learners what a flashback is and remind them of the work they did in Unit 1, both with *Voices at the Museum* and the listening text *Oliver Strange*. Ask them to explain to you how flashbacks work and where they are likely to find them.	Use the poem 'How to Cut a Pomegranate' to show that flashbacks can occur in poetry as well as in stories.

Starter idea

🎧 52 Persephone and the pomegranate seeds (10 minutes)

Resources: *Persephone and the Pomegranate Seeds* (Learner's Book, Session 9.5: Getting started); Track 52

Description: Ask if any learners have heard the story about Persephone and the pomegranate seeds. Tell them it is an ancient Greek myth.

Note that in the Roman myth, Persephone is called Proserpine, Demeter is called Ceres, Zeus is called Jupiter and Hades is called Pluto, but the story is the same.

Write the names of the key characters on the board: Persephone, Demeter, Hades and Zeus. Play Track 52 and, at the end, invite a volunteer to summarise the story to you.

Give learners time to go through the questions and see how much they can remember. Play the audio a second time to allow learners to listen for specific information to help them answer the questions.

The first three questions are lower order questions which require recall of information. The final question requires inference.

Help learners who struggle with the listening activity.

Audioscript: *Persephone and the Pomegranate Seeds*

Speaker 1: Persephone, daughter of Demeter, the goddess of the harvest, was out with friends when suddenly, the earth split open and Hades, god of the Underworld, snatched her away in his chariot. Demeter searched desperately for her and refused to allow plants to grow while she was missing. Meanwhile, in the Underworld, Persephone refused everything Hades offered her to eat or drink, knowing if she touched anything, she would have to stay in the Underworld. She discovered Hades was not so terrifying after all, but she still missed her mother and the world above.

Speaker 2: Eventually, Demeter discovered Persephone had been taken to the Underworld. She appealed to Zeus, ruler of the gods, to allow her daughter to return. Reluctantly, Hades prepared to take Persephone home but offered her one last thing to eat – a ripe, blood red pomegranate. When Zeus discovered Persephone had eaten six pomegranate seeds, he ruled that she could return home but would have to go back to be queen of the Underworld with Hades for six months every year, one month for each pomegranate seed eaten. And so, while Persephone is away, the world mourns; plants shrivel and die, only to be reborn in spring when Persephone returns.

Answers:

1 Demeter, the goddess of the harvest.
2 She knew that if she touched anything she would have to stay in the Underworld.
3 Because she ate six pomegranate seeds.
4 Because while Persephone is in the underworld her mother, Demeter, is distraught and the world mourns and plants shrivel and die. When Persephone returns, she is overjoyed, and plants flourish and grow once more.

Main teaching ideas

1 Read a flashback poem (25 minutes)

Learning intention: To read and respond to a poem with a flashback

Resources: *Pomegranate fact file* and *How to cut a pomegranate* (Learner's Book, Session 9.5, Activity 1); Tracks 53 and 54; a pomegranate and/or a picture of one

Description: Sensitively discuss memories that particularly stand out for learners – e.g. to do with a person, toy, event, place, food or first-time experience. Invite learners to describe an important memory to each other. If possible, ask two learners with the same experience to identify the differences in their memories. If learners seem reluctant to share their memories, then encourage them to listen attentively to others'.

How many of the class have seen, felt or tasted a pomegranate? If possible, pass pomegranates around and cut them open to help learners relate to the experience described. The pomegranate fact file (Track 53) contrasts with the poem's description of a pomegranate (Track 54). Although the fact file makes the pomegranate sound reasonably appealing (sweet, red, gelatinous flesh), the details are hardly poetic or the stuff of memories.

Explain the term *nostalgia* – perhaps make it the word of the week: 'a feeling of happiness mixed with sadness when you think about the past'. Ask: *Does the memory of the father and the pomegranate make the poet happy or sad? Does she wish she was back there, or does she just treasure the memory?*

Do learners think the image of the father cutting, talking about and eating a pomegranate is autobiographical or an invented moment and 'voice'? If the former, we cannot know whether the poet realised she would treasure the moment forever, or if it stayed as vividly in her father's mind. Encourage learners to articulate such ideas around the poem.

The poem is a combination of first-person narrative voice and dialogue – what the father says to the poet/narrator.

Spelling link: Explain that plants are classified within a framework to show related species. The names of plants can vary from region to region, so most plant reference books classify plants using their botanical Latin names, which can be used worldwide, regardless of the local language and local name for the plant. Some local names have clear origins in the Latin names, for example: pomegranate – *Punica granatum*; lettuce – *Lactuca sativa*; maize – *Zea mays*; mango – *Mangifera indica*; cocoa – *Theobroma cacao*.

> **Differentiation ideas:** Be aware of learners who may need input to understand the deeper meaning of the poem. Ask: *What is the narrator thinking*

about at the end? Where is her other home? What is it like? Where would she rather be? Also be aware of learners who seem uncomfortable discussing personal memories, and allow them just to listen to others rather than speak. Encourage confident learners to give their own meanings.

Answers:
1 a–c Learners' own answers.
   d The poet's voice – she is describing her own memory and recounting her father's words (first-person).
   e Learners' own answers.

2 Identify story features in the poem (20 minutes)

Learning intention: To analyse the features of the poem and compare them to the story genre

Resources: Learner's Book, Session 9.5, Activity 2

Description: The poem displays a number of story features, both technically and in terms of content. The narrative is punctuated by dialogue with two parts – the flashback to the father explaining how to cut and eat the pomegranate and the narrator's own attempts. There is no climax, but it concludes with a reflection.

Here, enjambment/sentences with the thought flowing over from one line into the next enhance the dialogue and makes the reader follow the thought as it would be said – some extended thoughts, some short (reflected by the end-stopped lines/sentences containing a single thought taking up a single line). The flow of the lines matches what the father is doing as he speaks – cutting the fruit and demonstrating, gesture by gesture. Lines with a complete sentence or thought are more common in poetry than having the thoughts run over one line into the next and even the next, partly because lines of poems do not match sentences and paragraphs. Here, the combination sentences ending at line end and running over into the next is very effective for giving the impression of what the father is doing as he speaks. We often mirror our actions with speech patterns.

Pull the activity together by making part c (How does the poet create the conversational feel?) a general question. Ask volunteers to build up the techniques the poet has used to create a conversational feel.

It is not just stories that use flashback techniques. The poem combines a vivid flashback with the narrator's subsequent memories. Learners should note in their learning journals that flashbacks can be used in poetry as well as stories.

Encourage learners to say honestly whether they enjoyed the poem and why/why not.

> **Differentiation ideas:** Support less confident learners by encouraging them to be more detailed in their learning journals when recording the poetic techniques, explaining the flashback and saying whether they enjoyed the poem. Encourage confident learners to give greater reflection and ask them for examples of techniques.

> **Assessment ideas:** Informally assess learners' ability to infer deeper meaning from the poem.

Informally assess how well learners have understood the effect of the variety of sentences, and how they run over lines or not in the poem through their responses in Activity 2.

Parts a–d could be answered in learners' notebooks for a more formal assessment.

Answers:
2 a The poem has a narrative voice (first-person narrative), it is past tense in narrative sections (present and future in the dialogue), it has a setting, a form of storyline (and a flashback), characters, dialogue and ends with a reflection.
   b The long and short sentences, with some running over more than one line reflect the father's actions relating to the pomegranate as he is speaking. They differentiate when he is explaining or, for example, holding it up to show what he means – gesture by gesture.
   c By using dialogue punctuation, juxtaposing dialogue and narrative, the mix of long and short sentences with some running over more than one line to match the natural rhythm and variety of speech patterns. Accept all sensible suggestions.
   d Learners' own answers.

Plenary idea

Talk about the poem (5 minutes)

Description: Write the words *nostalgia*, *memory* and *displacement* on the board. Invite learners to explain the poem's theme using the words written on the board.

CROSS-CURRICULAR LINKS

Science: Gather reference materials on pomegranates (including when and where they were first grown) along with how and where they grow.

Geography: Gather reference books on Pakistan – in particular its vegetation and climate.

Discuss as a class whether the memory is real or has acquired a power over time because it represents a time and a place that is lost to the poet.

> **Assessment ideas:** Informally assess learners' ability to understand how the theme of the poem is conveyed both explicitly and implicitly.

Homework ideas

Learners can research a pomegranate to extend the fact file in the Learner's Book.

They can also complete the Workbook activities for Session 9.5. Share answers in class, inviting volunteers to read out their paragraphs for Workbook Activity 3.

Answers for workbook

1–3 Learners' own answers.

9.6 'Encapsulate' a moment in time

LEARNING PLAN

Learning objectives		Learning intentions	Success criteria
Main focus	**Also covered**	• Plan a poem.	• Learners can plan a poem according to a model.
6Rs.02, 6Ww.07, 6Wv.02, 6Wv.04, 6Wv.05, 6Wv.06, 6Wg.02, 6Wg.04, 6Wc.04, 6Wp.03, 6Wp.04	6Rv.04, 6Rv.06, 6Ri.02, 6Wv.01, 6Wc.01, 6Wc.02, 6Wp.01, 6Wp.05, 6SLp.01	• Write a first draft, edit and improve it. • Present the poem with a fact file.	• Learners can write, edit and improve their poem using feedback and other tools. • Learners can finalise their poem and present it with illustrations and a fact file.

LANGUAGE SUPPORT

Remind learners about strong verbs (word choice) and command verbs (implied subject).

Common misconception

Misconception	How to identify	How to overcome
Command verbs have no subject.	Ask learners to give you examples of verb subjects – names of people, things and pronouns. Invite them to put them together with verbs noticing how the verb ending changes in the present tense. Now ask learners to give you a command or, e.g. an instruction such as, 'Go to the secretary's office'. Ask: *What is the subject of the verb 'go'?*	Use the poem *How to Cut a Pomegranate* to show the father using command verbs/instructions using similar verbs without an obvious subject. Ask learners whom the father is talking to (his daughter) and discuss that he is really saying (*you cut, you peel, you slice* but that the *you* is omitted). It is implied and not present. Look at a variety of recipes and instructions to consolidate this understanding.

Starter idea

Your favourite food (5 minutes)

Resources: Learner's Book, Session 9.6: Getting started

Description: Partners describe their favourite food to each other and why they like it. Encourage them to talk about what it looks like, tastes like, smells like and how they like to prepare it and eat it. Invite volunteer pairs to describe each other's favourite food to the class.

Main teaching ideas

1 Choose a food and plan a 'How to eat a …' poem (15 minutes)

Learning intention: To plan a poem following a model

Resources: Learner's Book, Session 9.6, Activity 1; Worksheet 6.32

Description: Food is a universal necessity and most people have a favourite, so 'How to eat a …' should be a topic learners can be inspired by. Spend a few minutes together as a class, following on from their starter discussions, thinking about favourite foods. Model talking about your own favourite food and explaining how best to eat it (in your opinion).

In the poem *How to Cut a Pomegranate*, the pomegranate is associated with a jewel – something precious – while the poem shows how worthless actual jewels are. Ask what is so valuable about the pomegranate. (They secretly carry in their seed the promise of a new generation – a world renewed.)

Move on to ask learners to think about what their food could be associated with.

Partners can discuss and suggest possible images for each other. The poem describes something very ordinary in an unusual way. You could use Worksheet 6.32 Imaginative comparisons to encourage creative comparisons to stimulate learners' thinking.

Learners might find it easier to imagine a specific audience for their explanation. It should be a personal moment so their audience should be someone close whom they genuinely want to share the experience with.

As with all writing, planning is essential. The planning for this poem is relatively straightforward if learners (roughly) follow the model: a conversation and memory followed by a personal response and reflective ending. Emphasise that learners do not have to follow this exactly. Importantly, remain sensitive to losses or other difficult events your learners might have experienced and try to avoid the themes of nostalgia and memory leading to disturbing thoughts.

Help learners to think about aspirational synonyms that they could use in their poem.

> **Differentiation ideas:** Support less confident learners by ensuring that they understand all the elements they should include in their plans.

Answers:
1 a–b Learners' own answers.

2 Write, edit and improve your poem (30 minutes)

Learning intention: To write, edit, improve and present a poem with a fact file

Resources: Learner's Book, Session 9.6, Activity 2; Worksheet 6.9; poem plans from Activity 1

Description: Learners do not have to follow the exact pattern of stanzas and lines in the poem; rather, encourage them to follow the pattern of ideas/action. The poem does not have a rhyme scheme, but it does have the strong conversational element enhanced by the actual dialogue and the strong command verbs. Remind learners that although it is a poem, the dialogue should be punctuated correctly. The lines can run on into each other and needn't all be the same length. Sentence variety can be very effective.

Encourage learners to follow the writing process they have learnt and applied over the year: plan using a mind map or other organising tool; write a first draft in a limited period concentrating fully; revise and incorporate feedback using a dictionary, thesaurus and personal word list; finally, proofread, edit and present.

This poem lends itself to hand-written presentation: neat joined-up writing interspersed with illustrations to enhance the content.

Finally, learners read poems to each other in a group. Give time for learners to discuss each poem.

> **Assessment ideas:** Use Worksheet 6.9 Writing assessment sheet or your own judgement to assess learners' understanding of the form and features of the poem model. Also, assess their creative content and capacity to include deeper or implicit meaning. Here are some possible success criteria.

- *The poem must follow the 'How to eat a …' model.*

- *The poem should have a conversational style and include actual dialogue.*

- *The poem should include some figurative imagery.*

- *The poem includes both short and long sentences.*

- *The poem should contain a reflection indicating a deeper level of meaning.*

> **Differentiation ideas:** Consider pairing less confident and more confident writers. Suggest they listen to (rather than read) each other's first drafts and make suggestions based on what they hear and visualise. Encourage more confident learners to write a fact file to accompany their poem.

Answers:
2 a–e   Learners' own answers.

Plenary idea

Let's listen and visualise (5 minutes)

Resources: Learners' poems from this session

Description: Invite volunteers to read their poems to the class. Ask the class to close their eyes while listening to heighten their capacity to visualise.

> **Assessment ideas:** Learners can identify the imagery and deeper meaning.

Homework ideas

Learners can do research on their food to write a fact file for the presentation.

Learners can also complete the Workbook activities for Session 9.6. Invite learners to share their final poems.

Answers for Workbook

1–3 Learners' own answers.

CHECK YOUR PROGRESS

1   An extended metaphor is when a metaphorical image continues to include more figurative images along the same theme.

2   Learners' own answers.

3   Internal rhyme – rhymes in the middle of a line: *Little Miss Muffet sat on a tuffet | Eating her curds and whey.* Half rhyme – words that almost rhyme: *Let your eyes hold the waists I of the colours and shapes.* End rhyme – rhymes at the end of lines: *Twinkle, twinkle little star | How I wonder what you are.*

4   **a**   False   **b**   True.

5   **a–e**   Learners' own answers.

PROJECT GUIDANCE

Group project: learners research poetry specifically about fruit (allow nuts as well and even the plants that bear them). They select poems to use in a dramatic reading for the class. They can hand write on large card or write onscreen to allow the audience to follow the words in the reading. Learners must take different roles in the dramatic reading and coordinate their ideas. They can use props and music to enhance the effect. Film groups for review later on.

Pair project: learners can research a fruit of their choice to prepare a presentation on. Focus on different sources, such as poems and stories as well as factual information. Encourage pairs to present to each other and give feedback – allowing time to improve their presentations. Learners can choose the most suitable medium for their presentation.

Solo project: learners look for specific information to create a fact file. Gather information or suitable sites for them to research either South Africa or Guyana. Remind them of the organisational tools useful for laying out fact files, such as bullets, headings, illustrations and numbering.

> Spelling activities answers

Term 1

A Revise common spelling sounds

1 Possible answers: b male, state, chafe, space; plaice, trail wait; reign, vein veil, abseil; grey; weigh, weight, neigh, neighbour, sleigh; in some words of more than one syllable you just need the letter *a* – crazy, acorn, alien, etc.

2 **a** f<u>e</u>te; g<u>au</u>ge; str<u>ai</u>ght; croch<u>e</u>t

   b Learners' own sentences.

B Recognising unstressed vowels

1 Learners stress the underlined syllable.

2 The underlined syllables here should be stressed: <u>bu</u>tterfly, <u>tri</u>angle, um<u>bre</u>lla, <u>al</u>phabet, com<u>pu</u>ter, <u>in</u>troduce.

3 The vowel part of the underlined syllables here are not stressed: choc<u>o</u>late, libr<u>a</u>ry, int<u>e</u>resting, busin<u>e</u>ss, med<u>i</u>cine, fam<u>i</u>ly, sep<u>a</u>rate, jew<u>e</u>llery, veg<u>e</u>table, mini<u>a</u>ture, hist<u>o</u>ry, di<u>a</u>mond.

C Prefixes can give clues to meanings

1 **a** Middle [of]

   b Do again

   c Many

2–3 Learners' own answers.

D Suffixes can change the meaning of words

1

add suffix –*less*	root word	add suffix –*ful*
careless	care	careful
hopeless	hope	hopeful
colourless	colour	colourful
thoughtless	thought	thoughtful
harmless	harm	harmful
powerless	power	powerful
helpless	help	helpful
tasteless	taste	tasteful

2 **a** adjectives

   b beauty, penny, plenty, mercy, bounty, fancy

   c nouns (abstract except for penny)

   d The *y* changes to an *i* when a suffix beginning with a consonant is added.

E Tricky endings

1 **a–b** audible–inaudible; divisible–indivisible; visible–invisible; possible–impossible; legible–illegible; responsible–irresponsible; flexible–inflexible; edible–inedible; manageable–unmanageable; capable–incapable; fashionable–unfashionable; comfortable–uncomfortable; acceptable–unacceptable; enjoyable–unenjoyable; workable–unworkable.

   c–d Learners' own answers.

2 action   mansion   session   electrician   satisfaction   fashion   expansion   musician   omission   cushion

F Not wrong, just different

1–2

UK	US	Rule
centre	center	re changes to er
kilometre	kilometer	
centimetre	centimeter	
colour	color	ou changes to o
mould	mold	
neighbour	neighbor	
favour	favor	
cancelled	canceled	double l changes to single l
dialled	dialed	

Term 2

A Revise common spelling sounds

1 a–c

k: k, c+consonant, ck, cc, ch, lk. cq, qu	*kind, kitten, comb, cattle, back, luck, bucket, acclaim, occupy, school, chemist, chorus, stomach, yolk, folk, chalk, acquire, racquet, antique, equator, conquer*
s: c + vowel, sc, cy ci, sci	*cent, city, science, scene, bicycle,*
sh: ce, ch	*ocean, machine, brochure*
ch: ch or tch	*chunk, chat, match, thatch*

d Learners' discussions.

2 **a–b** Learners' own answers. Possible words: bone, coat, show, foe, though, sew, brooch, chose, etc.

B Soft and hard c and g

1

Soft c	Hard c	Soft g	Hard g
census, citizen, cell	crisp, clasp, crave	gem, agile, age, logical, wedge	dialogue, garden

2 Learners' own answers.

C Forming nouns from verbs

1 payment–pay; treatment–treat; agreement–agree; replacement–replace; entertainment–entertain; government–govern; arrangement–arrange.

2–4 Learners' own answers.

D Tricky plurals

1 fungus–fungi; crisis–crises; medium–media; larva–larvae; cactus–cacti; axis–axes; formula–formulae; oasis–oases; antenna–antennae; datum–data; ellipsis–ellipses; focus–foci; analysis–analyses; octopus–octopi; stadium–stadia; hippopotamus–hippopotami.

2 sheep   salmon   squid   trout   deer   cod

3 sugar   wheat   money   bread   water   flour   salt   rice   sand

4 *less*

E Working with opposite prefixes

1 incorrect; irregular; unfair; disagree; illegible; anticlockwise; impossible; dishonest; unsuccessful; impolite; irresponsible; illegal; unofficial; informal; uneven; irreversible; imperfect; antisocial.

2 Learners' own answers.

F Revise a spelling rule

1 rebel; flap; run; admit; begin; regret; tipping.

2 spotted; flaked; stayed; referred; used; stepped; patted; equalled; committed; grabbed; slipped.

a Just added 'd'.

b snow; gaze; fax.

c Maybe if the last letter is w, z or x, the final consonant is not doubled before adding the suffix.

Term 3

A Revise common spelling sounds

1 a–d

(dge) *hedge,*	bridge, fidget, gadget, grudge, hedge, smudge, trudge, wedge
(dj) *adjust*	adjacent, adjective, adjourn, adjust
(ge) *privilege*	cage, challenge, encourage, foliage, genius, gorge, heritage, manage, privilege, refuge, siege, stranger, village
(j) *jam*	injure, jam, jealous, job, object
(gi) *gigantic*	gigantic, giraffe, region
(gy) *apology*	apology, gymnast

NB sol<u>di</u>er could be considered to also make a 'j' sound – depending on regional pronunciation.

2 Learners' own answers.

B Choose precise words

1–2 Learners' own answers.

C Homophones and homographs

1 **a** guest – guessed; idol – idle; sent – scent – cent; poor – pour – paw – pore; flaw – floor; allowed – aloud; vein – vain – vane; threw – through; site – sight; weather – whether; rode – road – rowed; knead – kneed – need; son – sun; muscle – mussel; shore – sure; their – they're – there; too – to – two; won – one.

b Learners' own sentences.

2 **a** bow – n. v.; fair – adj. n.; content – n. v. adj.; down – n. adj. prep.; object – n. v. adj.; refuse – v. n.; wind – n. v.; second – n. adj. v. adv.; tear – n. v.; wound – n. v.; wave – n. v.; bat – n. v.; lead – n. v.

b Learners' own sentences.

D The prefix *ad–*

1 **a–c** Learners' own answers.

E Revise a spelling rule

Learners' own answers.

> Acknowledgements

The authors and publishers acknowledge the following sources of copyright material and are grateful for the permissions granted. While every effort has been made, it has not always been possible to identify the sources of all the material used, or to trace all copyright holders. If any omissions are brought to our notice, we will be happy to include the appropriate acknowledgements on reprinting.

Excerpts have been taken from *Approaches to learning and teaching* series, courtesy of Cambridge University Press and Cambridge Assessment International Education.

(Texts in Learner Book) **Unit 1** *The Middle of Nowhere* by Geraldine McCaughrean, published by Usborne Publishing Ltd. Used by permission of David Higham Associates on behalf of the author; Excerpts from *East* by Edith Pattou. Copyright © 2003 by Edith Pattou. Reprinted by permission of Houghton Mifflin Harcourt Publishing Company. All rights reserved; Reproduced from *North Child* by permission of Usborne Publishing, 83-85 Saffron Hill, London EC1N 8RT, UK. www.usborne.com. Copyright © 2006, Edith Pattou; Excerpt from 'Oliver Strange and the Journey to the Swamps' by Dianne Hofmeyr, ISBN 9780624054931, Published by Tafelberg. Reproduced by permission of NB Publishers a division of Media24 Boeke (Pty) Ltd; **Unit 2** 'Indian Girl, 13, Becomes the Youngest Person to Climb Mount Everest' by Andrea Billups © 2014 TI Gotham Inc. All rights reserved. Reprinted/Translated/Adapted from People.com and published with permission of TI Gotham Inc. Reproduction in any manner in any language in whole or in part without written permission is prohibited; Excerpt from *Out of India: An Anglo-Indian Childhood* by Jamila Gavin, published by Hodder Children's Books, 2002. Used by permission of David Higham Associates on behalf of the author; Tenzing Norgay Biography,Copyright by Famous People; **Unit 3** 'Mawu of the Waters' by Abena P A Busia, Original publication Abena P.A. Buisa,*Testimonies of Exile*, Africa World Press, Trenton NJ, © Abena P.A. Busia,1990; 'A River Poem' by Mamta G Sagar. This poem originally in Kannada language by Mamta Sagar is published in this book with her permission; 'Right Here was the Ocean' by Zehra Nigah, Translated and used by permission of Yasmeen Hameed; **Unit 4** From *The Green Book* by Jill Paton Walsh. Copyright ©1982 by Jill Paton Walsh. Illustration copyright ©1982 by Lloyd Bloom. Reprinted by permission of Farrar, Straus and Giroux Books for Young Readers. All Rights Reserved, along with Reprinted by permission of Harold Ober Associates. Copyright 1982 by the Estate of Jill Paton Walsh; *The Diary of a Space Traveller and Other Stories* by Satyajit Ray, Copyright Satyajit Ray 2004. Used by permission of Penguin Random House India; Excerpt from *The Hitchhikers' Guide to the Galaxy* by Douglas Adams, Copyright 1979 by Pan Books. Reproduced with permission of the Licensor through PLSclear. Electronic use copyright © 1979 by Serious Productions Ltd. Used by permission of Harmony Books, an imprint of Random House and Penguin Random House Audio Publishing Group, a division of Penguin Random House LLC. All rights reserved, along with copyright by Curtis Brown **Unit 5** Excerpt from article *'Report Gives Strong Climate Change Warning'* by NFK Editors, October 10, 2018 Copyright NewsForKids.net 2018; Excerpt from article 'The shrinking world of penguins' by Les Line, Copyright 2007 National Wildlife Federation. Published with the permission of the copyright owner, the National Wildlife Federation®; **Unit 6** 'According to my Mood' by Benjamin Zephaniah from *Talking Turkeys* copyright © Benjamin Zephaniah 1995, published by Puffin, 1995. Reprinted by permission of Penguin Books Limited. Audio use of this poem is by permission of United Agents on behalf of Benjamin Zephaniah; 'Amaized' Copyright © 2010 by Amy Ludwig VanDerwater. First appeared on author's blog, the Poem Farm Blog. Reprinted by permission of Curtis Brown, Ltd; 'Jeremy, Jeremy Bishop' © Valerie Bloom 2000 from *Hot Like Fire* (Bloomsbury). Reprinted by permission of Eddison Pearson Ltd on behalf of Valerie Bloom; 'Glenelg puts a smile on my face' by Jim Haynes. Used by permission of the author Jim Haynes; 'There was a young boy from Peru' from *I Don't Want an Avocado for an Uncle: Poems by Chrissie Gittins* Published in 2006 by Rabbit Hole publications. Used by permission of the author Chrissie Gittins; **Unit 7** Text © 2013 Kate DiCamillo Illustrations © 2013 Keith Campbell From *Flora & Ulysses* written by Kate DiCamillo and illustrated by K.G. Campbell, Reproduced by permission of Walker Books Ltd, London SE11 5HJ www.walker.co.uk; Audio use of this excerpt by permission of Penguin Random House Audio Publishing Group, a division of Penguin Random House LLC. All rights reserved; *NO.6 Volume 1* by Atsuko Asano, art by Hinoko Kino, Published by Kodansha Comics;